ISRAELI CINEMA

Jewish History, Life, and Culture
Michael Neiditch, Series Editor

ISRAELI CINEMA

IDENTITIES IN MOTION

edited by **Miri Talmon**
and **Yaron Peleg**

university of texas press   austin

The Jewish History, Life, and Culture Series is supported
by the late Milton T. Smith and the Moshana Foundation,
and the Tocker Foundation.

♾ The paper used in this book meets the minimum
requirements of ANSI/NISO Z39.48-1992 (R1997)
(Permanence of Paper).

Library of Congress Cataloging-in-Publication Data

Israeli cinema : identities in motion/edited by Miri Talmon
and Yaron Peleg. — 1st ed.
    p.   cm.
  Includes index.
  ISBN 978-0-292-72560-7 (cloth : alk. paper)
  1. Motion pictures—Israel.   2. Identity (Psychology) in
motion pictures.   I. Talmon, Miri. II. Peleg, Yaron.
  PN1993.5.I86I87 2011   791.43095694—dc22
                                    2011003827

ISBN 978-0-292-73560-6 (E-book)

CONTENTS

INTRODUCTION

Motion fiction is, among many other things, a cultural medium for the articulation of collective identities. When we say "collective," we mean people who experience films, interpret them, and identify with them from a certain "subject position," which is always the intersection of individual experience and communal frameworks. Our national, ethnic, racial and religious, gender, and other communal affiliations, not necessarily in this order, guide our experience of the fictional world—the story, characters, setting, and our perception of the more subtle elements of the cinematic code, like composition and color, mise-en-scène, art, distance and angles, editing, soundtrack, and musical score.

When we say "identities," we refer to transient and always evolving cultural constructs, not fixed entities. Cultural identities are flexible and open identifications and self-perceptions that we keep developing as we go through life. They are reflected in and through our biographies and depend on cultural contexts (be they national, geographical, or ethnic) that are connected to our professional and personal, private affiliations.

Motion fiction is one of the most fascinating and relevant media for the study of such "moving" or evolving collective identities. Films are a spectacular vehicle for the dramatization of collective myths and for a ritual consumption of these myths through spectatorship. Through the reworking and retelling of familiar stories in variations, films articulate and form the collective unconscious that yearns to connect to an origin of fixed meaning that will anchor identity in the fertile common ground of the collective: stories that nations repeatedly tell themselves, ritualized mythologies which signify the dreams and the anxieties of these collectives, their utopian aspirations, and their dystopian nightmares.

Movies stir us because they tell us something about ourselves and our fellow humans; they can mobilize us to identify with common ideals, devote and even sacrifice our lives for them. They open a window to cultures we are curious about and hold a mirror to the cultures that create them, reflecting that culture, its highlights, and its discontents.

In our globalized, postmodern, condensed world, where populations are in constant motion and travel, identities become ever more fluid, contested terrains for negotiation and change. It is in this mobile world that films travel across borders and cultural boundaries and become intercultural arenas for the formation of meaning.

Israeli Cinema: Identities in Motion is a collection of essays that examine Israeli cinema as a prism that refracts collective Israeli identities through the medium and art of motion pictures. Israeli cinema, we believe, is a particularly fascinating test case, because it has been created within a national cultural context that has reflexively produced itself since its very beginning at the end of the nineteenth century and is still very much engaged in the formation of the evolving national/collective identity in the second millennium.

Israeli culture is a product of a utopian enterprise: Zionism, which started in the late 1880s, was conceived in the contexts of nationalism in Europe and realized in the land of Israel-Palestine as a pioneering endeavor, regarded by some contemporary historians and sociologists as a colonial enterprise. However it is conceptualized, this is clearly an intriguing case of a national community consciously imagining itself, writing its national revival as a new chapter in its ancient collective memory, and reviving its sacred texts and language as a new national secular culture. It is a fascinating case for studying the creation of a unified, cohesive national culture in a territory which existed virtually as a text, in a language used mostly in print and in oral sacred ritual, and on the basis of voluntary and forced immigration from diverse cultural and geographical backgrounds.

The evolution of Israeli culture can be placed on the long continuum of Jewish cultural and textual tradition. At the same time, it is also a disruptive revolutionary enterprise in that it forced diverse cultural traditions and collective biographies of the Jewish Diasporas into a "New Hebrew" collective-national mold, later termed "Israeli." In addition to these diverse ethnic-cultural challenges to the newly re-created community, the evolving national culture took root in the mythological ancient holy land of origin, in which other communal identities were and had been living and forming their own histories, collective memories, lived experiences, oral and print cultures. The encounter with the local Palestinian, Druze, and other communities in the Land of Israel yields a complex cultural clash over collective meanings and dominance. Articles in this anthology by Ben-Zvi-Morad, Gertz and Hermoni, Meiri, and Naaman offer a historical perspective and diverse theoretical positions on the intercultural and interethnic encounters, clashes, and conflicts between Israeli Jews and Palestinian Arabs and on their representations and historiographies in Israeli cinema.

Hebrew cinema took an active part in the mobilization and construction of the new national culture. The creation and dissemination of Zionism, the new ideology which in the late 1880s advocated the idea of the return of the Jewish people to their ancient homeland in the Land of Israel, coincided with the evolution and consolidation of cinema as a medium and art, both in Europe and in North America. The pioneering national Zionist enterprise mobilized the moving pictures to stir Jews in the Diaspora to join the efforts of construction and national revival in Palestine. Moreover, both silent and talking films made in Palestine itself as well as those co-produced abroad were a medium for the construction and articulation of the evolving national identity. Films such as *This Is the Land* (*Zot Hee Ha'aretz*, Agadati, 1934) documented scenes from the Land of Israel as well as staged scenes of pioneers settling the land, planting trees and expanding agriculture, building diverse communities, and creating new forms of social-communal living, including the urban Tel Aviv and the cooperative kibbutz.

The rebirth of the nation was depicted as a productive effort of building and taming the wasteland into a fertile abundance of life and creativity. This reproductive national project was imagined on the silver screen as a masculine teleological endeavor, a forceful movement through the territory to conquer it by a spectacular bodily effort: Western-like generic narratives of a mythic clash between frontier and homesteaders, wasteland and civilization. The persistent taming of the barren, desolate land was almost always by men and their phallic extensions: the body, the hoe, the rifle, the horse. The Palestinian inhabitants of the contested territory were ambivalently depicted as noble savages who thwart the attempt to bring civilization and harmonic order into the chaotic wild East; as model representatives of the ancient biblical forefathers, the shepherds and farmers of the ancient holy land; or as potent "Orientals," who represented the alternative to a feminized, passive, impotent, victimized Diaspora Jew.

This newly created cultural identity used the new medium of film to convey the creative momentum of the new nation. The aesthetics of Soviet cinema—with its dynamic montage editing style, magnifying oblique shooting angles, and ideologically committed pathos—was mobilized to create sequences of lively movement and visual and sonic excess, signifying the new life pulsating in the ancient, prehistoric land. At the same time, early Israeli films also borrowed narratives and iconographies from the American Western, with its resolute pioneers who tame the wasteland as well as the stylized encounters with the local natives as a setting for this spectacular national effort to seize and conquer the old-new frontier land.

The hybridization of Soviet and American genres and styles with additional futurist aesthetics—which glorified man and machine, mass production, labor, and industrialization—articulated the new nation as dynamic and Westernized. This pre-state Zionist cinema both expressed and determined the fundamentals of the inchoate Israeli culture, with its masculinist orientations, the centrality of territory and conflict, the emphasis on the collective rather than individual experience, and the primacy of the national over the familial and public over private sphere. Essays by Feldestein, Horak, and Peleg in this anthology offer diverse critical perspectives, interpretations, and re-visions of pioneering cinematic formulations of the Zionist enterprise.

The aftermath of the Holocaust and the 1948 war known to Israelis as the War of Independence brought waves of immigrants into the newly declared state of Israel: refugees from the death camps of Europe and Jewish refugees as well as voluntary immigrants from the Middle East. The encounter between Holocaust survivors and the veteran Yishuv is a formative chapter in Israeli history. The Holocaust, which had crucial consequences for the foundation of a state for the Jews in the Land of Israel, continues to fulfill a major role in the Israeli conscious and less conscious collective memory and psyche. Essays by Avisar, Steir-Livny, and Yosef in this anthology reexamine cinematic Israeli negotiations of the Holocaust and its ramifications in Israeli history, society, and identity politics in films from the 1940s to the 2000s.

During the 1940s and 1950s films in Hebrew and English were still consciously used to consolidate and create an Israeli community out of the diverse traditions and cultural heritages that the new immigrants brought to the country. In the 1960s and 1970s this intensive and deliberate effort, which cinema continued to deploy in a highly stylized manner, gave way to a "normalized" local cinematic idiom, created as part of the collective, lived everyday experience of a culture that began to be less self-consciously fabricated. Whereas in the United States and parts of Europe television became a popular medium for creating and projecting collective experiences in the 1950s, television in Israel was not genuinely legitimized as a productive commercial industry and medium for the collective dreams and anxieties before the early 1990s. That role was reserved for the film industry, which remained a significant medium for formulating collective identities that were often contested.

In the 1960s films affiliated with the "National Heroic" genre encapsulated the nationalist ethos of survival and cohesiveness, mostly in hybrid narratives and fictional worlds depicted in war films, melodramas, and comedies. These films featured pioneering collectives, warriors, and other socially significant peer groups. As such, they continued to uphold the national collectivist, group-oriented culture and represented the conservative gatekeeping of the boundaries of national identity. For the most part, these films presented a masculine world that relegated women to stereotypical representations, ignored the experiences of immigrants and diverse ethnic traditions, and privileged action and exteriority over the mundane and domestic sphere.

Eventually, however, the conservative nationalist genre lost its hold, as audiences increasingly preferred films that better articulated their real experiences and concerns. Israeli films from the 1960s and 1970s—melodramatic war films such as *He Walked through the Fields* (Yosef Millo, 1967), "group" movies and Bourekas films and comedies like *What a Gang!* (Ze'ev Khavatzelet, 1962), *Halfon Hill Doesn't Answer* (Assi Dayan, 1976), and *The Troupe* (Avi Nesher, 1978)—projected a cohesive collective, which coalesces out of a diverse and contested multiethnic and multicultural steaming melting pot.

The most popular films during the sixties and seventies highlighted the preoccupation of the local film industry, which, like Hollywood studio films, held a mirror to the nation, narrativized the formulaic stories, and projected the images that it wanted to see. The most popular genre of those years was the so-called Bourekas film: generic comedies and melodramas which adapted popular cinematic traditions from the Middle East and Eastern European Jewish folk traditions and re-created interclass and interethnic clashes that usually unfold in the familial sphere. Typically, the clashes of the Bourekas drama are resolved through intermarriage and integration or containment within the family unit. Such "happy endings" confirmed and endorsed the integrative-utopian thrust of the Israeli melting pot ideology by repeatedly dramatizing the merging of diverse identities in the communal mold. But with changing social and cultural realities this mythic and utopian model eventually became irrelevant. Essays in this anthology by Ben Shaul, Gershenson, Shemer, and Talmon offer a dynamic overview of the evolving cinematic idioms of ethnicity, immigration, and interethnic exchanges in Israeli films and their changing formations.

The Israeli military is another unique institution of social integration and co-option. War and the ongoing conflict in the Middle East continue to haunt Israeli consciousness, collective memory, and lived experience. Militarism and war have taken a painful and traumatic toll on Israelis, which Israeli cinema has dealt with directly over the years. Several essays in this anthology discuss the implications of war and its articulations in Israeli cinema through history: Cohen, Kaplan, Zerubavel, Zanger, Munk, and Ne'eman discuss ideological and mythic aspects of collective Jewish and Israeli memory in the cinematic depictions of war in Israel.

While popular films in the 1960s and 1970s continued to focus on commonplace themes of community, interethnic exchange, army camaraderie, and the emerging petit bourgeoisie, a counter-elitist genre developed that spoke against the egalitarian and integrative ethos articulated by the more commercial and conservative films. Expressing modernist sensibilities, these new films adopted the avant-garde artistic aesthetics of the French New Wave, Italian neo-realism, and American new Hollywood cinema. Highly stylized, these films proposed progressive as well as reactionary models of Israeli existence, an urban, alienated existentialism, and anti-ideological angst. Such films reversed the masculine worldview and integrative fervor of the collective ethos and offered alternative models of masculinity as well as alienated particularistic, individualistic, and privatized modes of existence. The reality of a nation at war, burdened by internal tensions among ethnic, national, and religious minorities, was suppressed in these aesthetically sophisticated films, reserved for the cinematic elite and detached from their Israeli audiences. These "personal" Israeli films, referred to as the "New Sensibility" cinema, strove to reverse the normative collectivist and masculine militarism of the past. Such films articulated a second transition, if not a real revolution, in Israeli cultural consciousness, setting in motion a new phase in the negotiation of collective identities.

At the end of the 1970s Israeli society and culture underwent crucial transitions. The long-lasting hegemony of the socialist labor party (Ma'arakh, Mifleget Ha'avodah) was challenged for the first time in Israeli history in the 1977 elections, which brought to power the nationalist-liberal party (Likud) headed by Menahem Begin. Later that year, the Egyptian president Anwar Sadat came to Jerusalem, initiating what was to become Israel's first peace treaty with an Arab state. Israeli cinema both reflected and took part in these transformations of Israeli culture toward a new social and political agenda. The vigorous revision of mainstream ideologies in 1980s films took place in the symbolic spaces that formerly defined the cohesive national ethos, such as the army and the kibbutz. These cultural sites, which allegorically dramatized and textualized the Sabra myth, were now used to deconstruct this very imagined epitome of collective identity. Israeli films from the late 1970s and throughout the 1980s renegotiate the altruistic tenets of the individual sacrifice of life and self-realization on the national altar in a variety of familiar contexts: the pioneer commune (*Once We Were Dreamers*, Barbash, 1987), the army (*Paratroopers*, Ne'eman, 1977; *One of Ours*, Barbash, 1989; *The Troupe*, Nesher, 1978; *Avanti Popolo*, Bukai, 1986), the kibbutz (*Noa at 17*, Yeshurun, 1982; *Atalia*, Tevet, 1984), and the peer group (*Late Summer Blues*, Schorr, 1987; *The Wooden Gun*, Moshenson, 1979; *The Summer of Aviya*, Cohen, 1988). These films retell the story of the committed and unified national collective as a countermyth of disintegration and oppression; they shatter the symbolic father and resurrect the repressed feminized diasporic Jew, Holocaust survivor, and excluded Palestinian Arab.

The 1990s saw the acceleration of these trends, especially as Israel increasingly opened up to outside influences. Millennial, postmodern sensibilities exercised a particularly strong hold on Israeli culture by emphasizing hybridity and ambiguity; the destabilization of grand narratives; and the fluidity of boundaries between national and global, masculine and feminine, real and virtual, and documentary and fiction. All of these global trends find their articulation in Israeli cinema. Alienated from its audiences by its subversive, deconstructivist political stance throughout the 1980s, Israeli cinema in the 1990s seems threatened by the rapid growth of viable commercial, cable, and satellite television, which have become the most productive sites in popular Israeli culture for the formation of identities.

This threat to cinematic dominance and expression was also an advantage, however, as commercial television uses Israeli cinema as a resource to anchor its discourse in a shared visual and narrative cultural memory as well as repertory. Israeli films are constantly recycled on TV, especially in ritual collective times such as national holidays (for example, Independence Day) and in special programming devoted to the screenings of past and contemporary Israeli cinema. Moreover, the commercial television industry frequently employs filmmakers, producers, cinematographers, and other film professionals for its own original productions, and an exchange of generic traditions as well as authorship feeds both arenas of cultural production.

Among the transformations created by the free market forces of the 1990s in Israel was an important change to the policies of the Israeli Fund for Quality Films, a public financing committee that dominated film production throughout the 1980s. As one of the only financial resources for Israeli filmmakers, the Israeli Fund traditionally supported more artistic and progressive, radically political films. In the 1990s, however, it began to adjust its support to fit the new and more popular cultural sensibilities. Together with the country's more commercial media, it became a resource for the formation of a new cinematic idiom, which under the slogan "films from here," strives for an authentic expression of real and sensually authentic Israeli life in its Mediterranean, Middle Eastern context.

The intense yearning for a change in the national agenda toward the end of the millennium was accompanied by a quest for authentic expression in the culture at large and in cinema in particular. A spate of second-generation films strove to express these changes through engagement with multiculturalism, collective and multiple biographies and histories, and an almost obsessive return to past traumas. Such films articulate revisionist approaches to representations of the Holocaust, Mizrahim, immigration, national history, and the kibbutz, along with new conceptualization of gender, sexuality, place, and cultural space. New social and cultural groups which were underrepresented within the homogenizing old cinematic discourses, or stereotypically represented in the service of collectivist-nationalist ideologies, are now more visible as well as self-represented. These new discourses of the minor and new sensibilities, which through cinematic expression offer "lines of flight" from obsolete cinematic and ideological paradigms, articulate processes within Israeli cinema and culture as well as larger formations in the postmodern world and global market. Articles by Dushi, Chyutin, Padva, and Kedem discuss such new discourses of old and newly visualized (sub)cultures as well as minorities in Israeli cinema of the current millennium.

The central role of gender formations in the cinematic negotiations of collective Israeli identity and the national history cannot be underestimated. National identities and their deconstruction formed mainly by adopting new masculine models and later shattering and dismantling them. The reaction against the victimized and marginalized Jewish positioning in the Diaspora brought hypermasculine overtones to the generic narrative and aesthetic features of early Hebrew and Israeli films. The opening of Israeli culture to alternative, new, and diverse directions is articulated through new approaches to gender and sexuality, which challenge by now obsolete cinematic and cultural models. Several essays in this anthology, although not included under this title, deal with gender and sexuality, as symptoms of ideological and cultural transitions in the culture.

The 1993 Oslo Accords were a political manifestation of a fundamental change in Israeli culture, signified in contemporary Israeli cinema by film noir–like dystopias reflecting Israelis' broken sense of place and control. The masculine paradigm, which had sustained the Zionist-national discourse, was replaced by a shift to the feminine aspects of mundane experiences within the private sphere and the legitimization of a personal pursuit of happiness and self-realization. This shift in cultural priorities, which sustained the great support for the peace process and the hopes for "normalization," was shattered in the early 2000s by the second Palestinian uprising and wave of terror known as the Al-Aqsa Intifada. The violent Palestinian revolt was preceded by the collapse of the peace process and reemphasized the severity of the internal fissures within Israeli society: the growing centrifugal pressures of subcultures, which no longer conform to a dominant Hebrew unifying cultural core, and the ever-growing quest for new leadership and "normalcy" that will finally end the pressures of war, terror, occupation, victimization, and other moral issues that keep haunting Israeli society and culture.

This anthology brings the discussion of Israeli cinema as a site of struggle over cultural meanings into this very transitional phase in Israeli culture in the first decade of the twenty-first century. Indeed, Israeli cinema has found a respectable place on the global cinematic scene, where the discourse about identity is integral to cinematic discourse. Yet, in addressing Israeli audiences, Israeli cinema remains a major site of negotiation and revisioning of history. This is an ongoing project of Israeli cinema, as demonstrated by the essays in this anthology, which chart a culture in constant motion that defies its deep longing for a stable and untroubled existence. The very conceptualization of Israeli identity and cinema, which we share as editors of this anthology, makes it difficult for us to conclude with tightly knit ends. We hope that readers will start a discussion rather than summarize and canonize one, because the stories we examine here are part of a history still in the making and a historiography much debated. We hope that those interested in the Israeli story will find these pages instructive and thought provoking.

Miri Talmon and Yaron Peleg

PART I

The Nation Imagined on Film

I Filming the Homeland

Cinema in Eretz Israel and the Zionist Movement, 1917–1939

ARIEL L. FELDESTEIN

The cinematic depiction of the historical return of the Jewish people to their homeland from 1917 through 1939 is the subject of this essay. After four centuries of consecutive Ottoman rule, which left a profound mark on the country, in 1917 the British conquered Eretz Israel, demarcating its political and administrative borders and shaping its regime and legal structure. These transformations contributed to the Zionist movement's endeavor to establish the Jewish National Home and to bring about the birth of the "New Jew" in Eretz Israel. Various creative disciplines began evolving in the country, including film, which was launched not only as a means of documenting and presenting the historical narrative but also as a method of constructing it. The development of cinema paralleled the fruition of other ventures initiated by members of the first generation of national revival, who experienced a tremendous metamorphosis as a result of their immigration to the country, and was later advanced by the second generation that was born into the new reality.

Most of the studies discussing the crystallization of cinema in Eretz Israel have defined the films produced during the first three decades of the twentieth century as "nonart," the result of filmmakers' adaptability and compliance with the national needs. Researchers maintained that the films lacked any artistic value, so there was no point in exploring them through that perspective. Some scholars have even gone so far as to point out similarities between the cinematic creation in Eretz Israel and films produced during the same period in totalitarian states such as the Soviet Union and Nazi Germany. Yet such an approach belittles the artistic aspect of the Eretz

Israel films. The present study questions this monolithic presentation and describes the diversity and differences that can be found among the various filmmakers and films.

This essay deals with two complementary issues. First, it is concerned with the way in which the Zionist idea was presented and realized through film. More specifically, it examines the translation or adaptation of the Jewish return to the homeland and the redemption and birth of the "New Jew" through visual expressions. At the core of this discussion is the premise that film is a bona fide historical document, a quintessential product of its time, whose power far exceeds that of written words. The films analyzed here provide a prism through which I explore the ideological components, the social characteristics, and the way real-life actions were interpreted at the time. The second issue I examine is the interaction between filmmakers and national institutions during a highly ideological era. The works analyzed here were all made by filmmakers who immigrated to Palestine to become an integral part of the Jewish Yishuv (Jewish community in Palestine). They include Yaacov Ben Dov, Natan Axelrod, Khaim Halakhmi, Barukh Agadati, and Helmar Lerski.

Yaacov Ben Dov

Yaacov Ben Dov immigrated to Eretz Israel at the beginning of December 1907, during the Hanukah holiday. Keren Kayemeth LeIsrael began acquiring lands in an organized manner at that time,[1] and infrastructures were built in preparation for the establishment of Jewish settlements. In order to implement the agency's policy efficiently, a Palestine Office was established in Jaffa, headed by Dr. Arthur Rupin. Ben Dov saw these developments as a chance to enhance his activity as a photographer and suggested that Rupin assist in securing him a position as the official photographer of the 1909 eighth Zionist Congress, convening in Hamburg. As far as we know, his request was denied. The Zionist institutions of the time were less than enthusiastic about cooperating with Ben Dov. But he was not discouraged. At every opportunity, he approached Zionist bureaucrats, imploring them to hire him as a photographer. Finally Rupin consented and commissioned him to take several photographs of Hebrew settlements around the country. Ben Dov's aspiration, however, was to direct films. But he faced an obstacle: he could not finance the purchase of a suitable camera. As a subject of the Ottoman Empire, Ben Dov was recruited into the Ottoman army during World War I and was positioned as a medical photographer in an Austrian unit.

As a token of their appreciation for his devoted service, his superior officers gave Ben Dov a motion-picture camera.

The progress of the British army toward Jaffa and Jerusalem at the end of the war, headed by General Edmund Allenby, excited the Yishuv population, who longed to be released from the Ottoman rule. Ben Dov perceived the transformations that occurred in Eretz Israel as a rare opportunity to immortalize history in the making on celluloid and filmed the entrance of Allenby and his troops into Jerusalem in the winter of 1917. That scene would constitute the opening of his first film, *Yehuda Ha'meshukhreret* (The Liberated Judea).

Through his camera lens Ben Dov witnessed the historical events and transformation transpiring in Eretz Israel. In shaping the historical memory of a nation which was beginning to crystallize its national identity and form as a geopolitical entity, he intended the filmed documentation not only for the people of his time but for future generations as well. This occurred while Eretz Israel was still in a state of war and suffered from a shortage of raw materials and means for filming a motion picture. But Ben Dov was not discouraged. Ignoring the dangers and the hardships, he traveled around the country to document with his camera the historical events and the evolution of the Zionist enterprise, prompted by the British occupation. Ben Dov perceived himself first and foremost as an artist-historian chronicling the drama on film. He considered every frame a testimony to the feats of the Zionist project in Eretz Israel. Most of the scenes were shot from afar, recording and immortalizing the events without intervening or influencing them. Some sequences are more reminiscent of still photos than of film. In addition, the cinematography lacks any aesthetic pretension, because Ben Dov wished to document the event as it "really" was and present it as a historical testimony. Perhaps he also hoped to evoke the viewers' trust in this way (as well as to express his own enthusiasm concerning the events) and to prevent any possible complaint concerning misleading camera effects. Ben Dov failed to interest Keren Kayemeth in purchasing the film and distributing it among the Jewish communities in the Diaspora. It was eventually lost, and only several sequences and its program have remained.

While preparing to produce another film, Ben Dov decided to realize his old dream: in April 1919 he founded the Menorah film company. The cofounder and associate manager was Mordekhai Schwartz. The Zionist Commission to Palestine (Va'ad Hatzirim) gave its blessing to the establishment of the company, recognizing it as a contribution to the effort of documenting "images of historical events, which have great national value."[2] Yet the commission was not quick to assist with the funding of this company, which fell apart in the early 1920s.

During the twenties and early thirties Ben Dov was often frustrated with his cinematic efforts. National institutions did not offer him the support and assistance he expected to receive. Over the years he repeatedly tried to reach the awareness of institutions and the general public, usually at his own expense. Ben Dov even failed in convincing the Keren Kayemeth and Keren Hayesod national funds to acquire the distributing rights for his films. As a last resort he decided to approach Khaim Weizmann, the president of the Zionist Movement, directly and offer his cinematic work to be preserved at the national library on Mount Scopus, for 2,000 Israeli liras. When his offer was declined, he decided to sell the collection to Barukh Agadati for 100 Israeli liras. His dream of presenting future generations with a visual historical documentation of the Jewish people's return to their national home in Eretz Israel was not realized. A substantial part of his work was lost or ruined over the years, and fragments from his films were integrated into other works without crediting their source.

In his cinematic work, Ben Dov focused on recording historical events related to Eretz Israel in general and the establishment of the national home in particular. Acting as a documentary filmmaker, he did not get involved with what was happening in front of the camera, preferring wide angles and long shots. The editing was simple: a depiction of the sequence of occurrences. He wrote the script himself and did not ask permission for the production from institutions. Many of the films were produced at his own expense and only later sold for distribution.

Ben Dov viewed himself as part of the Jewish national society forming in Eretz Israel; he defined himself as a Zionist and aspired to express this ideological perception in his work. Unlike filmmakers in other countries, such as the Soviet Union, Ben Dov assisted in national propaganda out of his own free will. No public or private resources could be found to invest in the film industry (as was the case in the movie industry in the United States), so he had to make do with incredibly inferior filming, developing, and editing equipment, which significantly lagged behind the accepted standards in Europe and the United States. Within the framework of these limitations he made an effort to produce high-quality films, in the hope that their content would uplift the spirit of the viewers and compensate for the technical flaws.

From a historical perspective, Ben Dov holds a place of honor as the herald of motion pictures in the Land of Israel and as the one who established its foundations. He paved the way for filmmakers who came after him, who relied on the experience that he had accumulated while laying the foundations of this creative project.[3]

Natan Axelrod and Khaim Halakhmi

During the late 1920s and early 1930s new attempts were made to produce films in Eretz Israel. The most prominent expression of these efforts was the establishment of a production company initiated by two people, Natan Axelrod and Khaim Halakhmi.

Oded Hanoded (Oded the Wanderer)

The first full-length Eretz Israel feature film, *Oded Hanoded*, was based on a Tzvi Liberman story. The book's protagonist is a boy who gets lost during a class field trip. Alone, Oded faces winds and storms but prevails and finds his way back home. During his long journey, Oded reaches a Bedouin tribe and befriends a boy his age who wishes to learn from him. The Bedouins assist Oded in his attempt to return home, and his friend finally joins him and integrates into Oded's school and the Jewish children's society. Oded "civilizes" the Bedouin boy, teaching him the secrets of the Western world. Thus the film expresses the approach which asserted not only the Zionist movement's transformation of the "Old Jew" but also its contribution to the redemption of the other peoples of the land. Oded represents progress and the benefits of Western culture compared to the Bedouin boy's way of life.

The most striking difference between the script of *Oded Hanoded* and the story it is based on is that the film does not mention the encounter between Oded and the Bedouin tribe. At the heart of the script are Oded and his classmates, who embark on a hiking trip with an American Jewish tourist near a village. They trek across rocky, rugged ground that is quite different from the luscious landscape of their native blooming valley. On the morning of the second day of the trip, Oded is lost. The teacher and the other students search for him with the village guard and some of the parents, including Oded's father, who join them on horseback. Oded wanders around, unsuccessfully attempting to find his way back. He is injured and his water canteen runs dry, but he does not lose hope and continues his effort to find his way back to the village. Eventually everyone returns safely home, and Oded is restored to his parents. The script, then, focuses on the individual's endeavor to overcome the natural elements, on the personal effort required for survival and the group's responsibility toward the individual. The spotlight has shifted from the initiation rite to concern for Oded.

The script translates Oded's effort to cope with the situation, the interaction between him and the group, and the Jewish settlement enterprise into images. The film opens with a long panoramic shot of the Jezreel Valley landscapes followed by a series of shots of large buildings, zooming in on village houses embedded in cultivated lands. These images glorify the Jewish settlement movement, before the viewer is even introduced to the movie's characters. The Zionist project is in fact the film's major theme, setting the foundation for the plot.

The movie's numerous visual statements integrate into a single plot based on the romantic image of the settlers' life in the Jezreel Valley in general and the lives of their children in particular. We are presented with a community that supports its members and vouches for them, offering values, serene country living, quality of life, and economic prosperity. The film takes a different turn due to the filmmakers' decision to exclude the Bedouin boy's initiation by Oded from the script and present the realization of the Zionist idea as a solution not just for Jews but for the rest of the country's population as well.

Although Ella Shohat mentions this factor, she also discusses the film's depiction of the tension embedded in the interaction between the pioneers and the land's "natives." But Shohat bases her claims on texts and other films of the era and of later periods rather than on *Oded Hanoded* itself. A movie should be analyzed in reference to the period and culture it was created in, so it seems inappropriate to find fault with it due to reservations about the Zionist endeavor or its approach to the "indigenous people of the land." "The wilderness toward which he feels alienation," writes Shohat, "includes the local residents, to whom the camera does not grant any autonomy or individuality beyond being part of the landscape. The teacher's history lesson, for example, ignores the Arab presence and strips it of any history and geography, as a kind of homological continuation to the Zionist discourse."[4]

Yet how can one praise a work of art that consciously ignores that particular disharmony and at the same time object to its disregard for that same factor? The creators of the film chose not to explore this issue. They described the importance of the settlement enterprise and its contribution to the development of the New Jew and to the construction of the identity, body, and soul of the New Jewish/Hebrew child. That was their concern, and hence their work had no room for a visual expression of "individual autonomy" or "the indigenous people of the land."[5]

The movie was screened for two months at the Eden movie theater in Tel Aviv, where the audience greeted it enthusiastically. Following the film's success at cinemas across the country, the producers hoped to distribute it across the Jewish world and searched for supportive philanthropist Jews for this purpose. The producers also approached Keren Kayemeth, which objected to the absence of images presenting pioneers or the rejuvenation of Eretz Israel. As a result, the filmmakers incorporated the settlement theme and the project of redeeming the Jezreel Valley in the second version of the script, hoping thus to receive assistance with the distribution of the film across the Jewish world.

The lack of resources also put a strain on the relationship between Axelrod and Halakhmi. The two argued about the film's production rights and about each author's part in it. Axelrod attempted to deny Halakhmi his title as the film's director, probably unjustly. The shortage of money and the personal animosity caused the bankruptcy of their production company. Khaim Halakhmi was compelled to shelve his dream to create films and gave up working in this field. But Natan Axelrod endured.

Barukh Agadati

In 1931, when Axelrod was in the middle of producing the *Homeland Newsreel* with Yerushalayim Segal, Barukh Agadati decided to quit his dancing career and focus on cinema. Together with his brother Yitzkhak, who was in charge of the technical and organizational aspects, he established a small laboratory in the shed where they were living and started producing *Aga Newsreel* to compete with *Homeland Newsreel*. Like other filmmakers in this field, the Agadati brothers requested assistance from the national institutions, but eventually they raised the necessary funds from private investors. One of them was Meir Dizengoff, a businessman and the mayor of Tel Aviv.

Zot Hee Ha'aretz (This Is the Land)

In the race to produce a feature film, Axelrod and Halakhmi preceded Agadati. Yet their motion pictures were silent, and therefore their triumph could only be considered relative. Aiming to achieve a complete victory, at the end of 1934 Agadati managed to buy the Ofek film company's equipment. A further step—the purchase of Yaacov Ben Dov's film archive for one hundred Israeli liras—brought him even closer to the fulfillment of his dream. Now he asked the author Avigdor Hameiri to write a script which incorporated the cinematic materials that had been accumulated. Meiri's script included sections from the Ben Dov films and newsreels which documented major historical events from the early days of Zionism and the British mandate in Eretz Israel and added sequences from the *Aga Newsreel* as well as new documentary and fictional footage.

The plot of *Zot Hee Ha'aretz* begins in 1881–1882, with the first wave of Jewish immigration. It depicts the pioneers' effort to build the country and ends with a display of the entire pioneering enterprise. In keeping with the Zionist ethos, the film presents Jews of the Diaspora as soulless and Eretz Israel as a wasteland: the consequence of the people's neglect of the land. After the Jewish people have returned to their land, the movie suggests, redemption begins. The symbiosis between the people and the land fills an important role in the construction of the Jewish nationality, and the religious yearning for the return to Zion is translated into a national longing. The immigration itself is described as a rebirth. The new life is based on the ideological "negation of the Diaspora" ("Shlilat Hagalut") and on the cultivation of the land.

One of the images representing this idea is a scene illustrating a pioneer's supreme sacrificial act: the pioneer is seen "redeeming the land" by plowing it, when he suddenly drops dead. A guard on horseback gallops toward the deceased pioneer, identifies him, and hurries to find a replacement. The body merges in a dissolve with the lumps of the plowed land while the dying man shouts, as if conveying a legacy: "Onward! Onward!" (in Hebrew: "Kadima"). The scene ends when the man's corpse and the land fuse into one, while the substitute pioneer continues to plow the land.

The plot also highlights one of the prominent features characterizing the metamorphosis of the diasporic Old Jew into a New Jew: the shift in the approach to the culture of the body. Zionist ideology has presented the rehabilitation of the Jewish body as one of its key goals and a countermeasure against the overly spiritual diasporic Jew. The mythic figure of the Israeli-born Sabra is muscular and powerful, as befits someone who is required to fill a historical role in the redemption of the land. The process of shedding the limp diasporic body is described in a sequence of images showing children and youths exercising in a variety of athletic activities.

Most of the scenes depicting Tel Aviv and its residents are teeming with activity and labor. Construction, athletics, and group activities are particularly emphasized. The discrepancy between the life of urban "comfort" and the hardships of the agricultural way of life in the settlements is minimized.

The movie culminates in a mass scene of an entire crowd singing "Am Israel Khai" (literally meaning "The People of Israel Live") while the volume increases along with the accelerated rhythm of the changing scenes. Groups of young men run in the open field toward a group of young women merging into a "Hora" dance circle. The pace of the dance and the spinning human circle gradually increase along with the swelling music, reaching great harmony. The statement is clear: "Am Israel Khai."

Zot Hee Ha'aretz was unfavorably received not just by contemporaneous film critics but by later film scholars as well. Thus, for example, Yehuda Harel disagrees with the claim that the production of the film, despite the meager means available at the time, was an achievement in its own right for the Agadati brothers.[6] He alludes to the revised version of the film and the adjustments inserted in a laboratory abroad, considerably improving its quality. Margot Klausner sums up her impressions of the film by asserting that its producers "did not provide the script with a main idea that will connect its disintegrated parts."[7]

Igal Bursztyn refers mainly to the film's quality and technique, which "includes two kinds of face shots: a horizontal camera movement (panning) across the faces of pioneers standing in a group and individual static close-ups of pioneers giving speeches."[8] He also criticizes the filming of the dialogues in the film and the acting therein: "It is not the words which are lying, but the actors' faces. The actors pretend that they are human while in fact they are nothing but a tool, an ideology's amplifier."[9] Furthermore, "conflicts are spoken about, but not shown. The film prefers words and stylized visual symbols as 'artistic' allegories."[10] Bursztyn mainly criticizes the film's use of actor positioning, acting, and filming techniques to communicate ideological messages. As a result of their desire to convey these messages, he claims, the filmmakers neglected to use the available arsenal of artistic tools at their disposal. Bursztyn reaches these conclusions without first finding out which professional tools Agadati indeed had at his disposal at the time and whether it was even possible for him to achieve the accepted professional levels in the Hollywood and European film industries of his time.[11]

Zot Hee Ha'aretz did not receive any financing or support from the national institutions. Therefore there was no outside interference with the contents, ideas, and filming of the movie. Keren Kayemeth and Keren Hayesod (literally, the Foundation Fund) even rejected Agadati's request to assist with the distribution of the film to Jewish communities abroad. The film, which was produced with the aid of private investment, expressed Barukh Agadati's personal artistic vision, which reveals enthusiasm about the national endeavor and its grandeur.

Barukh Agadati proved that with a relatively modest investment a talking movie could be made even in Eretz Israel and a proper level of filmic creation could still be achieved. In fact, this film should be regarded as part of the attempt to develop modern agriculture and industry with local means in Eretz Israel. The national institutions were mobilized in favor of the first two fields, however, while entrepreneurs in the field of cinema usually had to manage on their own.

Helmar Lerski

Helmar Lerski was a well-known portrait photographer in Germany who drew the attention of Paul Boroschek, a wealthy German Jew who decided to invest in a film about the achievements of the Zionist project. For that purpose, he established with Banuar Kelter a production company called Tzalmono'a, Inc. and allocated four thousand Eretz Israeli liras for the production of the film. Lerski agreed to Boroschek's offer to act as the film's cinematographer and arrived in Palestine at the beginning of the 1930s.

In his film, Lerski concentrated on water as a vital resource, perhaps the most important resource for the agricultural settlement in Eretz Israel. Most of the movie was filmed using a small amateur camera containing up to fifteen meters of film. He claimed that the small camera had great advantages: versatility, a dynamic movement free of a tripod, and the ability to shoot quickly from every angle and height. The professional camera of those days required heavy cranes and several operators to achieve the same effect. When Lerski photographed portraits, he used lighting to "sculpt" and design them in an expressive manner. The Palestinian sun gave him great pleasure and freed him of the need for artificial lighting.[12]

Avodah (Work/Labor)

The film begins with a quotation from Isaiah 11:12: "And He will lift up a standard for the nations / and assemble the banished ones of Israel / and will gather the dispersed of Judah / from the four corners of the earth," reminding viewers that the return to Zion in the modern age is a manifestation of the ancient divine promise. The opening sequence focuses on two feet walking resolutely along a railroad track. Closely focused on the marching feet, the "static" camera movement creates a sense of departure from an old place to a new one. Until he arrives in the Promised Land, the closed frame never reveals the identity of the walker, who functions as a symbol of the immigrants returning to Eretz Israel to transform the land. The "pilgrim's" personal story and exilic past are unimportant. Only his "rebirth" is significant: the moment when he arrives in the country and integrates into the collective that is laying the foundations for the Zionist endeavor.

Most of the film's plot involves the drilling of a water well in a scorched and barren expanse. The drilling sequence is presented in a series of close-ups showing pieces of the drilling machine and fragmented body parts of the pioneers who are operating it, with a harmony of rhythm and function between workers and machine. No faces are displayed. The right side of the frame displays a row of men's feet. At the center are silhouettes of the laborers, pulling the drill lever up and pushing it down in a coordinated movement. The rhythmic editing and the shadowy shapes of the drill pieces and the muscular body parts create an impression of a single organic body without clear boundaries. The tempo of the drilling, the close-ups of the drill penetrating the ground, and the exposed limbs converge into an erotic dance.

The in-and-out movement of the elongated iron rod clearly creates a kind of simulated intercourse between the men and the soil. Indeed, the sequence culminates orgasmically with the eruption of water, which finally bursts out of the ground. With the help of an improvised bell, a pioneer signals to his distant friends the coming of redemption.[13] Women show up for the first time in the film, and children swarm around the pump as the overflowing water fills the frame in a long series of images that compensate for the surrounding dryness. As the celebration continues the community's children sing and dance in a circle, embracing each other and moving together as one united body. Following the children, their parents join the circles of dancers. Water, the essence of life, gushes into the prepared canals and brings life to the land. Cattle, sheep, and children drink from the faucets: the next generation is already enjoying the fruits of the revolution.[14]

Even if Lerski's priorities were more aesthetic than ideological, it is clear today that the presentation of a new Jewish body in his films and others shaped Zionism profoundly. But this was not the way Zionist institutions perceived it at the time. Despite the challenges that the movement faced in Palestine and abroad, it failed to realize and utilize the potential of film to spread its word and propagate its cause.[15]

Conclusions

During the three decades addressed in this study and particularly in the first half of the 1930s, filmmaking in Eretz Israel contributed to the shaping of long-lasting Zionist symbols, inadvertently as well as by choice. Those filmmakers, who chose Palestine not only as the location for their films but also as their new home, combined the Jewish national idea and their aspirations to express it artistically. As such, they belonged to a larger group of contemporaneous Zionist artists: poets, writers, painters, photographers, and sculptors who were preoccupied with the transformation of Jewish life in Eretz Israel. Can their diverse creations be defined as propaganda? Were they an instrument in the service of national institutions? The answer is clearly no. Unlike Nazi or Soviet films, films in Eretz Israel during the 1930s were private, not institutional, projects. Consequently, filmmakers were not compelled to curb their artistic liberty. Impoverished Zionist institutions not only responded unfavorably to their requests for assistance but also did not understand cinema's potential to convey ideology. They invested in other forms of propaganda while almost completely ignoring film.

NOTES

1. Keren Kayemeth LeIsrael (Jewish National Fund: JNF) is a fund for the afforestation and reclamation of the land of Israel, originally established as the executive arm of the World Zionist Organization to purchase land on which the national homeland could be created. JNF was the brainchild of Professor Hermann Shapira. Action was not taken on the proposal until the Fifth Zionist Congress (1901).

2. The Zionist Commission to Palestine to Executive Office, November 25, 1919, Z3/37, Zionist Central Archives.

3. See Gross and Gross (1991: 19–30); Tryster (1995: 33); Tzimmermann (2001: 43–56).

4. Shohat (2005: 49).

5. Harel (1956: 219); Bursztyn (1990: 40–43); Gross and Gross (1991: 87–89); Talmon (2001: 81–83); Tzimmermann (2001: 95–103).

6. Harel (1956: 222).

7. Klausner (1974: 17).

8. Bursztyn (1990: 44; my translation).

9. Ibid., 46–47.

10. Ibid.

11. See ibid., 44–47.

12. During the 1920s sunlight and savings in lighting expenses were mentioned as advantages of filming in Eretz Israel. Most of the other filmmakers in Eretz Israel, however, were in fact looking for ways of reducing the effect of the sunlight. See Gross and Gross (1991: 153).

13. See Gertz (2004: 16–18); and Raz (2004: 42–43).

14. See Harel (1956: 220); Klausner (1974: 17); Bursztyn (1990: 51); Gross and Gross (1991: 123–124).

15. The way in which the Zionist body is filmed—the masculine nudity, the low angles, the contrast that accentuates the curves—suggests the way in which Russian filmmakers, and particularly Sergei Eisenstein, depicted the male body during that period. See Jay (1973).

REFERENCES

Bursztyn, Igal. *Face as a Battlefield (Panim Kisde Krav)*. Tel Aviv: Hakibbutz Hameukhad, 1990.

Gertz, Nurith. *Holocaust Survivors, Aliens, and Others in Israeli Cinema and Literature (Makhela Akheret: Nitzolei Sho'ah, Zarim Va'akherim Bakoln'oa Hayisra'eli)*. Tel Aviv: Am Oved, 2004.

Gross, Natan, and Yaacov Gross. *The Hebrew Film: The History of the Silent Film and Cinema in Israel (Ha'seret Haivri)*. Jerusalem: self-published, 1991.

Harel, Yehuda. *Cinema from the Beginning to the Present* (*Hakolno'a Mereshito Ve'ad Yamenu*). Tel Aviv: Yavne Publishing, 1956.

Jay, Leyda. *Kino: A History of the Russian and Soviet Film*. New York: Collier Books, 1973.

Klausner, Margot. *The Dream Industry: Herzliya Studios, 1949–1974* (*Ta'asiyat Ha'khalomot*). Tel Aviv: Herzliya Motion Pictures Studio, 1974.

Schnitzer, Meir. *The Israeli Films: All the Facts/Plots/Directors/and Criticism* (*Hakolno'a Ha'yisre'eli*). Tel Aiv: Kineret, 1994.

Shohat, Ella. *Israeli Cinema: East/West and the Politics of Representation* (*Hakolno'a Hayisra'eli: Historia Veidiologia*). Raanna: Open University of Israel, 2005.

Talmon, Miri. *Israeli Graffiti: Nostalgia, Groups, and Collective Identity in Israeli Cinema* (*Bluz Latzabar Ha'avud: Khavurot Venostalgia Bakolno'a Hayisra'eli*). Ramat Aviv: Open University of Israel, 2001.

Tryster, Hillel. *Israel before Israel: Silent Cinema in the Holy Land*. Jerusalem: Steven Spielberg Jewish Film Archive, 1995.

Tzimmermann, Moshe. *Signs of Film: The History of Israeli Cinema, 1896–1948* (*Simanei Kolno'a: Toldot Hakolno'a Hayisra'eli*). Tel Aviv: Tel Aviv University, Dyunon Publishing, 2001.

Yosef, Raz. *Beyond Flesh: Queer Masculinities and Nationalism in Israeli Cinema*. New Brunswick, N.J.: Rutgers University Press, 2004.

FILMOGRAPHY

Agadati, Barukh. 1935. *Zot Hee Ha'aretz* (This Is the Land).

Ben Dov, Yaacov. 1919. *Yehuda Ha'meshukhreret* (The Liberated Judea).

Halakhmi, Khaim. 1932. *Oded Hanoded* (Oded the Wanderer).

Lerski, Helmar. 1935 *Avodah* (Work/Labor).

2 Helmar Lerski in Israel

JAN-CHRISTOPHER HORAK

Helmar Lerski's first book of photographs caught the imagination and the spirit of the intelligentsia of the late Weimar Republic with its mixture of reality and artifice, working-class solidarity and high art aspirations, black-and-white earthiness and ethereal lighting. Lerski's *Köpfe des Alltags* (roughly translated as "Everyday Heads") brought together intense close-up portraits of supposedly normal working people, not the dregs or the celebrities of societies but rather those nameless masses who go about their daily chores: the butcher, the baker, the charwoman, the tailor, the stoker. Marked by strong lines, weather-beaten skin, deep shadows under pensive eyes, these faces of the commonplace were true to life and at the same time larger than life. Lerski's extreme camera perspectives and chiaroscuro lighting made them heroic, turning physiognomies into breathtaking landscapes of human desire and despair. His ambition went beyond the documentation of individual human faces to the depiction of the universal in humanity: his subjects are given occupations but no names. In his photographic magnum opus *Metamorphosis through Light*, Lerski took this tendency to its logical extreme, photographing the same face 175 different ways, bending and slicing rays of sun over Tel Aviv through mirrors to create radically different personalities.[1] It is this same dichotomy between Lerski's desire to reproduce a given social reality and his need to shape his artistic medium that characterizes much of his work, both as a photographer and as an independent filmmaker in Palestine.

Early Career in Germany

Born Israel Schmuklerski in Strassbourg in 1871, Helmar Lerski spent his childhood in Switzerland before going to the United States in 1893, where he was soon apprenticed as an actor on the German-language stage.[2] After leaving the stage Lerski began his career as a photographer in Milwaukee, shooting portraits of his former colleagues at the Pabst Theater. In 1915 Lerski decided to return to Germany, where he soon found employment as a cameraman in Berlin's film industry.

Helmar Lerski's film career can be divided into two periods. The second is the primary focus here. As a cameraman in Germany, Lerski subordinated his artistic persona to the commercial demands of his film directors: he was a technician who in the best of situations could develop elements of a visual style with directors who were sympathetic to his concerns. As an independent documentary filmmaker in Palestine, Lerski ideally had control over his films, but that freedom was often subject to the propagandistic demands of his Zionist financiers. Lerski's consistent formal strategies were common to his film practice in both countries: the use of extreme close-ups in the style of his portraiture and chiaroscuro long shots, which rejected the prevalent industry practice of lighting a scene evenly.

In 1916 Lerski was hired by William Wauer, a well-known painter and film director who hoped that Lerski's radical ideas would add artistic flair to his films. Responsible for "managing all photographic and technical aspects of the operation," Lerski indeed shaped the company's goals, as noted in a press release:

> As its specialty, the W. W. Film Co., Berlin, presents an original photographic treatment of the human face, with all the richness of its expressive features and forms. The photographic artist . . . achieves this perfection in living portraiture . . . through his artistically and technically new usage and placement of light sources, which allow him to capture the human soul, as reflected in the living reality of the face.[3]

The human soul's reflection in a face—a lofty goal—was thus central to Lerski's aesthetic even at this early date. Reviews of Wauer's films (of which no footage survives) continually mention the masterly use of light and shadow, although the films seem to have been somewhat literary in other respects.

In 1917 Lerski joined producer Hanns Lippmann's Deutsche Bioscop Film Co., Berlin, as technical director, producing both publicity stills and films for director Robert Reinert's film team. Between 1917 and 1921 Lerski and Reinert completed twenty-two films, including popular successes such as *Opium* (1919) and *Nerves* (1919). Although most of their films were apparently pretentious and overladen with symbolism, *Ahasver* (Ahasuerus, 1917) seems to have been an exception. Lighting and design in Lerski's portrait of Carl de Vogt as "the eternally wandering Jew" recalled Lerski's American portrait "An Arab Head" (1912) as well as serving as a precursor to his first project in Tel Aviv, "Jewish Heads" (1931–1935).

In 1921 Lerski followed Lippmann to the Gloria Film Co., working for directors such as E. A. Dupont and Hanns Steinhoff. Trade reviews noted repeatedly that Lerski achieved "beautiful, technically difficult" images but that the films failed "to rise above the well-trodden paths of German costume pictures."[4] Not until 1924 did Lerski receive an assignment worthy of his talents when he collaborated with Paul Leni on *Waxworks*, one of the most famous expressionist films of the era. Yet Lerski's cinematography has been unjustifiably ignored in favor of Leni's sets, although the final "Jack the Ripper" sequence was made possible through Lerski's lighting, which created filmic space solely with light by shooting the murderer against black backdrops and superimposing numerous images. This manipulation of cinematic space created through light matched Lerski's practice in making close-up portraits: he often used black velvet and wide-angle lenses to eliminate all superfluous visual information in order to explore the landscape of the face, using jupiter lamps and mirrors.

Lerski continued to utilize such techniques in films like *The Wig* (1924) and *The Adventures of a Ten Mark Note* (1926), both shot for Bertold Viertel; and *The Holy Mountain* (1926), directed by Dr. Arnold Fanck. Unfortunately, the technical and financial means necessary for Lerski's light and mirror experiments were substantial, so that the cost-conscious film industry soon labeled him a "commercially feared employee," whose "Rembrandt atmosphere" embodied aesthetic pretensions that film producers could ill afford.[5]

In October 1925 Lerski began working as head technician of the newly founded Deutsche-Spiegeltechnik Co., a subsidiary of Ufa (Universum Film Aktiengesellschaft), which had been founded for commercial exploitation of the "Schüfftan Process." Invented by Eugen Schüfftan, the special-effects system utilized a complicated set of mirrors—Lerski's specialty—to superimpose models, actors, sets, stills, and even other films onto one image. Companies wishing to use the process were required to hire the equipment and two technicians from the licensee. Although the process was featured in big-budget productions such as Fritz Lang's *Metropolis* (1927) and Joe May's *Dagfin* (1926), the Ufa staff was said to have sabotaged the undertaking by failing to utilize the process when the opportunity arose. After introducing the process in England in 1927, Lerski left the company.[6]

In 1929 Lerski completed his last "excursion" into German film before returning "regretfully" to photography. He was hired by novice film director and producer Carl Ludwig Achaz-Duisberg, son of the chairman of the board of the giant chemical combine I. G. Farben.[7] Utilizing a Soviet style of editing, Achaz-Duisberg's vanity production *Sprengbagger 1010* (1929) presented a paean to a giant steam shovel, which underscored the film's belief in economic progress and the redemption of the proletariat through socially enlightened capitalism. While the film was generally undistinguished, the experience certainly influenced Lerski's work on his masterpiece *Avodah*.

Avodah (1933–1935)

In late 1932, after a brief sojourn in Zurich, Lerski and his second wife, Anneliese, settled in Tel Aviv, where they remained until 1948. Since publication efforts of his "Jewish Heads" project had come to a standstill,[8] in 1933 Lerski began production on a Zionist documentary, *Avodah*, possibly at the suggestion of Dr. Ernst Aaron Mechner, the head of the Berlin office of the Keren Kayemeth LeIsrael. The film was financed by Paul Boroschek, a Berlin banker who had set up Palestine Pictures Ltd as an investment in the infant film industry of Eretz Israel. Boroschek, who may originally have planned the project with another director and cameraman, also sought financial support for the production, which was to cost approximately £3,000, from Leo Herrmann, general secretary of the Keren Hayesod in Jerusalem.[9] Using a small hand-held 35 mm camera which could only hold very short rolls (15 meters), Lerski was his own cameraman, shooting the film without synchronous sound. Although the camera allowed only relatively short shots, its lightness gave Lerski the capability of moving unobtrusively among the workers in the fields, in order to capture details and impromptu moments of the work process which would have been inaccessible to a director working with a larger camera and crew.[10] Postproduction, including a very complicated sound mix, was done at the Hunnia Studios in Budapest. The well-known German composer Paul Dessau wrote and recorded all the music in six weeks, with Laszlo Vajda handling the sound direction and Dr. Gerhard Goldbaum, formerly the head of Ufa's sound recording department, supervising the exactly timed postsynchronization.

The press acclaimed the film, although its artistic and propagandistic goals were thought to be in conflict at times. A critic at the press screening in Jerusalem in April 1935 noted: "It is not a paradox if one says that at times the artistry of Lerski is too great: viewing this supreme achievement one forgets the object of his depiction."[11] Another *Jüdische Rundschau* critic in Berlin wrote: "Work . . . That is the whole film's content, its images often intensifying to highest dynamism. Man and machine are its theme. The machine's stroke, the wheel's drive, the piston's hammering, the drill's clanking. Not since *Potemkin* have we seen such a rhythm."[12] The *Palestine Post* was equally ecstatic in its praise: "In this picture Lerski's artistic skill shows itself at its best. . . . Here the camera shows not only the light of the faces, but the very light of the souls."[13] Comparing the film to *Potemkin* and *Storm over Asia*, film critic Hans Feld, formerly of Berlin, wrote: "I have never felt more forcibly the compelling suggestiveness of an epos in pictures."[14] The Zionist newspaper *Selbstwehr* (Prague), however, complained about its lack of propaganda value:

> This Palestine film has the peculiar feature of not showing any Jewish cities, not a single settlement, and almost no human beings. Palestine is seemingly devoid of human life. One sees shoes, legs, hands, arms, faces— not whole human beings but only parts—not whole settlements, but only rooms, windows, doors, not complete landscapes, but only fields, beds, weeds.[15]

This last opinion seems to have been shared by other members of the Zionist community. Efforts to distribute the film through the Keren Hayesod Fund failed, although Paul Boroschek's belief that it was blocking exhibition in favor of its own film *Land of Promise* (1935) was apparently unfounded.[16] While Keren Hayesod correspondence demonstrated both positive and negative views of the film, Leo Herrmann agreed to distribute it; but Boroschek lacked the financial means to supply prints or acquire the negative, which was held as collateral by the Hungarian lab.[17] After a private screening (attended by an enthusiastic John Grierson) in the house of British Zionist leader Harry Sacher, the film was shown at the Academy Cinema in London's West End but failed to receive screenings in Germany, the United States, or South America.[18] The film did receive limited distribution in Europe through Otto Sonnenfeld's Slavia Films (Prague).[19]

In point of fact, *Avodah* was not really suitable as Zionist propaganda, unlike *Land of Promise*, which was a straightforward documentary with narration, emphasizing Jewish Palestine's economic boom and opportunities for capitalist investment while downplaying the more socialist aspects of the kibbutz movement.[20] *Avodah*, in contrast, was essentially a work of art with leftist tendencies and few references to Jewish reconstruction: a quotation from Isaiah, a Star of David, a Hebrew prayer (the only spoken words in the film), and *khalutzim* (pioneers) singing the anthem of the Hashomer Hatza'ir (literally, Young Guard, a Zionist-socialist youth movement). Small wonder that one Zionist official at Keren Hayesod characterized the film's image of Palestine as "a glorification of the dictatorship of the working class, rather than a Jewish land of the future."[21] Scenes of Jewish communal life, customs, religious rituals, and social gatherings were almost totally absent. In point of fact, three reels of outtakes reveal that Lerski originally shot much more traditional material (for example, a Purim festival, the Hebrew University, scenes of Tel Aviv, Allenby Street, the Jewish Agency Building, an Arab market, children playing, and the Western Wall), all of which was eliminated in the final version in favor of a very narrow selection of formal themes.[22]

The film opens with a pioneer walking to Palestine from Russia (an archetypical image of early Zionist documentaries) and a long, less typical sequence portraying Arab life in the British Mandate. The film's main theme, reinforced through a recurring image of a water wagon and Dessau's musical leitmotif, is the need for water for survival. Following sequences on the building of roads and houses in Tel Aviv, the film's final two reels focus on the often frustrating search for water, culminating in a symphony of gushing water as a drill strikes a subterranean reservoir. Through rapid editing that sequence becomes a symphony of water images flowing over parched land, recalling King Vidor's similarly constructed sequence in *Our Daily Bread* (1934), which Lerski may or may not have seen before finishing his own film. Both films are obviously indebted to the Russian montage techniques of Sergei Eisenstein and especially Alexander Dovzhenko. Typical of Lerski's style, the film utilizes extreme close-ups of machines and men, their facial features, the sweat on their bodies, and the dirt and oil of equipment, highlighted by intensely reflected light.

Lerski later circumscribed the photographer's aesthetic possibilities as follows: "The eye of the image maker is always looking at a portion of the whole, that area where his light falls. It is always merely a cut-out, a shot, a distant close-up."[23] The film is indeed nothing less than a visual symphony of hard physical labor in the desert, fragmented through editing into a formal play of movement, physical shapes, diagonally composed camera angles, shadows and light, music and sound effects. Rather than constructing a unified view of the Zionist project, the idea of work is lifted out of the historically concrete setting of Palestine in the 1930s into a timeless and idealized notion of human progress through labor, through which Lerski is again striving to capture the human spirit in images of beauty. Indeed, in its use of the film medium as raw material for abstract concepts instead of as a referent to the real world, *Avodah* has more in common with avant-garde Neue Sachlichkeit experiments such as Walter Ruttmann's *Berlin—Symphony of a City* (1926) than it does with the propagandistic documentary common to the era.

Zionist Film Production

Early in 1935 Lerski completed the short film *Hebrew Melody*, which he co-produced with another German Jewish refugee, Walter Kristeller, and the Jewish Kulturbund of Berlin. Lerski shot footage of the world-famous violinist Andreas Weissgerber walking through Jerusalem's old city and playing the popular tune by Joseph Achron of the film's title in front of Absalom's Pillar. Sound recording and postproduction were done by Shabtai Petruschka in Berlin's Tobis Klangfilm Studios, when Weissgerber toured Berlin in March 1935, with Joseph Rosenstock and the Kulturbund Orchestra accompanying him.[24] As in *Avodah*, Lerski edited numerous close-ups of Weissgerber's hands, face, and body into sequences that emphasized fragmentation rather than the unity of the musician's performance. While the film was distributed by the Keren Hayesod, it was apparently not widely seen.[25]

In spring 1939, after Lerski returned to Palestine from a long stay in England, the executive committee of the Histadrut under Golda Meir and Aharon Remez asked the sixty-eight-year-old filmmaker to help set up a film division. Lerski organized a modest 16 mm film unit, where he trained young filmmakers, including Robert Sziller, Rolf Kneller, and Naftali Rubenstein. In an interview Lerski noted: "At my age I cannot expect to make the Palestinian film of the future. I can only hope to train people who will stand on my shoulders. First small documentary films, then a real Palestinian picture. No Hollywood. Something sprung from the soil. Born out of strife and struggle of this hard land."[26] In 1939–1941 Lerski and his Histadrut film group produced at least four films: *Yaddei Hashemesh* (Children of the Sun), shot in the Kibbutz Givat Brenner; *Amal* (Labor), about a technical school of the Histadrut (the Hebrew Worker's Union in Eretz Israel); *Kupat Kholim*, about Histadrut's health care organization; and *Labour Palestine*, a history of the Histadrut.[27] In November 1941 the film workshop was forced to close down, due to the worsening war situation.

None of these films were known to have survived, since the labor organization placed little value on moving images. Recently a print of *Yaddei Hashemesh* was discovered, however, and is now preserved at the Steven Spielberg Film Archive in Jerusalem; it was released under the English title *Children of the Sun*.[28] As the title of this film indicates, its focus is on children in the kibbutz. We first see babies and toddlers in their cribs, outdoors, getting lots of fresh air. Older children are then seen playing on a jungle gym and also swimming in the kibbutz pool. Children of all ages are also shown working for the benefit of the kibbutz: feeding chicks, herding and milking cows, planting fields and saplings for new orange trees, and later clearing rocks from new fields for planting. Moving indoors, we see children playing, creating handicrafts, or reading, the implication being that they are also being educated properly and not just functioning as child labor. Another sequence shows slightly older children with paper hats and wooden swords forming teams for war games, a gentle reminder that vigilance and defense of the kibbutz's perimeter is a fact of life. In contrast to *Avodah*, Lerski and his team mostly eschew extreme camera angles, focusing instead on showing the children in the kibbutz as integrated members of the community. Given the collaborative nature of the Histadrut film collective, *Yaddei Hashemesh* is much less formalist and much less consciously aesthetic than *Avodah* and more of a document visualizing human beings. The last minutes of this short film make an overt pitch for the work of Histadrut, fulfilling the film's specific propagandistic intentions, which were probably to raise money for more pioneering work.

After World War II, Lerski directed another short film, *Balaam's Story* (1946), produced in conjunction with the puppeteer Dr. Paul Loewy. Financed by Keren Hayesod, the film was an adaptation of a puppet theater play, taken from the Old Testament Book of Numbers and probably based on Hugo Adler's play *Balak and Baalam* (1934). Kurt Weill was originally to have written the music, which was composed by Karol Rathaus, based on Weill's motifs. Giving human expression to an inanimate puppet through light, Lerski constructed scenes exclusively through close-ups, thus hiding the puppets' strings, developing their dynamism through camera movement and action within the frame. The animation of the puppets was to create a new kind of cinema, according to Lerski.[29] The film's narration states that "this was a story of a curse, of a people who are cursed with no land and no right to govern their own wish to live together." While this overt Zionist message could be culled from the story, it is not known whether it matched Lerski's intentions: the short was never released but instead was incorporated into the feature film *Out of Evil* (1951), directed by Joseph Krumgold.

Tomorrow Is a Wonderful Day (1947)

Lerski's final film, *Adamah* (1947), was produced by Otto Sonnenfeld for Hadassah (a Zionist women's organization) and was to become the first feature-length film of the new state of Israel. Shot at Ben Shemen boarding school and youth village, the film presented the fate of a young teenaged boy who, having survived the hell of Auschwitz, must learn to overcome his psychic wounds and trust his fellow humans again. The film's story, typical for the times, was to present Ben Shemen to the American Jewish community as a shining example of the educational work being done in Israel.[30] After completing the shooting, which was assisted by Lerski's pupils from the Histadrut collective, Robert Sziller and Naftali Rubenstein, Lerski sent the rough-cut to the United States for postproduction. As in the case of *Avodah*, Paul Dessau wrote the musical score, while Shabtai Petruschka handled the orchestration. In New York the film was shortened and reedited by Hazel Greenwald and released by Hadassah under the title *Tomorrow Is a Wonderful Day*. According to Anneliese Lerski, her husband "was beside himself with anger at the film's premiere at the Locarno Film Festival" in July 1948, "since it had been completely chopped up, destroying Lerski's best and most beautiful intentions," with scenes missing and others (not shot by Lerski) added.[31] Given that only the short version of *Tomorrow Is a Wonderful Day* was known to have survived, it has been difficult to ascertain to what degree the Americans had revised Lerski's original film or even whether this surviving short version was what was shown in Locarno.

Receiving a standing ovation at Locarno, the film was universally praised by the international press. The *Baseler Nachrichten* wrote: "The entire film makes the impression of a highly significant document through which a gifted film producer addresses to the world forum a life-affirming message in an emotional way." After the Israeli premiere, the critic for *Davar* (a Hebrew newspaper associated with the socialist worker movement) wrote: "This film teaches and elucidates, in a sublime form, the chapter of the absorption of the children from exile, and of love of the homeland."[32] The *New York Times* claimed that "the film's continuity and photography leave something to be desired" but otherwise praised the semidocumentary quality of the film.[33] After opening in New York in April 1949, the film earned four times its original production cost of 100,000 Swiss francs.

In terms of its lighting and photography, *Tomorrow Is a Wonderful Day* was a typical Lerski film. Utilizing numerous close-ups, reflecting the bright sun through mirrors into his youthful actors' faces, and presenting the skewed vision of its young hero, Benjamin, through oblique camera angles, Lerski gives the village of Ben Shemen a larger-than-life presence. At the same time, Lerski's fragmented editing and the multitude of spoken languages (reflecting the origins of the children) create a sense of emotional chaos that certainly reflected the atmosphere of the times. In one classroom scene, all the children reveal their origins in various European countries, making it evident that Benjamin is not the only one to have suffered during the Shoʾah. Only slowly does Benjamin learn to sort out at times confusing impressions and come to grips with his new reality. He initially hoards food and refuses to take part in either the play or the work of the children and young adults. Finally, with the help of a young girl his age, Miriam, he begins to realize that this is his new home. He is chosen to carry a torch to the Hanukah celebration, the Festival of Light. Moving from darkness to light, Benjamin's path from the darkness of the concentration camp to the light of the kibbutz Hanukah celebration thus completes his integration into the community and gives the short version of the film its dramatic high point. Given the discovery of a long version, it can now be surmised that the short version was probably put together by Hadassah for nontheatrical distribution to American audiences after the New York theatrical release.

In 2009 a more complete version of *Tomorrow Is a Wonderful Day* was found in France and rescued by the Steven Spielberg Film Archive in Jerusalem.[34] This version is only slightly different from the previously known short version for its first five reels. For example, the scene in the classroom where children name their home countries includes an Arab Jew from Syria, who was later removed. Was he left on the cutting room floor to keep American sympathy focused on the European Shoʾah (Holocaust) victims? In any case, the long version adds two more reels, after the concluding Festival of Light. Included in this edition is a substantial amount of footage of athletes marching in Maccabi-like games, which was probably not shot by Lerski and was at least partially the cause of his irate response at Locarno. Indeed the footage makes little sense and is edited somewhat chaotically. Furthermore, the film now ends with the news of the founding of the state of Israel on May 14, 1948, footage that was most certainly added by Hazel Greenwald at the last minute before the film's July premiere at Locarno. But most of the footage in the final two reels involves following Benjamin as he joins a group of older teenagers who establish a new kibbutz in an undeveloped desert area.

Like *Avodah*, this section of the film focuses on the absolutely backbreaking work of building barricades, clearing fields, constructing housing, digging wells, defending the land against Arab attacks, and eventually harvesting a first crop. At one point, Lerski centers the frame on a sign in Hebrew that reads "Adamah" (earth, soil), indicating that this new generation of Israeli youth is rooted in the soil. That soil has been Jewish for thousands of years, as a walk through ancient ruins by the youths demonstrates, while an announcer on the radio underscores the notion of this "old-new" Jewish homeland. Another scene shows young girls dancing, dressed in what are supposed to be ancient Hebrew costumes. The film concludes with a montage of the pioneers, plows, aerial shots of Israel, and close-ups of children's faces, "the hope of Israel," an apotheosis that once again recalls *Avodah*. The long version of *Tomorrow Is a Wonderful Day* thus moves from the intense subjectivity of Benjamin and his narrative of rescue to the larger story of the founding and development of the modern state of Israel, with its youth firmly leading the way.

According to an early treatment of the script, this subjectivity, which was reinforced by concentrating solely on Ben Shemen and the activity of the young immigrants (youth Aliyah), seems to have been what Lerski was striving for. That subjectivity was undermined by Hadassah's insertion of stereotypical and historical images of Israel's reconstruction as well as the scenes of independence. In other words, just as *Avodah* had been pared down to the essential theme of work, *Adamah* was to be about the rebirth of hope, nourished in the soil of Ben Shemen. To include documentary shots that broadened and generalized the film's view defeated Lerski's aesthetic intentions. It is conceivable, however, that Hadassah preferred a more directly propagandistic narrative that could be used for fund-raising purposes and eventually distributed the short version of *Tomorrow Is Another Day* in America because it focused on the rescue of European Jewish children from the concentration camps while deemphasizing the harshness of life in the kibbutz, which would have been unpleasant for American viewers.

Of all the filmmakers to work in Israel before statehood, Helmar Lerski was certainly the most original as a film artist. The single-mindedness of his artistic vision, his formal concerns as a "writer with light," and his desire to shape his documentary visions into something timeless, a "metamorphosis into eternity," beyond the more narrow propagandistic concerns of his Zionist funders, have given his films their lasting value. At the same time, it is clear that Lerski's films failed to accomplish their overtly propagandistic missions as advertisements for Eretz Israel, given their limited distribution and their distribution in "unauthorized" versions. Yet for the Israeli cinema of the future Helmar Lerski's aesthetic legacy as the nation's first gifted filmmaker was certainly an auspicious beginning.

NOTES

1. See Ute Eskildsen (ed.), *Helmar Lerski: Metamorphosis through Light/Verwandlung durch Licht*.

2. For a complete biography of Lerski, see Ute Eskildsen and Jan-Christopher Horak (eds.), *Helmar Lerski, Lichtbildner* (catalogue published in German and English in conjunction with the exhibition shown at the Tel Aviv Museum, March 1983).

3. *Der Kinematograph*, July 19, 1916.

4. Reviews in *Der Kinematograph*, December 4, 1922, 10; *Licht-Bild-Bühne*, December 16, 1922, 16.

5. Quoted in *Der Film*, January 25, 1925; *Die Filmtechnik* 2, no. 23, November 13, 1926, 463.

6. See *Kinematograph Weekly*, January 13, 1927, 105.

7. Unpublished letter, Helmar Lerski to Bertold Viertel, January 18, 1930 (Helmar Lerski Estate Collection, Museum Folkwang, Essen).

8. According to Anneliese Lerski, the Nazis had threatened Lerski because of his proposed book "Jewish Heads." See Eskildsen and Horak, *Helmar Lerski, Lichtbildner*, 15, note 55.

9. Unpublished letter, Gal Esser to Leo Herrmann, March 22, 1934, Central Zionist Archives, Keren Hayesod (KH, 4B/1202).

10. See Curt Kramarski, "The Palestine Film for Palestine: An Interview with Helmar Lerski," *Palestine Post*, vol. 11, no. 2679, July 12, 1935.

11. M. Y. Ben-Gavriel, "Lerskys Palästina-Film," *Jüdische Rundschau* 40, nos. 33–34, April 26, 1935.

12. Dr. Karl Schwarz, "Lerskis Film *Awodah*," *Jüdische Rundschau* 40, no. 65, August 13, 1935, 7.

13. Curt Kramarski, "*Avodah* at the Rimon Cinema, Tel Aviv," *Palestine Post* 11, no. 2786, July 19, 1935, 10.

14. Quoted in "The Film of Palestine," *Palestine Post* 11, no. 2727, May 21, 1935.

15. Arthur Engländer, "Gedanken über den Palästinafilm *Awodah*," *Selbstwehr* 32, no. 13, April 1, 1938, 6.

16. Letter, Leo Herrmann to Palästina Filmstelle, Berlin, March 11, 1936 (KH 4B/1290).

17. Letter, Manfred Epstein to Leo Herrmann, April 30, 1937; letter, Leo Herrmann to Paul Borochek, July 8, 1937; letter, L. Herrmann to Epstein, April 26, 1938 (KH 4B/1202, 378).

18. Letter, Hans Feld to Helmar Lerski, June 28, 1935 (Lerski Estate Collection, Museum Folkwang, Essen, Germany). Lost for over fifty years, a nitrate print of *Avodah* was discovered in the Academy Cinema, where Lerski also exhibited his *Metamorphosis through Light* in 1938. It was preserved by the British Film Institute, and a print is now available at George Eastman House and at the Israel Film Archive.

19. Letter, Leo Herrmann to Dr. Arthur Bergmann, Prague, March 15, 1936. See also letter, Leo Herrmann to Kol Noa Institute, April 26, 1938 (KH 4B/1202, 378).

20. See Jan-Christopher Horak, "Zionist Film Propaganda in Nazi Germany," 49ff.

21. Letter, Arthur Hantke to Leo Herrmann, March 27, 1935 (KH 4B/1202).

22. I found this footage in Hungary when I organized a Lerski exhibition in 1982. It has been preserved by the Bundesarchiv, Koblenz, Germany.

23. Quoted in Eskildsen and Horak, *Helmar Lerski, Lichtbildner*, 25.

24. Interview with Shabtai Petruschka, Jerusalem, March 9, 1983. See also *Jüdische Rundschau* 17, February 26, 1935. Weissgerber also performed "Hebrew Melody" publicly on April 11, 1935, in Berlin at a benefit concert for the Keren Kayemeth.

25. Letter, Dr. Max Prager (Vienna) to Leo Herrmann, March 3, 1936 (KH 4B/1202).

26. "Lerski at Seventy," *Palestine Post*, February 21, 1941.

27. According to officials at Histadrut, three of these films must be considered lost, although I hope they will be found in the archives of the Labor Council.

28. Thanks to the Steven Spielberg Film Archive (Jerusalem) for making a screening of this title possible.

29. Manfred Geis, "Helmar Lerski at 75," *Palestine Tribune* 2, no. 9, February 28, 1946, 11; "Vortrag Helmar Lerski," *Mitteilungsblatt Alija Chadascha* 10, no. 12, March 22, 1946.

30. Compare Norman Bertwich, *Ben-Shemen: Children's Village in Israel* (Paris, 1956). Films with similar narrative lines are *Our Father's House* (1946), *The Great Betrayal* (1947), and *Out of Evil* (1951).

31. Letter, Anneliese Lerski to Ernst Loewy, July 15, 1961; letter, Anneliese Lerski to Stettner, April 2, 1962 (Lerski Estate Collection, Museum Folkwang, Essen, Germany).

32. Quoted in press brochure for *Adamah*.

33. *New York Times*, April 11, 1949. See also *New York Herald Tribune*, April 11, 1949.

34. Thanks again to the Steven Spielberg Film Archive in Jerusalem for allowing me to see a video transfer of this newly discovered version of *Tomorrow Is a Wonderful Day*.

BIBLIOGRAPHY

Downing, Taylor. *Palestine on Film*. London: Council for the Advancement of Arab-British Understanding, 1979.

Eskildsen, Ute (ed.). *Helmar Lerski: Metamorphosis through Light/Verwandlung durch Licht*. Freren: Luca Verlag, 1982.

Eskildsen, Ute, and Jan-Christopher Horak (eds.). *Helmar Lerski, Lichtbildner*. Essen: Museum Folkwang, 1982.

Horak, Jan-Christopher. "Zionist Film Propaganda in Nazi Germany." *Historical Journal of Film, Radio and Television* 4, no. 1 (1984): 49–58.

———. *Making Images Move: Photographers and Avant-Garde Cinema*. Washington, D.C.: Smithsonian Press, 1997.

Tryster, Hillel. *Israel before Israel: Silent Cinema in the Holy Land*. Jerusalem: Steven Spielberg Jewish Film Archive, 1995.

———. "The Land of Promise (1935): A Case Study in Zionist Film Propaganda." *Historical Journal of Film, Radio and Television* 15, no. 2 (1995): 187–217.

FILMOGRAPHY

Achaz-Duisberg, Carl Ludwig. 1929. *Sprengbagger 1010*.

Eisenstein, Sergei. 1925. *Potemkin*.

Fanck, Dr. Arnold. 1926. *The Holy Mountain*.

Krumgold, Joseph. 1951. *Out of Evil*.

Lang, Fritz. 1927. *Metropolis*.

Lehman, Juda. 1935. *Land of Promise*.

Leni, Paul. 1924. *Waxworks*.

Lerski, Helmar. 1933–1935. *Work (Avodah)*.

———. 1937. *Hebrew Melody*.

———. 1939–1941. *Amal* (Labor).

———. 1939–1941. *Children of the Sun (Yaldei Hashemesh)*.

———. 1939–1941. *Kupat Kholim*.

———. 1939–1941. *Labour Palestine*.

———. 1946. *Balaam's Story*.

———. 1947. *Tomorrow Is a Wonderful Day. (Adamah)*.

May, Joe. 1926. *Dagfin*.

Pudovkin, Vsevolod. 1928. *Storm over Asia*.

Reinert, Robert. 1917. *Ahasuerus (Ahasver)*.

———. 1919. *Nerves*.

———. 1919. *Opium*.

Ruttmann, Walter. 1926. *Berlin—Symphony of a City*.

Vidor, King. 1934. *Our Daily Bread*.

Viertel, Bertold. 1924. *The Wig*.

———. 1926. *The Adventures of a Ten Mark Note*.

3 Ecce Homo

The Transfiguration of Israeli Manhood in Israeli Films

YARON PELEG

This chapter examines the metamorphosis that the image of Israeli men has undergone on the screen: from engaged, enterprising, daring, bold, brash, brave New Jews or New Hebrews—Palmakhniks (volunteer warriors in the pre-state Jewish Yishuv), soldiers, and womanizers—in earlier films to the detached, retiring, confused, tenuous, and subdued men that appear on the screen in the 1990s and 2000s. The chapter traces these changes in various films, including *Siege* (*Matzor*, 1969), *Peeping Toms* (*Metzitzim*, 1972), *The Wooden Gun* (*Roveh Khuliot*, 1979), *Time of Favor* (*Hahesder*, 2000), and *Campfire* (*Medurat Hashevet*, 2004).

The creation of masculine Jews in early Zionism in opposition to the perceived effeminacy of diasporic Jews has been exhaustively discussed in the past, most recently as part of the post-Zionist debates during the 1990s.[1] These discussions form the basis and background for the present examination, without referring to them directly. Moreover, numerous studies of Israeli literature and cinema, including a number of essays in this anthology, are premised on this analysis and demonstrate plausibly and conclusively how early Israeli fiction and films promoted this new Jewish-Israeli masculinity.

To mention two of the most representative works which do that, I would point out Moshe Shamir's 1951 novelistic memoir of his fallen brother, *Elik: With His Own Hands* (*Bemo Yadav: Pirkei Elik*) and the 1955 film *Hill 24 Doesn't Answer* (*Giv'a 24 Eina Ona*). In his best-selling novel, Shamir set up one of the most comprehensive images of the Sabra in Israeli literature.[2] Like the mythological founder of Athens, Elik is described as symbolically emerging out of the earth or in his case the sea. He is a consummate New Hebrew: tall, handsome, free-spirited, independent, yet loyal, responsible, hard-working, determined, and brave. Elik is dedicated to his family and his friends and above all to his emerging nation, for which he dies in battle as a young officer. The film *Hill 24 Doesn't Answer*, which focuses on several fighters in Israel's War of Independence, presents Elik as the brash and brave David Amiram. The film expands the salubrious effects of Israel and Zionism on Jewish manhood even more in the image of Yehuda Berger, a weak and frightened Holocaust survivor who in the course of the film is transformed into a confident captain in the nascent Israeli army.

The history of Israel and its escalating conflict with its Arab neighbors deepened the connection between masculinity and military service, which persisted in Israeli films in the decades that followed independence and continues to this very day. Again, the subject has been well researched, as even this anthology attests. Instead I would like to focus on the gradual changes in the representation of Israeli masculinity, which are already hinted at in the 1969 film *Siege* (*Matzor*). I begin with this film precisely because it continues to make the connections between masculinity and militarism. The film takes place immediately after the Six Day War and deals with some of its aftermath by following the life of a war widow, Tamar, who is reluctant to occupy the hallowed position in which society wants to put her.

One of the most interesting aspects of *Siege* is its casting. Tamar (Gila Almagor) is practically the only female character in the film. She is surrounded by men: her dead husband, her dead husband's best friend Elli (Yehoram Ga'on) and other friends who fought in the war with them, her new lover David (Dan Ben Amotz), and finally her young boy. The most disturbing sense of siege in the film comes from this very imbalance. These are all good men, to be sure, paragons of Israeli manhood. Her brave husband died for his country. His friends, foremost Elli, continue to stand guard over their country's borders as well as over Tamar, whom they wish to help and protect, and her kind new lover, David, provides her with the opportunity for a new life. But Tamar is not interested in what these men have to offer. Herein lies the film's critique about the grim side of a war that otherwise was considered miraculous and spectacular and the men who waged it. The memory of her dead husband haunts Tamar, who resents the sanctity it bestows on her. Elli and her husband's other friends coddle and suffocate her rather than help her, and David ultimately betrays her in a way by leaving to do his reserve duty. It matters little that he does not have a choice. From Tamar's perspective he is a deserter of sorts, risking their fledgling love by answering the nation's call to arms.

Siege is not a straightforward antiwar film. Rather, its civic agenda quietly undermines the militarizing effects of the war, the Spartan ethics it promotes. Some of this critique is folded into the notable gender economy of the film, the imbalance between the men and the woman. One result of this imbalance is the aspersions that are cast on the men in the film. None of them is denigrated outright, yet the female narrative perspective from which they are all seen erodes their traditional roles as Israeli husbands, soldiers, friends, and lovers.

Another conspicuous aspect of Israeli masculinity is sexual prowess. The 1972 *Peeping Toms* (*Metzitzim*) is probably the most unabashed illustration of this in the history of Israeli cinema. Made in the wake of the 1967 triumph and indicative of both the conceit and indulgence that followed it, the film follows the vapid adventures of a bunch of self-satisfied beach bums, who live an empty life on a Tel Aviv beach, occupied primarily by the juvenile pursuit of casual sex. They try to bed every eligible woman they lay eyes on, sometimes forcefully, and, most pathetically, spend a lot of time peeping into the women's changing rooms on the beach.

Peeping Toms received a lot of critical attention.[3] The film gained cult status fairly early on. Cult status is an illusive quality. It is not only impossible to predict but almost as difficult to explain. The silly frivolity of the film and the resonance it found in the culture were clearly a product of the postwar atmosphere in Israel. It was an expression of the sheer giddiness and exuberance of victory, a celebration of the release of tension and perhaps most importantly the relaxation of the harsh pioneering resolve of the past in favor of a lighter mood, eased by the opportunities that the new life promised. Among these new opportunities was the chance to express manhood in different, less regimented ways.

My own description of the film above belies the way we look at it today. From almost half a century away, the ditzy antics of Gutte, the film's protagonist (Uri Zohar), and his friends seem not only pathetic but downright offensive, if not worse. But they did not seem so at the time. In some ways, they provided one of the first legitimate opportunities to be a different kind of Israeli man: not a hardworking pioneer or a brave soldier or an earnest young man in the service of his developing nation. If we consider the life of the nation in human terms and think of pre-independence as infancy and post-independence as childhood, then the period after the 1967 war was young adulthood or "teenage" years. Gutte and his cinematic friends fit that mold neatly.

Sometime in the 1970s the image of the New Hebrew began to undergo a "transvaluation of values" of sorts, to evoke an early Zionist parlance.[4]

The 1978 film *Lemon Popsicle* (*Eskimo Limon,* Boaz Davidson, 1978) records that shift pretty clearly in its nostalgic depiction of the carefree life of petit bourgeois Israeli adolescents in the 1950s. The film's focus on urban youth culture in pursuit of individual happiness by emphasizing fashion, music, and leisure—hitherto unsanctioned by official Israeli culture—is a drastic departure from the more ideological and at times heavy-handed works that preceded it.[5] In the way it serves up the slender and sensitive Bentzi as the moral hero over the manlier but craven Momo, *Lemon Popsicle* depicts one of the first transformations in the image of Israeli masculinity, especially among Ashkenazim. Historically speaking, this shift can be described thus: if the creation of a more powerful Jewishness was useful during the early stages of Zionism, and indeed shaped the image of the New Hebrew at that time, the starkness of that image later became less useful, irrelevant, and finally even problematic when it stood in the way of developing a more normal civic society in Israel. This is one of the main foci of *Lemon Popsicle,* which, as a backlash against an increasingly outdated state ideology, ironically promotes the kind of weak, sensitive, and brainy men that Zionist pioneers denigrated.[6]

Peeping Toms is the link between the first phase of manhood and the second, between the mighty New Hebrews—as seen in *Hill 24*—and their wispy heirs—as seen in *Lemon Popsicle.* The great energies of the forefathers are not harnessed or focused constructively by their young. Instead, they are frittered away. Gutte has prodigious energy. He is full of life, constantly in motion, and has plenty of vigor and a great many schemes. But all of his plans and all of his vitality are dedicated to the procurement of casual sex. As such, and in historical context, they signal an ironic change from the past. The immense foundational energy that enabled the creation of Israel from scratch lacked an overt or acknowledged sexual aspect. The ascetic picture that we have today of the pioneers no doubt stems from the little attention their intimate lives, especially their love lives, received in the art of the period.[7] Their private affairs, of the heart and of the body, were silenced by the great din of national construction. In *Peeping Toms,* director Uri Zohar reverses this trend and overcompensates for it by creating a bunch of salivating young men who work hard—at love.

Uri Zohar continued to make a few more films about this species of Israeli man until he abandoned his artistic career completely in 1977 and became an orthodox Jew. Zohar's personal history was ironically adumbrated in his art. Conceivably, his own turn to faith was a result of the kind of frustrations that his protagonists experience in his films, the dead end of their meaningless lives as young Israeli men. None of these men ever manage to mature and take on the responsibilities of adulthood. Zohar's last film, *Save the Lifeguard* (*Hatzilu et Hamatzil*, 1977), rehashes the earlier *Peeping Toms:* now the protagonist is not twenty-something and single anymore but a pathetic forty-year-old family man.

A new direction in the metamorphosis of Israeli manhood was suggested by another film, *The Wooden Gun* (*Roveh Khuliot*, 1979), which ends with a curious reference to the mythic literary Elik from Shamir's novel, the autochthonous Sabra who in this case emerged out of the sea. The film is an iconoclastic allegory that was part of the first wave of criticism directed against the labor hegemony after the 1973 Yom Kippur War. It uses a feud between two "gangs" of young boys in the early 1950s as a distorted mirror that reflects the contemporaneous corruption of the pioneering ethos and its excesses. Set shortly after independence at a time of national triumph and alleged unity, the film depicts a heartless and cruel Israel: the boys torture one another, disrespect their pioneering elders, and are especially mean to the weak and the disenfranchised, including an unhinged Holocaust survivor symbolically named Palestina (Palestine). More than being an accurate historical representation, the film paints a picture that highlights the society's mutation from a cohesive community inspired by a liberating ideology into a callous and belligerent Sparta.

In the final climactic scene of the film, Yoni, the leader of one of the gangs, runs away to hide on the beach in fear that he has killed a member of a rival gang during a battle. He falls and hurts himself while escaping and is tenderly nursed by Palestina, who finds him on the beach and takes him into her shack by the water. The walls of the dark hut are covered with old photographs of Palestina's family, which was murdered by the Nazis, including her children. Yoni, who observes them in bewilderment, suddenly realizes the consequences of his former actions: not just his taunting of Palestina and his ruthlessness but also the wider implications of such hatred, violence, and brutality. Shocked by the intimate proximity to the family photos, and embarrassed by Palestina's tenderness, he briefly imagines himself as a Holocaust victim. When his former gang members come calling for him and start throwing stones at Palestina's shack, he bursts out of it and in defiance of his stunned friends runs from them and climbs away from the beach.

In some ways, Yoni can be said to have a birthing experience. After straying and losing his way, he is called back into the depth of historical Jewish consciousness, represented by the womblike darkness of Palestina's hut, from which he reemerges kinder and more considerate. We do not know this for sure, of course, because the film ends at this point. But his newfound empathy for Palestina and his disdain for his former friends hint at it. Unlike Elik, however, who emerges pastless out of the sea as a clean slate on which a new kind of Hebrew manhood was to be etched, Yoni is reborn with a conscience, the moral progeny of valuable experience. There may be more than a little naïveté in this symbolic gesture, but it becomes a significant benchmark in the transformation of Israeli manhood—all the more so because Yoni is a young teenager on the verge of adulthood.

Throughout the 1980s and 1990s Yoni-like figures come up again and again in Israeli films, men who shed the resolute heroism of earlier types to exhibit a more complex and humane image.[8] We see this in *Hide and Seek* (*Makhbo'im*, Wolman, 1980), *Eastern Wind* (*Khamsin*, Wachsmann, 1982), *Beyond the Walls* (*Me'akhorei Hasoragim*, Barbash, 1984), *Atalia* (Tevet, 1984), *Avanti Popolo* (Bukai, 1986), *Himmo, King of Jerusalem* (*Khimmo Melekh Yerushalayim*, Guttman, 1987), *One of Ours* (*Ekhad Mishelanu*, Barbash, 1989), *Shuru* (Gavison, 1991), *Cup Final* (*Gmar Gavi'a*, Riklis, 1992), *Life according to Agfa* (*Hakhaim Al-pi Agfa*, Dayan, 1992), *Amazing Grace* (*Khessed Mufla*, Guttman, 1992), *Song of the Siren* (*Shirat Hasirena*, Fox, 1994), and *Pick a Card* (*Afula Express*, Shles, 1997). All of these films, which can broadly fit under what Ella Shohat calls personal cinema, present two complementary images of men: introverted, shy, or minority figures (like gays) and seriously flawed strong men, who are criticized or punished for abusing their privilege and power.[9]

Two films by Joseph Cedar illustrate this new masculine order that has come to prevail on Israeli screens in the first decade of the twenty-first century, *Time of Favor* (2000) and *Campfire* (2004). In *Time of Favor*, Cedar returns to examine the military aspects of Israeli manhood in ways that are curiously reminiscent of earlier films from the 1950s like *Hill 24 Doesn't Answer*. The film, which focuses on the dynamics of an army unit and its place in society, is anachronistic in some respects, because it does so in an era that is decidedly postmilitaristic if not altogether antimilitaristic. Even more anachronistic or perhaps old-fashioned is the film's keen study of the soldiers themselves, especially the ties between the commanding officer and his men. Exploring relations between the individual and the group has been a hallmark of Israeli literature and films, but such inquiries have dwindled since the 1980s and the advent of a more postnational age in Israel.

But *Time of Favor* is not anachronistic at all. The film's innovation is that the members of the army unit are all religious and the society consists of religious settlers in the West Bank. As such, it examines the great ideological changes that transformed Israeli society after 1967, especially the messianic trends that were inspired by the spectacular military victory and the rise of the religious settlement movement in the West Bank and the Gaza Strip in their wake. What began as a slow and sporadic occupation in the name of the old Zionist settlement ethos eventually turned into a mass movement that took over large areas of the occupied territories. In time, as the movement grew and increased its political clout, it also used its influence to establish quasi-religious military units, called Yeshivot Hesder,[10] whose allegiance hovers dangerously between their own religious leaders and those of the state.

In *Time of Favor,* Cedar examines old labor Zionist paradigms through their distorted modern interpretation embodied in Yeshivat Hahesder. Whereas Labor Zionism extolled military duty as the ultimate service to the state, the religious soldiers in the film pervert that secular dogma by putting God before state. Inspired by their radical rabbi, and in defiance of their army commander, a few of the soldiers hatch a plot to blow up the Dome of the Rock mosque on Temple Mount in Jerusalem in order to make room for a third Jewish temple. *Time of Favor* takes the kind of fighting Sabra image developed in films like *Hill 24* to an extreme, exaggerates it, and creates a monster that inevitably rises against its master. Thus the perversion of one of Zionism's oldest masculine mythologies in *Time of Favor* effectively ends it, discarding that species of manhood as nonviable or illegitimate.

Cedar's other film, *Campfire,* continues the logic of his previous work. Since the men in *Time of Favor* are such deviants, *Campfire* punishes them by removing them almost completely from the screen. The film, which also revolves around the national religious community, is reminiscent of *Siege* in its gender casting ratio, albeit in reverse: all of the major characters in *Campfire* are women, whereas the minor roles are a cast of sorry men. Taking place in 1981, the film is the story of a family of three, a widow and her two teenaged daughters, who struggle for recognition and respect as independent women in an oppressive masculine world. The mother, Rachel (Michaela Eshet), tries to qualify as a member of a group of settlers who plan a new community in the West Bank by trying to conform to their righteous requirements. In the meantime, both she and her daughters are subjected to the demeaning pious, patronizing, and sexual predatory practices of the men in their religious community.

The leader of the group, Motkeh (Assi Dayan), is a prig who presents his plan to start up a comfortable suburban community in the West Bank as a great sacrifice and service to the nation. The people he selects for the future community are all made in his image: smug, self-satisfied burghers who search for an affordable suburb while pretending to be ideological pioneers. Motkeh regards Rachel's widowhood as a handicap. When a few young seminary students try to rape her daughter, Tami (Hani Furstenberg), he clucks at her and, predictably, blames Tami for the boys' violence. His son Yair follows in his father's footsteps when he tries to force himself on Tami because he has heard that "she puts out." The first date that Motkeh and Shula (Idit Teperson) arrange for Rachel is with an obese and self-absorbed cantor (Yehoram Ga'on). Even the man Rachel is finally interested in, Yossi (Moshe Yivgy), another of Shula's arranged matches, is a nebbish, a forty-something-year-old virgin, who is a self-proclaimed loser.

At no time is the sad state of this marginal cast of masculine "role models" clearer than when a religious youth group watches reruns of the 1977 action film *Operation Thunderbolt* (aka: *Operation Jonathan*, *Mivtza Yonatan*, *Golan*), about the daring 1976 Israeli commando operation for the release of an Air France airliner hijacked to Entebbe, Uganda, by German and Palestinian terrorists. The young religious boys and girls are shown watching one of the most patriotic highlights of the über-Zionist film, during which the operation's commander, Yoni, gives his men a pep talk about their duty as soldiers and citizens of the Jewish state. The scene ends symbolically enough with an excerpt from *Operation Thunderbolt* in which we hear the announcement that "Yoni is dead." This statement suggests an intriguing proposition: the death of the exemplary manhood of earlier times, the demise of the mythological citizen-soldiers of the past. The new model of manhood in *Campfire* is not only represented by the gentler and more ambivalent young Rafi, Tami's romantic interest, who tacitly participated in the attempt to rape her. It is also represented by the women themselves, by their position in the center of the story as a reflection of a paradigmatic cultural shift.

The focus on Rachel and her daughters and their gradual ascendancy as a matriarchy seems both to compensate and to suggest a more balanced or normalized future with respect to the social roles of men and women. The removal of the men from their usual place front and center appears to be a corrective measure which *Campfire* takes against the problematic roles of the men in *Time of Favor* and in the culture at large. Having betrayed their traditional positions of moral leadership and responsibility—by waging unnecessary wars, by abusing their power in dealing with the Palestinians, by perpetuating the conflict with the Arabs, and by militarizing Israeli society as a result—the men in *Campfire* are punished by being shoved aside. When they are allowed to return and assume constructive roles in the story it is only by the women's invitation. Rachel accepts her suitor Yosi because he is a virgin in more than one respect. Tami seeks out Rafi because she knows he is weak and unable to do the right thing without her guidance. Even Esti (Maya Miron), the oldest daughter, who rebels against her controlling

mother by flaunting her soldier-lover, finally dismisses him when she finds
out that he is not her equal. The film ends symbolically enough with the
three women driving their car with Yosi in the back seat. Although it was
Yosi who fixed the car, which had stood idle ever since the death of Rachel's
husband, he is not invited to drive it. Instead, the film suggests a healthier
order of moderation, balance, and cooperation.

Similar gender alignments are repeated in a number of subsequent films,
including *Year Zero* (*Shnat Effes*, Pitchhadze, 2004), *Frozen Days* (*Yamim
Kfu'im*, Lerner, 2005), and *Aviva My Love* (*Aviva Ahuvati*, Zarkhin, 2006).
None of these films and others like them permit a categorical division into
traditional masculine/feminine roles anymore. Almost half a century after
the creation of a native Hebrew or Sabra superman in the Land of Israel, his
iconic image has been gradually replaced, not necessarily by another definitive image but by more variant and ambiguous ones. More importantly, the
transformation of these men is inseparably connected to the growing visibility of women and the greater balance that is created between men and
women in recent Israeli films.

NOTES

1. For some of the most well-known examples, see Daniel Boyarin, *Unheroic
Conduct: The Rise of Heterosexuality and the Invention of the Jewish Man;* and Mi-
chael Gluzman, *Haguf Hatziyoni: Le'umiyut, Migdar U-miniyut Ba-sifrut Ha-'Ivrit
Ha-khadashah.*

2. Moshe Shamir, Bemo Yadav: Pirkey Elik.

3. For a comprehensive and representative example and additional references,
see Miri Talmon, *Bluz Latzabar Ha'avud: Khavurot Venostalgia Bakolno'a Hayisra'eli*,
220–228.

4. The reference here is to the popular early Zionist slogan or motto about changing
traditional Jewish values and transforming them into new ideological values inspired
by nineteenth-century European nationalism. The slogan succinctly expresses the
core idea of the Zionist cultural revolution.

5. Quite naturally, most of the films that were produced in the first few decades
after independence, when Israel was still fighting for viability as a fledgling political
entity, reflected official state ideology to some degree. This is true even for films that
ostensibly defied that ideology, like the 1964 immigration comedy *Sallah Shabbati*
(Ephraim Kishon, director).

6. For further discussion of this, see my article "From Black to White: The Changing
Image of Mizrahim in Israeli Cinema, 1960–2000."

7. One notable exception is the well-known case of Bitaniya, an agricultural settlement founded in 1920 in the Galilee by a group of revolutionary pioneers from the
Hashomer Hatza'ir youth movement. In his 1922 record of their short-lived community, entitled Kehilatenu, one of the members of the group, the writer Natan Bistritzky-
Agmon, records the fierce ideology of the group, which was augmented by equally

intense sexual tensions among the four women and over twenty men who made up the isolated community. For a general sexual history of the period, see David Biale, *Eros and the Jews: From Biblical Israel to Contemporary America.*

8. See Yael Yisrael, "The Image of Men in Israeli Cinema."

9. See Ella Shohat, *Israeli Cinema: East/West and the Politics of Representation.* From the late 1980s on, Shohat's definition of "personal cinema" becomes less valid.

10. Yeshivot Hesder is a Jewish seminary that combines advanced Torah study with military service. It originated in the 1950s as a way to enable religious youth to combine their strict religious lifestyle with their military duty and become more fully integrated into Israeli society. In 1999 the ad hoc custom became law and popularized the service among religious youth, who have since raised their military profile and credentials, supplanting those of soldiers affiliated with the Labor Movement, such as kibbutz members.

BIBLIOGRAPHY

Biale, David. *Eros and the Jews: From Biblical Israel to Contemporary America.* Berkeley: University of California Press, 1997.

Boyarin, Daniel. *Unheroic Conduct: The Rise of Heterosexuality and the Invention of the Jewish Man.* Berkeley: University of California Press, 1997.

Gluzman, Michael. *Haguf Hayhudi: Le'umiyut, Migdar U-miniyut Ba-sifrut Ha-'Ivrit Ha-khadashah* (*Nationalism, Gender, and Sexuality in Modern Hebrew Literature*). Tel Aviv: Hakibbutz Hameukhad, 2007.

Peleg, Yaron. "From Black to White: The Changing Image of Mizrahim in Israeli Cinema, 1960–2000." *Journal of Israel Studies* 13, no. 2 (Summer 2008): 122–145.

Shamir, Moshe. *Bemo Yadav: Pirkey Elik* (Elik: With His Own Hands, 1951). Merkhavia: Sifriyat Po'alim, 1967.

Shohat, Ella. *Israeli Cinema: East/West and the Politics of Representation.* Austin: University of Texas Press, 1989.

Talmon, Miri. *Bluz Latzabur Ha'avud: Khavurot Venostalgia Bakolno'a Hayisra'eli* (Israeli Graffiti: Nostalgia, Groups, and Collective Identity in Israeli Cinema). Tel Aviv: Open University Press, 2001.

Yisrael, Yael. "The Image of Men in Israeli Cinema" ("Dmut Hagever Bakolno'a Hayisra'eli"). E-mago.co.il, an online magazine for culture and content, http://www.e-mago.co.il/Editor/cinema-2287.htm.

FILMOGRAPHY

Amazing Grace (*Hessed Mufla*, Amos Guttman, 1992).
Atalia (Akiva Tevet, 1984).
Avanti Popolo (Rafi Bukai, 1986).
Aviva My Love (*Aviva Ahuvati*, Shemi Zarkhin, 2006).
Beyond the Walls (*Me'akhorei Hasoragim*, Uri Barbash, 1984).
Campfire (*Medurat Hashevet*, Joseph Cedar, 2004).
Cup Final (*Gmar Gavi'a*, Eran Riklis, 1992).
Frozen Days (*Yamim Kfu'im*, Danny Lerner, 2005).
Hamsin (aka: Eastern Wind) (*Khamsin*, Daniel Wachsmann, 1982).

Hide and Seek (*Makhvo'im*, Dan Wolman, 1980).

Hill 24 Doesn't Answer (*Giv'a 24 Eina Ona*, Thorold Dickinson, 1955).

Himmo, King of Jerusalem (*Khimmo Melekh Yerushalayim*, Amos Guttman, 1987).

Lemon Popsicle (*Eskimo Limon*, Boaz Davidson, 1978).

Life according to Agfa (*Hakhaim Al-pi Agfa*, Assi Dayan, 1992).

One of Ours (*Ekhad Mishelanu*, Uri Barbash, 1989).

Operation Thunderbolt (aka *Operation Jonathan*; *Mivtza Yonatan*, Menahem Golan, 1977).

Peeping Toms (*Metzitzim*, Uri Zohar, 1972).

Pick a Card (*Afula Express*, Julie Shles, 1997).

Sallah (*Sallah Shabbati,* Ephraim Kishon, 1964)

Save the Lifeguard (*Hatzilu et Hamatzil*, Uri Zohar, 1977).

Shuru (Savi Gavison, 1991).

Siege (*Matzor*, Gilberto Tofano, 1969).

Song of the Siren (*Shirat Hasirena*, Eytan Fox, 1994).

Time of Favor (*Hahesder*, Joseph Cedar, 2000).

The Wooden Gun (*Roveh Khuliot*, Ilan Moshenson, 1979).

Year Zero (*Shnat Effes*, Joseph Pitchhadze, 2004).

PART II

War and Its Aftermath

4 From Hill to Hill

A Brief History of the Representation of War in Israeli Cinema

URI S. COHEN

This essay is not an attempt to tell the complete story of the representation of war in Israeli cinema, which is far beyond its reach. Instead of a complete history I offer a selective view of the field, deriving from the present. The films I have chosen to discuss here all seem to me to have succeeded in capturing and representing essential nodes of the Israeli culture of war as it has evolved into its present state. They also seem to me the most artistically accomplished, and the two obviously go together.

The arc of representation is wide. It begins with the war of 1948, Israel's War of Independence and the Palestinian Naqba, as they are represented (or not) in *Hill 24 Doesn't Answer* (Thorold Dickinson, 1955) and concludes with the film *Beaufort* (Joseph Cedar, 2007) and the end of the First Lebanon War, which is also the beginning of the second, as the book on which the film is based makes clear.[1] The cultural shift between the two films can be understood as a process in which the whole of culture takes part, creating a kind of change in the perception of war that is almost a full inversion of the way it was seen, yet without changing or defying the conventions of Zionism in a major way. The films I discuss in detail are two central cinematic works of national cinema that have fifty years between them.[2] Both are about a hill representing war and the sacrifices made on it in a cinematic manner that makes it possible to see them as the beginning and endpoint of a discussion about war and its meaning in Israeli culture and cinema.

....

Hill 24 Doesn't Answer, directed by Thorold Dickinson and written by war veteran and minor writer Tzvi Kolitz together with Peter Frye, is in many ways the first large-scale Israeli film production and certainly the first influential cinematic representation of the war.[3] The structure of the story is slightly confusing: it is constructed as a flashback telling the stories of the four dead soldiers clenching the Israeli flag and determining the inclusion of Hill 24 in the territory of the newborn state.[4] The film and the story heavily depended on international support to approve the justness of the cause and of the war. The border is determined by a United Nations official and is discussed calmly by Israeli and Jordanian officers. In the same way it is necessary that two out of the four soldiers on the hill be foreigners. One is a complete stranger, an Irish detective serving the British who fell for a female resistance fighter he was following on assignment. The other is an American Jew caught in the besieged old city who joins the fight. This kind of international support is needed to enhance the point of view of the film, which claims justice without considering the enemy's catastrophe.[5] Even if the outcome of the war was inevitable, the inability to see the enemy precludes any meaningful discussion of justice. Instead the film is a clear manifestation of the Israeli Jewish point of view taking form as the camera's field of vision.[6]

The opening sequence is rather odd and defines the paradigm that is in place. The film opens with a shot of a Judean hill: framed by the local flora, three shells explode. Opening titles appear against the backdrop of a series of changing pictures of the land. The latter part of the sequence is particularly interesting: it moves through various pictures of portal elements that are part of a seemingly impenetrable wall, later revealed to be elements of the wall of the Old City in Jerusalem. Visually this seems to say that the story of the 1948 war being told is one of setting out against such a wall (a war of survival fought with their "backs against a wall"); the outcome, though, points in the direction of the 1967 war and the conquest of Jerusalem as a fulfillment of a millennial longing, visually positioned at the heart of Zionism. After an inscription thanking the Israel Defense Forces (IDF) and El Al (the Israeli airlines) appears, a highly authoritative voice introduces us in the most didactic manner to a map of the partition:

> The eastern shore of the Mediterranean. Palestine. On May 14, 1948, the state of Israel [a pointing stick appears in the frame, tracing the differently colored borders of the state] sanctioned by the United Nations was declared and the British mandate ended on that day. Seven Arab countries challenged the borders set by the United Nations. Thus began the war of liberation in which Israel fought for survival. Here are the boundaries held

at 5:45, July 18, 1948, when a general truce between the Arabs and the Israelis was established by the United Nations.

We return to a repeat of the shot watching the hill while three shells explode then cut to an image of a pale dead man, eyes looking into the distance within a face unspoiled by death. When a voice calls out the name "James Finnegan," we cut to Finnegan rising from his seat eagerly smiling and saying: "Here." We then cut to the overturned dead body of Allen Goodman, who rises with a "Yup." Ester Hadassi, obviously a Yemenite girl, rises with a local Hebrew "Ken" (Yes). The body of David Amiran (Arik Lavi) has a golden Palmakh necklace and blood coming out of his mouth: he rises reluctantly and, full of casual "Palmakh" attitude, answers "Yesh" (a cooler and more "Israeli" way to say "present").

The whole sequence and especially the didactic part seems pompous, almost comic, in retrospect even though it was earnestly intended at the time.[7] The four faces and modes of saying "present" as symbols of the nation's diversity are hardly an artistic achievement. The didactic part is unthinkable today; it proposes that it is that easy: a map showing the meagerness of the partition plan together with its rejection by the Arabs in itself illustrates justice. Tellingly, the place where the film is set is called Palestine, ironically illustrating the Palestinian view that, whatever Israel's borders may be, they were carved out of the carcass of Palestine. Besides ignoring the first part of the war, which began on November 29, 1947, after the UN decision on partition, the didactic lecture also shows us that the borders of July 18, 1948, represent serious progress on all fronts by the Israelis. The date marks the end of the battles that followed the end of the "First Truce" (Hafuga Rishona) imposed by the UN on June 10, 1948. After the truce the Israeli side was determined to improve its position. In the battles that followed, known as the "Battles of Ten Days" (Kravot Aseret Hayamim), the Israeli army made immense progress on most fronts, including the capture and emptying of the Palestinian cities of Ramla and Lod.[8] It is hard to know why this date was chosen to end the timeline, and the only explanation seems to be pride in the achievement of enlarging the state's territory.

The ubiquity of this view is underlined by the opening briefing to the soldiers, in which we learn that taking the hill is precisely an operation enacted "in time" to capture territory before the cease-fire takes effect. This premise has little to do with the stated "fighting for survival" and seems less than heroic. If a battle for survival has the undeniable justification of saving lives, insisting on the capture of an empty hill declares rather bluntly that territorial expansion deserves the same sacrifice. This is the political claim of the settlement movement in embryo and perhaps a less pronounced feature of Zionism in general. It is certainly not a view of Zionism or war embraced by the post-1967 peace movement or by the films produced in its wake.

This sequence is also important because it defines the relation between life and death and the camera. The twice-repeated opening shot is crucial in establishing the point of view of the film. The camera, the gaze, the line of vision, anticipates the plot in determining the ideological message by presenting the film through the eye that is seeing all of this unfold.[9] The vision is static: the camera seems to be unmanned, because any camera attached to an operator would have been shaken as the shells exploded; in essence the gaze is a figure of history seeing its making and lovingly giving tribute to its fallen heroes.[10] The structure of the roll call and the characters visually rising from death further establishes the sequence and the film itself as a memorial service. The arrival of the voice a few seconds after seeing the dead visage is the traditional way a memorial service is enacted in schools, youth movements, and the media; and it stands in direct contrast with the story that is beginning to unfold. The present tense of the film, which tells of how these people arrived at their fates, is caught between the end (death) and the future (the state). The confusion of the tenses is part of the cinematic enunciation, expressing a view in which the dead are present and alive in memory and in history and in the annals of the people.

This kind of view has been widely discussed. Its quintessential figures are usually the living dead, a defining feature of the cultural production of the time.[11] What is revealed here is the structure of this figure in cinema. Though this may not hold true of all films portraying the war, it is the clear beginning of the representation of war in Israeli society. As such it suggests that war is seen through eyes beyond and above the existential condition of the individual. The film does not suffer from understatement; it takes great care to underline this view in the form of the ending. Starting from the briefing in the beginning, the film moves along two lines: the present tense moving from the briefing in the commander's office to the hill and the flashbacks showing how each character except the woman came to join the struggle. This insistence on exploring the motivations of the characters instead of their actions seems to express the humanistic side of the film. The dead all have stories that are interesting and worthy of telling because they have sacrificed. This is also a main feature of the cultural response to the war, which insisted on publication of the rather puerile ruminations and correspondences of these young heroes that some critics mistook for works of great art and thought.[12] Strikingly, the film forgoes the telling of Ester's story; we know only that "she grew up in these hills" and that she helped patch up the American, who is obviously planning to marry her.[13] The film then tells Amiram's story, in which an enemy soldier he spares turns out to be an SS officer. The officer dies while hurling insults at the Israeli Jew, who is visually turned into a ghetto Jew, underlining the Holocaust as a justification for the overall survivalist nature of the conflict.[14] Back in the truck the four drink to the future capture of Hill 24 as a "link in the chain."

The night on the hill remains untold. The film moves from the silhouettes ascending the hill to a peaceful view of the landscape. A UN jeep arrives carrying a printed sign: "United Nations Truce Supervision."[15] The camera dwells on the UN flag and on the sign, investing much symbolic stock in the international gaze, in what can also be seen in retrospect as a colonial moment. The French and American officers call out to the hill in French and in English but receive no answer. A Jordanian officer with a face not unlike young King Hussein calls in Arabic, and the Israeli calls in Hebrew. They climb the hill, only to reveal the gruesome opening frames of the cadavers. Ester is found dead in a crouching position. She is knocked over by the Israeli officer, who is climbing the stairs, and rolls onto her back into a position that is not without sexual innuendo. All modes of love—for the man, for the land, and for the people—are visually aligned as the French officer covers her face with the flag and declares the hill to be an Israeli possession. A rather inflated version of the national anthem "Hatikva" takes over the soundtrack (composed by the brilliant Paul Ben Haim).[16] The theorem is complete when the mounting sound of the anthem is coupled with the camera rising above the hill and a slideshow of aerial views of Israel at the end of the film. These aerial views are rather restricted, presenting limited slivers of land and carefully concentrating on classical Zionist postcard views. The final view is of the Eilat hills, which were captured only at the very end of the war during Operation Uvda, which ended the war (March 10, 1949). The film finally achieves closure as the words "The Beginning" zoom into full view, dominating the screen as it goes dark.

The ideological insistence of the movie is clear, and yet it is important to see how the representation of war in Israeli cinema begins with an alignment of the cinematic gaze with the people in history and a soundtrack full of unfulfilled hope and longing, as the national anthem is. The characters and their stories are in part a demonstration of the humanistic drive to "give the fallen a name," yet the film still does not go beyond a symbolic treatment of these characters as an illustration of history. All aspects of the film are dominated by a symbolizing gaze that endows the hill with highly expressive significance. As the opening shot gazes on Hill 24 all we see is a hill; but by the end of the film we are supposed to feel that the whole tale of the war is enfolded in that hill, as a story of the Jewish people struggling for survival. The cinematic eye, symbolizing the people, is now an enlightened gaze that can see history in the land and heroism in its "blood-soaked" soil. It is therefore clear why the end is only the beginning: not only, as the film suggests, because this war has created a new beginning for the Jewish people but because the gaze has been symbolized. Everything it sees, as the aerial views claim, is endowed with the same story. The glaring irony is that the end of the film is also "the beginning" of an endless chain of wars that the state will be involved in, when the control of territory as a dominant political view becomes an undeclared aim in itself, already in the 1956 war but more clearly after the 1967 expansion.[17]

.....

As already hinted by the way Ester's body is knocked over by the climbing Israeli officer, the representation of war in Israeli culture found its "antiwar" voice by seeing what *Hill 24* envisioned as the noble and worthy sacrifice as victimization of the individual by a callous public and unworthy commanders.[18] In Hebrew this is rendered possible by the ambiguity of the term *korban*, which can mean "sacrifice" or "victim," depending on the context.[19] This is a collaborative effort that takes place in all spheres of Israeli culture over the years leading from *Hill 24* (1955) to the contemporary depiction of another embattled hill in Joseph Cedar's rendering of Ron Leshem's novel *Beaufort* (2007). Much could be gained by a comprehensive study of the many films representing war made in these years, which has yet to be written.[20] The following discussion is only a sketch of the major modes of resistance to war developed in Israeli cinema, read as taking part in the movement between the two "Hills"; obviously this is not an exclusive reading and does not preclude other interpretations of the films.

One way to think of this process is as a steady inward inversion of the gaze that reveals the unfathomable complexity of the sacrificed individual, rendering death almost impossible to justify. It is possible to claim that this had been achieved already in the representation of the 1948 war in literature. One can see signs of these changes in the major films made in the sixties, especially Uri Zohar's *A Hole in the Moon* (*Khor Balevana*, 1964) and Micha Shagrir's *Scouting Patrol* (*Sayarim*, 1967), but it seems safe to say that the deep changes in the representation of war in Israeli cinema began to take place especially after the 1967 war.[21]

Films made after 1967 continued to develop the complexity of the individual but also brought into the discussion the role of the military and political powers-that-be in defining impossible missions and pursuing erroneous political aims with the lives of simple soldiers. Perhaps the earliest movie to pursue this line of resistance is Uri Zohar's *Every Bastard a King* (U.S. title: *Every Man a King*, 1968). The unveiling of military arbitrariness matched with political blindness increasingly became the focal point of the representation of war in Israeli cinema (as in Rafi Bukai, *Avanti Popolo*, 1986; Renen Schorr, *Late Summer Blues*, 1987; Amos Gitai, *Kippur*, 2000).

Another line of resistance pursued in earnest after 1967 cinematically engages the devastating effect that the death of the soldier has on surviving friends and family. It is telling that the first film with this loaded subject at the heart of its plot is the fine film *Siege*, made by Italian theater director Gilberto Tofano in 1969.[22] Others in this vein include Shimon Dotan's *Repeat Dive* (1982), a notable film within this tradition, as well as Shmuel Imberman's adaptation of Dan Ben Amotz's novel *Don't Give a Damn* (1987).

Perhaps the most important role in Israeli cinema's resistance to war is played by comedies, which had an important part in changing the perception and representation of war. In the terms that have been established here military comedies expose the military establishment's arbitrary and corrupt nature. Most of them are fully intent on deconstructing the self-importance of the military command, and they had a significant impact on the way Israeli culture sees war. The seminal military comedy is a take on *Hill 24 Doesn't Answer*: Assi Dayan's *Halfon Hill Doesn't Answer* (1976). This is the first real film to satirize the war machine itself and is among the earliest cinematic reactions to the 1973 war, dwelling affectionately on the degeneration of the Israeli military. Like *Hill 24*, the film opens with a shot of a hill, but it is a small, insignificant hill. The frame split between sand and sky is immobile as a pole penetrates it; at first it appears to be an antenna, but it soon turns out to be a disheveled soldier returning with two fish from the sea. The plot is all slapstick yet serious in its own way, telling of the capture and rescue of one Victor Khasson (literally "strong winner") by the Egyptians. The main parts are played by a popular comedy trio Hagashash Hakhiver (the Pale Tracker Trio), and the captured Victor is rescued by his friends posing as the UN peacekeepers, who show up *ex machina* pretending to be Swedes in search of a good time. Not only is the international order ineffectual in resolving the conflict, but the line between friend and foe has grown hazy. In one telling moment it turns out that the interrogating Egyptian officer and the captured Israeli cook Victor both come from Alexandria. They end up reminiscing about the good old times, obviously the times before a Jewish state existed. If death is the cause for the lack of response in *Hill 24 Doesn't Answer*, in *Halfon Hill Doesn't Answer* the soldiers do not answer because they are too busy goofing around. The serious question they raise is "Who shall I say is calling?" Is it a call that needs to be answered? Answering that call could end your life because you may be asked to gain another hill before the cease-fire.

This view of the history of Israeli cinematic representation of war needs further elaboration, which is beyond the scope of this chapter. This kind of outline by nature does not do justice to the many divergent details, yet such a view is helpful in understanding the development of the Israeli cinema of war. It allows us to discuss Joseph Cedar's *Beaufort* as standing at the end of this trajectory with a point of view that is diametrically opposed to that of *Hill 24*, incorporating all of the previously discussed modes of resistance into a film which is the summa of the Israeli antiwar cinematic culture. By looking at *Beaufort* as standing in direct contrast to *Hill 24* with *Halfon Hill* in the middle, we can talk of these changes in terms of cinematic enunciation: *Beaufort* can be said to realize the full potential of the Israeli Zionist antiwar discourse. It also provides some explanation for the appearance of a new way of representing war at precisely the same moment in *Waltz with Bashir* (Ari Folman, 2008).

....

Beaufort, not unlike *Halfon Hill* and *Hill 24*, is a film about a hill. In the 1950s representation of the 1948 war, the hill was anonymous, one of many hills with (Arab) buildings on top but no name, just a number. In present-day Israel it is a mythological hill. Beaufort is a name that dominated Israeli newscasts after the Palestine Liberation Organization (PLO) took control of the crusader stronghold in 1976 and used it for bombings of Israel. The ruins and later the Israeli bunker on the hill were further mythologized during the first day of the First Lebanon War. After the mountain was taken at an unnecessary price, prime minister Menahem Begin was flown in to view the spoils. In a moment that symbolized the whole conduct of the war, Begin was told a lie—that there were no casualties. He also inquired whether the "terrorists had machine guns" and if many of them surrendered (though none had), exposing how little he understood and controlled the war he had declared. All of this is relevant because the movie stands directly on this symbolic residue.

The film *Beaufort* is based on the eponymous book (in English: in Hebrew the book is titled *If There's a Paradise*) and remains quite faithful to it, following the last days of the Israeli presence on the mountain before the retreat from Lebanon on May 24, 2000. In the book the story takes the form of the diary of the hill's last commander, Liraz Liberty, famously prophesying the inevitability of a second Lebanon War as a direct result of the one-sided retreat. The plot remains relatively untouched in the film adaptation. Yet on the visual level the film does not adopt the commander's point of view; instead it directly engages the tradition of Israeli war films, creating a point of view that is the direct opposite of the perspective in *Hill 24*.

The opening sequence of Beaufort makes this quite clear. The film begins with one production credit followed by ten seconds of dark and silent screen, which then opens to a shaft of light: it is the view from inside the bunker looking out, saturated with light. Suddenly Liraz materializes from the outside, weary and enveloped in dust. Once inside he leans on the wall and sighs. The whole frame then shrinks into the Hebrew title forming the inside of the Hebrew letter Vav as it appears in the logo of the film. Oddly, the point of view of this first shot of the film is from inside the hill. To some extent, the hill itself is gazing indifferently upon human folly. This is the exact opposite of the point of view established at the beginning of *Hill 24*, where the camera omnisciently observes the hill from the distance of an ideologically committed and historically informed gaze. Like the mountain, we too are gazing indifferently as the young men that we sent to occupy the hill go about losing their lives to no avail. The gaze of a figure in history or the nation viewing the worthy occupation of the hill is now turned 180 degrees. It incorporates the various antiwar discourses into a point of view that sees the soldiers as victims of political folly, military mismanagement, indifference to life, and a public sphere capable of protest but incapable of a meaningful political discussion. The hill has eyes, but all they see are the pity and folly of it all.

Liraz continues to walk in the frame within the name of the film and, much as in *Hill 24*, a didactic text appears:[23]

> [Frame 1] *Beaufort*, a crusader castle from the twelfth century, has been changing hands between armies for centuries. Bloody battles have turned it into a mythological symbol of heroism.
>
> [Frame 2] In 1982, on the first day of the Lebanon War, the Israeli flag was flown over it, after a difficult and disputed battle.
>
> [Frame 3] Eighteen years later, following public protests, the Israeli government decided to get out of Lebanon.

More than being a reference to *Hill 24*, this didactic information is mainly the expression of a need to explain the Israeli position and introduce the viewer to the context. Even so, it is already part of the film's national form. Without engaging in a lengthy debate over the nature of national cinema, the need to "explain" Israel already qualifies the film as generically "national." It is remarkable, however, that the premise of *Beaufort* is almost diametrically opposed to that of *Hill 24*. Both films begin with a deadline, yet in *Beaufort* the time limit is for retreat, not for a cease-fire and the "last" opportunity to conquer. Following this premise, the deaths that ensue serve no real object. The fallen soldiers are plainly useless victims of the callousness of the large organization and the leadership failure of the IDF. Their sacrifice is meaningless and futile: the hill they are occupying is eventually blown up.

From the opening shot it is clear that the film makes a conscious effort visually to engage all aspects of Israeli antiwar culture. The difficulty inherent in this position can already be sensed in the didactic text itself as it makes an effort to stay neutral. As critical of war as the film may be, describing the fortress as "constantly changing hands between armies" undermines the film's critical edge and enhances the view of the war being depicted as also just a constant feature of life in the Middle East.

The next shot is perhaps the most intriguing. It is taken from the bottom of the hill looking up and frames it beautifully. The hill is massive and distant, filmed on a cloudy day with soft light. The frame lasts ten seconds, and until the bunker is blown up at the end we do not see it again from this perspective. The next frame is of the mythological Israeli flag put up there by the soldiers in 1982. It is shot from a defending post, and sandbags form the edge of the frame. Next we see the courtyard of the military stronghold. We gradually begin to move into the bunker, following a soldier who crawls into a secluded tunnel, filmed from the inside of the hill. We are then introduced again to commander Liraz and another soldier who will be killed later, as they wait for a helicopter carrying a bomb squad specialist. The following shot of the helicopter arriving under fire is reminiscent of Francis Ford Coppola's *Apocalypse Now* (1979), and certainly the film shows the same attitude toward the military command.[24] It is also part of the film's remarkable ability to be extremely local yet also about war and its representation in the larger sense. The specialist (fair and blue-eyed) is brought in to investigate an improvised explosive device planted on the road leading to the base. As the helicopter lands, the shelling begins and the three scramble breathlessly into the bunker. The arrival of the specialist and his subsequent death in useless action are important: his presence provides proof of the indifference and thoughtlessness of the military command and hints at a homoerotic subplot in the form of the relationship between him and Liraz.[25]

The first frame of this sequence is almost the same as the one that opens *Hill 24*. The mountain stands there as if to be taken. But the camera's movement from the outside to the inside suggests a perspective at once intimate and indifferent, providing a much more complicated and tragic view of war.

Such an opening sequence is also a declaration that we are about to see the inside of what has always been seen from the outside. The insistence on not offering another outside view of the hill is remarkable, even if symbolically clear: a view of the hill is only possible after the hill has been deconstructed by the horror of war lived and viewed from the inside. The film treats not only the private-public and soldiers-commanders dynamic but the hill as an object of desire. Against the very belief that territory is worthy of sacrifice that drives *Hill 24*, *Beaufort* reminds us constantly that the deaths we view have no significance.

The film tells the story of the last days on the hill. Hunted by a totally invisible enemy and haunted by memories and a numbing fear, the characters pass the days like sitting ducks. Perhaps the most interesting character is Liraz, the young commander of the post, complexly driven to execute the mission in a manner that makes it difficult to see where ambition ends and duty begins. The composition of the group of soldiers also makes it clear that this is a national movie. If the composition of the group in *Hill 24* is almost too symbolic, *Beaufort*'s is not much less symbolic. It indicates the shift in Israeli society from the older, salt-of-the-earth type of soldiers to the new lower-class, mostly Mizrahi, and religious men who are now serving. This is the reality of military service, and the film is more aware of it than the book. This awareness also gives the film just the slightest hint of class consciousness.[26] In this inevitable symbolism of the cast shared by the two films it becomes clear that even after making a U-turn one still remains on the same road.

A closer look at the details of the film confirms what already has been disclosed: all the modes of resistance to the culture of war are engaged. The impact of the soldier's death on his surroundings is described when the bereaved father of the bomb specialist Ziv appears on television, seen on the set inside the bunker. The father delivers a chilling speech blaming himself for having educated his son to become a victim of the state and not teaching him that his life is supremely important. A meeting between Liraz and his commanders is quite effective in illustrating the inability to trust the higher command with the lives of the simple soldiers and the infinite gap between the reasons of state and the individual.[27] Together with showing the obvious conflict between the individual and the collective and the degenerated level of public discourse, in its final sequences the film makes it quite clear that the older way of representing and justifying war has been thoroughly deconstructed.

The film begins to end with the evacuation of the hill and the preparations made to demolish the bunker. In a symbolically charged moment Liraz and another soldier attempt to take down a memorial plaque for the soldiers who fell taking the hill in 1982. After a few attempts Liraz says that it is obvious that the soldiers want to stay on the mountain, and they proceed with the evacuation. Mounted on the armored vehicles, they are all ordered inside to avoid the blast. Only Liraz remains with his head out as the hill explodes, unable to turn his eyes away, like Lot's wife. Viewed from afar, the blast burns the night. Then the camera returns inside the hill to see the plaque being hit by the blast, unhinged and illuminated. It is the state itself, and the way it uses power and soldiers, that causes the crisis of faith. As the plaque is engulfed by fire one can only feel the uselessness of the sacrifice. Liraz is a real idealist. His actions make it clear that he saw the Beaufort just as Hill 24 and the deaths for its capture are presented in *Hill 24:* as a place worthy of defending unto death. Why? Because the trusted people in charge told him to. If he is sent to defend it, then it must matter in some grand scheme of things. In this sense the journey of Liraz in the film is exactly the unraveling of the old way of seeing the hill. Had the film ended with the explosion, this would undoubtedly have been the message. But the film has another closing sequence.

As the armored vehicles start their journey from the hill to Israel, they are viewed in a static shot that lasts five seconds and discloses the hill's point of view. The decision not to end the film with this shot means that the point of view of the hill is subjected to yet another gaze. In the next shot, early in the morning from inside the state, we see the vehicles cross the border. The soldiers dismount, hug each other, and call home; their obvious relief is punctuated by the Israeli flags in many of the frames. Like Liraz, who commands the driver to "drive home," the soldiers all refer to the Israeli side of the northern border as "home." It turns out that the film is not about war and hills in general but rather about this specific one or at most about all hills outside Israel. This allows ample room for a Zionist public to enjoy and accept the film, as it seems to refer only to hills outside the "consensus."

The final closure of the film arrives as Liraz moves to the side and begins to shed his military gear; he collapses into a sitting position, starts to pant hard, and then sobs. He raises his head and regains control: framed against a field in sunrise, he looks ahead with a firm, resolute gaze, perhaps seeing the mountain, perhaps not. The position clearly refers to the iconic image from *Platoon* (Oliver Stone, 1986), but without the raised hands asking "why?" Instead of a question we have acceptance, a feeling of catharsis: the aberration has been removed and the city is once again made whole. Or at the very least Liraz looks ready for another war that will be quick to come.

....

By way of conclusion it seems fair to say that *Hill 24* and *Beaufort* are two very connected films that stand at two ends of representation of war in Israeli cinema from the 1948 war to the end of the Israeli occupation of southern Lebanon. In essence the two films have almost opposite points of view, as can be seen in their very form of cinematic enunciation, but in the end they offer opposing directions on the same road. The discussion here cannot do justice to the many works in film and in other genres that led up to *Beaufort*. Just as *Hill 24* sums up the discourse of the 1948 War of Independence in Israel's early years, *Beaufort* aptly incorporates the various discourses that deconstruct the view of war from a perspective which is not existential, ignoring the real pain and loss of the individual. *Beaufort* has gone as far against war as it is possible to go in a film that after all remains national: the point of view of the camera is still an allegory of the nation at some level. *Beaufort* deconstructs the heroic view of war in a very deep and thorough way, perhaps not breaking new ground in the representation of war but creating a cultural space for a completely new way of representing war in Israeli cinema, as in *Waltz with Bashir*.[28] In turn we can only hope that these are the harbingers of equally new political modes of discussing war in Israel.

NOTES

1. Ron Leshem, *Beaufort*, 365.

2. The term "national cinema" is notoriously difficult to define. In this context it means that the point of view of the film is at least to some extent an allegory of the nation and the action captured is part of a national allegory. For a discussion of this point of view in the field of Israeli cinema, see Ella Shohat, *Israeli Cinema: East/West and the Politics of Representation*, 14–20.

3. *Hill 24 Doesn't Answer* is not the first representation of the war on film and is in English, necessarily marking it as a work of propaganda, as critics at the time pointed out. Still, it is an Israeli film and highly representative of the cultural moment. See Nathan Gross, "The Second Five Years of Israeli Film"; David Greenberg, *Cinema*.

4. This, of course, is far from being a neutral structure, as the backward movement in time comes to symbolize the reactionary forces in Sergei Eisenstein's *October* (1927); see Susan Buck-Morss, *Dreamworld and Catastrophe*, 80–81. As different as these movies might be, they share the discussion of a revolutionary moment toward which the backward movement in time is always deliberate. In this case the temporal movement does not stress the opposing forces as much as it underlines the worthiness of the sacrifice.

5. This argument is hardly new: see Nurith Gertz, *Motion Fiction*, 13–62.

6. This point is shared in Igal Bursztyn's discussion of the face in Israeli cinema, *The Face as a Battlefield*, 166–167.

7. For both perspectives, see Ella Shohat, *Israeli Cinema: East/West*, 58–76; and Nitzan Ben Shaul, *Mythical Expressions of Siege in Israeli Films*, 15–21.

8. Benny Morris, *1948: A History of the First Arab-Israeli War*, 316–325.

9. The terms used here can be discussed at length. As with the rest of this essay, the view here is almost literary, questioning the figure of the gaze for its allegory.

10. For a penetrating discussion of the gaze and its role in the theory of cinema as well as a way of seeing the gaze as working to undermine the spectator's sense of identity, see Tod McGowan, *The Real Gaze*, 1–38 (esp. 8–10).

11. Nurith Gertz, "The Book and the Film: A Case Study of *He Walked in the Fields*," 22–26; Hanan Hever, "Gender, Body, and the National Subject," 225–260. There are noticeable exceptions to this mode: for a detailed discussion, see Dan Miron, *In Front of the Silent Brother*.

12. B. Michali, *The World of the Native Sons*. There are noticeable exceptions to this rule and some of the material published is truly beautiful, yet the state tends to fetishize such expressions, as can be seen in the endless publication of these writings in an interminable series of *Burnt Scrolls* (*Gvilei Esh*) by the Ministry of Defense.

13. On this issue and more about the film, see Shohat, *Israeli Cinema: East/West*.

14. It should be noted that Kolitz, the writer and producer of the film, is the author of a work of prose called *Yossel Rakover Speaks with God*, supposedly found in the ashes of the Warsaw Ghetto. Kolitz did very little to correct the impression that this was a genuine document, leading even Levinas to comment on it in an eloquent piece: "To Love the Torah More Than God"; *Yossel Rakover Speaks with God*.

15. The odd wording of the UN sign has direct and very funny consequences in *Halfon Hill Doesn't Answer* (Assi Dayan, 1976).

16. See Yoash Hirshberg, *Paul Ben Haim—His Life and Work*.

17. Officially the 1956 war was a reaction to terrorist activity encouraged by the Egyptian army. The declassification of documents and the accounts of those involved show quite clearly that the war was a willful act of the military establishment, asserting war as a determining mode of Israeli policy. See Mordechai Bar-On, *The Gates of Gaza*.

18. See Miri Talmon, *Israeli Graffiti: Nostalgia, Groups, and Collective Identity in Israeli Cinema*; and Judd Ne'eman, "The Death Mask of the Moderns: A Genealogy of New Sensibility Cinema in Israel."

19. For a comprehensive discussion of the subject, see "Grief and Bereavement in the National Library."

20. Many excellent works tell different parts of that story, however. Raz Yosef's work is a good example of an examination of war and soldiering through a critically queer perspective: *Beyond Flesh: Queer Masculinities and Nationalism in Israeli Cinema*.

21. A novel such as *He Walked through the Fields* by Moshe Shamir (Tel Aviv: Poalim, 1947) provides a good example. The book is habitually understood as a text justifying sacrifice, yet in retrospect the protagonist Uri is revealed to be a far more complex character than first perceived. This complexity eventually brings us to see him as a martyr and a victim to the same extent, though the film made by Yosef Millo in 1967 follows a script changed by Shamir himself in an attempt to be less ambiguous in terms of the nation; the complexity remains in part due to an outstanding performance by Assi Dayan as Uri. There is much commentary on the book; for a more recent account, see Shai Ginsburg, "Between History and Myth."

22. An important distinction should be made here in the discussion of the gendered depictions of this problem: see Régine-Mihal Friedman, "Between Silence and Abjection."

23. The need to explain, the assumption that the viewer does not have the information needed to understand the film "correctly," is a curious phenomenon. It is in part due to the distance from the imperial metropolis but also because the morality play itself needs the national framework outside of the film in order to make sense. See Orly Lubin, *Women Reading Women*, 259–260.

24. The film contains references to Coppola's work as well as to other movies about Vietnam in general or to those films engaging Michael Herr's seminal work *Dispatches*.

25. The film thus joins the whole field of works dealing with homoerotic relations and the military life: see Yosef, *Beyond Flesh*, 48–83.

26. No one has made this point more eloquently or forcefully than Ella Shohat in *Taboo Memories*, 330–358.

27. As can be understood better from Nir Toyeb's film *Every Mother Should Know* (*Teda Kol Em*, 2007), this kind of critique is not always against war; sometimes it is a thinly disguised jab at the softness of the current Israeli army. In the case of this film it is clear that the visual aspect goes against the text of the book in discouraging this point of view.

28. As might be expected, Folman's previous work on war and especially his 2001 film *Made in Israel* are a rare exception.

BIBLIOGRAPHY

Bar-On, Mordechai. *The Gates of Gaza*. London: Palgrave, 1995.

Ben-Shaul, Nitzan. *Mythical Expressions of Siege in Israeli Films*. New York: Edwin Mellen, 1987.

Buck-Morss, Susan. *Dreamworld and Catastrophe*. Cambridge, Mass.: MIT Press, 2000.

Bursztyn, Igal. *The Face as a Battlefield (Panim Kisde Krav)*. Tel Aviv: Hakibbutz Hameukhad, 1990.

Cohen, Uri S. "Grief and Bereavement in the National Library" ("Shkhol Va'evel Basifria Ha'leumit"). In Avriel Bar Levav (ed.), *War and Peace in Jewish Culture (Milkhama Veshalom Batarbut Hayehudit)*, 277–312. Jerusalem: Zalman Shazar, 2006.

Friedman, Regine-Mihal. "Between Silence and Abjection: The War Widow in Israeli Cinema" ("Bein Shtika Leniduy: Hamedium Hakolno'I Vealmanat Hamilkhama Hayisra'elit"). In Nurith Gertz, Orly Lubin, and Judd Ne'eman, eds., *Fictive Looks: On Israeli Cinema (Mabatim Fiktivi'im Al Kolno'a Yisra'eli)*, 33–43. Tel Aviv: Open University, 1998.

Gertz, Nurith. *Motion Fiction (Sipur Mehasratim: Siporet Yisra'elit Ve'ibudeihah Lakolno'a)*. Tel Aviv: Open University, 1993.

———. "The Book and the Film: A Case Study of *He Walked in the Fields*." *Modern Hebrew Literature* (Fall/Winter 1995). 153–174.

Ginsburg, Shai. "Between History and Myth." In Yasir Suleiman and Ibrahim Muhawi, *Literature and Nation in the Middle East*, 110–127. Edinburgh: Edinburgh University Press, 2006.

Greenberg, David. *Cinema (Kolno'a)*. Tel Aviv: Am Oved, 1967.

Gross, Nathan. "The Second Five Years of Israeli Film" ("Hakhomesh Hasheni Bakolno'a Ha'yisra'eli"). *Kolnoa* 75, no. 4: 69–86. Reprinted in Yaacov Gross and Natan Gross, *The Hebrew Film (Ha'seret Haivri)*, 131–134. Jerusalem: Self, 1991.

Herr, Michael. *Dispatches*. New York: Vintage, 1991.

Hever, Hanan. "Gender, Body, and the National Subject." In Edna Lomsky Feder and Eyal Ben Ari (eds.), *Military and Militarism in Israeli Society*, 225–260. Albany: SUNY Press, 2000.

Hirshberg, Yoash. *Paul Ben Haim: His Life and Work (Paul Ben Khaim: Khayav Vitzirato)*. Tel Aviv: Am Oved, 1983.

Kolitz, Zvi. *Yossel Rakover Speaks with God*. Hoboken: Ktav, 1995.

Leshem, Ron. *Beaufort*. New York, Random House, 2007.

Lubin, Orly. *Women Reading Women (Isha Koret Isha)*. Haifa: Haifa University Press, 2006.

McGowan, Tod. *The Real Gaze*. Albany: SUNY, 2007.

Michali, B. *The World of the Native Sons (Olamam Shel Bnei Ha'aretz)*. Tel Aviv: Neuman, 1951.

Miron, Dan. *In Front of the Silent Brother (Mul Ha'akh Hashotek)*. Tel Aviv: Open University, 1998.

Morris, Benny. *1948: A History of the First Arab-Israeli War*. New Haven: Yale University Press, 2008.

Ne'eman, Judd. "The Death Mask of the Moderns: A Genealogy of New Sensibility Cinema in Israel." Israel Studies 4, no. 1 (Spring 1999): 100–128.

Shohat, Ella. *Israeli Cinema: East/West and the Politics of Representation*. Austin: University of Texas, 1989.

———. *Taboo Memories*. Durham: Duke University Press, 2006.

Talmon, Miri. *Israeli Graffiti: Nostalgia, Groups, and Collective Identity in Israeli Cinema (Bluz Latzabar Ha'avud: Khavurot Venostalgia Bakolno'a Hayisra'eli)*. Tel Aviv: Open University and Haifa: Haifa University Press, 2001.

Yosef, Raz. *Beyond Flesh: Queer Masculinities and Nationalism in Israeli Cinema*. New Brunswick: Rutgers University Press, 2004.

FILMOGRAPHY

Avanti Popolo. Rafi Bukai, 1986.

Beaufort. Joseph Cedar, 2007.

Don't Give a Damn (Lo Sum Zain). Shmuel Imberman, 1987.

Every Bastard a King (Kol Mamzer Melekh). Uri Zohar, 1968.

Every Mother Should Know (Teda Kol Em). (Nir Toyeb, 2007).

Halfon Hill Doesn't Answer (Giv'at Khalfon Eina Ona). Assi Dayan, 1976.

He Walked through the Fields (Hu Halakh Basadot). Yosef Millo, 1967.

Hill 24 Doesn't Answer (Giv'a 24 Eina Ona). Thorold Dickinson, 1955.

A Hole in the Moon (Khor Balevana). Uri Zohar, 1964.

Kippur. Amos Gitai, 2000.

Late Summer Blues (Bluz Lakhofesh Hagadol). Renen Schorr, 1987.

Made in Israel. Ari Folman, 2001.

Repeat Dive (Tzlila Khozeret). Shimon Dotan, 1982.

Scouting Patrol (Sayarim). Micha Shagrir, 1967.

Siege (Matzor). Gilberto Tofano, 1969.

Waltz with Bashir (Vals Im Bashir). Ari Folman, 2008.

5   From Hero to Victim

The Changing Image of the Soldier on the Israeli Screen

ERAN KAPLAN

In a country with universal conscription which has been in a declared state of war since its inception—officially and frequently in actuality—it should be of little surprise that the military has figured prominently in Israeli cinema.[1] What might be somewhat surprising is that—although the army has continued to be a constant factor in Israeli life and war (despite several attempts at peace) continues to rage within and without Israel's borders—the image and perception of the IDF have undergone profound changes in the cultural and social arenas that have manifested themselves on the Israeli screen as well.

In the early years of the state the IDF was regarded as the epitome and fulfillment of the Zionist dream, the people's army that manifested the strength and resolve of the young nation and its inhabitants, the New Jews. Over the years, however, the army came to be seen more and more as a necessity rather than as an ideal. Service in the IDF was no longer viewed as participating in a grand national undertaking but as just another phase—following high school and preceding the university—in the *cursus honorum* of Israeli Jews. In the early decades after Israeli independence the IDF was a venerable institution that stood high above the fray, an Israeli "holy cow" of sorts; but with time the army became the source of constant criticism and questioning, if not outright derision.

The young state of Israel was a highly communalist society that embraced government-run austerity programs.[2] Or as the sociologist and social anthropologist Haim Hazan put it, "From Zionist thinkers to Israeli citizens, collectivism has been long perceived not as threatening the autonomy of the individual but rather as an emancipatory force. Collectivism became the 'civil religion' of Israel."[3] This was a country that by and large celebrated collectivism and eschewed most manifestations of individuality, whether in the economic marketplace or in the cultural arena. The military fit within this national ethos perfectly. It was the ideal vehicle both to carry out and to exhibit society's core values: sacrifice and uniformity are at the heart of the military way of life. But since the 1960s and especially after the 1967 war, in which it seemed that in a mere six days Israel transformed from a country in a constant battle for its survival into a regional power (both militarily and economically), the country began to shed its collectivist identity and embrace the opportunities and possibilities of individual freedoms.[4] Israelis seemingly had more choices: in the grocery stores and in boutiques as well as in the political arena (in 1977, the Labor party, which had dominated Zionist and then Israeli politics for over five decades, was dethroned by the Likud).[5] And with greater choices and opportunities for personal expression, the old institutions that were once the extolled symbols of the Zionist enterprise began to lose their prestige and centrality: chief among them was the military. The changing images of the Israeli soldier on film have reflected the evolving place of the military in Israeli life.

In this essay I delineate four distinct images of the Israeli soldier in Israeli cinema, which correspond to the overall social and cultural changes that Israel and its military have undergone. First, from the 1950s and 1960s, the heyday of Israeli collectivism, when films celebrated and helped form the national narrative, the dominant image of the Israeli soldier was of a hero who captures the very essence of the New Jew. The second image, which took hold in the 1970s and 1980s, reflects the growing criticism of the military and its violent legacies and presents the soldier not as a moral hero but rather as an agent of rage and violence. The third period corresponds to what Slavoj Zizek has described as the "happy 1990s" or the post-Zionist era, when under the umbrella of the Oslo Accords many Israelis felt that the Arab-Israeli conflict was nearing its end and that the country was about to enjoy a period of peace and prosperity (a kind of Pax Israeliana). The image of the Israeli soldier that emerged at that time is that of a detached slacker, someone who is interested not in the overall mission of the military but rather in his own personal fate.[6]

The fourth period is the first decade of the twenty-first century, after the Second Intifada, when peace for most Israelis again seemed like a distant fantasy and the realities of war (though this time not against large national armies but against smaller paramilitary groups) and terror once more dominated the Israeli experience. The image of the Israeli soldier came to symbolize the prevailing national sentiment: feeling like helpless victims of irrational and indiscriminate violence.

These are quite naturally broad lines of historical demarcation, and one could easily find counterexamples to the images that certain movies have produced during these decades (heroic images of soldiers continued to inform Israeli movies and culture well beyond the 1960s).[7] But these four categories do reflect some fundamental changes in Israeli society and culture that are accentuated (and perhaps even better understood) through the cinematic representation of the Israeli soldier.

For Israelis, at the beginning was the War of Independence, which a plurality of Israelis viewed as a classic battle of David (Israel) versus Goliath (the Arabs) until the emergence of the New Israeli History in the late 1980s.[8] In the early Israeli collective consciousness, the war of 1948 was etched as a war of liberation in which a fragile Jewish community fought for its survival against five invading Arab armies and miraculously prevailed through sheer determination and willingness to sacrifice everything (and certainly with full moral and historical justification).[9] *Hill 24 Doesn't Answer* (*Giv'a 24 Eina Ona*), which was directed by the notable British director Thorold Dickinson in 1955, created that very image of the war for Israelis but also for the rest of the world in this mostly English-speaking film.

The hill in the movie's title is captured by the military in the last days of the war. A UN commission surveys the armistice lines between Israel and Jordan and finds an Israeli flag among four dead Israeli soldiers who fought on the hill, clutched by the only female warrior among them. Therefore Israel is granted sovereignty over the hill. The movie proceeds by way of a series of flashbacks to recount the individual stories of the four fighters and of their commanding officer: a Holocaust survivor who came to Palestine as an illegal immigrant. The soldiers are an American Jew who came to Israel to understand the conflict and was taken over by the Zionist idea; an Irish detective who served as part of the British administration in Palestine and fell in love with a member of the Jewish underground; a woman who served as a nurse during the Arab Legion's siege of Jewish East Jerusalem; and a Sabra (native born Israeli) played by Arik Lavi, one of Israel's first musical and theatrical stars, whose blond hair and self-assurance symbolized the very idea of the New Jew, the subject of the Zionist program.[10] All the members of this unit exemplify the various aspects of Zionism in a rather crude way; through their personal stories we learn about notions such as the ingathering of the exiles as well as the moral and historical necessity of the Zionist cause. We find out very little about the personal past of the Sabra soldier, seeing him only on the battlefield in the Negev desert in his flashback sequence. Unlike the diasporic Jew—the man of language and learning, steeped in history and tradition—the Sabra that we encounter in *Hill 24* is all action and resolve, a New Jew indeed.[11]

The battle scene in which we learn about the young Sabra soldier is quite extraordinary, if not outright fantastic. Escaping artillery shells in the desert, he comes across a wounded enemy soldier and drags him into a cave. There, much to his surprise, he learns that his captive is not an Arab but a former SS officer, probably one of several mercenaries who fought for the Egyptian army then. In this scene the Israeli soldier hardly says a word; it is the Nazi who tries to appeal to the soldier to free him. As the Nazi, in his great agony, grows more and more delusional, for a minute he sees the Israeli soldier as a Jew in the ghetto, in traditional Jewish garb, wearing a yellow star. But within seconds we again see the Israeli soldier in his khaki fatigues, smiling confidently and brandishing a handgun. This is a vivid representation of one of the quintessential Zionist tropes: the idea of the negation of the exile and of Jewish history. The scene offers a clear contrast between the Old Jew of the Diaspora, who is weak and passive, the victim of gentile aggression; and the Sabra, the New Jew, strong and determined, who laughs as the Nazi lying at his feet dies.[12] And this is the image of the Israeli soldier that comes across in this period of nation building: the celebration of heroism in the face of incredible odds (he was fighting not only Arabs but also the perpetrators of the greatest atrocity against the Jews) and a willingness to sacrifice it all for the sake of the national collective, like his unit mates who died on Hill 24.[13]

If the first two decades of Israel featured movies that celebrated the soldier as a hero fighting for the general cause, some notable Israeli movies of the 1970s and 1980s came to question the cost that the ethos of militarism and heroism brought upon Israeli society. One interesting way in which two important movies from that era, *Hide and Seek* (*Makhvo'im*, 1980) and *The Wooden Gun* (*Roveh Khuliot*, 1979), chose to examine the limits and impact of militarism on Israeli society was to focus on children. Both movies portray groups of kids (in the late 1940s and early 1950s, respectively) who try to participate in the greater national struggles by creating military gangs and engaging in war games. The films show the consequences of this militaristic ethos and how it can turn society into a mobilized and potentially violent mob. As Ella Shohat wrote of *Hide and Seek*, "the main interest of the film is the ambient violence and its effect on children and outsiders."[14]

A scene at the end of *The Wooden Gun* draws these arguments to a radical conclusion. Yoni, the movie's protagonist and leader of one of the gangs, has just shot the leader of a rival gang with a wooden sling gun. Fearing that he might have killed his adversary, he runs to the beach and ends up at a cabin, the home of Palestina, an enigmatic Holocaust survivor harassed by the children earlier. As the woman attends to the wounds of the young boy, Yoni sees in the cabin pictures of her children in the ghetto. For a brief moment his own image is superimposed on that of the young Jewish boy in the ghetto: Yoni sees himself as a ghetto Jew. This scene is almost the exact reverse of the scene that pitted the Sabra soldier against the Nazi in *Hill 24*; now it is the young Sabra, the boy who wants to be a brave soldier like his father and who plays war games with his friends, who embraces the image of the suffering Jew. The message that the director seems to be conveying, in a not so subtle way, is that once Jews have embraced the culture of militarism and national heroism they can easily find themselves the oppressors, the perpetrators of indiscriminate violence. The way out of this violence, the movie suggests, is by accepting weakness and passivity and renouncing the hero worship of soldiering.

Paratroopers (*Masa Alunkot*, 1977), which Shohat describes as pertaining to the cycle of "personal cinema," explores the attendant violence of the militaristic ethos by focusing on the dynamics within an elite paratrooper platoon. According to Raz Yosef, this was the first Israeli film to deconstruct Israeli military manhood.[15] The film's protagonist, Weissmann, is a young recruit who chose to volunteer for an elite unit out of a desire to please his parents and to conform to the expectations of his social milieu, but in fact he does not have the physical or mental skills to make an elite fighter. Weissmann draws the wrath of his commanding officer, who torments and humiliates him on a regular basis. In an attempt to prove his bravery, Weissmann dies in what may be interpreted as a training accident, suicide, or even murder by his officer, who pushed him over the brink by his constant harassment. Here the very image of the brave Sabra soldier comes under scrutiny. In this film the military violence is not seen as serving the national good but rather as the outcome of a Spartan society and the enormous expectations it places upon the individual member. In *Paratroopers* the military becomes a metaphor for Israeli society as a whole: by embracing the ethos of militarism, Israel has become a vindictive and unforgiving society that, like Weissmann's officer, crushed the individual will for no apparent greater cause. The image of the Israeli soldier that emerges in this film is of a brutal dispenser of cruel violence, not of someone who sacrifices himself for the greater national good.[16]

If the 1970s and 1980s were a time for introspection and self-criticism, the 1990s seemed to be a time to celebrate a new postconflict Israel that was in the midst of an economic boom infused with high tech. In the 1990s

Israelis were busy consuming goods from all over the world (in the face of a diminished Arab boycott on international firms dealing with Israel), traveling abroad, and becoming full-fledged members in the newly constituted, Internet-based global village.[17] And the image of the Israeli soldier that best fit this era of hedonism was that of the aloof slacker.

The historian Daniel Guttwein has defined the 1990s as a post-Zionist era marked by a total privatization of the Zionist collectivist ethos. In that period the entire edifice of the Israeli welfare state, the hallmark of Israeli collectivism, was being dismantled.[18] The Israeli military underwent similar processes. Some elements of the military, like its counterparts in the civilian sector, were privatized (food and laundry services were outsourced to private companies). But the privatization of the IDF went deeper. The very ethos of the military was also being transformed: for a growing number of Israelis (especially those groups who in the earlier decades had constituted the very establishment of both the IDF and Israeli society more broadly: Ashkenazi Jews from kibbutzim and the major urban centers) the military was no longer seen as an arena for fulfilling one's collective duty but rather as a place to maximize one's individual potential.[19] In the 1990s the social prestige of serving in certain intelligence units that have produced some of Israel's high-tech pioneers eclipsed service in the more traditional elite units (such as pilots and commandos). A growing number of Israelis simply avoided military service.

In the critically acclaimed short movie *The Second Watch* (*Mishmeret Shniya*, 1995), Berkovich, a reservist serving in a remote outpost on the Jordanian border (at a time when Jordan and Israel already had established diplomatic relations), is the quintessential slacker in uniform. Berkovich has no idea what he is supposed to do at his guarding post. He spends the hours reading, listening to music, and playing mindless games. Eventually he makes contact with his Jordanian counterpart across the fence, and the two share a *Playboy* magazine. Berkovich is cynical, apathetic, and detached. He has no idea what he is doing in the middle of the desert (a far cry from the soldier in *Hill 24*) and would much rather be somewhere else. When he comes to the guard post, Berkovich asks the soldier that he replaces: "What are we doing in this place? Making sure the Jordanian doesn't run away? Why don't we all just go home?" A soldier ready for the ultimate sacrifice he is not.

A more subtle but no less poignant portrayal of the Israeli soldier as an unwilling actor in the grand theater of war can be seen in the film *Cup Final* (*Gmar Gavi'a*, 1992). Set during Israel's invasion of Lebanon in the summer of 1982, it tells the story of two Israeli reservists who were captured by a group of PLO fighters trying to escape the Israeli forces in southern Lebanon and make it safely to Beirut. One of the two Israeli soldiers is an officer from a kibbutz who exhibits many of the characteristics of the classic soldier as hero both in his typically Ashkenazi appearance and in his proud demeanor, but he dies early in the film. Cohen, the other Israeli soldier, who already has his tickets ready to go to Spain to watch the soccer World Cup tournament, is a typical antihero. Disheveled, diminutive, and disinterested, he is all but the antithesis of the classic Sabra image of the New Jew captured so powerfully by Arik Lavi in *Hill 24* (Cohen is played by Moshe Ivgy, the actor who brought the antihero to perfection in movies like *Shuru* and *The Revenge of Itzik Finkelstein*). All Cohen wanted was to attend the World Cup games. Throughout the surreal journey with his captors (in an interesting twist, the leader of the Palestinians, played by Mohammed Bakri, looks like a classic cinematic military hero), he tears his game tickets on the days when he was supposed to attend the games. Unlike his captors, he has no discernible political views. The war was forced on him, and politically he seems to have no real stake in it except his personal well-being. He projects weakness and fear; all he wants is to return home safely to his clothing store. He has typical middle-class aspirations, which are perfectly suited to the spirit of the 1990s, not the collectivist idealism of the previous generation of Israelis.

The "happy 1990s," as Slavoj Zizek called them,[20] came to a crushing end with the Second Intifada, which erupted in late 2000 and turned the entire country of Israel, especially urban centers, into combat zones. The exuberance of the 1990s quickly gave way to a sense of existential fear. But unlike the earlier decades, this time the enemy was not the armies of foreign nations but clandestine terrorists, bringing a strong and wealthy country with a reported nuclear arsenal to a seemingly permanent state of emergency.[21] In this climate of terror, the Israeli soldier is neither a disinterested slacker nor a fierce fighter in the open battleground; rather, like the rest of society, he appears to play the role of victim of a hidden, menacing enemy.

As If Nothing Happened (Ke'ilu Klum Lo Karah, 1999) captures the essence of the terror of the time. At the start of the movie we see a young paratrooper officer, who looks and acts the part, getting ready to return to his base after a weekend leave at home. His father drops him off at a bus station and heads off to his office. We then see ambulances and other emergency vehicles on the road, and the father learns from the radio that a terrorist attack has occurred near the place where his son was heading. From that point the movie focuses on the officer's family (the officer's parents and his two siblings) as they struggle to learn what happened to him. Along the way despair takes over the life of the family, while quick shots of clocks reveal the agonizingly slow passage of time. At one point we see three soldiers from a unit that informs families of the death of their sons driving in a car, heightening the suspense. What we do not see is the officer, who appears only at the very end when he returns home at the same time that the soldiers reach his building to notify another neighbor that her son died in the suicide bombing. The suspense is similar to the suspense that viewers might experience in watching a war film taking place in a traditional battle zone as they fear for the life of the military hero. But here the soldiers are absent; they are only helpless victims. The real drama takes place in the house, as the family comes undone under the immense pressure. This sense of terror is what many people felt at the time of intense attacks on the home front, and it was only intensified by a sense that the military was all but incapable of providing adequate security. In a reversal of the old model, here it was not the individual who was asked to contribute for the sake of the collective but the exact opposite: the collective was being torn apart in an attempt to preserve the well-being of the individual (soldier).

Beaufort, which was nominated for an Academy Award for best foreign film in 2007, offers another image of the soldier as vulnerable victim. Set in the last days before Israel's withdrawal from southern Lebanon in May 2000, it focuses on a group of soldiers in an outpost located alongside an old crusader-era fort that was the site of one of the bloodiest battles of the 1982 Israeli invasion of Lebanon. The movie, which is based on a best-selling novel that became a cult hit at the time of the Second Lebanon War of 2006, depicts a small group of soldiers who man the post as they are routinely attacked by Hezbollah forces (though we never see the enemy) and suffer several fatal casualties. The film takes place mostly in the dark and narrow tunnels of the outpost. The scene is highly claustrophobic—like the soldiers, the audience just wants out of that hellhole. The soldiers know that Israel is about to withdraw from Lebanon, which adds to their growing feeling that they are engaged in a futile battle that is doomed to fail. As their commander pleads with his superiors to let him lead an expedition outside the post to attack the Hezbollah forces, he is denied permission to do so. The soldier is not allowed to fulfill his true destiny as a fighter; his true role in the twenty-first century is to be a sitting duck, an idle victim waiting for the order to evacuate, while back home politicians and the greater public bicker over how to resolve the situation. With the home front torn by political strife (as opposed to the perceived uniformity of early Israeli society), the soldiers are being sacrificed not as warriors in battle but as victims of an unseen enemy. In the twenty-first century, it would seem, the soldier has again become a necessary part of the public (and cinematic) sphere in Israel. His heroism, though, has changed; it is up to the public to protect the soldiers, while they are passively awaiting their fate. This is true of Gilad Shalit, the Israeli soldier held captive by Hamas in the Gaza Strip, and it seems to be the fate of the soldiers in *Beaufort* and in *As If Nothing Happened*.

NOTES

1. The term "universal conscription" here is part of the Israeli law regulating military service, but in reality it applies only to the Jewish population in Israel, because several groups are exempted from service. Arab citizens of the state, by and large, do not serve in the Israeli military. Even among the Jews a fairly substantial group (the ultra-Orthodox Haredim) is exempted from service in the IDF.

2. See Tom Segev, *1949: The First Israelis* (New York: Henry Holt, 1998), 296–323; Mordechai Naor, "Tzena," in *Olim U-Ma'abarot 1948–1952* (Immigrants and Transit Camps, 1948–1952) (Jerusalem: Yad Ben Zvi, 1986), 97–110.

3. Haim Hazan, *Simulated Dreams: Israeli Youth and Virtual Zionism* (New York: Berghahn Books, 2001), 14. See also Motti Regev and Edwin Seroussi, *Popular Music and National Culture in Israel* (Berkeley: University of California Press, 2004), 18.

4. See Yaron Ezrahi, "Individualism and Collectivism in Zionist Culture and the State of Israel," in Steven J. Zipperstein and Ernest S. Freirichs (eds.), *Zionism, Liberalism, and the Future of the Jewish State* (Providence, R.I.: Dorot Foundation, 2000), 35.

5. See Ariella Azoulay, "Bidlataim Ptukhot: Museonim Lehistoria Bamerkhav Hatziburi Beyisra'el" (Open Doors: Historical Museums in the Israeli Public Sphere), *Te'oriah Uvikoret* 4 (Fall 1993): 81.

6. Uri Ram, *Hazman Shel Ha"Post": Le'umiyut Vahapolitika Shel Hayeda Beyisra'el* (The Time of the "Post" Nationalism and the Politics of Knowledge in Israel) (Tel Aviv: Resling, 2006), 158.

7. These historical divisions broadly follow the periodization offered by Ella Shohat in her 1989 book *Israeli Cinema: East/West and the Politics of Representation*. Shohat described the post-1948 period as the heroic nationalist genre in Israeli cinema and contrasted it with the more personal cinema of the late 1960s and the 1970s and 1980s that was more concerned with the limitations of the power of the constituting myths of the state of Israel. Naturally, Shohat's book did not deal with Israeli cinema of the 1990s and first decade of the twenty-first century.

8. On the emergence of the New Israeli History and its "revisionist" image of the 1948 war, see Uri Ram, "Historiographical Foundations of the Historical Strife in Israel," in Anita Shapira and Derek Penslar (eds.), *Israeli Historical Revisionism: From Left to Right* (London: Frank Cass, 2003). For a critical assessment of the New Historians, see Anita Shapira, "The Strategies of Historical Revisionism," in ibid.

9. On the mythical aspects of the 1948 war, see Benny Morris, "The New Historiography: Israel Confronts Its Past," *Tikkun* 3 (6) (Autumn 1988).

10. On the Sabra "ideal type" in the Israeli imagination, see Oz Almog, *The Sabra: The Creation of the New Jew* (Berkeley: University of California Press, 2000), 78.

11. On the idea of the Sabra as a person devoid of (diasporic) history who emerges as a tabula rasa, see Anita Shapira, "Le'an Halcha Shlilat Ha-Galut" (What Ever

Happened to the Negation of the Diaspora), in *Yehudim, Tzionim U-Ma She-Beineham* (Jews, Zionists, and In Between) (Tel Aviv: Am Oved, 2007), 74.

12. See Shohat, *Israeli Cinema*, 69–70.

13. On the Sabra, see Almog, *The Sabra: The Creation of the New Jew*, 78.

14. Shohat, *Israeli Cinema*, 222. See also Yosefa Loshitzky, *Identity Politics on the Israeli Screen*, 156.

15. Shohat, *Israeli Cinema*, p. 179; Raz Yosef, *Beyond Flesh: Queer Masculinities and Nationalism in Israeli Cinema*, 57.

16. See Judd Ne'eman, "The Death Mask of the Moderns: A Genealogy of New Sensibility Cinema in Israel," 125.

17. See Oz Almog, "The Globalization of Israel: Transformations," in Anita Shapira (ed.), *Israeli Identity in Transition* (Westport, Conn.: Praeger Publishers, 2004), 233–256; Uri Ram, "Bein Ha-Neshek Ve-Ha-Meshek: Yisra'el Be-Idan Ha-Olamekomi" (Between the Gun and the Market: Israel in Globalocal Era) *Sotziologiah Yisra'elit* 2 (1999): 99–145.

18. Daniel Guttwein, "Post Tzionut, Mahapechat Ha-Hafrata Ve-Ha-Smol Ha-Hevrati" (Post-Zionism, the Privatization Revolution and the Social Left), in Tuvia Friling (ed.), *Teshuvah Le-Amit Post Tzioni* (An Answer to a Post-Zionist Colleague) (Tel Aviv: Yediot Aharonot, 2003).

19. Yoram Peri, "Land versus State: Israel and Its Army after the Disengagement," *Dissent* (Winter 2006) (http://dissentmagazine.org/article/?article=154).

20. Slavoj Zizek, "The Subject Supposed to Loot and Rape: Reality and Fantasy in New Orleans," *In These Times*, October 20, 2005 (http://www.inthesetimes.com/article/2361/).

21. On the relationship between terrorism as subjective, irrational violence and the way nations employ a "state of emergency" to fight it (in the name of objective, systematic violence), see Slavoj Zizek, *Violence* (London: Verso, 2008), esp. 8–12, 34–38. On Israel and the rise of terror-related existential fears in the twenty-first century, see Benny Morris, "Why Israel Feels Threatened," *New York Times*, December 29, 2008; Guttwein, "Post Tzionut, Mahapechat Ha-Hafrata Ve-Ha-Smol Ha-Hevrati," 243.

BIBLIOGRAPHY

Loshitzky, Yosefa. *Identity Politics on the Israeli Screen*. Austin: University of Texas Press, 2001.

Ne'eman, Judd. "The Death Mask of the Moderns: A Genealogy of New Sensibility Cinema in Israel." *Israel Studies* 4(1) (Spring 1999): 100–128.

Shohat, Ella. *Israeli Cinema: East/West and the Politics of Representation*. Austin: University of Texas Press, 1989.

Yosef, Raz. *Beyond Flesh: Queer Masculinities and Nationalism in Israeli Cinema*. New Brunswick, N.J.: Rutgers University Press, 2004.

FILMOGRAPHY

As If Nothing Happened (Ke'ilu Klum Lo Karah, 1999). Dir.: Ayelet Bargur.

Beaufort (2007). Dir.: Joseph Cedar.

Cup Final (Gmar Gavi'a, 1992). Dir.: Eran Riklis.

Hide and Seek (*Makhvo'im*, 1980). Dir.: Dan Wolman.
Hill 24 Doesn't Answer (*Giv'a 24 Eina Ona*, 1955). Dir.: Thorold Dickinson.
Paratroopers (*Masa Alunkot*, 1977). Dir.: Yehuda (Judd) Ne'eman.
The Revenge of Itzik Finkelstein (*Nikmato Shal Itzik Finkelshtein*, 1993). Dir.: Enrique
    Rotenberg.
The Second Watch (*Mishmeret Shniya*, 1995). Dir.: Udi Ben-Arieh.
Shuru (1991). Dir.: Savi Gavison.
The Wooden Gun (*Roveh Khuliot*, 1979). Dir.: Ilan Moshenson.

6 The Lady and the Death Mask

JUDD NE'EMAN

The question I ask myself, above all:
what is the meaning of resisting death?
Antonio Tabucchi

Many films produced in Israel in the 1960s and 1970s may be grouped within the modernist genre of film. It has been said of modernism that it is a genre of "anti-art" aimed at "negating every accepted style and, ultimately, at negating itself."[1] The roots of that negating approach lie in ancient times, such as the Platonic idea of the "perfect being," a being unlike anything the senses perceive. Aspiring to an artistic purity characterizes modernism, emulating the philosopher's distant gaze, insisting on aesthetic distance. Alongside purity and aesthetic distance, modernist films have other attributes, such as elitism and an individual "handwriting" that discloses the mechanism of the cinematic endeavor and reflects its conventions.[2] Aesthetic distance in modernism engenders a divide between film and spectator, providing a means for considering film an artistic artifact. Distance produces a sense of alienation, breaks the audience identification with the image on the screen, and prevents the addiction to the illusions of the film's materiality. While the illusion of materiality underlies mainstream cinema, modernist film challenges it and encourages the awareness that, after all, film is an artifact.

Modernist film did not begin with the French New Wave auteur theory in 1950s Paris. Its roots lie in the classic French avant-garde, in surrealist films, in Soviet constructivism and 1920s German expressionism. They lie in the work of directors such as Dziga Vertov and Luis Buñuel. However, the post–World War II new modernist film sparked a revolution and engendered a radicalism of cinematic form whose shock waves resonate today on television and on the Internet. The innovative approach impacted the form of moving images, transforming film into a self-conscious medium. Balint Andras Kovacs argues that modernist film is a strategy for expressing urbanization and industrialization, whose subtext is imbued with references to previous myths. Integrating the archaic and the modern is illuminating and fits the interpretation I suggest here for the film *A Woman's Case* (*Mikre Isha*, Jacques Katmor, 1969), which belongs to the 1960s modernist trend in Israeli cinema.

In a previous essay, I suggested that the iconography and cinematic rhetoric of the 1960s–1970s Israeli modernist films express a common motif: the death mask.[3] The death mask cinematic motif is associated in this corpus of films with the myth of the fallen and the concept of the "living dead," both emerging from the killing fields of World War II and the Holocaust and the 1948 War of Independence. The mark of the twentieth century lies mainly in the violent death on the battlefields and in the memory of the fallen. Where the mass destruction of young men is conceived as the definitive negation of life, a young man wearing a death mask stands for the negation of a negation. The death mask becomes a symbolic mold on the features of a flawed reality.[4] Disruption and flawing are the antipathetic aesthetic foundations of modernist cinema, reflected in a range of expressive forms, such as minimalism, temporal and spatial distortion, representation of the human body dismembered into its components, replication and confinement of representations within series of montages, and grotesquerie. To the human eye, nothing is more grotesque than the corpse.

In Jacques Katmor's film *A Woman's Case*, set in Tel Aviv and Jerusalem one year after the 1967 Six Day War, the very beautiful actress Helit Yeshurun appears in the main role. As the film opens, this young and delicate woman has her body encased in a plaster cast. She then walks toward the death that her lover offers to her. The young man in the film has gone through war and must feel around him the shadows of the fallen. The chill expression on his face with a touch of distance and alienation expresses this elegant young man's intense efforts to subdue the memory of the battlefield horrors, the view of shattered male bodies. This modernist film embodies, in its protagonists and plot, the death-mask motif that repeats in many films of the genre that followed. The film structured as a set of progressions draws together two characters, a shell-shocked veteran and a woman who provokes his suppressed misogyny. This specific reaction to combat stress, transformed to a modernist cinematic style, reaches its climax in the murder of the woman.

The corpus of modernist feature films of the 1960s and 1970s constitutes a unique cinematic cycle that I have called the "New Sensibility" cinema.[5] For the most part, these were debut films made by filmmakers of the post-1948 generation,[6] whose early lives were overshadowed by the events of World War II, the Holocaust, and the 1948 War of Independence. It was a challenging task to represent in words, photography, and moving images the horrors and terror of war, and so the tendency was to convey this horrifying impact on the memory through what Fredric Jameson calls "compensatory structures."[7] These formal conventions, tailored as symbolic substitutes, were mainly minimalism and grotesquerie. Ludwig Wittgenstein's statement "about what one cannot speak, one must remain silent" holds true for the futile attempt to reconstruct an image of a war that has ended and that can better be represented by stylized metaphors.[8] When we cannot reconstruct the Holocaust gas chambers and crematoria, when we cannot photograph young men killed in combat and their bodies shattered, when we cannot capture on film the suffering of people uprooted and expelled from their homes, then style assumes a very particular task. What cannot be told in a realistic mode will be told through minimalism, aesthetic distance, alienation, and grotesquerie.

The New Sensibility films focus on the picturing of the myth of youth, the downhill slide toward death, and the actual moment of death. In Israel, in the years following World War II and the 1948 War of Independence, the myth of the "living dead" related to the Holocaust and to the fallen of the War of Independence took shape in Hebrew poetry and literature.[9] In the generation that came of age after the wars, paradigmatic poems such as Haim Gouri's "Here Lie Our Bodies" ("Hine Mutalot Gufoteinu") inscribed in the collective consciousness a sense of solidarity with the fallen. No security zone remained, though, between solidarity with the youthful dead and a subconscious death wish. The modernist discourse of the New Sensibility films expressed the negating of a negation. The chill expression, the distanced gaze, obsessive repetitions, grotesquerie, and aesthetic distance created a death mask of sorts. The death mask functioned to identify with the dead and at the same time as a defense mechanism against the unacknowledged death wish. The avant-garde film *A Woman's Case* sketches the trajectory of a war veteran compelled to abandon himself to death or instead ruthlessly to murder the young woman with whom he falls in love. By killing her he rips away her death mask and himself uses it as a protective camouflage against his own death on the battlefield. The murder of a loved woman becomes a "supplementary mold" for the combat memories that haunt and unsettle him. Erich Neumann describes an archetype that he calls "the terrible female," whose identity he relates to the "dragon of the depths," a monster that threatens "pure masculinity" and seeks to annihilate it. In this way, the pure nature of masculinity that comes into play on the battlefield can be preserved.[10]

A Woman's Case has a minimalist plot, a small number of characters, very few events, several montage sequences of realistic and surrealistic moving images, and a montage of still photography. As opposed to the rules of mainstream cinema, the film has little dramatic development and few turning points in the plot until its very ending. Like *A Hole in the Moon*, the first New Sensibility film that radically differs from most films that followed, *A Woman's Case* is an avant-garde, surrealistic film that does not comply with the realism of most other New Sensibility films. At the same time, in its iconography and plot *A Woman's Case* explicitly embodies the death-mask motif that other films of the same corpus conceal in their subtext. Close reading of the film allows us to illuminate the postwar situation of the combatant and see the relationship between the memory of the threat of destruction of the male body and the film's modernist style, both under the sign of the terror of the female body.[11]

The film opens with several shots of old women in a hospital, an operating room, and surgical instruments. Then we see the corpse of the woman protagonist of the film covered by a white sheet, wheeled on a stainless steel gurney along a hospital corridor. A good-looking young man is watching a beautiful woman who is modeling for the artist Yigal Tumarkin. The artist is covering her body with moist plaster bandages. She is asking: "Will it hurt?" The artist makes a plaster mold of her whole body, to reproduce her form. The young man is watching the woman's naked body encased in plaster bandages; once the process ends, her body is uncovered and revealed. Following this is a sequence of metal sculptures with angular components, forming male and female bodies, and invoking weaponry.

The man and woman are walking along an avenue of concrete pillars. He says: "He took a beautiful woman like you and turned you into something broken and torn . . . did you know what he would do with your body?" They talk in a café, and she says that through her body mold she will learn what her body looks like. When he asks her about the men in her life, she speaks about the repetitions and ritual elements in her relationships: "Repetition turns it into a kind of ritual . . . I love rituals . . . ceremonies." In the man's apartment, another young woman lies asleep in his bed. The woman takes a cane and lifts the sheet that covers the sleeping woman. Then she systematically describes the woman's body. "I love her face . . . it has an expression of pain when she's asleep," says the man as he looks at the naked woman in

his bed. As he is driving his car, he says, "For you that girl was just an object
. . ." She replies: "Isn't any woman just an object for you?" Later the two are
in his advertising agency, where the woman looks at models' photographs
on the wall. Lying on a desk are passport photos of old women dressed in
the European style of World War II. In a restaurant they meet a girlfriend of
the woman, and the two swap clothes by the table. The man notices another
woman at a nearby table. He imagines her in a series of close-ups; at the
end of the montage, she is seen wearing a combat helmet. They are in his
office, where photos of women are scattered on his desk: a woman holding
a sword; a photograph of a naked woman. With a paper cutter, he cuts the
photograph into sections then passes the knife over her throat and makes
an incision in the paper. We see a woman's body: thin plastic wire is being
wrapped around her belly and chest, with the pressure creating folds and
creases in her flesh. After that comes a montage of female bodies.

Many sequences include a large number of representations of the female
body: a nude woman; a plaster mask being placed on a woman's face and
body; distorted metal statues of female forms; discussions in the dialogue
about the body as an object, as a broken and torn statue, as a signifier of
pain; a line of dialogue addressing ceremony and ritual connected to the
body and sex; a montage of photos of old women; a close-up montage of
parts of a woman's body; a montage of stills showing dancing young women;
and a montage of high-heeled shoes. The male protagonist constantly examines the woman's body when he is leading her from place to place. He may
be Hermes, the messenger of the gods who accompanies the dead souls to
the underworld and then returns to the world above. The sequence outlines
several themes—the woman's body as a death mask, the woman's body signifying pain, the woman's body as an object to be taken apart, the woman's
body on her way to the afterlife.

The film continues, in a kind of second act. The two are driving in a car,
and the woman talks about a man who constantly asked to see her legs. In
juxtaposition, we see a montage of high-heeled shoes and machines manu-
facturing shoes. They arrive in Jerusalem, where they are photographed
against the backdrop of the Old City. They rent a hotel room, and the woman strips. Taking off his tie, the man passes it over her naked body. Then
he winds the tie around her throat and tightens it gently until she emits
a sigh. On the way back to Tel Aviv, they stop by a car damaged in an accident. Two corpses are lying on the ground, covered. Another driver who
halts says, "I think they're dead." In a Tel Aviv café the woman asks: "What
are you thinking?" He answers: "About the dead in the accident . . . the first
dead body that I saw in the war was lying on the road, too . . . an Egyptian

soldier lying on his back, with round open eyes . . . he didn't seem dead . . . he looked just like a doll." Now the woman leads the man: "Come, I want to show you something." The two are in the studio of an artist who creates life-sized rubber dolls. The artist breathes into the trembling doll, which slowly inflates to the size of an adult woman. "At first I built them in sections, but they wouldn't fit together . . . it was too difficult to attach the head," the artist notes. A montage of makeup appears on the screen—eyelashes, lips, nails—and then a transition to a woman's body bound with leather strips.

Several montage sequences are interwoven in the plot of the second section of the film. The opening montage of high heels and the closing montage of makeup serve as a frame for the central theme: "The Lady and the Death Mask." The road-accident casualties evoke memories of the battlefield and the war dead. The dead bodies look unreal, like dolls, and the man compares them with his memories; that is how the artist produces them, using his models. The woman models a corpse. For a moment in a liminal state, she hovers between the live male and the corpse. But her liminal state cannot stay for too long. Once a layer of plaster covers her body and hardens into a plaster cast, from which she removes herself into the embrace of her shell-shocked man, she is marked as condemned to death. The roadside corpses draw him back to his "crime scene"—the battlefield. From then on, she will lead him, as if he has abandoned his role as Hermes and has been handed over to Aphrodite, who will lead him to awareness of the ultimate tribulation—a body emptied of all its content, an inflatable rubber doll, a corpse. It is said of the corpse on the battlefield that it is a blank sheet devoid of any identity, a tabula rasa onto which any law can be inscribed. The mystery of the body count in war: the side that harvests more enemy bodies can apply to them the ideology in whose name it set out for battle.[12]

Throughout the film, in a series of montages with feminine motifs, the patriarchal law is inscribed on a woman's body and not on the bodies of the fallen. The post-traumatic male dismisses the patriarchal order as soon as he realizes, after the furor of battle, that his body and the bodies of his fellow combatants were abandoned to death by and on behalf of the state that represents that order.[13]

In the third section the couple spends an evening at a party, where they meet a theater director who demonstrates an element of his new play; he plans to direct a ritual scene of strangling with a shoelace that is wound around the throat with a pencil inserted between the throat and the shoelace. He demonstrates the method on the throat of a young woman. The woman (actress Helit Yeshurun) then goes to the bathroom, puts on makeup, and dons a wig in a gamine style. Next to her stands another woman making up, who remarks: "You look just like a boy." Other guests at the party practice the gimmick until the "victims" start choking. In the man's apartment, the woman holds an hourglass and tells a story: once upon a time, a woman brought home her husband's ashes, put them in a hourglass, turned it upside down, and said, "Now you get to work." The man and the woman lie naked on the bed. He remembers that he forgot to turn over his wristwatch, which the woman had put face down to hide the watch hands. They get up and get dressed. The man reads a long paragraph from Rainer Maria Rilke's *The Notebooks of Malte Laurids Brigge* about the deaths of an old nobleman and of pregnant women. The woman stands facing a mirror, wraps black fabric around her body, up to her neck, and laughs. The man walks toward her, winds the fabric around her throat, and tightens it until she says, "Enough." Then the woman's body on a metal bed covered with a white sheet is wheeled along a hospital corridor.

The third section opens with a ritualistic strangling performed on a woman's neck. With her boyish wig, actress Helit Yeshurun has taken on a male role, and her task as a young man is to place a death mask on her face. As she tells the story of the male ashes running through the hourglass, she is endorsing the contemporary logocentric order, grounded on the division of time and on the capitalist regime's subjugation to the work ethos. In a previous scene, she turned the man's wristwatch face down, making him unaware that time—the principal patriarchal resource—is progressing and running out. In this way, the concealed watch face signals the wounded male's abandoning of the logocentric order. The montages featured in this section typically engage with the wounded female body and focus on female skin. Another montage of women's bodies is held within medical devices, while performing physiotherapy exercises and peeling off a piece of plastic adhering to a woman's skin. Then we see a series of naked women lying on the floor, moving and caressing each other. The focus on soft skin and representations of a torn-apart body prepares us for the moment of the murder. After reading the section on death in Rilke's *Notebooks*, the man murders the woman by strangling her. The head is the Achilles heel of control and rational criticism. The repeated provocations to the neck throughout the film—several times at the party and later at the ending of the film, with the act of murder—stem from an urge for control, since murder is the act of ultimate control.

The next scene shows the woman's body on a morgue trolley, covered with a white sheet and being wheeled down a long hospital corridor. The man's reading of the passage from Rilke's book takes place in a space graphically demarcated as the male space, dominated by the logos of the wristwatch, the wheel, and the written word—all of which have a prominent presence. Against that backdrop, Rilke's text is a kind of elegy to the woman, before her murder. The passages from *The Notebooks of Malte Laurids Brigge* that the man, seated in an armchair, is reading aloud in the film deal with the perpetual presence of death as an autonomous entity that has a separate existence from the human being who is about to die:

> The death at Ulsgaard of Chamberlain Christoph Detlev Brigge.
>
> Christoph Detlev's death had already been living at Ulsgaard for many many days now, talking with everyone and demanded—demanded to be carried, demanded the blue room, demanded the little salon, demanded the large drawing room, demanded the dogs, demanded that people laugh, talk, play games and remain silent and all at the same time, demanded to see friends, women, people who had died, demanded to die itself: demanded, demanded, screaming.
>
> For, when night had fallen and those among the overtired servants who were not keeping watch were trying to go to sleep, Christoph Detlev's death would scream and scream again and groan and roar for such a length of time without stopping that the dogs, which at first had joined in the howling, fell silent and didn't dare lie down but remained standing on their long, slender, trembling legs, overcome with fear.
>
> And when I think of the others I have seen or heard of: it's always the same. They've all had a death of their own. Those men who carried it in their armor, shut inside it like a prisoner; those women who grew very old and small and then on an immense bed like the ones on a theatre stage, in front of the whole family, the servants and the dogs, discreetly and with dignity passed away. The children, even the really small ones, didn't have just any child's death; they braced themselves and died as who they were already and who they would have become.
>
> It wasn't the death of somebody suffering from some kind of dropsy; it was the evil regal death that the Chamberlain his whole life long had carried inside him where it had fed. Every excess of pride, of will and of dominance that he had not been able to use up himself on his calm days had gone into his death, the death that now sat at Ulsgaard squandering them. What a look Chamberlain Brigge would have given to anyone who demanded he die a different death from this one. His was a hard death.
>
> And what a wistful beauty that gave to the women when they were pregnant and stood there with their slender hands resting naturally on the large shape where two fruits were: a child and a death. And that tight, almost nourishing smile that took over their faces, didn't it sometimes come from sensing that both were growing?

Rilke's work, a novella with a fragmentary structure, is considered a masterpiece of twentieth-century German literature and a precursor of modernist literature in general. The narrator, Malte Brigge, is afflicted with an obsession over the question of death, and the tangible death of the character is a permanent escort throughout the book's pages. According to Michael F. Davis, "This is a text on the fragmented body, the unstable ego . . . it is a text that undermines walls, flows into and out of the body, into and out of literature. . . . I find that the mother motif is problematic from the outset, a problem stemming from the Law of the Father against which there is no resistance."[14] This passage in the book that the male protagonist reads to his lover before strangling her tells us about death in a multifaceted polyphony. In Rilke's words death appears as an autonomous entity, above all as the death of the narrator's father. Rilke challenges it in every possible way: the death of women in childbirth—such a common event in the past, the death of newborn infants, the death of old women gazing from their high beds at their family, the death of cows while calving, "and one calf together with all the mother cow's entrails was dragged out dead," and the death of men who carry death inside their chest. Death appears here as tangible and powerful, manifest "inside them like the stone inside a fruit" that grows until exiting the body. Moreover, a woman should have "two fruits . . . : a child and a death." The link between birth and death has an association with the warrior going to the battlefield, since "after making love with a woman the warrior abandons his body to death. Heterosexual relations constitute a 'red light' for warriors, signaling the immediate danger of death."[15]

The film and the book are both characterized by fragmentary structure and an obsession with death. And like death, the film itself flows in and out of the body, in and out of the man trapped in the patriarchal order. In *A Woman's Case* it is the Law of the Father that ultimately dictates to him the killing of a woman. However, the male character's fundamental trust in the Law of the Father has eroded after he was injured by combat trauma. Men who return home after injury or trauma in battle no longer believe the "framework story" they were born into and in whose lap they were raised and matured. They find difficulties in isolating and containing the trauma's traces, and as a result the destructive forces of war inculcated in them are channeled from then on, as Kaja Silverman has indicated, "less into destroying the enemy and more into the positivist structure of the male self. . . . Male control reaches the edge of the abyss and the repetition with which it is meant to re-crystallize is destroyed by an earlier repetition that still exists in the present, linked to a death wish."[16] From this point of view, *A Woman's Case* presents a series of threatening images of decay and death that leads the post-traumatic male character to commit his object of desire to her death, since for him she only represents the sign of death on the battlefield.

Many scenes in the film consist of a cinematic montage not related directly to the characters or to the plot. Several of the elements that appear in these sequences foreshadow the destruction of the woman's body: a montage of surgical instruments, gloves, sinks, an infusion stand, gloved hands washing off the blood, old men lying on hospital beds, hands holding a woman's naked body and winding black fabric around it, a montage of painting and photographs of women that imply threat, passport photos of old women, a photograph of a woman's body cruelly depicted as a machine, a woman holding a sword to her body, naked women stretched out on the floor, and an installation of piled-up high-heeled shoes.

These paraphernalia engage with aging, the dismembering of the female body, and death. Together they form a symbolic substitute for a failed desire to achieve eternal youth that the beauty of the young woman character stands for. Made one year after the 1967 Six Day War, the film includes many scenes of symbolic dismembering of the female body. These scenes mirror the shattering of the male body on the battlefield and emanate from a profound fear of women hosted in the man's mind. Erich Neumann says that "[t]he consequence of the patriarchal male's haughtiness toward women leads to the inability to make any genuine contact with the Feminine, i.e., not only in a real woman but also with the Feminine in himself, the unconscious "[17] Neumann also holds that this fear finds collective expression in going to war, in men's readiness to be subjugated to the dictatorial combat regime conceived as pure virility. In various mythologies, the image of the terrible Great Mother has certain male body traits, such as a beard and a male sexual organ. Thus the characteristic behaviors of men—in war, hunting, and killing—are also attributed at the mythic level to the terrible Great Mother. "Hence the fear of the Feminine includes also the fear of the masculine."[18] When set against the traumatic memories of the Six Day War, the woman's murder at the very end of the film means simultaneously the destruction of the "terrible Great Mother" and of the male enemy that the man in the film confronted in battle.

Adrienne Rich speaks of an immanent link between women and men's death. In her view, the mother-son relationship is, in some ways, connected to death. The newborn looking at his mother's face feels his existence to be a small, weak, blind part of her body. Dependence on the mother's body and the extreme sense of weakness in infancy are precursors of the future when he will once again be weak and dependent on others. From the beginning of humankind, men have always chosen caves, graves, and other hollows designated for burial—all spaces replicating the female form.[19] In Rich's opinion, romantic sexual love has an indivisible connection with death.[20] In the film *Alien* (Ridley Scott, 1979), when the crew members leave the spaceship to investigate the planet, they enter a bizarre maze that turns out to be the body of an alien creature. One crew member who touches the creature's body fluid becomes pregnant and gives birth to a monstrous embryo that erupts through his stomach and causes the man's death. Only the female crew member aboard the spaceship succeeds in restraining the alien creature that continues to live in the ship. The grown-up alien that stays alive in the domain of the woman in the spaceship resembles a dragon with tough scales.

In *A Woman's Case*, when the artist encases the woman protagonist's body in plaster and then removes it, a rigid mold results. That mold evokes the association with a mythological dragon, whose body is also covered with tough scales. In the scene where the plaster mold is removed from her body, we see the young man watching the model, fascinated. From here on, she accompanies the man until meeting death at his hands. Erich Neumann argues that "pure masculinity" must shake off any trace of "otherness,"[21] and in this film otherness is the woman. The tender infant is forced to overcome the matriarchal sphere that he perceives as infantile, archaic, and chaotic. These characteristics are associated with the "terrible mother" embodied in myth as the vicious dragon from the depths. The "terrible mother" serves as a threat and an obstacle for the developing ego and for flourishing energy; she is emblematic of death, regression, and fixation. Represented as a dragon, this "terrible mother" is not passive; she draws men downward and backward, like Sigmund Freud's description of the psychological drive to return to the most primal state—the prebiological, inanimate state.[22]

Another mythical image of the "terrible mother," familiar from the ancient Egyptian myth of Isis and Osiris, tells an even darker story. In this myth a brother and sister are also a couple. The threatening side of Isis comes into play when her brother-husband Osiris, whom she revives and brings back to life, remains castrated. The part of the myth relating how Isis becomes impregnated by her dead husband and gives birth to their son Horus is not clear. It becomes more understandable if we accept the assumption that impregnating the "terrible mother" requires the man's death. "Mother Earth" can only be fertile through death, slaughter, castration, and sacrifice. Horus, the son of Isis by her dead husband Osiris, mates with his mother, who gives birth to his son. This step repeats the events in the matriarchal sphere throughout all generations: "the terrible mother" always remains one and the same;[23] and men are replaceable and transient. In *A Woman's Case*, there is an inherent radical feminist position that views men as redundant. While modernism is a style that negates every other style, and ultimately itself too, one can say that once the project of modernity has deconstructed all forms of the social order that preceded it, it will be totally fulfilled with the destruction of the order on which the nation-state and the "Name of the Father" are grounded. That may also become the historical moment of altogether conceding human existence in the male configuration. That will be the end of men.

NOTES

1. Daniel Bell, *The Cultural Contradiction of Capitalism*, 46.

2. Balint Andras Kovacs, *National Cinema—International Modernism*, 211.

3. Judd Ne'eman, "The Modernists: The Manifest of the Israeli New Sensitivity."

4. Fredric Jameson, "Realism and Desire: Balzac and the Problem of the Subject," 183.

5. "The New Sensibility" cinema was the title of the corpus of modernist films that I used for the first time in my lectures "Introduction to Israeli Cinema," a course that I taught in mid-1985 at the Department of Film and Television at Tel Aviv University. The title "The New Sensibility" first appeared in print in 1992, in a short article in French, "Les modernes, le manifeste inédit," and in a comprehensive Hebrew article in 1998, "A Genealogy of New Sensibility Cinema in Israel."

6. Among them are *A Hole in the Moon* (Uri Zohar, 1964), *The Woman in the Next Room* (Yitzhak Tzcpel Yeshurun, 1966), *Three Days and a Child* (Uri Zohar, 1967), *Slower* (Avraham Hettner, 1968), *Louisa, Louisa* (Igal Bursztyn, 1968), *Iris* (David Greenberg, 1968), *Siege* (Gilberto Tofano, 1969), *A Woman's Case* (Jacques Katmor, 1969), *The Dress* (Judd Ne'eman, 1969), *The Customer of the Off Season* (Moshe Mizrahi, 1970), *From the Other Side* (Menachem Binetzky, 1970), *The Dreamer* (Dan Wolman, 1970), *The Snail/Shablul* (Boaz Davidson, 1971), *The Pill* (David Perlov, 1972), *I Love You Rosa* (Moshe Mizrahi, 1972), *But Where Is Daniel Wax?* (Avraham Heffner, 1972), *Rose Water from Port Said* (Ram Loevy, 1972), *Light Out of Nowhere* (Nissim Dayan, 1973), *Shalom, Prayer for the Road* (Yaki Yosha, 1973), *Hagiga La-Eynaim/Saint Cohen* (Assi Dayan, 1975), *A Little Night Music* (Avi Nesher, 1975), *My Father* (Daniel Wachsmann, 1975), *Meir in Seven Pictures* (Shimon Dotan, 1976), *Nachum Glickson: Two Days in Israel* (Eitan Green, 1976), *After* (Renen Schorr, 1977), *The Honey Connection* (Yeud Levanon, 1977), *Piano Lesson* (Tzipi Trope, 1977), *The Black Banana* (Binyamin Haim, 1977), *Moments* (Michal Bat-Adam, 1979)—and this of course is only a partial list.

7. Fredric Jameson, *Signatures of the Visible* (New York: Routledge, 1992), 25.

8. Ludwig Wittgenstein, *Tractatus Logo-Philosophicus*, proposition 7.

9. Hannan Hever has often noted in his research the roots of this perception/notion and its appearance in modernist Israeli poetry.

10. Erich Neumann, *The Fear of the Feminine and Other Essays on Feminine Psychology*, 239–242; Klaus Theweleit, *Male Fantasies*.

11. For further discussion of the representations of the warrior in Israeli films, see Judd Neʾeman, "Camera Obscura of the Fallen: Military Pedagogy and Its Accessories in Israeli Cinema."

12. Elaine Scarry speaks about the structure of war in her book *The Body in Pain*.

13. Kaja Silverman depicts the post-traumatic condition in discussion of post–World War II Hollywood films, in a chapter devoted to an analysis of *The Best Years of Our Lives* (1946), a film dealing with the basic loss of trust in men who were physically or psychologically injured in war. Kaja Silverman, *Male Subjectivity at the Margins*, 65.

14. Michael F. Davis, "Writing the Mother in *The Notebooks of Malte Laurids Brigge:* The Rhetoric of Abjection." The quotations from *The Notebooks of Malte Laurids Brigge* come from the film dialogue rather than from the printed text.

15. Neʾeman, "Camera Obscura of the Fallen."

16. Silverman, *Male Subjectivity at the Margins*, 65.

17. Erich Neumann, *The Fear of the Feminine*, 264.

18. Ibid., 228.

19. Adrienne Rich, *Of Woman Born: Motherhood as Experience and Institution*, 223.

20. Ibid., 224.

21. Neumann, *The Fear of the Feminine*, 279.

22. Ibid., 241.

23. Erich Neumann, *The Origins and History of Consciousness, Part I*, 67.

BIBLIOGRAPHY

Bell, Daniel. *The Cultural Contradiction of Capitalism*. London: Heinemann, 1976.

Davis, Michael F. "Writing the Mother in *The Notebooks of Malte Laurids Brigge:* The Rhetoric of Abjection." *Germanic Review* 68 (1993), http://www.questia.com/googleScholar.qst?docId=97923561.

Hever, Hannan. *Suddenly the Sight of War: Nationality and Violence in Hebrew Poetry of the 1940s (Lefetah Marʾeh Hamilkhama)*. Tel Aviv: Hakibbutz Hameukhad Publishing House Ltd, 2001.

Jameson, Fredric. "Realism and Desire: Balzac and the Problem of the Subject." In *The Political Unconscious: Narrative as a Socially Symbolic Act*, 151–184. Ithaca, N.Y.: Cornell University Press, 1981.

Kovacs, Balint Andras. *National Cinema—International Modernism*. Studies in Cinema and Television. Tel Aviv: Kolnoʾa, 1998.

Neʾeman, Judd. "The Modernists: The Manifest of the Israeli New Sensibility" ("Hamodernim: Megilat Hayokhasin Shel Haregishuth Hakhadasha"). In *Fictive Looks: On Israeli Cinema (Mabatim Fiktiviʾim Al Kolnoʾa Yisraʾeli)*, edited by Nurith Gertz, Orly Lubin, and Judd Neʾeman, 9–32. Tel Aviv: Open University of Israel, 1998.

———. "Camera Obscura of the Fallen: Military Pedagogy and Its Accessories in Israeli Cinema" ("Kamera Obskura Shel Hanoflim: Pedagogia Tzvaʾit Vaʾavizareihah Bakolnoʾa Hayisraʾeli"). In *Security and Communications: A Dynamic of Relations (Bitakhon Vetikshoret: Dinamika Shel Yekhasim)*, edited by Udi Lebel, 347–386. Beersheva: Ben-Gurion University of the Negev, 2005.

Neumann, Erich. *Amor and Psyche: The Psychic Development of the Feminine*. New York and Evanston: Harper Torchbook/Bollingen Library, Harper and Row Publishers, 1956.

————. *The Origins and History of Consciousness, Part I*. The Bollingen Library. New York: Harper Torchbooks, 1962.

————. *The Fear of the Feminine and Other Essays on Feminine Psychology*. Bollingen Series 61.4. Princeton, N.J.: Princeton University Press, 1994.

Rich, Adrienne. *Of Woman Born: Motherhood as Experience and Institution* (1976). Hebrew translation by Carmit Guy. Tel Aviv: Am Oved Publishers, 1989.

Scarry, Elaine. *The Body in Pain*. New York: Oxford University Press, 1985.

Silverman, Kaja. *Male Subjectivity at the Margins*. New York and London: Routledge, 1992.

Sivan, Emanuel. *The 1948 Generation: Myth, Profile, and Memory* (*Dor Tashakh: Mitos, Dyokan Vezikaron*). Tel Aviv: Israel Ministry of Defense Press, 1991.

Theweleit, Klaus. *Male Fantasies*. Vol. 2. Minneapolis: University of Minnesota Press, 1989.

FILMOGRAPHY

After (Renen Schorr, 1977; short).

The Black Banana (*Habanana Hashkhora*, Binyamin Haim, 1977).

But Where Is Daniel Wax? (*Le'an Ne'elam Daniel Vaks?* Avraham Heffner, 1972).

The Customer of the Off Season (*Ore'akh Be'ona Metah*, Moshe Mizrahi, 1970).

The Dreamer (*Hatimhoni*, Dan Wolman, 1970).

The Dress (*Hasimlah*, Judd Ne'eman, 1969).

From the Other Side (*Mineged*, Menachem Binetzky, 1970).

A Hole in the Moon (*Khor Balevana*, Uri Zohar, 1964).

The Honey Connection (*Kesher Ha-Dvash*, Yeud Levanon, 1977; short).

I Love You Rosa (*Ani Ohev Otakh Roza*, Moshe Mizrahi, 1972).

Iris (David Greenberg, 1968).

Light Out of Nowhere (*Or Min Hahefker*, Nissim Dayan, 1973).

A Little Night Music (*Musikat Laila Ze'ira*, Avi Nesher, 1975; short).

Louisa, Louisa (Igal Bursztyn, 1968; short).

Meir in Seven Pictures (*Meir Be-Sheva Tmunot*, Shimon Dotan, 1976; short).

Moments (*Rega'im*, Michal Bat-Adam, 1979).

My Father (*Avi*, Daniel Wachsmann, 1975; short).

Nachum Glickson: Two Days in Israel (*Nakhum Glikson: Yomaim Beyisra'el*, Eitan Green, 1976; short).

Piano Lesson (*Shi'ur Psanter*, Tzipi Trope, 1977; short).

The Pill (*Haglulah*, David Perlov, 1972).

Rose Water from Port Said (*Mei Vradim MePort Said*, Ram Loevy, 1972; TV drama).

Saint Cohen (*Hagiga La-Eynaim*, Assi Dayan, 1975).

Shalom, Prayer for the Road (*Shalom, Tfilat Haderekh*, Yaki Yosha, 1973).

Siege (*Matzor*, Gilberto Tofano, 1969).

Slower (*Le'at Yoter*, Avraham Heffner, 1968; short).

The Snail (*Shablul*, Boaz Davidson, 1971).

Three Days and a Child (*Shlosha Yamim Vayeled*, Uri Zohar, 1967).

The Woman in the Next Room (*Isha Bakheder Hasheni*, Yitzhak Tzepel Yeshurun, 1966).

A Woman's Case (*Mikre Isha*, Jacques Katmor, 1969).

7 Coping with the Legacy of Death

The War Widow in Israeli Films

YAEL ZERUBAVEL

Given Israel's long and unresolved conflict with the Palestinians and its continuing toll on human life, one might expect that the character of the war widow would occupy an important place among the cinematic representations of the war experience in Israeli society. Yet the war widow has been a relative latecomer to Israeli films and has thus far received limited attention. During the pre-state and early state periods, the tendency was to highlight the national heroic aspects of nation building, the War of Independence and the foundation of the state and its governing organs. Israeli films, like other expressive forms of that era, showed a preference to feature Jewish youths in their social spheres of action and their mobilization for the national cause.[1] In this context, male characters often took the center stage, while female characters were assigned to supporting roles.

The fact that the war widow was largely overlooked in Israeli cinema reflected the social attitudes prevalent in the post-1948 years. At the time, the parents of fallen soldiers were seen as representing the entire community of mourners, and women who lost their spouses or companions in the war received little attention. It was only after the 1967 Six Day War that the media focused on widows' plight and the public pressure led the government to establish new procedures of care for the widows and their children.[2] Whereas the bereaved parents' organization Yad Labanim (literally, "the memorial to the sons") had been established in 1949, war widows founded their own organization in affiliation with it only in 1973, following the Yom Kippur War. It may not be surprising, therefore, that the war widow emerged as a major character in films only in the 1960s. The study of the cinematic portrayals of the war widow can thus draw on a limited number of examples. In spite of this limitation, such a study provides an important venue to learn about changing attitudes toward the war widow and her experience following her husband's death.

The loss of a husband during his military service confers on his wife the status of a war widow. In this new position, she enters a new set of rights and obligations as the symbolic extension of the fallen soldier in her relation with the state and becomes a member of the national "bereaved family."[3] The war widow becomes the carrier of her husband's memory and embodies the connection between a personal and a national sacrifice. While she copes with her often complex response to her husband's sudden death and with being left behind as a young woman with or without children, she also faces the challenge of dealing with the social expectations that she should behave in conformity with her new status. These expectations, which are often un-clear and even contradictory, inevitably place her in a new and vulnerable situation. The war widow is expected to go through a process of mourning, grief, and recovery but also to remain loyal to her social role as a living memorial, an obligation that is likely to inhibit the recovery process.

The analysis of the cinematic portrayals of the war widow reveals an im-portant dimension of the consequences of war and the direct impact it has on women. The discussion addresses the new sensibilities that transform the representation of the war widow and broadens our understanding of the interrelations of gender, memory, and patriotic sacrifice.[4]

The 1960s: The Struggle with Memory

Two cinematic works mark the direct exploration of the war widow's expe-rience in Israeli film in the 1960s: *The Hero's Wife* (*Eshet Hagibor*) in 1963 and *Siege* (*Matzor*) in 1969. Turning the widow into the lead figure and casting the male characters in supporting roles, these films invert the ac-cepted gender representation of the national heroic films. They focus on the war widow and her social environment, while the fallen soldier whose death looms large as the trigger for the unfolding story is represented only through photographs, flashbacks, and occasional references to him. Both these films were shot in black and white, a choice that enhances the empha-sis on the widow's personal and subdued life under the shadow of death.

The Hero's Wife and *Siege* are clearly Israeli productions, shot locally with an Israeli cast and in Hebrew. Yet both films were made by foreign directors. Peter Frye, who directed *The Hero's Wife*, is a Canadian who came to Israel in his mid-thirties; and Gilberto Tofano, who directed *Siege*, is an Italian. In

both films, however, the female lead actors—Batya Lancet and Gila Almagor—were married to men involved in the film production and contributed
to the script writing. Thus the first films to focus on the Israeli war widow
were made by men who were not raised in the national Hebrew culture that
shaped earlier films and benefited from their female leading actors' insights
into their characters' experiences.[5]

In spite of these similarities, there are major differences in the representation of the war widow in these two films. *The Hero's Wife* introduces
the widow fifteen years after her husband's death. In spite of the passage
of time, the widow is reluctant, or unable, to unlock the hold of the past
over the present and continues to see herself as "the hero's wife." Although
she is a well-liked and respected member of the kibbutz where she works
as a teacher, her life continues to be defined by her loss, and her private
living space is constructed as a shrine to the dead. The widow still lives
under the shadow of her husband's memory and ignores the special feelings
that another kibbutz member has for her, while he respects the boundaries
of her role as the hero's wife. An earlier shot of a warning sign near their
kibbutz—"Stop! Border ahead!"—thus becomes a metaphor for the invisible
walls around the war widow.

The plot is propelled forward, however, by the appearance of a foreign
volunteer who unabashedly expresses his attraction to the heroine and disregards the legacy of her position as the hero's wife. Although the widow
rejects his advances out of her own commitment to the dead and to the
collectivist ethos of the kibbutz, which the cynical, carefree young man
dismisses, the young volunteer eventually wins her over when he risks his
life to save the kibbutz. The widow becomes his lover, as if his heroic deed
entitled him to serve as an appropriate replacement for the dead hero. *The
Hero's Wife* allows the outsider to occupy this role only within the set boundaries of a liminal phase: having released the widow from her entrapment in
the role of "the hero's wife," the young man leaves the country soon after. As
the ending of the film suggests, his departure allows the widow to follow a
more suitable and long-term relationship with her fellow kibbutznik, whose
love she previously ignored.

The Hero's Wife's shortcomings are evident in its unidimensional characters, overly ideological script, and outdated theatrical style. Its portrayal of
the kibbutz society as caring, nonjudgmental, and nurturing would be highly contested by later films such as *Atalia* (Akiva Tevet, 1984) and *Sweet Mud*
(*Adamah Meshuga'at*, Dror Shaul, 2006). In spite of these weaknesses, one
should credit the film for being the first full-fledged cinematic portrait of an
Israeli war widow that brought to light the social constraints of her role as

a living memorial for the dead hero and the ways in which the expectation that she should continue this role undermines her prospects for recovery.

Siege, made in the aftermath of the 1967 Six Day War, provides a much more mature and sophisticated portrayal of the war widow and her struggle to reshape her life following her husband's death. Influenced by the French New Wave, the film provides an intimate portrayal of her process of mourning, social withdrawal, and slow recovery as it follows her interacting with her young son, friends, and gossiping neighbors; coping with loneliness and pain in her private space; or deciding to return to work. The film is particularly powerful in showing the ambivalence that underlies her relations with her husband's close friends, whose friendship and care are a major source of support yet are also experienced as a form of social control. Although the friends encourage her to enter a new relationship with potential suitors to whom they introduce her, tensions surface when she pursues a new relationship without the friends' knowledge. Resentful and alarmed at first, the husband's best friend eventually accepts her choice. His symbolic gift to her—a photo album for her husband's photographs that fill the house—represents her release from the burden of the past and a tacit acceptance of her choice to move on with her life. The sensitive exploration of the widow's recovery might have appeared to end on an optimistic note similar to that of The Hero's Wife, yet this redemptive trajectory is subverted by the introduction of a new theme that would later emerge as central to the 1980s films.

The 1980s and 1990s: Double Besiegement

The last episode of Siege radically transforms its message when it raises the possibility that the continuing violence of the Israeli-Palestinian conflict might endanger the widow's lover, who is called for reserve duty. Upon hearing on the radio the news that Israeli soldiers were critically wounded, the widow drives with her husband's best friend to find out what happened to her lover. Leaving the outcome ambiguous, the film narrative abruptly shifts from the fictional drama to documentary footage of the film shooting and of the news broadcast about what was to become recognized as the "War of Attrition" that followed the Six Day War. "Siege" as a theme thus receives a broader meaning than the widow's personal sense of besiegement in her role, becoming a collective representation of Israel's besiegement in a cycle of violence and death.

Repeat Dive (Tzlila Khozeret), Shimon Dotan's 1982 film about the War of Attrition, revolves around a group of friends from the marine commando and their response to their comrade's death in action. The dead marine's best friend brings to his widow a video recorded at a party, in which her husband boasts about his sexual pursuits and jokingly bequeaths his wife to this friend in case he dies in a military action. Although she responds with anger to the disclosure of her husband's infidelity and to being passed as an object to another man, the widow follows her dead husband's will and marries that friend. The lack of sexual and emotional intimacy between them and her fears that he too might be killed in action cripple their relationship from the start. The second husband's decision to extend his military service in spite of his wife's objections and the beginning of his extramarital affair at the military base suggest that "repeat dive" refers not only to the military operations performed by the marine commandos but also to the characters' "dive" into a recurrent cycle of marriage and betrayal, heroism and death, that might result in the wife's return to the role of a war widow.

Repeat Dive's interest is directed to the exploration of male companionship and the impact of the military on Israeli life. The film tries to offer a critical view of the national heroic films, highlighting the soldiers' psychological immaturity and inability to form intimate relationships. Yet the film ultimately fails to offer a powerful critique and remains locked within the gender stereotypes that it sets out to examine. Although the film features the widow as a distinct figure, she remains an underdeveloped character: a woman who is erratic and lacks integrity or an independent will and who pursues a predetermined path carved out for her by others.

Based on a short story by Yitzkhak Ben-Ner,[6] the film *Atalia* (directed by Akiva Tevet, 1984) reestablishes the war widow as the lead character. Like *The Hero's Wife*, the film introduces her long after her husband's death and examines her experiences within the kibbutz society. Unlike the main character of the earlier film, the widow of the 1980s is portrayed as a lonely and malfunctioning woman who becomes increasingly alienated from her immediate social environment and is eventually driven over the edge into a revengeful act aimed at the entire kibbutz. The film opens seventeen years after her husband's death in 1956, when she was pregnant with their daughter, now a high school senior.

Atalia is portrayed as a loner whose adolescent behavior and open sexuality become the subject of vicious gossip in the kibbutz and a source of embarrassment to her own daughter. In the story version, Atalia is falsely accused of being promiscuous when she invites three foreign volunteers to her room for a cup of coffee. When she eventually becomes involved with a married man, years after her husband's death, she feels she has nothing to lose in terms of her social standing. The film presents Atalia as a self-centered, immature, and provocative woman who fails to function as a mother and has no qualms about having an affair with a married kibbutz member. Furthermore, the film version adds a subplot to Ben-Ner's story—a relationship between the war widow and a young kibbutz member who is a year older than her own daughter and whose character borrows biographical details that the story version attributes to her dead husband. This added relationship, which occupies a central place in the film plot, enhances its portrayal of the widow as a social misfit, provoking other kibbutz members' hostility toward her.

The outbreak of the 1973 Yom Kippur War compounds the widow's troubled situation. Her daughter's boyfriend is killed in action. Although this development introduces the theme of widowhood as a legacy that is being passed on from mother to daughter, its direct impact on Atalia receives little notice in the film. The young man's death moves Atalia's young lover to leave the kibbutz and return to the army, and his departing words echo her earlier account of her husband's departing words in 1956. This repeated experience of desertion and betrayal by men throws the war widow into rage and despair. Her response—to set the kibbutz's barn on fire—is not only interpreted as the act of a madwoman;[7] it is also presented as a criminal act typically associated with the Palestinians.[8] The war widow's expulsion from the kibbutz thus turns her formally into an outcast. Whereas the film emphasizes her immature and self-destructive behavior, the original story mitigates this portrayal by highlighting the kibbutz's complicity and lack of compassion that drove her into this madness.

The story version also provides a more complex view of Atalia's difficulty with the social role of the war widow. She protests to her dead husband against living with the burden of his memory: "Almost twenty years have passed. A third of my life I knew you, and only one-tenth of this time I was with you. I left you when you were twenty-four years old and I am already a bit over forty now. How dare you direct my path, stop me, caution me? I am a grown woman and you are still a boy."[9] Atalia admits that their relationship had been distant even before he died; and her knowledge that he died in an accident and not in the war further makes it difficult to accept his official commemoration as a fallen soldier of the 1956 Sinai Campaign. Atalia's rejection of the heroic ethos is articulated in the film through her attempt to stop her young lover from joining the 1973 war, arguing against the famous saying that "it is good to die for our country."[10] "They lied to you, Matti, don't you understand?" she screams in despair.

It is significant to note that this spirit of defiance of the ethos of patriotic sacrifice is articulated in *Sex, Lies, and Dinner* (*Sex, Shkarim Va'arukhat Erev*), a 1996 made-for-TV drama directed by Dan Wolman, featuring three war widows' get-together. In this setting the two women who have been widows for a while offer two opposing models of widowhood to a younger woman who recently lost her husband. One of the veteran widows, who is a kibbutz member, acknowledges her reluctance to pursue relationships with men for fear that it might undermine her social standing. The other, a seemingly carefree urban woman who serves as their host, refuses to embrace the war widow role as a symbolic extension of her dead husband. She cynically describes society's expectation that the war widow will attend every memorial service for fallen soldiers, "an awesome entertainment for a twenty-four-year-old woman," and decries the duplicity that marks the perception of the widow. "Once," she tells the others, "someone even tried to come on to me in the cemetery . . . I told him I am already taken, I already have a tombstone here." She dryly notes that her female friends disappeared because they were afraid she might steal their men and prides herself on being uninhibited and determined not to have her life slip by.

As the evening progresses, however, the war widows discover that in spite of their different choices they all struggle with a continuing sense of loss and loneliness. Moreover, *Sex, Lies, and Dinner* brings to light more clearly than earlier works the war widows' social marginalization, a process that leads them to associate with persons on the margins of Israeli society or further down the social ladder. The scene in which the three widows invite foreign workers to join them for drinks late at night creates an analogy between the women and those foreigners, highlighting their shared loneliness, marginality, and lack of ability to communicate the predicament of their respective situations. This theme also appears in *The Hero's Wife* (the widow bonds with a foreign volunteer) and in *Siege* (the lover is a blue-collar worker, unlike the professional, middle-class men to whom her friends introduce her earlier); in *Atalia*, the heroine's attraction to "loners" within the kibbutz society adds to her marginalized position as a widow.

The films of the 1980s and 1990s thus present the widow as doubly besieged by a conflict that continues to demand human lives and by the dual attitude of the society that sees the war widow as a symbolic extension of her dead husband but also as an available young woman who poses a potential threat to the social order. In the polarized environment after the 1973 war, at a time when the national heroic myths became the subject of heated controversies and peace movements challenged the continuing toll of war, the focus on the war widow became a venue to explore a broader situation. The besiegement of the woman in the role of the widow has become an allegory for an entire society entrapped in a vicious cycle of war, injuries, and death.

The 2000s: From Double Widowhood to Double Happiness

A more recent film, *Noodle* (2007), directed by the female director Ayelet Menahemi, moves the cinematic representation of the war widow to a new plane and, as if to complete the circle, returns to a more optimistic note about her prospect of recovery, similar to the ending of *The Hero's Wife*. *Noodle*'s point of departure, however, differs from earlier films that presented the possibility of recurrent widowhood as their dramatic climax. The 2007 film refers to the heroine's status as a twice-widowed woman as a biographical fact almost in passing, as if it is marginal to the plot, which appears to be centered elsewhere. Two photos of her dead husbands and related military mementos placed on a single shelf function as the mute evidence of her double widowhood, and the film makes only fleeting references to her experiences as a war widow. It is only by piecing together these fragmented allusions that the viewer can make inferences about the extent to which this experience shaped the widow's life.

A flight attendant, the war widow appears to be literally and metaphorically on a flight, escaping from the void in her life. When she returns home from a flight as the film opens, her apartment is not empty: her sister has moved in after separating from her husband, who lives next door and has a strong attachment to the widow. A Chinese cleaning woman who is working for her leaves her young child in their care for an hour, yet fails to come back and get him. The presence of this foreign child with whom they cannot communicate destabilizes the complex web of interlocking yet broken relationships in the war widow's life. "Noodle," as they call the Chinese boy, thus becomes the trigger that awakens the widow from a prolonged state of emotional numbness and opens the door for a change.

Mobilized to find his missing parent with the help of her sister and friends, the widow learns from the police that the mother, an illegal foreign worker, has been expelled back to China by the Israeli immigration authorities. Faced with a bureaucratic malaise that leaves the child without proper documents and devoid of either Israeli or Chinese citizenship, the widow chooses to hide his existence from the authorities and resolves the bureaucratic deadlock by smuggling the child back into China, hidden in her suitcase.

As the relationship between the widow and Noodle develops, their broken communication provides the only affirmation of the heroine's double widowhood. The war widow explains to him who the men in these two photographs are and what happened to them in gestures and sounds that convey their deaths in combat. The husbands' stories, her own relationships with them, and her responses to their deaths thus remain absent from the film, highlighting the widow's avoidance of dealing with that painful past. As the dramatic plot thickens, however, she and her sister are forced to reflect on their own respective situations and to begin a more revealing, if painful, dialogue between them. It becomes increasingly apparent that the sisters' inability to move on with their lives is a direct outcome of their responses to the widow's double trauma of loss. The widow's experiences led her to prefer an unhappy present rather than risk changes in her life or in the lives of those around her. She appears more intent than her sister and her brother-in-law on seeing their broken marriage glued together, while her sister avoids telling her about a love affair that occurred when she became a widow for the second time and therefore attempts to suppress this episode and deny her love for that man.

At a critical moment, the widow's strong aversion to risk ("If something bad is going to happen to someone," she says, "it is going to happen to me") almost prevents her from embarking on her rescue mission, but with the support of those around her she goes through with her plan. As a result of this process, she manages to disentangle her larger family from the trappings of their own situations. "Double Happiness"—the name of the Chinese restaurant in Beijing where they locate the boy's mother—thus serves as an allusion to the promise of a double redemption: for the boy as well as the war widow and her sister.

Unlike earlier films that emphasized the role of the continuing Israeli-Palestinian conflict as undermining the possibility of a personal redemption, *Noodle* remains focused on its characters' private lives and ends with the message of hope for a possible recovery. At the end, the family's realignment develops out of their active participation in the mission of rescuing a foreign child who, in turn, brings hope into their lives. On the flight to China, the widow's sister finds courage to share the secret of her relationship with a former lover who became part of the rescue mission, and the widow now encourages her to join him. The brother-in-law finds courage to confess his deep attachment to the widow before she leaves for Beijing; and she appears to be empowered by the discovery of her own ability to feel again and to take charge of her life and the boy's fate. One assumes that the door may be open for her relationship with her brother-in-law to grow with her sister's blessing or for her to find another way to move on with her life.

Unlike earlier films that raised the possibility of recovery, *Noodle* takes a feminist stance that attributes the change to the widow rather than to men who rescue her from her predicament as the eternal widow (as is the case in *The Hero's Wife* and *Siege*) or fail to do so (in *Repeat Dive* and *Atalia*). *Noodle* presents the change as emerging out of the feminine base of the characters involved: the sisters' strong bonding, their female friends, the sensitive men who help them along the way (the brother-in-law and the sister's lover), and ultimately the child himself.

Unlike some of the films that highlighted the widow's difficulty within the context of the kibbutz society, *Noodle* is situated in the highly urban, middle-class environment of Tel Aviv, which is typically identified with the individualistic ethos, urban alienation, and materialistic approach to life. Yet the film challenges these stereotypes. *Noodle*'s fairytale-like framework portrays the power of humanity, compassion, and personal courage to overcome materialism, alienation, bureaucracy, and even international law as a way to personal redemption. It attempts to make us believe that with the appropriate social support, care for human values, and the courage to take risks, recovery is possible even for someone deeply hurt by the continuing state of war. The war widow may thus find her own voice and assume agency to free herself from the double prison of memory and war.

NOTES

1. For an extensive analysis of the development of these themes in Israeli film, see Miri Talmon, *Israeli Graffiti: Nostalgia, Groups, and Collective Identity in Israeli Cinema.*

2. Lea Shamgar-Handelman, *Israeli War Widows: Beyond the Glory of Heroism,* 22–32.

3. Yoram Bilu and Eliezer Witztum, "War-Related Loss and Suffering in Israeli Society: A Historical Perspective"; Yael Zerubavel, "Patriotic Sacrifice and the Burden of Memory in Israeli Secular National Hebrew Culture," in *Memory and Violence in the Middle East and North Africa.*

4. For an earlier discussion of the portrayal of the war widow in Israeli film and fiction, see Régine-Mihal Friedman, "Between Silence and Abjection: The Film Medium and the Israeli War Widow"; and Yael Zerubavel, "Female Images in a State of War: Ideology, Crisis, and the Politics of Gender in Israel."

5. Batya Lancet was married to Frye, the director of *The Hero's Wife,* at the time, and Gila Almagor was married to Yaacov Agmon, the producer of *Siege. The Hero's Wife* was Frye's second film, following *I Like Mike* in 1961, and was based on a short story by Margot Klausner. For further information, see Meir Schnitzer, *Israeli Cinema.*

6. Yitzhak Ben-Ner, "Atalia." It is important to note that the cinematic version introduces major changes into Ben-Ner's story. For a detailed analysis of the differences between the fiction and the film, see Nurith Gertz, *Motion Fiction: Israeli Fiction in Film,* 289–317.

7. It may be interesting to compare this story to Lea Eini's novel *Sand Tide.* The war widow serves as the narrator, describing her responses to her husband's death. The end of the novel reveals that her apparent recovery after her husband died disguised a growing process of internal withdrawal that ultimately drove her to an act of defiance that appeared to others as madness. The war widow is thus hospitalized in a clinic for

the mentally ill. For further discussion of this novel, see Zerubavel, "Female Images in a State of War."

8. See Yael Zerubavel, "The Forest as a National Icon: Literature, Politics, and the Archeology of Memory"; see also Gertz, *Motion Fiction*, 315.

9. Ben-Ner, "Atalia," 11 (my translation).

10. Atalia refers to the famous last words of Joseph Trumpeldor, a Jewish hero who was killed in Tel Hai, a small Jewish settlement in northern Galilee, in 1920. Tel Hai emerged as a key national heroic myth in Israeli culture, and Trumpeldor's words "it is good to die for our country" became a major educational slogan during the pre-state and early state periods. The Tel Hai myth has suffered from a gradual decline since the 1970s and became a subject of harsh criticism and a public controversy in the late 1970s and 1980s. For a more extensive discussion of the rise of the myth and the politics of its interpretation, see Yael Zerubavel, *Recovered Roots: Collective Memory and the Making of Israeli National Tradition*.

BIBLIOGRAPHY

Ben-Ner, Yitzkhak. "Atalia." In *After the Rain: Three Stories (Aharei Hageshem: Shelosha Sipurim)*, 5–40. Jerusalem: Keter, 1979.

Bilu, Yoram, and Eliezer Witztum. "War-Related Loss and Suffering in Israeli Society: A Historical Perspective." *Israel Studies* 5, no. 2 (2000): 1–31.

Eini, Lea. *Sand Tide (Ge'ut Hakhol)*. Tel Aviv: Hakibbutz Hameukhad, 1992.

Friedman, Régine-Mihal. "Between Silence and Abjection: The Film Medium and the Israeli War Widow." *Filmhistoria* 3, nos. 1–2 (1993): 79–89.

Gertz, Nurith. *Motion Fiction: Israeli Fiction on Film (Sipur Mehasratim: Siporet Yisra'elit Ve'ibudeihah Lakolno'a)*. Tel Aviv: Open University Press, 1993.

Schnitzer, Meir. *Israeli Cinema (Hakolno'a Hayisra'eli)*. Or Yehuda: Kineret, 1994.

Shamgar-Handelman, Lea. *Israeli War Widows: Beyond the Glory of Heroism*. Massachusetts: Bergin and Garvey, 1986.

Talmon, Miri. *Israeli Graffiti: Nostalgia, Groups, and Collective Identity in Israeli Cinema (Bluz Latzabar Ha'avud: Khavurot Venostalgia Bakolno'a Hayisra'eli)*. Tel Aviv and Haifa: Open University and Haifa University Press, 2001.

Zerubavel, Yael. *Recovered Roots: Collective Memory and the Making of Israeli National Tradition*. Chicago: University of Chicago Press, 1995.

———. "The Forest as a National Icon: Literature, Politics, and the Archeology of Memory." *Israel Studies* 1, no. 1 (Spring 1996): 60–99.

———. "Female Images in a State of War: Ideology, Crisis, and the Politics of Gender in Israel." In *Landscaping the Human Garden: 20th Century Population Management in a Comparative Framework*, ed. Amir Weiner, 236–257. Stanford: Stanford University Press, 2003.

———. "Patriotic Sacrifice and the Burden of Memory in Israeli Secular National Hebrew Culture." In *Memory and Violence in the Middle East and North Africa*, ed. Ussama Makdisi and Paul A. Silverstein, 77–100. Bloomington: Indiana University Press, 2006.

FILMOGRAPHY

Atalia. Directed by Akiva Tevet (1984).
The Hero's Wife (*Eshet Hagibor*). Directed by Peter Frye (1963).
Noodle. Directed by Ayelet Menahemi (2007).
Repeat Dive (*Tzlila Khozeret*). Directed by Shimon Dotan (1982).
Sex, Lies, and Dinner (*Sex, Shkarim Va'arukhat Erev*). Directed by Dan Wolman, 1996.
Siege (*Matzor*). Directed by Gilberto Tofano (1969).
Sweet Mud (*Adamah Meshuga'at*). Directed by Dror Shaul (2006).

8

The Privatization of War Memory in Recent Israeli Cinema

YAEL MUNK

Preface: Wars in Israeli Cinema

The memory of war has been etched in the consciousness of Israel since its bloody birth in 1948. Expressions such as "war of survival" and "War of the Sons of Light against the Sons of Darkness" became central to the way Israelis perceived themselves. Yet military struggle in modern Hebrew culture became important prior to the state's independence as part of the notion of the New Jew, who, in contrast to passive ancestors in exile, had to fight for the right to live in the old-new land. Israeli cinema did not overlook these perceptions and turned the various expressions of the war narrative into the foundation stone of its first feature films. As part of the pre-state cinematic narratives or in the national ones at the beginning of the state's existence (*They Were Ten*, Baruch Dienar, 1960; *He Walked through the Fields*, Yosef Millo, 1967),[1] war images were to play a central role in Israeli cinema's iconography. In the second half of the 1960s this theme was exhausted in *Every Bastard a King* (Uri Zohar, 1968), dedicated to the glorification of the Israeli soldiers' bravery during the Six Day War. Financed by the IDF, Zohar's film demonstrated that under certain circumstances the patriotic ideal of defending one's country could provide a shallow sense of meaning to those threatened by an existential anxiety of meaninglessness.[2]

Already after the Six Day War in 1967 but progressively more so after the traumatic 1973 Yom Kippur War and the confusing and expensive Lebanon War in 1982, representations of war in Israeli cinema diminished. This change was expressed in Ido Sela's documentary *Earthquake* (1997), produced for the public television series *Tkumah*. Sela's film describes the chronology of the Yom Kippur War as a continuum of indecision and hesitation that cost the lives of many. Through interviews with various soldiers and government ministers who witnessed the conduct of defense minister Moshe Dayan and chief of staff David El'azar, the film undermined the trust between the individual and the state and showed that this war was a turning point in Israeli history. Other films, like *Shell Shock* (Yoel Sharon, 1988) and *Burning Memory* (Yossi Somer, 1989), continued the shift in Israeli cinema by developing stories that explicitly portrayed individuals trapped in a post-traumatic condition that derived from the ongoing state of war with the neighboring Arab countries.

The civilian uprising of the Palestinians, the Intifada of 1987, which was the first conflict during which Israel lost control over the "battlefield," minimized the discourse of war in Israeli cinema even further until its total disappearance in the 1990s.[3] Thus the appearance of the three Israeli war movies produced in the new millennium—*Kippur* (Amos Gitai, 2000), *Beaufort* (Joseph Cedar, 2007),[4] and most recently *Waltz with Bashir* (Ari Folman, 2008)—represented an unusual and noteworthy phenomenon.[5] This essay argues that these films express a new historiographical stance regarding Israel's national narrative. Focusing on the space in which trauma is created,[6] the films bring back the repressed war discourse. By portraying the battlefield in a hyper-realistic manner, they play a central symbolic role, producing disorientation and agoraphobia in *Kippur* and suffocation and claustrophobia in *Beaufort*. By doing so, both films express aspects of the spatial experience characteristic of the old Jewish Diaspora,[7] including the defenselessness of abandonment in a hostile territory and the claustrophobia of life in the ghetto. These aspects defy Israeli nationalism by presenting the privatization of Israeli war memories as a resistance to Zionism's metanarrative.

The Return of Repressed Wars

In *Kippur* Amos Gitai sought to mark the twenty-seventh year of the personal trauma he experienced in the Yom Kippur War, deliberately releasing the film in October 2000. Like most Israelis, however, Gitai did not imagine that Israel would cope with a second Intifada—the Al-Aqsa Intifada.[8] Even though the "external" events influenced the film's cold reception in Israel,[9] the proximity of the historical events and the actual ones can shed light on the change that took place in Israeli society's attitude toward the notion of war.

Moreover, during the seven years after the release of *Kippur*, no distinct war movie was produced in Israel until the release of Cedar's *Beaufort* (2007). Although *Beaufort* deals with another war, the First Lebanon War in 1982, it continues Gitai's Israeli argument about armed conflicts: the growing disconnection between the soldiers on the battlefield and the politicians who sent them there as well as the soldiers' trauma of abandonment. The portrayal of this detachment seems to be part of the process of undermining the military pedagogic values, expressed, among other ways, through "a process of traumatization which frees the urge to die from any inhibitions and allows the soldier to become comfortable with the need to kill the enemy as well as the inevitability of getting hurt or dying on the battlefield."[10]

Both films return to two dramatic events that have been "mythicized" in the Israeli discourse. *Kippur* depicts the first days of the Yom Kippur War (1973) on the Syrian front.[11] *Beaufort* portrays the last days of Israeli presence on Lebanese soil after eighteen years of occupation, which began symbolically with the strategic conquest of the Beaufort crusader fortress in a fierce battle on July 6, 1982. Both films adopt muted tones, however, and prefer symbolism over the explicit representation of war. Moreover, in both plots overt patriotism, which characterized the national cinema of the 1960s and was then widely criticized in the 1980s,[12] is abandoned, making room for low-ranking soldiers to express their ambivalence toward war. Both films also show a random group of men who would not have met as civilians and who are thrust into intimate situations that make them jointly face the struggle for survival and the possibility of death. The patriotic meaning of military service, which figured as a conceptual and ideological framework in previous films, seems to have lost its validity. Fighting to survive, the Israeli soldiers in both films demonstrate the arbitrariness of their condition.[13]

Kippur: Disorientation as an Expression of Abandonment

"War is a chaotic event, which creates a split in the continuity of life," claims Gitai. "It rips people away from their normal, daily lives, thrusting them into a different existence and different territories. War itself is a chaotic event, especially in the case of the Yom Kippur War, which hadn't been planned ahead but was rather imposed on us and took us by surprise. . . . The state of chaos is the conceptual starting point of the experience we deal with."[14] Gitai describes this event as the place where trauma is created. Those who are "thrown" into a different, chaotic existence will never fully return to the place they came from, since, as psychiatrist Judith Lewis

Herman describes it, they "feel and act as if their nerve system has been detached from the present."[15]

Kippur opens with an unconventional lovemaking scene: in a slow sequence shot from a variety of angles and accompanied by a soundtrack of a lone saxophone, Weinraub and his female partner hand-paint each other's bodies in a variety of primary colors that eventually turn into khaki.[16] Their act is brutally interrupted when war breaks out and Weinraub is called to join his unit. He passes quickly through the empty streets of Tel Aviv and then continues toward the front on the Golan Heights together with a friend who picks him up in his car. When they arrive at the front, however, they realize that this war, as opposed to previous ones, is out of control and their chances of finding their unit are slim. Determined to help, they quickly join an airborne medical rescue unit that they encounter by chance. The rest of the film consists of their Sisyphean efforts to rescue wounded soldiers and airlift them from the battleground on the Golan Heights to hospitals in Israel. Recurring images of wounded soldiers, wading through dark mud, are shown repeatedly, lending the battle the air of a dreary and never-ending journey. Time and again the protagonists try to rescue injured soldiers who are shown languishing on a deeply rutted battlefield where the enemy is significantly absent and invisible.

The sense of abandonment that the soldiers experience is depicted through their spatial disorientation. As they move toward the choppers, they are unable to distinguish between south and north. Unlike the authentic representation of Tel Aviv's empty streets, the monotonous description of the battlefield seems almost abstract. The gray sky that hangs low over the soldiers seems to emblematize the absence of a guiding hand, and their constant circles in the mud intensify the sense that they have been betrayed by a seemingly confident leadership that tried to pretend that everything is under control.

The protagonists' journey comes to an end as they find themselves deliberating the evacuation of yet another fatally wounded soldier. While the doctor wants to airlift him, claiming that he is not dead yet, another soldier insists that they leave him behind because they were ordered to take "no dead soldier in the chopper." The scene ends as Weinraub covers the soldier with his coat, pronouncing him dead. The death of this anonymous soldier marks the end of their mission. The heroes get on the chopper and begin their journey back home. Weinraub's gaze reveals the Israeli green landscapes now plowed by tank marks, a reflective vision that is brutally interrupted by a missile that hits the chopper. After thinking that their mission was over, the soldiers now find themselves almost fatally trapped.

As two members of the crew are transferred to a hospital, Weinraub picks up his car and drives home after meeting with the pilot, who declares his intention to fly to Tel Aviv to meet those responsible for the war. The next sequence opens in Weinraub's house. His girlfriend is peacefully engaged in yoga exercises outside. This scene, in contrast to the previous sequence of the muddy and chaotic battlefield, leads to a repetition of the opening love-making scene: a splash of paint on the white canvas, followed by splashes of primary colors. Again the painted naked bodies of the lovers fill the screen, tying the lovemaking with the battlefield. Unlike the opening scene, however, during which the camera followed the dynamic lovers, now the camera stays still and remains stationary even when the naked, painted lovers roll out of frame. The white stain left by their bodies remains on the sheet in the center of the frame, an emblem of the war's traumatic memory.

In *Kippur* Gitai argues that the trauma of the Yom Kippur War is one of abandonment. The soldiers who went to war in order to fulfill their national duty found a battlefield that did not resemble the image of past wars, leaving them in a fighting situation for which they had not been trained. This sense of abandonment is validated through a small personal story incorporated in the narrative, through a rhetorical form known as *mise-en-abyme:*[17] the doctor's memory of his childhood during the Nazi occupation of Belgium. He recalls how, before their deportation to the concentration camp, his parents gave him away to a Christian family that raised him as their son. After the war, he considered himself Belgian and at first refused to return to his Jewish family.

According to historian Anita Shapira, the specific situation created by the Yom Kippur War brought forth repressed Jewish memories and reawakened the repressed Holocaust narrative in Israeli consciousness. She writes:

[The Yom Kippur War] undermined the validity of certain axioms in the Israeli society. Pictures of Israeli defeat, soldiers in captivity, weakness, and anxiety were shown on national television and undermined the country's image of invincibility. The anxiety evoked by the war reawakened images of the Holocaust, which no longer belonged to the past, as part of a nation's history, but became an ongoing presence in Israel's collective memory. Israeli history was no longer solely a story of success, but also a story of failure and weakness. The collective memory now included the story of hardship and suffering, defeat and victimhood [which paved the way for] Holocaust survivors to become bearers of the national memory as well. The glorified Hebrew warrior of the ancient past made room for those who came to Israel by the skin of their teeth, encountered a hostile environment, and acquired their place in it by participating in the war and shedding their blood.[18]

Hence the narrative's *mise-en-abyme* allows Gitai to emphasize the survival issue in the Yom Kippur War, which was never openly discussed before because of the way Israeli wars were officially portrayed. It was only during the Yom Kippur War that Israelis began to fear for their very existence as Jews, just like Jews during the Holocaust. And they too were permanently traumatized. Thus the Holocaust intertext allows an additional interpretation of the disorientation that haunts the entire narrative: the distancing from the sense of national belonging and subsequently the expropriation of the private memory from it.

Beaufort: Claustrophobia or Back to the Ghetto

Just like *Kippur*, Joseph Cedar's *Beaufort* consciously undermines the realistic rendition of the battlefield by portraying a metonymic war zone.[19] Whereas Cedar's previous films (*Time of Favor*, 2000; and *Campfire*, 2004) dealt with the way the establishment of settlements in various sites of the West Bank sacralized these empty spaces, his latest film applies to a sacralized site in Israeli collective memory, one of the most symbolic sites of the First Lebanon War: the Beaufort fortress. In a similar way, it introduces the viewers to those Israelis whose voice has hardly been heard in Israeli society: low-rank soldiers who operate from within what may be the last melting pot in today's Israel society, the IDF.

Beaufort tells the story of Israel's last days on Lebanese soil through the eyes of the soldiers who are left to man the fortress and are waiting for the official evacuation order. As in *Kippur*, the soldiers are in a limbo, living in an indeterminate state. Prohibited from firing back, they must absorb enemy fire and casualties without retaliation. The film tells the story of the injury and death of four of them: Ziv, a sapper who arrives at the post to deactivate a large explosive charge, understands the futility of his dangerous mission but undertakes it nevertheless; Zitlawy, a bored soldier who entertains his comrades with pornographic tales over the wireless; Oshry, a veteran soldier who eagerly awaits his discharge so that he can join his beloved girlfriend in America; and Shpitzer, a talented musician who doubts his artistic ability.

Two contrasting characters are at the center of the story, Koris and Liraz. Koris, who toys with the idea of disobeying orders, is a combat medic from a well-off family. A dedicated soldier who risks his life to save his wounded comrades, he is also not ashamed to cry under pressure. Liraz, the post's commander, is an ambitious and controversial Mizrahi young man who becomes an officer, contrary to what is usually expected of men from his so-

Figure 8.1. The Israeli soldiers left to man the fort. Liraz (Oshri Cohen) and
Ziv (Ohad Knoller) in *Beaufort* (Joseph Cedar, 2007). Photograph by Karin Barr.
Courtesy of United King Films Ltd.

cioeconomic background. The film's narrative unfolds through his painful
disillusionment with the Beaufort myth, upon which he was raised, as well
as his bitter disappointment with the IDF's ability to provide some kind of
father figure for its soldiers.

Even though the film includes no combat scenes and Liraz is never called
to actual action, his dedication, his eagerness, and his resolve paint him as
an ideal officer. Yet his stay at the Beaufort undermines his firm beliefs in
the IDF and its mission. In one of the film's dramatic climaxes, he dares to
question his admired commander, Kimkhi, about his part in the mythological battle over the fortress. To his great surprise, he learns that they had no
clear military instructions to take the fortress and that Kimkhi himself did
not take part in the battle, since he was injured just before it began.

This revelation is followed by a scene set in the bunker's dark control
room, in which Liraz watches an interview with the father of Ziv, the sapper
who died in the film's opening scene. Symbolically, the interview is shown
on one half of the frame, while the other half is filled with official state
regalia—the Israeli flag and portraits of present-day policy makers, chief of
staff Shaul Mofaz and the prime minister Ehud Barak. While at first the tele-

vision screen seems to amplify the state's official voice, echoing the hegemonic voices of the pictured politicians on the right (the prime minister and
the chief of staff), the TV screen gradually fills the entire frame, as if the
speakers were addressing Liraz (as well as the viewers). The shot/reverse
shot editing technique of the scene, which includes cross gazes between the
bereaved father on the screen and Liraz watching him in the bunker, creates
the impression that the father's words about the hollowness of the heroic national narrative on which he educated his son are in fact addressed to Liraz.

> One can blame the army, the generals. But these generals are really not
> responsible for my son. They don't even know him. I'm responsible for him.
> He is my son. I brought him up. Apparently, I did a bad job. . . . Perhaps I
> didn't make him understand how precious his life is. That if something bad
> happens to them a whole world collapses. That's our duty as parents. I feel
> as if I've abandoned my child.

In these words, the father unequivocally declares the bankruptcy of
national values and the urgent need to abandon the collective spirit that
animated the Israeli culture for so long. In fact, he calls for a privatization of Israeli identity, far from the accepted national ethos and the human
sacrifices it requires. His speech suggests his wish to replace this ethos by
familial norms that characterized the Jewish family in the Diaspora, where
the father as head of the family would do everything to guard his family's
physical and spiritual well-being. When Ziv's father adopted the Zionist ideology with its inherent heroic death myth, he relinquished the primal Jewish instinct that allowed the survival of the Jewish people in the Diaspora.

Just as the diasporic Jew experienced the open space outside the ghetto
as unexpected and therefore dangerous, Ziv's father blames himself for forgetting this traditional Jewish behavior and sending his son to unknown
and dangerous territories, where war usually takes place. In fact, he admits
on television that the state cannot replace a father's care and guidance for
his son and implies that those who (like Liraz) believe that the IDF could
provide a father figure will eventually be disillusioned. Indeed, the following sequence depicts Liraz's assertive handling of the evacuation. "Leave it,"
Liraz says to a soldier who is trying in vain to remove a memorial plaque
to the casualties of the first battle over the Beaufort fortress that is hanging
on the wall. "They probably want to stay here," he adds with a mixture of
resignation and resolve.

The ghetto-like experience in the Beaufort enables Liraz to grasp the
empty rhetoric of war and patriotism. In the final sequence, when he returns
to Israel with his soldiers, Liraz finally cries over the loss of what has been

most precious to him: belief. In the commotion of rejoicing soldiers, when Koris cheerfully announces "I'm home" to his mother over his cell phone, Liraz continues to walk toward the camera. Falling on his knees, he bursts into tears, crying like a baby who has just been born into a meaningless world, the post-ideological era of the state of Israel.

The Return of Jewish Values?

Indeed, one of *Beaufort*'s subversive aspects is that it dares to replace some of the Zionist values with Jewish ones. The father's speech about his son's pointless death is just one of them. These themes appear throughout the narrative. They show up for the first time just after Ziv's death. Soldiers are shown praying before Shabbat in the dining room. These soldiers, who were not shown previously (in fact, the viewer gets the impression that the fortress is almost empty), give the impression that the walls of the fortress have fallen. When the Talmudic verse from the Shabbat service prayer—"last in creation, first in God's thought" (meaning: "First think, then act")—is heard offscreen, the camera turns to Liraz, who is standing quietly in the corner. The juxtaposition of these meaningful words with the man who sent Ziv on his deadly mission evokes a well-known Jewish concern: can a person waive responsibility for damage inflicted upon others by claiming it was not his or her fault? The question of responsibility is obviously more complicated in this case, since Ziv did not receive his order from Liraz but from an unspecified senior command. Yet Liraz realizes that as commander he is an accomplice to the death. Following the emotional shock from Ziv's death, the words of the prayer welcoming the Shabbat (Kabbalat Shabbat) seem to be the sanest ethical option. Sinking into his consciousness, these words become the first expression of his gradual distancing from blind obedience.

The second prayer is shown at the end of the film. While most of the secular soldiers are aimlessly sitting in the front of the frame, waiting for the evacuation order to come, the religious soldiers are shown in the background, wrapped in praying shawls and intensely praying. The dynamic, jump-cut editing, intended to accelerate the passage of time, can also be interpreted as an expression of the difference between two positions. For those who believe in mortals (the failed representatives of the state and the IDF), time has stopped, whereas for those who converse with God a possible future can still be envisaged. Both representations of Jewish religious practices are significant, because they draw attention to a Jewish alternative that has been discarded by Zionism. Like the doctor's story in *Kippur*, the presence of Jewish symbols in *Beaufort* offers an alternative for soldiers who feel that they are sacrificed by other men on the altar of empty ideology.

Only toward the end of the film, after experiencing these Jewish humanistic insights, can Liraz begin to prepare for the evacuation and the explosion of the fortress. The universal axiom that he now bears in his heart gives precedence to human life over political-national considerations. These insights, which radically change his attitude, turn him into the film's tragic hero. He finally understands that he must let go of a heroic myth in order to prevent death and that his duty obligates him to stand between the system's blindness and his soldiers' survival. The evacuation of the fort thus becomes a symbol for the breaking of the ideological chains with which the country shackled its sons, which led to their abandonment and exposed them to danger as it fenced them inside an ersatz Jewish ghetto on enemy soil.

A Journey into the Depths of the Traumatic Lacuna

Both *Beaufort* and *Kippur* were released after a few decades during which wars had been absent from Israeli cinema. In the interim, however, wars have dramatically changed from confrontational affairs involving two distinct armies to battles between more amorphous forces (as in the Gulf War and the Palestinian Intifadas).

This change in the nature of war brought about disillusionment with romantic nationalistic attitudes, doubts regarding concepts of heroism, and a rethinking of the reciprocal relations between the individual and the state. "Whereas in the past individuals interpret[ed] intense national events like wars by weaving them into the stories of their lives . . . [and] most [Israeli] soldiers [did] not represent the experience of war as a traumatic one, but rather as normal, natural, and expected aspects of their lives,"[20] the two films analyzed in this essay reveal a distancing from that national ethos and a privatization of war memories that opened the way to the appearance of individual trauma and legitimized its public discussion.

The normalization of war memories by Israeli soldiers is therefore destabilized here by the revision of historical processes, which implies that the course of history inevitably affects individuals in traumatic ways.[21] Psychiatrist Judith Lewis Herman defines the individual's experience of historical trauma as one that undermines a nation's distinction between interior and exterior and causes the collapse of time and the cancellation of the distinction between "here and now" and "there and then," which creates the traumatic lacuna. The historical trauma, according to her, represents the disaster of the helpless experienced in those moments when the social systems that provide individuals with a sense of control, context, and meaning collapse due to traumatic events.

It seems that both films reconstruct the lacuna in the heart of the nation through a subjective depiction of the space of trauma, seeking to depict that which cannot be represented. They do so through representations of radical spaces: disorientation in the case of *Kippur* and claustrophobia in the case of *Beaufort*. Their focus on the lives of a limited number of soldiers enables them to show the way in which canonical history is experienced through the eyes of individuals. Revealing the gap between historical narrative and individual experience, both films attempt to reconstruct the lacuna in which the trauma was created, as a tool intended to challenge the validity of history and to expropriate war from the hands of policy makers and historians.

Kippur and *Beaufort* express the painful disillusionment with the amnesias required for the building of nations.[22] As these amnesias disappear, the repressed narrative of the exilic Jew denied by Zionism reappears in both films through their experience of siege and abandonment. Hence the diasporic Jewish narrative hovers over the described traumas and as such offers a new political interpretation of the recent history of the state of Israel, an interpretation based upon the disillusionment with national myths and the privatization of war memories.

NOTES

1. Nurith Gertz, *Holocaust Survivors, Aliens, and Others in Israeli Cinema and Literature*, 16–41.

2. Miri Talmon, *Israeli Graffiti: Nostalgia, Groups and Collective Identity in Israeli Cinema*, 64.

3. Yael Munk, "Introduction," in "Borderline Cinema: Space and Identity in Israeli Cinema of the 1990s."

4. *Beaufort* is based on Ron Leshem's bestseller *If There Is a Heaven* (Tel Aviv: Zmora Bitan Publishers, 2005).

5. *Waltz with Bashir* (Ari Folman, 2008) presents a similar approach in a most interesting way: the animated documentary form. This impressive film, based on the filmmaker's memories as a soldier during the First Lebanon War, deserves a separate discussion, however.

6. This essay uses the notion of trauma in its psychiatric meaning: an emotionally, painful, distressful, or shocking experience, which often results in lasting mental and physical effects. According to Caruth ("Introduction," 4–5), "to be traumatized is precisely to be possessed by an image or an event. And thus, the traumatic symptom cannot be interpreted simply as a distortion of reality, nor as the lending of unconscious meaning to a reality it wishes to ignore, nor as the repression of what once was wished."

7. The Zionist ideological discourse marked the difference between the Jew in the Diaspora (referred to as the Old Jew) and the New Jew, the Sabra, living in the independent state of Israel.

8. The Al-Aqsa Intifada, also known as the Second Intifada, is the second Palestinian uprising, which began in September 2000 after Ariel Sharon's visit to the sacred mosque of the Temple Mount in Jerusalem. The visit triggered riots between the Israeli police and the Palestinian worshippers. Whereas Palestinians consider the Second Intifada to be a part of their ongoing struggle for the end of the Israeli occupation, Israelis consider it to be a wave of Palestinian terrorism preplanned by the late Palestinian leader Yasser Arafat. The Palestinian strategy included general strikes as well as armed attacks on Israeli civilians and security forces and suicide bombings. Israel reacted by creating checkpoints, demolishing suicide bombers' houses, and building the West Bank Wall.

9. As opposed to its Israeli reception, *Kippur* was extremely well received abroad, being given, among other awards, the Palme d'Or of the Cannes Film Festival.

10. Judd Ne'eman, "Camera Obscura of the Fallen: Military Pedagogy and Its Accessories in Israeli Cinema," 369.

11. The Syrian front is along the southern part of the strategic Golan Heights, which were heroically captured by the IDF during the Six Day War and became the site of fierce battles during the Yom Kippur War.

12. The first feature films made in the new state of Israel served to approve and reinforce the national ethos. For example, *They Were Ten* (Baruch Dienar, 1960) told the story of the hardships encountered by a group of Zionist settlers (nine men and a woman) who arrive in Palestine at the end of the nineteenth century in order to build their home. This national tendency did not last long. Already in the late sixties the influence of Western cinemas and ideologies on Israeli cinema was evident. The result, among other effects, was distancing from the national discourse. This discourse was to reappear in Israeli cinema after the 1977 political upset that brought the right-wing Likud party to power for the first time since the establishment of the state and subsequently encouraged many Israelis to look for the blind spots in national narratives such as the Palestinian narrative or the Holocaust survivors' story.

13. In her fascinating book *Recovered Roots: Collective Memory and the Making of Israeli National Tradition*, cultural historian Yael Zerubavel deals with the metamorphosis of the heroic narrative of the Masada myth and how it influenced the development of a new approach toward the Holocaust: "During the last two decades, another commemorative narrative of Massada has emerged in Israeli culture, offering a competing reading of Josephus's historical narrative. Whereas the activist commemorative narrative emphasized the contrast between Massada and the Holocaust, the new narrative highlights the analogy between the two events. The new commemorative narrative thus underscores the importance of the suicide as the tragic climax of an extreme state of besiegement and persecution. In this framework, the situation, not the act of suicide, is strongly condemned. The new commemorative narrative continues to define suicide as an act of defiance in a situation that leaves no other dignified alternative, but *it shifts the commemorative focus from armed resistance to the Romans to the situation of utter helplessness and despair, epitomized by the suicide*" (93; emphasis added). The very emphasis on helplessness and despair in the commemorative narrative seems to me the beginning of a new era in which the private sphere is finally allowed to exist.

14. Cited by Irma Klein in *Amos Gitai: Cinema, Politics, Aesthetics*, 336.

15. Judith Lewis Herman, *Trauma and Recovery*, 52.

16. "Weinraub" is not an arbitrary name. It was Gitai's name before he decided to adopt a Hebrew one. The use of the filmmaker's own name reinforces the biographical dimension of the film.

17. According to Lucien Dällenbach (*Le récit spéculaire: essai sur la mise en abyme*, 8), the *mise-en-abyme* is a technique by which the work (text) turns back to itself in a kind of reflection. Its essential property is that it brings out the meaning and form of the work (text).

18. Anita Shapira, "Historiography and Memory: The Case of 1948 Latrun," 26. Yael Zerubavel continues that line of thought and adds that "it was the major trauma of the 1973 Yom Kippur War that made Israelis more aware of their own vulnerability and more open to empathy with the Holocaust victims and survivors. The Lebanon War, the Intifada, and the tensions surrounding the future of the Palestinians, the West Bank, and the Gaza Strip continue to place matters of survival and death at the foreground of Israeli collective consciousness" (*Recovered Roots*, 192).

19. In the case of *Beaufort*, the symbolic part that the fortress played in the narrative of the First Lebanon War enables the filmmaker to depict the IDF occupation of this limited geographical space as representative of the entire IDF situation during this war.

20. Eyal Ben-Ari and Edna Lumsky-Feder, "Cultural Construction of War and the Military in Israel," 9–10.

21. Intellectual historian Dominique LaCapra argues that "there are reasons for the perception of history as traumatic, especially in postmodern culture and especially as a symptomatic response to excess and disorientation which may have to be undergone or even acted out. . . . The after effects—the possessive haunting ghosts—of traumatic events are not fully owned by anymore and in various ways affect everyone" (*Writing History, Writing Trauma*, x–xii).

22. Benedict Anderson, *Imagined Communities*, 240.

BIBLIOGRAPHY

Anderson, Benedict. 2006. *Imagined Communities*. London/New York: Verso.

Ben-Ari, Eyal, and Edna Lumsky-Feder. 1999. "Cultural Construction of War and the Military in Israel." In Ben-Ari and Lumsky-Feder (eds.), *The Military and Militarism in Israeli Society*, 1–35. Albany: SUNY Press.

Caruth, Cathy. 1995. "Introduction." In Cathy Caruth (ed.), *Trauma: Explorations in Memory*, 3–12. Baltimore: John Hopkins University Press.

Dällenbach, Lucien. 1977. Le récit spéculaire: essai sur la mise en abyme. Paris: Editions du Seuil.

Gertz, Nurith. 2004. *Holocaust Survivors, Aliens, and Others in Israeli Cinema and Literature (Makhela Akheret: Nitzolei Sho'ah, Zarim Va'akherim Bakolno'a Uvasifrut Hayisra'eli)*. Tel Aviv: Am Oved and Open University Publishers.

Herman, Judith Lewis. 1992. *Trauma and Recovery*. New York: Basic Books.

Klein, Irma. 2003. *Amos Gitai: Cinema, Politics, Aesthetics (Amos Gitai: Kolno'a, Politika, Esthetika)*. Tel Aviv: Hakibbutz Hameukhad Publishing House.

LaCapra, Dominick. 2001. *Writing History, Writing Trauma*. Baltimore: John Hopkins University Press.

Munk, Yael. 2005. "Borderline Cinema: Space and Identity in Israeli Cinema of the 1990s" ("Kolno'a Gvul: Zehut Umerkhav Bakolno'a Hayisra'eli Bishnot Hatish'im"). PhD dissertation. Tel Aviv University.

Ne'eman, Judd. 2005. "Camera Obscura of the Fallen: Military Pedagogy and Its Accessories in Israeli Cinema" ("Kamera Obscura Shel Hanoflim: Hapedagogia Hatzva'it Va'avizareha Bakolno'a Hayisra'eli"). In Udi Lebel (ed.), *Security and Communications: A Dynamic of Relations*, pp. 347–386. Beersheva: Ben Gurion University Press.

Shapira, Anita. 1994. "Historiography and Memory: The Case of 1948 Latrun" ("Historiografia Vezikaron: Mikreh Latrun Tashakh"). *Alpaim* 10: 9–41.

Talmon, Miri. 2001. *Israeli Graffiti: Nostalgia, Groups and Collective Identity in Israeli Cinema (Bluz Latzabar Ha'avud: Khavurot Venostalgia Bakolno'a Hayisra'eli)*. Haifa: Haifa University Press and Tel Aviv: Open University Press.

Zerubavel, Yael. 1995. *Recovered Roots: Collective Memory and the Making of Israeli National Tradition*. Chicago and London: University of Chicago Press.

FILMOGRAPHY

Beaufort. Joseph Cedar, 2007.

Burning Memory (Resisim). Yossi Somer, 1989.

Campfire (Medurat Hashevet). Joseph Cedar, 2004.

Earthquake (Re'idat Adamah). Ido Sela, 1997.

Every Bastard a King (Kol Mamzer Melekh). Uri Zohar, 1968.

He Walked through the Fields (Hu Halakh Basadot). Yosef Millo, 1967.

Kippur. Amos Gitai, 2000.

Shell Shock (Helem Krav). Yoel Sharon, 1988.

They Were Ten (Hem Hayu Asarah). Baruch Dienar, 1960.

Time of Favor (Hahesder). Joseph Cedar, 2000.

Waltz with Bashir (Vals Im Bashir). Ari Folman, 2008.

PART III

An Ethno-Cultural Kaleidoscope

9   Disjointed Narratives in Contemporary Israeli Films

NITZAN BEN SHAUL

Ethnicity has always posed a challenge to secular national culture. Therefore it usually has been articulated in cultural production in relation to the question of nationality, often in terms of the degree of incorporation of ethnicity into the national culture. Through the character of Michael Corleone (Al Pacino), an Italian American war hero who gradually becomes the head of the Corleone Mafia family and is married to an ethnically unidentified non–Italian American (Diane Keaton), Francis Ford Coppola's *The Godfather: Part II* (1974), for example, both opposes American Italian ethnicity to the American national ethos and allegorizes American politics through the Mafia. The way cultural products represent and negotiate this tension between ethnicity and national culture is an index of the stability of national culture and, by extension, the stability of the state. Hence *The Godfather: Part II* can also be seen as an index of the destabilization of American national culture and of the state apparatus as brought about by the Vietnam War and the Watergate affair.

The challenge posed by ethnicity to secular national culture has usually been contained within the particular frame of reference of the respective state despite the subnational or supranational nature of ethnicity. In the past two decades, however, due to processes of globalization, the challenge posed by ethnicity to the nation-state, particularly in peripheral states, transcends the confines of the state. This seems to be so because globalization adds pressures to deregulate the economy in the periphery, as led by the core elites, weakening the legitimacy and bargaining power of peripheral national governments. Thus it seems that ethnicity and religion, particularly in peripheral states, have become a more effective frame of reference for the individual than that offered by the nation-state. This process is supported by what may be called a core-elite generated "glocalization" (Robertson 1995) discourse whereby differing communities or lifestyles (particularly peripheral ones) are presented as different-yet-equal in relation to core-elite communities. This global-reaching multicultural "democratic" perception expedites the obscuring of the economic-political dependence of peripheral communities on the core elites by detaching culture from political economy. Hence peripheral ethnic groups are economically and politically neutralized in this discourse by their presumed equal and legitimate cultural variety. In other words, the glocal legitimating of peripheral communities allows them to express their culture so as to alleviate the denial of their economic-political interests (Ben-Shaul 2006b).

This essay focuses on the figuration of ethnicity in the highly acclaimed film *Khatuna Me'ukheret* (Late Marriage), released in 2001 and directed by Dover Koshashvili, an Israeli Jew of Georgian heritage. The film deals with the failed attempt of Zaza (played by Lior Ashkenazi), a thirty-one-year-old doctoral student of philosophy, to escape his Jewish Georgian ethnic origins and family. While his parents repeatedly attempt to find him a proper engagement with a young Georgian girl, Zaza reluctantly joins his parents in all these peculiarly funny tradition-laden visits to different candidates' families but conducts a secret passionate love affair with Yehudit (played by Ronit Elkabetz), a thirty-four-year-old Israeli divorcée of Jewish Moroccan heritage with a six-year-old daughter. When Zaza's father Yasha (played by Moni Moshonov) finds out about his son's love affair, he and a bunch of relatives break into the woman's apartment, where the loving couple is. They humiliate Zaza; his father picks up a sword hanging on the wall (left there by the woman's Moroccan ex-husband and symbolizing Moroccan tradition and male chauvinism) and threatens to decapitate the woman. The terrified woman, noticing her lover's passivity in the face of his relatives and realizing that he had spotted them coming and actually left the door open for them to come in, brokenheartedly asks him to leave. Now alone, Zaza reluctantly conforms to his family's traditional demand that he should marry a younger Georgian girl in a prearranged marriage. In the film's final wedding scene Zaza, standing half-drunk beside his young bride, picks up the microphone and invites his real love to come onstage. The suspense and embarrassment are relieved when one of the relatives urges the protagonist's mother to step forward to the stage. The film ends with Zaza joining his father in a traditional Georgian dance.

As the latest expression of ethnicity in the historical trajectory of Israeli cinematic representation of the subject and in relation to contemporary tensions between globalization and nation, *Khatuna Me'ukheret* is a fascinating index of the present decentered character of Israeli culture and of the related declining legitimacy of the Israeli dominant national culture. It indicates the wider process which is slowly eroding the power of peripheral nation-states in the age of globalizing capitalism. The film's immense popularity in Israel (as one of the most financially successful Israeli films ever made and winner of ten Israeli academy awards) and its unprecedented widespread screening and film festival successes abroad may be taken as further evidence for the reverberation of these trends among audiences.

A first indication of this glocal ethnic trend is that *Khatuna Me'ukheret*, unlike previous Israeli films, was mostly advertised abroad as a film about Georgian ethnicity made by an ethnic auteur. As Kevin Thomas of the *Los Angeles Times* wrote: "*Late Marriage* marks the arrival of a unique artist in world cinema" (May 22, 2002). Thus the film was circulated as part of a general tendency in popular culture toward what might be termed "world ethnicity" (replicating the trend of "world music"). Other examples are Mira Nair's *Monsoon Wedding* (2001), which is focused almost exclusively on Punjabi culture, and Joel Zwick's *My Big Fat Greek Wedding* (2002), where the ethnically undifferentiated American groom manages to marry his Greek American lover but instead of drawing her toward American secular culture is drawn together with her into Greek American culture. From a "world ethnicity" perspective, the film *Khatuna Me'ukheret* offers an apparently highly detailed and concrete ethnic hetero-cosmos that affirms the power of ethnic traditions, which are posited as the most relevant frame of reference for the individual.

Upon a closer look, however, this sense of ethnic concreteness is revealed to be a detached floating ethnicity, as evidenced in its use of universal tropes connoting ethnicity which transcend the specific ethnic community dealt with. Thus, as in all "world ethnicity" films, ethnicity is embellished aesthetically through the warm colors used for the interiors, the ethnically detailed decoration of the apartments, the casting of exaggerated, often caricatured ethnic representatives whose peculiarly funny body and facial features are enhanced (for example, the grotesque portrayal of Zaza's excessively fat mother, played by the director's own mother), and the recurring rendition of odd yet homologous ethno-general rituals, dances, customs, and superstitions.

Particularly funny in *Khatuna Me'ukheret* is a lengthy scene portraying the visit of Zaza, his parents, and various relatives to another family whose young daughter is offered as a potential bride. They all cram into a little

living room to discuss the issue, mostly focusing on the income and future earning prospects of Zaza and of the potential bride's family. Beyond
such homologous specificities are some tropes connoting ethnicity but un-
related to the specific ethnic group portrayed. For example, the sword in
Khatuna Me'ukheret, while symbolizing Moroccan ethnicity, looks more like
a samurai sword than an Arab sword. The ornaments in the apartment of
Zaza's rich and violent uncle include a golden Chinese statue of a tiger. In a
sense, the ambience in this apartment recalls cinematic ethnic figurations of
American Italian Mafia families, also recalled in the elegant and expensive
black suits that the Georgian men wear to the wedding ceremony. Viewed
within the context of globalization processes, *Khatuna Me'ukheret* attempts
to communicate a virtual ethnicity that bypasses its concrete national setting, signaling the slowly eroding power of peripheral nation-states in the
age of globalizing capitalism.

Within the trajectory of the Israeli cinematic presentation of ethnicity,
this film signals a further distancing of ethnicity from the dominant national culture, a process that began in the 1980s. Israeli films of the fifties promoted Jewish interethnic intermingling and erasure of the diasporic
ethnically differentiated East-West past of Jewish immigrants to Israel, as
in Leopold (Aryeh) Lahola's 1951 film *Ir Ha'ohalim* (Tent City). Films of the
sixties and seventies celebrated ethnic diversity while also promoting interethnic marriages among the younger generation, as in Menahem Golan's
1971 film *Katz VeKarasso* (Katz and Carraso). Films of the eighties (particularly after the 1977 political upset that brought the right-wing Likud party
to power, mostly due to the votes of low-income Jews of Eastern origin) reversed this nomenclature ideology and began to articulate the tragic failure
of interethnic commingling and the dead-end situation of interethnic tensions (as in the 1984 film *Kurdania,* by Dina Zvi-Riklis), signaling the deep
split in Israeli society at the time.

This reversal of the trend toward ethnic nomenclature in pre-1977 films
was intensified during the 1990s, when Israeli films began to offer authentic
self-representation of a variety of "others" (such as recent Russian immigrants, Holocaust survivors, and gays) whose voices had been mediated by
the dominant national discourse or silenced altogether in earlier cinematic
cultural production (Gertz 2001). This 1990s cinematic trend evidenced the
splintering of Israeli society into various power groups, as also indicated in
the composition of the Israeli parliament. Since then it has included a variety of ethnic parties (such as the mostly Jewish Moroccan Orthodox party
Shas and the Jewish Russian party Israel Beitenu) whose power and sectar-
ian politics have weakened any government's ability to rule effectively. This

splintering can be seen in 1990s films relating to ethnicity. For example, *Hakhaverim Shel Yana* (Yana's Friends, 1999), directed by Russian-born Arik Kaplun, deals with the 1990s Russian immigration to Israel during the first Gulf War. *Shkhur* (1994), directed by Shmuel Hasfari and scripted by Hannah Azoulai-Hasfari, an Israeli author of Moroccan Jewish heritage, exalts the return of a contemporary Israeli Moroccan woman to the mystical aspects inhering in Jewish Moroccan ethnicity in reaction to her forced secular "Israelization" during the 1950s.

Koshashvili's *Khatuna Me'ukheret* furthers this splintering trend in its representation of the ethnicity of Georgian Jews. It goes far beyond merely offering an authentic presentation of a previously unrepresented "other" Israeli ethnic group. What is peculiar to this film, signaling a break with films of the 1990s, is that it does not articulate ethnicity in relation to the Israeli dominant national culture. Hence while the 1990s films *Hakhaverim Shel Yana* and *Shkhur* authentically represent previously silenced ethnic voices, they also portray ethnically undifferentiated Israelis: through their interaction with the ethnic representatives the relation of ethnicity to nation is negotiated. *Hakhaverim Shel Yana* presents Eli, an Israeli of unmarked ethnicity, who falls in love with Yana, a Jewish Russian immigrant. Their love is consummated within the context of the first Gulf War, thus signaling a possible incorporation of Yana's marked ethnic difference into Israeli national culture through the major tenet of Israelis coming together in the face of their shared besiegement by a hostile world (Ben Shaul 2006a). In *Shkhur* Moroccan ethnicity and Israeliness are negotiated within the consciousness of the protagonist, Kheli Ben-Shoshan, suggesting that her alienated modern secular Israeliness and her repressed Moroccan heritage may coexist and even revitalize each other once the repressed ethnicity is reevaluated for what it offers in terms of warmth and communality.

Like previous Israeli films, these 1990s films ultimately strive to negotiate the relationship between "other" ethnicities and the national "self." Indeed, Nurith Gertz's study of otherness in films of the 1990s is properly articulated from the point of view of the national self in relation to which these others define themselves. *Khatuna Me'ukheret* and other contemporary Israeli films, however, contain no representation whatsoever of the national self. In *Khatuna Me'ukheret* most of the dialogue is spoken in Georgian; the bulk of the film is set in apartments that are ethnically Georgian (decorated down to the smallest detail and with no sense whatsoever of Israeli ambiance); the few exterior shots are in undifferentiated and explicitly alien (to the interiors) parking lots, empty sidewalks, and building staircases to which the characters are indifferent; and the only non-Georgian interiors (such as the Moroccan woman's apartment and the student's apartment) are decorated "internationally" (with an agglomeration of Western look-alike furniture, posters, and other items).

Hence "Israeliness" either is drained from this film altogether or, when represented (as in the few exterior shots), is vague and alien to the interiors and to the characters. Furthermore, the film makes clear that Zaza's Jewish Moroccan lover Yehudit is also haunted by her ethnic origin while willingly submitting to it, as evidenced in the omnipresent sword left by her Moroccan ex-husband and by her ethnic superstitions (as when she burns the underwear stained with her lover's semen while praying that his heart will burn with desire for her). While the film positions passionate love against ethnic secular universality, the notion of love is actually couched in terms of witchcraft (defined by the protagonist as the effect of one body over another without physical contact), resonating with her ethnic Moroccan heritage of superstition rather than secular rationality.

Moreover, the powerful and lengthy portrayal of carnal passion, unprecedented in Israeli cinema in its flowing, uninhibited, and natural handling of lovemaking, further signals the film's detachment from "Israeliness." Previous Israeli cinematic representations of sexual intercourse, characterized by avoidance, inhibition, or vulgarity, may be taken as an index of a tribal shame of exposure in public (the film's daring eroticism was criticized by many Israelis). If some Israeliness can be read into the image of Yehudit by negation, in that her divorce and rejection of her lover negate the pressures of ethnicity, her terrorized and forced isolation implies that this vague Israeliness is in a threatened situation.

Hence, unlike the other-self paradigm evident in films of the 1990s, *Khatuna Me'ukheret* signals a decentered Israeli culture, which contains only others without an overarching national self; or, alternately phrased, there are only ethnic selves. This decentered trend can also be seen in other recent films such as *Ushpizin* (The Guests; directed by Giddi Dar, 2004) and *Sof Ha'olam Smolah* (Turn Left at the End of the World; directed by Avi Nesher, 2004). *Ushpizin* is a parable dealing from an Orthodox Jewish religious point of view with a "born-again" Jew and his beloved wife, whose belief in God is tested by the deeds of two escaped convicts who know the man from his "secular" past. This secular past is abstract, universal, and symbolic, however, rather than concretely Israeli. *Sof Ha'olam Smolah* deals with the personal interrelations between Jewish immigrants from Morocco and India placed by the Israeli government in an isolated southern desert town during the sixties. It pictures them in total seclusion from Israeli society and revolves around their frustrated attempts to maintain French and British customs irrelevant to the desert surrounding them (such as the Indians' attempts to play cricket wearing white sweaters in the midst of the summer desert heat). Hence, rather than dealing with Israeli national culture, *Sof Ha'olam Smolah* deals with European cultural imperialism.

In sum, Israeli films of the past decade do not deal with the "Israelization" of ethnic immigrants, whether lauded or contested as in earlier Israeli films. Rather, these films are framed within the confines of a detached ethnicity, bypassing Israeli national culture and identity altogether.

BIBLIOGRAPHY

Ben-Shaul, Nitzan. 2006a. "Israeli Persecution Films." In *Traditions in World Cinema*, edited by Linda Badley, R. Barton Palmer, and Steven Jay Schneider, 160–176. Edinburgh: Edinburgh University Press.
———. 2006b. *A Violent World: TV News Images of Middle Eastern Terror and War.* Lanham, Md.: Rowman and Littlefield Publishers.
Gertz, Nurith. 2001. "Gender and Nationality in the New Israeli Cinema." *Assaph Kolnoa: Studies in Cinema and Television*, section D, no. 2: 227–246.
Robertson, Roland. 1995. "Glocalization: Time-Space and Homogeneity Heterogeneity." In *Global Modernities*, edited by Mike Featherstone, Scott Lash, and Roland Robertson, 25–44. London: Sage.

FILMOGRAPHY

The Godfather: Part II. Directed by Francis Ford Coppola, 1974.
Hakhaverim Shel Yana (Yana's Friends). Directed by Arik Kaplun, 1999.
Ir Ha'ohalim (Tent City). Directed by Leopold (Aryeh) Lahola, 1951.
Katz VeKarasso (Katz and Carasso). Directed by Menahem Golan, 1971.
Khatuna Me'ukheret (Late Marriage). Directed by Dover Koshashvili, 2001.
Kurdania. Directed by Dina Tzvi-Riklis, 1984.
Monsoon Wedding. Directed by Mira Nair, 2001.
My Big Fat Greek Wedding. Directed by Joel Zwick, 2002.
Shkhur. Directed by Shmuel Hasfari, 1994.
Sof Ha'olam Smolah (Turn Left at the End of the World). Directed by Avi Nesher, 2004.
Ushpizin (The Guests). Directed by Giddi Dar, 2004.

10 Trajectories of Mizrahi Cinema

YARON SHEMER

The popular Bourekas genre of the 1960s and 1970s, marked by its stereo-typical treatment of ethnicity, is often considered the harbinger of Mizrahi cinema—a corpus of films featuring the dilemmas of a subjugated Israeli collective whose origins are in the Arab/Muslim Middle East. Although recent Mizrahi films often steer away from the hitherto derisive representations of its Mizrahi characters, the discussion of Mizrahi films from the early 1990s to the present enables us to trace the genre's legacy and reveals the marks that the Bourekas has left on the narratives, characters, and discourses of contemporary Israeli films. My discussion of the Bourekas legacy is not meant to provide a comparative study of Mizrahi cinema then and now. Nor does it suggest that the Bourekas genre should be the yardstick by which all Mizrahi films should be measured and studied; clearly, some important Mizrahi films have no recourse to the Bourekas genre.[1] Rather, the analyses of *Turn Left at the End of the World* (*Sof Ha'olam Smolah*, 2004), *Lovesick on Nana Street* (*Khole Ahava Beshikkun Gimmel*, 1995), and *James' Journey to Jerusalem* (*Mas'ot James Be'eretz Hakodesh*, 2003) are designed to probe into the tensions between the reification of ethnic identities on the one hand and the playful postmodern rendering of indeterminate individual and group identities on the other.

Introduction: The Bourekas Legacy

The term "Bourekas" was coined in the mid-1970s as a derivative of the popular *bourekas* Middle Eastern pastry. Bourekas cinema, consisting primarily

of comedies or social (melo)dramas, generally foregrounds Mizrahi characters. These characters in most Bourekas films lack depth, complexity, and
agreeable traits. The Mizrahi is often portrayed as irrational, emotional,
oversexed, traditional, primitive, chauvinist, patriarchal, and manipulative.
The titular character in *Sallah* (*Sallah Shabbati*, Ephraim Kishon, 1964) is a
frenzied, lazy, primitive, rude, and sexist Mizrahi immigrant. He aspires to
leave his residence in the *ma'abara* (transient camp) for a permanent housing in the *shikkun* (a cheaply built and undistinguishable apartment complex), but he is unwilling to seek a job due to laziness or to let his son earn
an income due to his reluctance to violate the familial patriarchal structure.

Despite genre-related differences, both the musical *Kazablan* (Menahem
Golan, 1974) and *Sallah* resort to a similar cluster of stereotypes. Kaza, the
hero of the film's title, is traditional, brutish, physical, and emotive, like Sallah. He lives in the old city of Jaffa in a mixed neighborhood of immigrants
from various countries. Kaza leads a (quite benign) gang of young men; in
accordance with genre conventions, they sing and frolic but never seem to
work. Finally, Charlie of the comedy *Charlie and a Half* (*Charlie Vakhetzi*,
1974) is a petty criminal who lives in a slum. He is vulgar and manipulative
and does not hesitate to recruit a young neighborhood boy as his "appren-
tice." Interestingly, even the redeeming and charming characteristics of Sallah, Kaza, and Charlie—brevity, hospitality, warmth, and physical attrac-
tiveness—hark back to the stereotypical exotic markers of the "Oriental"
subject, as pointed out by Edward Said (1978) and his followers.

Paradoxically, reiteration of the Mizrahi predicament in the Bourekas
and its often carnivalesque play with ethnicity amount to an elision of the
ethnic *problem*.[2] The formulaic narrative of the Bourekas social comedy calls
for a happy ending not by offering the Mizrahi a cathartic new understanding but by demanding oblivion. Narratively, Sallah, Kaza, and Charlie might
have missed the train of modernism, but the younger generation is fully
ready to be co-opted into a putatively progressive Israeli society. Sallah's
son and daughter are marrying Ashkenazim and the baby Kaza was born
to an Ashkenazi father and a Mizrahi mother, so the world of enlightenment is awaiting these "Ashkenized" younger people. The films' seemingly
benign discourse clearly suggests that the social, economic, and political
power disparity is not structural and is thereby bound to disappear in the
next generation. The Bourekas narrative in which Mizrahi children—native
Israelis who are cultured, educated, and fluent in Hebrew—are often pitted
against their parents (primitive, illiterate, and diasporic) further defuses the
contentious problem of the ethnic dilemma by turning it into a generation-
gap issue.

As suggested by Rami Kimchi (2008: 269–270), contemporary films that employ the generic conventions of the Bourekas may be categorized as neo- or post-Bourekas. Accordingly, I consider neo-Bourekas those films that reiterate the narrational and discursive paradigms of their sixties and seventies predecessors, resorting to stereotypical representations of the Mizrahi community and pitting Mizrahim against Ashkenazim only to offer a denouement where the ethnic schism is deemed a matter of the past. The term "post-Bourekas," rather than connoting a continuation of the genre both chronologically and discursively, attests to a break from the genre on which it is predicated and, indeed, uses the genre against itself. Consequently, post-Bourekas shares with most other "posts" a playful rendering of conjectural and fluid identities in lieu of the construction of essentialist selves.

My discussion of the Bourekas in this analysis provides me with a hermeneutic analytical framework. To wit, I am sidestepping the question of whether we ought to censure contemporary filmmakers for reinscribing ethnic stereotypes in neo-Bourekas or, conversely, commend them for the liberty they take in revisiting trite stereotypes and charging them with new, even subversive values in post-Bourekas. Instead my focus is on the problematics of "identity politics" in contemporary ethnic cinema.

Turn Left at the End of the World (Sof Ha'olam Smolah, Avi Nesher, 2004)

Set in 1968 in an unidentified development town on the edge of the Negev desert, the film features two "clans"—Moroccan and Indian. The Moroccans, who were settled in that place by the government ten years earlier, are dismayed to realize that the "primitive blackies" who have just arrived in Israel are going to live in the *shikkun* across from them. For their part, the members of the Indian family, in particular the mother, are just as derisive of the others' lack of basic mores. Considering the generic paradigm of the Bourekas the film has a twist: the clash of cultures is not so much between Mizrahim and Ashkenazim but within two incompatible Mizrahi clans. Early in the film the two adolescents—Nicole of the Moroccan family and Sara of the Indian one—become best friends, signaling the thawing of the fractious relations between the families. In a scene that marks the apex of this comity between the two clans, the Moroccan family, which thus far has disparaged the Indians' obsession with cricket, joins them in a historic match against a British team that deigned to play in the Israeli desert. Yet, when the British unmercifully beat the local team, leading 68 to 0, havoc ensues as the Moroccans take out their frustration and anger on all the "foreigners"—Indian immigrants and British players. The preparation for the game and its aftermath coincide with three personal stories of separation

Figure 10.1. Sara (Liraz Charchi, left) and Nicole (Netta Garty, right) in *Turn Left at the End of the World* (Avi Nesher, 2004). Courtesy of Artomas Communications, Metro Communications, and United King Film.

and grief. Nicole, who had sexual relations with her Tel Aviv teacher, is now disenchanted by this first lover; the Indian father, Roger, terminates his affair with Simone, a titillating Moroccan widow (who also coaches Nicole on matters of love); and Nicole's mother, Jeannette, is diagnosed with incurable leukemia.

Turn Left situates Tel Aviv as a topos, in Said's term.[3] In an interview Nesher called it "a state of mind."[4] Mentions of the big city as the indexical opposite of the local town are strewn throughout the film—the handsome, energetic Ashkenazi teacher who comes from Tel Aviv to teach for one year, magazines that feature the luminous media stars from the big city, and Nicole's impatience to leave for Tel Aviv as soon as she is done with school. Draft calls to the Israeli military that Sara and Nicole receive in the mail render another promise of life outside the stifling town; they both cherish the reward that mandatory military service has to offer them—life away from their town. *Turn Left* and some other contemporary films which focus on the Mizrahi community, including *Bonjour, Monsieur Shlomi* (*Hakokhavim Shel Shlomi*, Shemi Zarhin, 2003), *Shkhur* (Shmuel Hasfari and Hannah Azoulai-Hasfari, 1994), and *Shuli's Fiancé* (*Habakhur Shel Shuli*, Doron Tzabari, 1997), situate their stories of departure from home exactly at the film's dramatic juncture. The Mizrahi characters' move to the center(s) leads to a breach between life in the periphery (shown throughout the films) and the unknown life at the unknown center (rarely present in the films' diegesis).

Yet *Turn Left* renders unique relations between the town's locality and its topos. The elision of the place's name casts this town as indistinguishable from other towns on Israel's geographical and socioeconomic periphery and indeed renders it a "nonplace." When Nicole's mother returns from her medical diagnosis in Tel Aviv, a road sign at the entrance to the town indicates the distance to Tel Aviv. At the end of the film, another road sign shows the distance to the southern city of Eilat and then, within the same shot, the same Tel Aviv road sign seen earlier. The town therefore is defined by its distance from other localities, while the place itself is obscured (not having a name) but also forsaken. When local employees go on strike in protest against their working conditions and low pay in the town's bottle plant—this community's sole major livelihood—the plant manager and government officials do not even deign to meet with the strikers.

The "nonplace" status of the town is paradoxically inscribed precisely by the film's exclusive focus on this one location secluded from the rest of the country. Early in the film Nicole notices that Sara is taking notes in her diary of what she is experiencing in the place her family just moved into. Nicole tells her dismissively in this first exchange between them: "Here you'll have only blank pages. Nothing happens here." In panoramic shots of the landscape, the desert stretches as far the camera's eye can reach. The excessive use of warm colors and the anachronistic contemporary Israeli music played at the end of the film underscore this town's lacuna and thus defy the film's sense of a real place. Instead of the emplacement of the community, the film offers its displacement, its "nonplacement." Significantly, the absence of the town as an actual locality signifies the otherwise abstract topos as real.

The film's chronology is sometimes rendered through references to world events. Ultimately the "nonplace" that the film intimates corresponds to the "nontime" as a characteristic of the town. The death of the mother in the film's penultimate scene alludes precisely to a time warp; at the moment when she slips into death the radio is announcing the historic moment of landing on the moon. As Nesher suggests in his commentary on the DVD version, this scene is meant to mark the end of an era and the commencement of a new stage in human history. One of the film's first scenes mentions the 1968 student riots in Paris, and it concludes with another historic event. Thus it renders the town and its inhabitants as a community sealed off in time and space—a "slipchronotope" between spatial and temporal markers which point outward.

Clearly, the film's treatment of time and place is reminiscent of the ahis-torical treatment of the Mizrahi in the Bourekas, and its comedic and ste-reotypical rendering of the Mizrahi invites us to think about Nesher's film as neo-Bourekas. And yet, in place of the common cinematic ethno-sexual economy of the Bourekas, *Turn Left* proffers a new order implicated by sepa-ration. In addition to the return of the (Ashkenazi) teacher to Tel Aviv and the return of Roger to his loving wife, the ethnic/cultural disengagement in the film reaches its climactic point at the end: Sara leaves town to join the Israeli army, whereas Nicole is bound to stay home and take care of the family due to her mother's death. The bond between the two triggered some cultural exchanges involving other characters; the separation between them is the final seal of segregation. The possibility (fantasy?) of ethnic and cul-tural exchange "at the end of the world" slips off, leaving only the insular self. The song at the film's end reinforces this interpretation; the refrain "you will not be able to run away from yourself" is played against the image of Nicole entrapped between the two road signs, far from both Eilat and Tel Aviv.

Notwithstanding the sweeping, nearly unprecedented success that *Turn Left at the End of the World* enjoyed at the box office, it was critiqued for its escapist treatment of real social and ethnic problems and its affinity with the Bourekas films and its reinscription of the demeaning depiction of the Mizrahi.[5] Arguably, however, this film offers also a somewhat progressive notion of ethnic identities; instead of the pejorative "melting pot," the film recognizes the incommensurability of ethnic identities and thus can even open a discursive space for identity politics. Furthermore, the film chal-lenges the construction of an all-encompassing Mizrahi identity and thereby intimates the notion of intragroup differences.

Whereas Nesher's neo-Bourekas film maintains the Bourekas paradigm but without making direct references to the genre, post-Bourekas films lay the generic conventions bare, but only to turn the paradigm on its head. These films share elements of citationality with other "posts": "origin" is nothing but a springboard to a playful and performative (nonessentialist) take on identities.[6]

James' Journey to Jerusalem (Mas'ot James Be'eretz Hakodesh,
Ra'anan Alexandrowicz, 2003)

In *James' Journey* Israeli society and, more specifically, the film's Mizrahi characters are revealed through the eyes of James, a devout young Christian whose African community sends him on a pilgrimage mission to the Holy Land. Upon his arrival at the airport, he is mistaken for an illegal migrant laborer seeking employment in Israel and is hauled off to jail. In a shady deal between the jailer and Shimi, a Mizrahi businessman (played by the Palestinian actor Salim Dau) who hires out illegal foreign workers, James is bailed out. But he is now at the mercy of Shimi, who keeps his passport away. Therefore James has no choice but to join the herd of other laborers exploited by Shimi. One day James is sent to work at the house of Shimi's father (whose name is Sallah). The two form such a close friendship that, to Shimi's chagrin, he finds it difficult to separate the two men and reassigns James to other jobs. Sallah teaches James all the ins and outs of the Israeli version of "how to beat the system." James, now more sober and pragmatic, successfully applies the lessons that Sallah has taught him and turns out to be a successful and manipulative subcontractor who hires out his fellow illegal migrants.

James' Journey is replete with references to the Bourekas exemplar *Sallah*. Like the titular character of the earlier film, Sallah of *James's Journey* is a scheming, dishonest, dependent, and lazy Mizrahi. For both Sallahs, their love of backgammon has its financial incentives and rewards; they beat and bankrupt their fellow players (often neighbors and friends). Interestingly, whereas the "old" Sallah simply relies on his good luck to win the game, the contemporary Sallah has to rely on the (black?) magic throw of James to bring him the best possible dice combination time and again.

It is blatantly obvious that the film is not meant to comply with the generic codes of the Bourekas, however, but to use the genre against itself in jiu-jitsu fashion. The film can be read as an ironic and critical fable on Zionism from the standpoint of a contemporary Sallah. As filmmaker Alexandrowicz put it, his Sallah becomes the lone figure who can point to Israel's social maladies, and the film critically revisits these ailments—substandard work ethics, the exploitation of laborers, and widespread racism.[7] Alexandrowicz conceives of this filmic play with the Bourekas ethnic characterizations as an artistic liberty that the passing of time affords him. In this filmic fable, Alexandrowicz is not interested in the issue of empowered versus subaltern groups; instead his film is a mockery of Zionism as a whole. Returning to our main inquiry here, we may wonder what to make of that filmic "freedom" where what initially and primarily seems to be a commentary on ethnicity becomes secondary to a performative play. Specifically, does the playful (re)enactment of stereotypical representations attest to acquiescence or subversion? Is the citationality of the Bourekas paradigm in the post-Bourekas films *James' Journey* and *Lovesick* meant to propose the dissolution of ethnic identities or, conversely, to reinscribe them in what amounts to the demarcation of ethnic identities and the reiteration of identity politics?

Lovesick on Nana Street (*Khole Ahava Beshikkun Gimmel*, Savi
Gavison, 1995)

Set in the small town of Kiryat Yam, Gavison's' *Lovesick* features the bach-
elor Victor, who is a mix of the slacker, the village fool, and a Mizrahi nebbish. But Victor also single-handedly runs a popular pirate cable TV station
from the apartment he shares with his mother. On his station Victor plays
mostly tearjerker Middle Eastern melodramas and pornographic films. He
rents them from a local video store and reads the films' synopses off the
video covers to his viewers.

Lovesick opens with a prolonged ribald story in which Victor uses graphic
language to tell his audience of two elderly men about a fantastic/fantas-
matic sexual experience he had. This scene before the credits concludes
when one of the old men has a fatal heart failure just as Victor is fully im-
mersed in his depiction of the woman's orgasm. This scene sets the pattern
for the rest of the film—performativity and fantasy are disrupted by the
intrusion of "reality." Performativity and desire are predicated on a circular
and nonconsummated movement (like Victor's climax that is missing in his
invented tale of sexual experience), so fantasy is destined to crop up time
and again.

Although Kiryat Yam is located on the outskirts of the city of Haifa (the
"center" of Israel's northern region), it is depicted as one of Israel's derelict
and nondescript towns populated mostly by Mizrahim. The film's iconog
raphy immediately marks Victor's neighborhood as a part of the periphery—the charmless gray housing projects, the rows of apartments dotted
with small windows, the laundry drying in public areas between apartment
blocks, and the place's often shabby inhabitants. Similarly, the inclusion of
the word *shikkun* in the film's Hebrew title conjures up "second Israel"—
poverty, unemployment, and crime.

Victor's seemingly uneventful life is about to change when the dainty
Ashkenazi actress Michaella moves from Tel Aviv to Kiryat Yam. Constructed within the parameters of the Mizrahi/Ashkenazi sexual economy of
the Bourekas—the romance between the affluent, cold, sophisticated Ashkenazi and the poor, warm, gregarious, and simple-minded Mizrahi—the
film ought to place the relationship between this newcomer and Victor at
center stage. Victor believes that he and Michaella are destined for each
other; even when he realizes that Michaella lives with her boyfriend Gadi (a
drama teacher at the local youth community center with whom she moved
to town), he is convinced that she desires him and that only the boyfriend
keeps her from falling into his arms.

The first encounter between the dark, hirsute Victor and the blonde, light-skinned Michaella early in the film establishes the center/periphery thematic dyad. Looking at Michaella, Victor guesses that she is from Tel Aviv. When she confirms this, Victor boasts of his acquaintance with that city—"oh, I have been there" (read, "oh, I have heard about it"). This first meeting also contrasts Victor's "local time" with Michaella's "Tel Aviv time."[8] The sophisticated, urban Michaella is always conscious of time—she is on the move and often in a hurry. Conversely, time is both expansive and dispensable for Victor; he expatiates on his (imagined) sexual experiences; plays a pornographic film at the wrong time slot, when children still watch television; and (even before his hospitalization in a psychiatric hospital in the film's second part) spends an immeasurable amount of time waiting for Michaella to join him. Along the lines of the dichotomous representation of the Mizrahi/Ashkenazi dyad in the Bourekas, whereas Victor and the asylum inmates traverse the lines between public and private spaces, the conduct of Michaella and her boyfriend and specifically their treatment of Victor's courting clearly eschew such behavior. Victor's body language, his uncalled-for verbal intimacy, and intrusion into the lives of others are constantly contrasted in this film with Michaella and Gadi's reserved behavior and their acknowledgment of boundaries.

But the seemingly romantic comedy of the Bourekas that characterizes the film's first part is aborted as Michaella becomes more assertive in her rejections of Victor's incessant courting. His obsession with Michaella eventually lands him in an asylum adjacent to his neighborhood, a narrational breaking point after which the film switches gear and mood—it becomes a slow-paced moving drama about people trapped in their fictive worlds. Sympathetic to Victor's heart-breaking love story, the asylum inmates warmly welcome him.

Lovesick's flirtation with the Bourekas genre attests to its postmodernist stand, which favors citationality and indeterminacy over ontological or essentialist positions. As indicated above, the film utilizes the sexual economy of the Bourekas, but the allusions to this genre come with a twist. For example, this film does not offer the comforting conclusion of the Bourekas comedies, where the young people's ethnic disparities evolve into love affairs that are consummated in interethnic marriages. The screening of the emotionally charged Middle Eastern films on Victor's station is another allusion to the Bourekas. The melodramatic narratives involving unrelenting love and the suffering lover (characteristic of both the Bourekas and the films aired) gradually implicate Victor's own story. Indeed, *Lovesick*'s characters are part of the postmodern game of indeterminacy; they are echoed and mirrored in others, thus creating fluid, porous, and indistinct identities. Similarly, soon after Victor is sequestered in the asylum, he makes love with his fellow inmate Levana. Not surprisingly, Victor fantasizes that he is making love to Michaella, not Levana, and in turn Levana assures him of this imaginary transformation.

In addition to the quotational feature of the film and its provision of conjectural selves, the frequent employment of media—videos, cable station, television, and the video rental store—further propels us to identify the diegetic space created in *Lovesick* as a contingent, virtual space and to place the film in the postmodern sphere. In the articulation of what W. Edward Soja (1996) calls Thirdspace, the realms that the media create and employ are the loci where subjectivity and objectivity, the abstract and the concrete, structure and agency intersect and therefore, I would add, are implicated by duplicity and reflexivity. When Victor decides to air on his cable station a desperate love message for Michaella from the asylum in which he is staying, the whole place turns into a (sound) stage—its inhabitants and objects are positioned strategically to achieve an increased effect for the film *Lovesick* itself and for the aired love message. Likewise, the real-life filmmaker Dan Wolman is cast in *Lovesick* as a filmmaker inmate who deems Victor's tragedy most suitable to be made into a film "because it is a story that contains both love and drama."

According to Homi Bhabha, one of the modalities of cultural translation taking place in Third Space is as "a way of imitating, but in a mischievous, displacing sense—imitating an original in such a way that a priority of the original is not reinforced but by the very fact it *can* be simulated, copied, transferred, transformed, made into a simulacrum" (Bhabha 1990: 210; original emphasis).[9] The diegetic space of *Lovesick* is a playing field where events/scenes are replicated and reproduced time and time again during the course of the film. The town's residents, who in the first part are mostly inhospitable to Victor, metamorphose into a sympathetic crowd debating Victor's predicament empathically and in public. This crowd scene of the people engaged with Victor's "real-life" melodrama is visually refashioned after a previous scene in which these people gather down the street to listen to the sounds of a woman panting while having sex in one of the apartments above. An intertextual analysis of *Lovesick* enables us to take this chain of allusions and cinematic referentiality even further. In the former street scene where the crowd follows the shadow image of the panting woman as it moves from one window to another, the mise-en-scène and lighting conjure up the crowd scene in Vittorio De Sica's *Miracle in Milan* (1951), where the people, cold and shriveled, try to warm themselves by following a ray of sun as it is cracking through the clouds.

The Material Marks in the Performance of Identity

As an alternative to essentialist articulations of identities, postmodern thought embraces indeterminacy. "Performativity" is meant to smack of light air and insubstantiality and "Thirdspace" to effuse fluidity, liminality, and porosity. Yet, arguably, the characters that Thirdspace envelops neither are ephemeral themselves nor operate in a power-free realm. Hamid Naficy (2001: 286) turns to the problematics of performance of identity as free play by pointing to the sediments that it leaves behind. Intersecting and evolving identities are fashioned within regimes of power—"coercion, sanction, or reward"—and they leave their marks "at individual, group, or national levels that cannot with impunity be erased, ignored, discarded, or replaced with new ones—as some proponents of postmodern fluidity seem to suggest" (ibid.). Guided by this argument and qualms expressed by Ella Shohat (2004) about the celebratory postmodern discourse about ephemeral and hybrid selves, I seek to identify the "material" staples generating and generated by Thirdspace. Ultimately, it becomes blatantly clear that, instead of eliding or reducing entrenched identities by marking them merely as free-floating signifiers, the films discussed here often propose difference in order to draw boundaries and reaffirm incommensurable cultural and ethnic identities.

The cinematic construction of the asylum as a fluid and liminal Thirdspace in *Lovesick* is undermined in the film's conclusion; there the asylum resonates as a Foucauldian regime of power sanctioning and disciplining its subjects. The last scene reinscribes identities and affiliations along ethnic lines. Upon Victor's arrival at the asylum, borders are traversed (literally, when women inmates join Victor in the shower) and identities are confused (for example, Levana, who substitutes for Michaella), but at the end spatial boundaries are drawn again. Victor cancels his trip to Tel Aviv to see Michaella, who has moved back to that city with her boyfriend. He returns to the asylum, but this time he desires Levana for herself. Indeed, unlike the Bourekas sexual economy, *Lovesick* and *Turn Left* render an even more restrictive order by which the marginalized Mizrahi and the dominating, often Ashkenazi members of Israeli society are destined to inhabit two distinct and separate societal and geographic spaces. The former (Victor and Levana) may love and live only with members of their own ethnic group (but only in an asylum?). The others, who cannot acclimate to life in the periphery, inevitably move back to the center, free of the nuisances or interferences of the overbearing periphery and its inhabitants. *Lovesick on Nana Street*, like *Turn Left at the End of the World*, points to the collapse of the "melting pot" discourse and offers instead a depiction of a society marred by ethnic divisions.

In the final analysis, the "performance of identity" with its overemphasis on ethnicity in a playful manner is intimately connected to what is seemingly an opposite phenomenon in Israeli cinema—the structuring absence of the Mizrahi and elision of Mizrahi markers even when they are expected to be present (as rendered, for example, in Shemi Zarhin's *Passover Fever* [*Leilasede*, 1995]). In both cases, the attempt to steer away from essentialist treatment of Israeli identities ends up with a postmodern take on the artificiality and constructivist nature of collective identities, thus sidestepping issues of power disparity and the questionable advantage for the subalterns to participate in the postmodern play. Yet not only *Turn Left*, which resorts unabashedly to facile ethnic characterizations, but also the post-Bourekas/postmodernist films ultimately reiterate ethnic identities rather than deeming them a thing of the past. By embracing identity politics and the power struggle it involves, the Mizrahi films discussed here expose the societal seams which the discourse on hybridity and multiculturalism often obfuscates.

NOTES

1. Most noticeably, Mizrahi protest films, such as David Benchetrit's documentary *Ancient Winds: Moroccan Chronicle* (*Ru'akh Kadim: Kronika Maroka'it*, 2002) and Eli Hamo and Sami Shalom Chetrit's documentary *The Black Panthers [in Israel] Speak* (*Hapanterim Hashkhorim Medabrim*, 2003) are in no way informed by the Bourekas genre.

2. See Shohat (1989) for an elaborate discussion of Bourekas.

3. In *Orientalism* (1978: 177), Said distinguishes between the "geographical" and the discursive Orient: "In the system of knowledge about the Orient, the Orient is less a place than a *topos*, a set of references, a congeries of characteristics, that seems to have its origin in a quotation, or a fragment of a text, or a citation from someone's work on the Orient, or some bit of previous imagining, or an amalgam of all of these." Likewise, I employ "topos" as the referential and ideological construct for Tel Aviv as the Israeli center, which is mostly independent of the location of the place in strictly geographical terms.

4. Author's interview with Avi Nesher, June 30, 2004.

5. See Schnitzer (2004), Klein (2004), Mizrahi (2004), and Shuv (2004).

6. As in the work of Judith Butler (1993), "performativity" purports to destabilize conceptualization of "origin," "self," and "identity." Consequently, individual and

group identities ought to be articulated based not on what they supposedly *are* but on what they *do* (i.e., their enactments).

7. Author's interview with Ra³anan Alexandrowicz, June 8, 2005.

8. See Ne³eman (1998) for a discussion of "Mizrahi time" in the Bourekas cinema.

9. Bhabha (1990) employs "Third Space" rather than "Thirdspace."

BIBLIOGRAPHY

Bhabha, Homi. 1990. "The Third Space: Interview with Jonathan Rutherford." In *Identity, Community, Culture, Difference*, ed. Jonathan Rutherford, 207–221. London: Lawrence and Wishart.

Butler, Judith. 1993. *Bodies That Matter: On the Discursive Limits of "Sex."* New York: Routledge.

Kimchi, Rami. 2008. "A Shtetl in Disguise: Israeli Films and Their Origins in Classical Yiddish Literature." PhD dissertation. University of Michigan, Ann Arbor.

Klein, Uri. 2004. "Sand and Sand Only" ("Rak Khol Vakhol"). *Ha³aretz*, June 25, 2004, p. 23.

Mizrahi, Iris. 2004. *"Campfire/Ushpizin/Turn Left at the End of the World"* (*"Medurat Hashevet/Ushpizin/Sof Ha³olam Smolah"*). *Kedma Portal*, October 22, http://www.kedma.co.il/index.php?id=408&t=pages.

Naficy, Hamid. 2001. *An Accented Cinema: Exilic and Diasporic Filmmaking.* Princeton: Princeton University Press.

Ne³eman, Yehuda (Judd). 1998. "The Cup of Coffee and the Glass of Tea: The Bourekas Films and Social Realism" ("Sefel Hakafeh Vekos Hateh"). In *Social Realism in the '50s; Political Culture in the '90s*, ed. Gila Ballas, 41–47. Haifa: Haifa Museum of Art.

Said, Edward. 1978. *Orientalism.* New York: Vintage Books.

Schnitzer, Meir. 2004. "There Were Times in the Middle East" ("Hayu Zmanim Bamizrakh Hatikhon"). *Ma³ariv*, June 25, p. 10.

Shohat, Ella. 1989. *Israeli Cinema: East/West and the Politics of Representation.* Austin: University of Texas Press.

———. 2004. "The 'Postcolonial' in Translation: Reading Said in Hebrew." *Journal of Palestine Studies* 33:3 (Spring): 55–75.

Shuv, Ya³el. 2004. "There Were Times in the South" ("Hayu Zmanim Badarom"). *Tel Aviv Time Out*, June 24, p. 58.

Soja, W. Edward. 1996. *Thirdspace: Journeys to Los Angeles and Other Real-and-Imagined Places.* New York: Blackwell.

FILMOGRAPHY

Ancient Winds: Moroccan Chronicle (*Ru³akh Kadim: Kronika Maroka³it*, 2002). Dir. David Benchetrit.

The Black Panthers [in Israel] Speak (*Hapanterim Hashkhorim Medabrim*, 2003). Dir. Eli Hamo and Sami Shalom Chetrit.

Bonjour, Monsieur Shlomi (*Hakokhavim Shel Shlomi*, 2003). Dir. Shemi Zarhin.

Charlie and a Half (*Charlie Vakhetzi*, 1974). Dir. Boaz Davidson.

James' Journey to Jerusalem (*Mas³ot James Be³eretz Hakodesh*, 2003). Dir. Ra³anan Alexandrowicz.

Kazablan (1974). Dir. Menahem Golan.

Lovesick on Nana Street (*Khole Ahava Beshikkun Gimmel*, 1995). Dir. Savi Gavison.

Passover Fever (*Leilasede*, 1995). Dir. Shemi Zarhin.

Sallah (*Sallah Shabbati*, 1964). Dir. Ephraim Kishon.

Shkhur (1994; a film by Hannah Azoulai-Hasfari). Dir. Shmuel Hasfari.

Shuli's Fiancé (*Habakhur Shel Shuli*, 1997). Dir. Doron Tzabari.

Turn Left at the End of the World (*Sof Ha'olam Smolah*, 2004). Dir. Avi Nesher.

11 Immigrant Cinema

Russian Israelis on Screens and behind the Cameras

OLGA GERSHENSON

In 2005 the new reality show *Israeli Project Greenlight* premiered on local cable. As in the original American show, the prize was half a million dollars and a chance to make a first film. The competition attracted hundreds of aspiring filmmakers. Against all odds, a twenty-three-year-old Russian immigrant from the Israeli periphery, Felix Gerchikov, won. He went on to make *The Children of USSR*, which took the first prize in the drama category at the 2005 Jerusalem Film Festival. This is a story of the "Israeli dream" come true. But it is also a sign of changes in Israeli culture.

Since *The Children of USSR* was produced as part of *Israeli Project Greenlight*, every step of its production was documented and televised. This footage revealed the immigrant filmmaker and cast, speaking Russian and variously accented Hebrew on and off the screen. The film itself was populated by immigrant characters struggling with drugs, gangs, and drabness of life in the Israeli backwater. If the film placed these normally marginalized characters at the core of the plot, the reality show brought their equally marginalized creators not only into the cultural mainstream but also into the audience's living rooms. This was not just a new reality show but a new reality.

Mass migration from the former Soviet Union brought about 1 million people to Israel, which means that today every sixth Israeli is a Russian speaker. Such a population influx, and its arguably destabilizing influence on the Israeli culture, became a media sensation. Newspapers and television news were full of reports of "Russian prostitutes" and "Russian mafia." Immigrants who took an enormous step down in their social status were portrayed as either parasites of the Israeli welfare system or shrewd invaders taking over the Israeli job market. Soon characters representing the new immigrants started popping up on screens too—a new "cultural other" was added to the Israeli cinematic repertory, joining women, Holocaust survivors, Mizrahim, and Palestinians. At the same time, a handful of immigrant filmmakers slowly started breaking into the Israeli film industry. These filmmakers not only increased the visibility of their community but also introduced the immigrants' point of view to the Israeli cinema.

In this essay I survey the representation of Russian immigrants both in Israeli films and in the emerging field of Russian Israeli filmmaking. This survey continues the research on the representation of cultural others in Israeli film (pioneered by Ella Shohat and continued by Yosefa Loshitzky and Nurith Gertz), which so far has focused mainly on Mizrahim and Palestinians.[1]

Figure 11.1.
DVD cover of *The Children of USSR* (Felix Gerchikov, 2005). Slava (Daniel Brook) is in the foreground. Courtesy of NMC United Entertainment.

History Lessons

Historically, Russian characters have not always been the "other" in Israeli films. Their representation, including their gender, nationality, and class, has been a product of an ideological climate and cultural needs at a particular historical moment. Thus the films of the heroic-nationalist genre, as Shohat points out, aimed to create heroic narratives reaffirming national unity and Zionist values.[2] One such film, *They Were Ten* (1960, dir. Baruch Dienar), is a heroic tale of Zionist pioneers. As they are working the land, they transform not just the fields but themselves into New Jews. Unsurprisingly, most of these characters are male; the only woman among them is the beautiful Manya (Ninette Dinar), who works dutifully beside her husband and his comrades. Historically, Zionist pioneers were Russian Jews, whose Zionist-socialist ideology was equally fueled by their revolt against traditional Jewish and bourgeois values. Their pioneering ethos was deeply influenced by the contemporary Russian culture, including the veneration of Russian letters and the nascent revolutionary movement. But the film downplays its characters' ethnicity. On the screen they speak fluent, unaccented Hebrew: only one phrase in the entire film is spoken in Russian and not a single one in Yiddish. And even though the diegetic songs have Russian melodies, the pioneers sing them in Hebrew.

As the Israeli cinema moves away from the nationalist genre, its characters lose their propaganda poster appeal, but cinematic Russians remain in the cultural center. In *The House on Chelouche Street* (1973, dir. Moshe Mizrahi), Russian Sonia (Michal Bat-Adam) is positioned as a local both culturally and socially, in contrast to the Mizrahi Clara and her son Sami. Sonia speaks flawless Hebrew and has the clout to introduce Sami to the Israeli Zionist cultural capital (including Russian literature). In all these films, the characters' Russian culture of origin, however downplayed, constitutes an integral part of the Israeli Zionist cultural capital. So when do Russian characters become cultural others?

The first film to introduce Russians as foreign newcomers was the now forgotten drama *Lena* (1980, dir. Eytan Green). This film reflects the era of the 1970s, when a ban on emigration from the USSR was eased and the first wave of Soviet Jews landed in Israel. *Lena* portrays Russian characters as immigrants and moves them from the Israeli cultural center to the margins. In many ways, it typifies the representation of Russian immigrants on Israeli screen for years to come.

The film's heroine Lena (Fira Cantor) is a young and beautiful woman, torn between her loyalty to her Zionist activist husband, still in a Soviet jail, and a newfound love for an Israeli man (incidentally, a Hebrew teacher), or metaphorically between maintaining her Russian identity and assimilating to Israel. Consistent with the Zionist tenets of immigration, she chooses to leave her Russian husband. Lena herself, with her poor control of Hebrew, her non-Israeli looks, and her struggle to negotiate a new society, is represented as a classic immigrant—the "other." Such a portrayal is typical of later films.

The representation of gender is also typical. As is common in Israeli films, interethnic tension is expressed through mixed coupling, similar to the Ashkenazi-Mizrahi Bourekas comedies. Lena is inducted and assimilated into Israeli society via the narrative strategy of a romantic-sexual relationship with a local male. In contrast, Russian male characters are confined largely to their self-contained, predominantly homosocial world that evades assimilation into Israel. In *Lena* Russian male immigrants are portrayed as ardent Zionists—they are activists campaigning for immigration rights for other Soviet Jews. Despite this positive ideological allegiance to Israel, however, Russian male immigrant characters appear to be aggressive, irrational, and violent. None has any potential for developing relationships with Israeli women. Even more outrageous are Russian immigrant male characters used for comic relief in other films. For instance, the Russian thug in *Kuni Leml in Cairo* (1983; dir. Joel Silberg) is violent and stupid and barely speaks any Hebrew.

Finally, the casting and use of language in *Lena* are also typical. From the 1980s on, immigrant characters are played by actual Russian immigrant actors. Their accent and occasional Russian dialogue are authentic but also foreign-sounding within the "Hebrew only" text of the film.

From Bourekas to Pierogi

In the 1990s Russian characters started appearing more often on Israeli screens. They were mostly stereotypical, representing dangerous and abusive men and exotic and sexualized women. Such characters are featured in many films, including *Saint Clara* (1996; dir. Ari Folman and Ori Sivan), *Circus Palestina* (1998; dir. Eyal Halfon), *The Holy Land* (2001; dir. Eitan Gorlin), *What a Wonderful Place* (2005; dir. Eyal Halfon), *Schwartz Dynasty* (2005; dir. Amir Hasfari and Shmuel Hasfari), and *Love & Dance* (2006; dir. Eitan Anner) as well as the TV serials *A Touch Away* (2007, dir. Ron Ninio) and *Loving Anna* (2008–2009, dir. Tzion Rubin). At present, it is difficult to find an Israeli film which does not feature a "Russian" at least as a minor character. Subplots involving secondary Russian immigrant characters appear in mainstream hits such as *Broken Wings* (2002, dir. Nir Bergman) and *Nina's Tragedies* (2003; dir. Savi Gavison) and popular TV serials such as *Florentine* (1997–2001; dir. Eytan Fox) and *The Mediator* (*Haborer*, 2007; dir. Shai Kanot). Some of these films conflate an image of a Jewish immigrant with an image of a trafficked non-Jewish sex worker or mail-order bride, but their narratives and casting overlap with the immigration stories in other films. To various degrees, Russian characters in these films remain limited by stereotypes.

The films representing Russian immigrants indicate the emergence of a new cycle, which, to parallel Bourekas, I call the Pierogi films.[3] Bourekas were the well-known ethnic comedies of the 1970s and 1980s about Mizrahi-Ashkenazi relations. They often featured "stereotypical characters with whom it is easy to identify, and the divided reality in which everything exotic or sentimental is emphasized."[4] As in Bourekas, characterization in Pierogi films is also stereotypical. Ashkenazi-Mizrahi relations in Bourekas took the form of a crossover romance, when, as Shohat writes, "ethnic/class tensions and conflicts are solved by a happy ending in which equality and unity are achieved by means of the unification of the mixed couple."[5] Similarly, Pierogi films bring together a Russian immigrant and a local Israeli, their private union being symbolic of the national unity. Like Bourekas, Pierogi films pose assimilation into Israeli culture as an ultimate goal for the immigrants.

Historically, interethnic romance in Israeli cinema has revolved around the "Orient question," as in the Mizrahi-Ashkenazi intermarriages of Bourekas films and forbidden Jewish-Palestinian loves. According to Shohat and Loshitzky, the prohibitive impetus of the latter plots was fueled by the fear of miscegenation.[6] In pierogi films, as in Bourekas, this fear is completely removed, and the interethnic relationships are celebrated, as they facilitate the induction of an immigrant into the Israeli-Jewish nation.

Following in the footsteps of *Lena*, most cinematic romances in Pierogi films involve an immigrant woman and a local male.[7] In most cases, the women are portrayed as young, beautiful, helpless, and seductive. They often have distinctly Russian looks (blonde hair, blue eyes, round face) and are frequently shown in frontal close-ups, disassociated from their surroundings, even in shots that are not structured into the film's narrative as reaction shots or eye-line matches. These close-ups depict Russian women in the manner reminiscent of a Russian Orthodox icon, emphasizing their foreignness and fetishizing their beauty. Russian women on Israeli screens are mysterious, exotic, and at times dangerous. Such heroines appear, for instance, in *Saint Clara*, *Yana's Friends* (1999; dir. Arik Kaplun), and *Schwartz*

Dynasty. Usually the heroine's nonassimilable foreignness is overcome by a romantic involvement with a local male.

But in some respects Pierogi films depart from Bourekas conventions. In Bourekas films Ashkenazi actors often portray Mizrahi characters; in pierogi films Russian actors play Russian characters. Their accents are authentic and are not used only for comic effect (as in Bourekas). Yet most Pierogi films still subscribe to the "Hebrew only" convention of Israeli cinema. Recently some films, such as *Love & Dance*, have started introducing more Russian dialogue. This is another departure from the Bourekas genre.

Schwartz Dynasty is a good example of the emerging Pierogi conventions. The film's narrative conflict hinges on the presence of a beautiful and seductive Russian woman, Ana (Anya Bukstein), who comes to Israel not to immigrate but to fulfill her late father's will and to bury his ashes in the soil of Israel. As the daughter of a non-Jewish mother, Ana is not considered Jewish according to Jewish law. Consequently she runs into endless bureaucratic obstacles trying to bury her father's ashes in a Jewish cemetery without the proof of his Jewishness. While trying to resolve this problem, she falls prey to various exploiters and crooks. An older woman (Miriam) who is originally Russian herself tries to help Ana, perhaps out of ethnic solidarity. Miriam's grandson (Avishai) also helps Ana. Predictably, Ana and Avishai fall in love and get married. In its use of the interethnic marriage plot device and conventions of romantic comedy, *Schwartz Dynasty* recalls the Bourekas films.

Despite the sympathetic treatment of immigrants, *Schwartz Dynasty* represents them from the local Israeli vantage point. For instance, its Israeli Jewish characters go to great length to lure secular, pork-eating Russian immigrants to a synagogue on Yom Kippur, the Day of Atonement, and thus include them in a national religious ritual. The perspective of the immigrants themselves does not figure into the narrative.

The question is: what will happen to Ana and Avishai (and other Russian-Israeli couples) in the "happily ever after"? *Love & Dance* further explores Russian-Israeli intermarriage. Framed according to the generic conventions of romantic-comedy-cum-melodrama and adopting the style of cinematic realism, *Love & Dance* depicts Khen (Vladimir Volov), a young boy battling a cultural conflict between his Russian-born mother and Israeli father. Like other Russian women in Pierogi films, Khen's mother is beautiful and charming but also helpless and frivolous. Khen's own identity is caught between his frustrated parents. The rift in his identity is emphasized linguistically in the way his mother speaks to him in Russian and his father in Hebrew. The Hebrew title of the film, *Sipur Khatzi Russi* (A Half-Russian Story), exemplifies this tension in Khen's identity.

Moreover, Khen's father wants him to take up judo, but Khen is drawn to ballroom dancing—a hobby imported and spread in Israel by the Russian immigrants. Khen's father ridicules ballroom dancing for being "too Russian" and too effeminate, but the boy sticks with it. If Khen uneasily negotiates his Russianness and his Israeliness, his parents fail to reconcile their cultural differences and must part. Thus the film's prognosis for intermarriage as a vehicle of assimilation is not optimistic. Even the offspring are somewhat nonassimilable into the mainstream Israel.

And yet at the end *Love & Dance* avoids this pessimistic conclusion and comes back to the Bourekas formula: as the characters are swirling on the floor in the final dance, it becomes clear that Khen is leaving behind his obsession with the beautiful but dysfunctional Russian Natalie and is falling in love with Sharon, the down-to-earth and reliable Israeli. In the narrative logic of the film, even the nonassimilable hybrid Khen makes the right choice between his Russianness and his Israeliness.

In contrast to bicultural Khen, immigrant men almost never become protagonists in Pierogi films. In those rare cases where a romance between an immigrant man and a local Israeli woman is featured, it is a failed or an illegitimate connection. For instance, *A Touch Away* presents an aborted romance between the secular immigrant from Russia, Zorik (Henry David), and the ultra-Orthodox Rokhale (Gaya Traub). Despite her love for Zorik,

Figure 11.2. Khen (Vladimir Volov) and Natalie (Valeria Voevodin), dancing on a rooftop in *Love & Dance* (Eitan Anner, 2006). Courtesy of July-August Productions.

Rokhale ultimately chooses to marry an ultra-Orthodox man. An earlier show, *Florentine*, featured a subplot about an illicit affair between a married immigrant (Israel Demidov) and a young Israeli woman (Karin Ofir). In the logic of these film and television narratives, a successful union between a Russian male immigrant and a local woman is unlikely. For the most part the Russian male characters are depicted as unreliable husbands and fathers (for example, in *Yana's Friends* and *Love & Dance*) or worse, as swindlers and mafia thugs (as in *The Mediator* and *What a Wonderful Place*), or just as nonassimilable strangers with dangerous hobbies and precarious habits (in *Saint Clara* and *Schwartz Dynasty*). Most importantly, whether male or female, stereotypical or nuanced, Russian immigrants are represented in these films from the Israeli perspective.

Russian-Accented Cinema

As Russian immigrants are increasingly gaining cinematic representation on Israeli screens, they still rarely find themselves in the position to control or contribute to the production and circulation of such representations. The films discussed above were made by Israeli filmmakers, representing immigrants from the local vantage point. This is why the few films that have been made by Russian immigrant filmmakers present an opportunity for understanding their perspective. Within contemporary Israeli cinema, these films, which I call Russian Israeli cinema, form a body of work distinguished by the immigrant filmmakers' vantage point.

As such, Russian Israeli cinema can be viewed as "accented film," which, according to Hamid Naficy, can be defined not only by the actual languages and accents on the screen but also by the diasporic or displaced identities of the filmmakers.[8] The "accent" of Russian Israeli films is expressed in their narrative strategies, use of language, self-referential casting, and style.

Naficy notes that accented films often critique the "universal" dominant cinema, and yet they are not entirely oppositional.[9] Indeed, in contrast to Pierogi films, Russian Israeli films subtly subvert both ideological and cinematic Israeli conventions. At the same time, like the mainstream Israeli cinema of which they are part and parcel, they are preoccupied with the integration of immigrants into the Israeli Jewish nation. To various degrees, Russian Israeli films walk a thin line between asserting the immigrants' belonging in Israel and insisting on their cultural distinctiveness. Sociologists call this position "integration without acculturation."[10]

Russian Israeli films are most distinguished by their narrative strategies. Unlike the Pierogi films, which are preoccupied with assimilation via interethnic romance, Russian Israeli films do not feature interethnic Russian Israeli couples (*Yana's Friends* is the only exception to this rule, making it closer to Pierogi films). In the rare cases of an interethnic romance, the relationships have no future. Most couples are intraethnic, and the protagonists are often male immigrants.

The very first Russian Israeli film, *Coffee with Lemon* (1994; dir. Leonid Horowitz), is a case in point. At the center of the plot is a famous Moscow actor (Russian film star Alexander Abdulov), who immigrates to Israel with his family only to discover that he cannot bridge the cultural gap and is doomed to failure. In part he comes to realize this due to his brief affair with his Hebrew teacher (recalling the romance in *Lena*). He returns to Moscow and is killed in a freak accident. At the end the immigrant protagonist fits neither here nor there. Not only his interethnic affair fails; his immigration to Israel and his return to Russia result in tragedy. This is not a typical immigration narrative for an Israeli film.

A more recent example is *The Children of USSR*. Like *Coffee with Lemon*, this film features a male protagonist, Slava (Daniel Brook), once a soccer star in his native town and now an immigrant suffocated in the remote town of Netivot, working random jobs and struggling to support his young family. The main romantic relationship of the film is Slava's failing marriage to Sveta, a fellow Russian, who wants him to leave behind his dreams of soccer and to be like her father (the proud manager of a garbage business). But Slava is unwilling to give up the male camaraderie—he lives in a world of other young Russians whose dreams have also been crushed. With the help of his ex-coach (Vladimir Friedman), Slava succeeds in putting together a soccer team.

Slava and his friends populate the margins of Israeli society—the locals that they encounter are marginalized minorities themselves, including the corrupt Mizrahi officials, an Ethiopian immigrant soccer player, and an oddball Hassidic soccer fan nicknamed Messiah. The "model Israeli" is nowhere to be seen, which explains why the film does not insist on assimilation. The only reference to it is ironic: Messiah promises Slava to buy uniforms for his team if the players put on phylacteries and pray with him. Slava agrees. In the next scene the camera pans over the motley immigrants, who, being entirely unfamiliar with the Jewish ritual, senselessly parrot Messiah's words and movements. Whether they intend it or not, their mimicry transforms into mockery, serving as a parody of the entire Israeli institution of immigrant "absorption."

Yet the film is not all gloom and doom. Despite its raw realism, *The Children of USSR* succeeds in being both funny and lyrical. Its immigrant characters are represented from an insider's perspective: Russian teenagers rarely appear as a group or in a long shot. The camera frequently moves to let the audience see from Slava's perspective. The plot, which could have produced a stereotype of immigrant social cases, turns into a complex and sympathetic narrative.

Another intraethnic romance is at the center of *Paper Snow* (2003, dir. Lena Chaplin and Slava Chaplin). The plot focuses on a love affair between two mythological Russians in 1930s Tel Aviv: Hannah Rovina, a star of the Habima national theater, which originated in Moscow, and Alexander Penn, a Communist poet from Siberia. Other literary giants (Avraham Shlonsky, Avraham Halfi, and Khaim-Nakhman Bialik, all of them hailing from Russia) surround Rovina and Penn. The film emphasizes their culture of origin, their Russian literary and theater training. In this way it focuses on the Russian roots of Israeli culture, emphasizing the role of Russian Jews (both past and, by extension, present) in building the nation. This particular vantage point on Israel's national past is an important characteristic of the Russian immigrant perspective.[11]

Ironically, as other Israeli groups try to contest the images of the Russian Jewish fathers-founders, contemporary Russian immigrants try to reassert it.[12] In a more subtle form this use of the past also appears in *Yana's Friends*. A subplot of the film involves an ostensibly Israeli woman and an immigrant war veteran who recognize each other as lovers separated by World War II (in which they both fought on the Soviet side). Their son died defending Israel in the Six Day War. This subplot both pays tribute to the heroic Israeli past and claims the new immigrants' right to be part of this grand narrative of the nation. In the narrative logic of the film, it is the Russian immigrants' lost sons and daughters, mothers and fathers, who fought the Nazis, founded Israel, and defended it.[13] A similar motif appears in the short film *Dark Night* (2005; dir. Leonid Prudovsky), which opens with a scene of an Israeli patrol in the occupied territories. One of the soldiers, who comes from a Russian family, is singing a famous Soviet song of the World War II era—*Dark Night*. Driving the army Jeep through the night, he explains to his fellow soldiers the significance of the song, which accompanied the Soviet troops, including his Jewish grandfather, as they went to defeat the Nazis. In another film, *A Trumpet in the Wadi* (2002; dir. Lena Chaplin and Slava Chaplin), an accented variation of a Jewish Palestinian cinematic romance, a Russian immigrant protagonist is killed while on army duty, presumably by Palestinian militants. All these representations emphasize the identification of Russian immigrants with the Israeli Jewish nation while simultaneously affirming their Russianness.

In addition to these narrative strategies, Russian Israeli films are marked as accented by their extensive use of Russian. The use of the filmmakers' native language, according to Naficy, is a marker of belonging and authenticity.[14] Indeed, in contrast to Pierogi films, dialogue in Russian Israeli films moves freely between Russian and Hebrew, with the majority of the dialogue in Russian. This difference becomes particularly tangible in films representing the national past, such as *Paper Snow*, where Israeli historical figures are portrayed speaking to each other in Russian. The use of Russian dialogue challenges Israeli cinematic convention, according to which the national past is portrayed in Hebrew. Even today, as other Israeli films (especially coproductions) have become more multilingual, this convention still holds true.

Clearly, Israeli films about immigration are made to appeal to the mainstream Hebrew-speaking audience, whereas Russian Israeli films are also made for Russian speakers, who can access Russian dialogue without subtitles. More importantly, Russian Israeli films give center stage to the Russian language and accent, usually relegated to the margins. In one case, even the film's title is Russified: *Yaldey CCCP* (pronounced *yaldey sssr* and translated as "the children of the USSR"; see figure 11.1). The filmmakers insist on a Russian spelling of the abbreviation for USSR, part of the Soviet iconography. This idiosyncratic title not only introduces a Russian word into Hebrew but also uses a Cyrillic acronym as a nostalgic icon.

The "accent" of the Russian Israeli films is further emphasized through casting. According to Naficy, in accented cinema the actor's ethnicity and the character's ethnicity coincide.[15] Moreover, filmmakers are often engaged in multiple tasks in accented films, directing as well as acting in their own films. Regardless of the motivation behind them (usually limited resources), such casting decisions function as self-inscription and are often autobiographical.

Indeed, casting in Russian Israeli films is often self-referential, as when Russian-Israeli filmmakers, actors, and other cultural figures are cast as similar figures in the past. For instance, in *Paper Snow* Leonid Horowitz (a Russian Israeli director mentioned above) is cast as Tzvi Friedland, a key Habima actor and director. Vladimir Friedman, a famous Russian Israeli film actor, is cast as Aharon Meskin, a Habima actor since its Moscow days. Hanna Rovina is played by Yevgenya Dodina, a leading actor from Gesher—a contemporary theater founded by Russian immigrants in Israel.[16] For Israeli audiences Dodina blends the two figures: she is both Rovina—a legendary Habima star—and herself—an immigrant actor starring in many Israeli films discussed here. Such casting works as a collective or communal self-inscription, by means of which the Russian Israeli filmmakers inscribe themselves (and by extension their community) on the narrative of Israeli history.

Russian Israeli films are marked by an emerging accented style: *Yana's Friends* offers sophisticated metacinematic commentary by intercutting deep-focused color film footage with variably focused black-and-white homemade video. *Paper Snow* creates the visual nostalgia of a sepia photograph by shooting the film through a yellow filter. *A Trumpet in the Wadi* is shot entirely by an unstable handheld camera to achieve the veracity of a documentary and the urgency of news footage. Russian Israeli cinematography, with its raw, highly personalized methods, conveys the sense that the lives depicted on camera and those lived behind it are one.

....

So what does all this mean for Israeli cinema and culture? In terms of cinematic style, Pierogi films continue to tap into the Bourekas legacy. Russian Israeli films present greater challenges to the local cinematic conventions, offering not only an immigrant vantage point but also accented narratives and styles. At the same time, accented films are an integral part of Israeli cinema, which is increasingly engaged in multilingual, multicultural co-productions appealing to the international cinema markets.

The treatment of immigration in both Pierogi and accented films is emblematic of larger cultural trends. The two cycles of films reflect competing discourses on immigration—"nativist" and "accented." The nativist discourse is preoccupied with cultural preservation and with the threat of further destabilization of the allegedly unified Israeli national identity. In contrast, an accented or immigrant-centered discourse insists on the value of the diasporic cultures and languages. Instead of focusing on assimilation, it is preoccupied with finding the balance between the old and the new. The emergence of accented discourse in the public sphere is part of a larger shift in Israeli culture toward post-Zionist politics, including a positive attitude toward the diasporic heritage and a greater orientation toward multiculturalism. This is a new reality.

NOTES

1. Ella Shohat, *Israeli Cinema: East/West and the Politics of Representation*; Yosefa Loshitzky, *Identity Politics on the Israeli Screen*; Nurith Gertz, *Makhela Akheret: Nitzolei Sho'ah, Zarim Va'akherim Bakolnoā Uvasifrut Hayisra'elit.*

2. Shohat, *Israeli Cinema*, 57–114.

3. Pierogi are a kind of Russian pastry. For the initial definition of the term, see

Olga Gershenson and Dale Hudson. "New Immigrant, Old Story: Framing Russians on the Israeli Screen," 29. For discussion of Bourekas, see other chapters in this anthology.

4. Judd Ne'eman, "Kolno'a Darga Effes," 21.

5. Shohat, *Israeli Cinema*, 134.

6. Ibid., 239–253; Loshitzky, *Identity Politics*, 112–154.

7. This cinematic trend is an accurate reflection of the actual demographic reality: in the surveys, twice as many Russian immigrant young women as men report having had a romantic involvement with an Israeli partner (Larissa Remennick "The 1.5 Generation of Russian Immigrants in Israel: Between Integration and Socio-cultural Retention," 51). Russian immigrant women are clearly seen as more acceptable partners than Russian men.

8. Hamid Naficy, *An Accented Cinema: Exilic and Diasporic Filmmaking*, 4.

9. Ibid., 26.

10. For articulations of this position by Israeli sociologists, see Tamar Horowitz, "Integration without Acculturation: The Absorption of Soviet Immigrants"; and Larissa Remennick, *Russian Jews on Three Continents: Identity, Integration, and Conflict*, 109–117.

11. For an expanded analysis of *Paper Snow*, see Olga Gershenson, "Accented Memory: Russian Immigrants Reimagine the Israeli Past."

12. For an analysis of a critical rereading of history in Israel and a proliferation of jokes about previously taboo historical topics, see Yael Zerubavel, *Recovered Roots: Collective Memory and the Making of Israeli National Tradition*, 167–177.

13. For analysis of *Yana's Friends*, see Olga Gershenson and Dale Hudson. "Absorbed by Love: Russian Immigrant Woman in Israeli Film," 309.

14. Naficy, *An Accented Cinema*, 122.

15. Ibid., 24.

16. For background on Gesher's history and reception in Israel, see Olga Gershenson, *Gesher: Russian Theatre in Israel—A Study of Cultural Colonization*.

BIBLIOGRAPHY

Gershenson, Olga. *Gesher: Russian Theatre in Israel—A Study of Cultural Colonization*. New York: Peter Lang, 2005.

———. "Accented Memory: Russian Immigrants Reimagine the Israeli Past." *Journal of Israeli History* 28, no. 1 (2009): 21–36.

Gershenson, Olga, and Dale Hudson. "Absorbed by Love: Russian Immigrant Woman in Israeli Film." *Journal of Modern Jewish Studies* 6, no. 3 (2007): 301–315.

———. "New Immigrant, Old Story: Framing Russians on the Israeli Screen." *Journal of Film and Video* 60, nos. 3–4 (2008): 25–42.

Gertz, Nurith. *Makhela Akheret: Nitzolei Sho'ah Zarim Va'akherim Bakolno'a Uvasifrut Hayisra'elit* (Holocaust Survivors, Aliens, and Others in Israeli Cinema and Literature). Tel Aviv: Am Oved, 2004.

Horowitz, Tamar. "Integration without Acculturation: The Absorption of Soviet Immigrants." *Soviet Jewish Affairs* 12, no. 3 (1982): 19–33.

Loshitzky, Yosefa. *Identity Politics on the Israeli Screen*. Austin: University of Texas Press, 2001.

Naficy, Hamid. *An Accented Cinema: Exilic and Diasporic Filmmaking*. Princeton: Princeton University Press, 2001.

Ne'eman, Judd. "Kolno'a Darga Effes" (Cinema Degree Zero). *Kolnoa* 5 (1979): 20–23.

Remennick, Larissa. "The 1.5 Generation of Russian Immigrants in Israel: Between Integration and Socio-cultural Retention." *Diaspora: A Journal of Transnational Studies* 12, no. 1 (2003): 39–66.

———. *Russian Jews on Three Continents: Identity, Integration, and Conflict*. New Brunswick, N.J.: Transactions, 2006.

Shohat, Ella. *Israeli Cinema: East/West and the Politics of Representation*. Austin: University of Texas Press, 1987.

Zerubavel, Yael. *Recovered Roots: Collective Memory and the Making of Israeli National Tradition*. Chicago: University of Chicago Press, 1995.

FILMOGRAPHY

Broken Wings (*Knafaim Shvurot*). Directed by Nir Bergman, 2002; DVD: Culver City, Calif.: Sony Pictures Classics, 2004.

The Children of USSR (*Yaldei CCCP*). Directed by Felix Gerchikov, 2005; DVD: Globus United, 2008.

Circus Palestina (*Kirkas Palestina*). Directed by Eyal Halfon, 1998; DVD: New York: SISU Home Entertainment, Inc., 2000.

Coffee with Lemon (*Kafe im Limon*). Directed by Leonid Horowitz, 1994.

Dark Night (*Laila Afel*). Directed by Leonid Prudovsky, 2005; DVD: Tel Aviv: Pimpa Film Productions, 2005.

Florentine (*Florentin*). TV series. Directed by Eytan Fox. Totzeret Haaretz Production, 1997–2001.

The Holy Land. Directed by Eitan Gorlin, 2001; DVD: New York: Hart Sharp Video, 2004.

The House on Chelouche Street (*Habayit Birkhov Shlush*). Directed by Moshe Mizrahi, 1973; VHS: New York: Jewish Media Fund, 1997.

Kuni Leml in Cairo (*Kuni Lemel BeKahir*). Directed by Joel Silberg, 1983; DVD: Netanya, Israel: Globus United, 2000.

Lena. Directed by Eytan Green, 1980.

Love & Dance (*Sipur Khatzi Russi*). Directed by Eitan Anner, 2006; DVD: Netanya, Israel: Five Stars, 2007.

Loving Anna (*Le'ehov et Annah*). TV series. Directed by Tzion Rubin; Herzliya Studios, 2008–2009.

The Mediator (*Haborer*). TV series. Directed by Shai Kanot. JCS Productions, 2007.

Nina's Tragedies (*Ha'asonot Shel Nina*). Directed by Savi Gavison, 2003; DVD: New York: Wellspring Media, 2005.

Paper Snow (*Haya O Lo Haya*). Directed by Lena Chaplin and Slava Chaplin, 2003.

Saint Clara (*Klara Hakdosha*). Directed by Ari Folman and Ori Sivan, 1996; DVD: New York: Kino International, 2007.

Schwartz Dynasty (*Shoshelet Shvartz*). Directed by Amir Hasfari and Shmuel Hasfari, 2005; DVD: Netanya, Israel: Globus United, 2006.

They Were Ten (*Hem Hayu Asarah*). Directed by Baruch Dienar, 1960; VHS: Teaneck, N.J.: Ergo Media, Inc., 1987.

A Touch Away (*Merkhak Negi'ah*). Directed by Ron Ninio. 2007; DVD: Netanya, Israel: Globus United, 2008.

A Trumpet in the Wadi (*Khatzotzra Bavadi*). Directed by Lena Chaplin and Slava Chaplin, 2002.

What a Wonderful Place (*Eize Makom Nifla*). Directed by Eyal Halfon, 2005; DVD: Or Yehuda, Israel: Hed Artzi, 2007.

Yana's Friends (*Hakhaverim Shel Yana*). Directed by Arik Kaplun, 1999; DVD: Netanya, Israel: Globus United, 2000.

PART IV

Holocaust and Trauma

12 The Holocaust in Israeli Cinema as a Conflict between Survival and Morality

ILAN AVISAR

The global discourse on the linkage between the Holocaust and Israel is subject to intense political debates regarding the implications of the connection between the Holocaust and Israel. The spectrum of the political views ranges from support for the Jewish state because of the massive suffering of the genocide to Holocaust denials and open calls for a new Holocaust against the Jewish state. The conflicting political views suggest either historical closure or a historical cycle. Historical closure is suggested by the assertion about Jewish statehood arising out of the ashes of Auschwitz; a historical cycle underlies the observation that the Jews continue to face threats of annihilation in their own state; another sinister cycle is perpetrated by Israel's detractors with the claim that the victims of the past have become new Nazi victimizers.

The Israeli discourse often contains elements of global views, but the place of the Holocaust in Israeli collective consciousness has been profound and traumatic. Israel's engagement with the genocide and its legacies has been an intriguing and complex process that exceeds the forms of cycle or closure; it has been a dramatic narrative of turns and reversals unfolding in the volatile history of the young Jewish state.

Films, as players and articulators of historical narratives and national dramas, offer a valuable insight into the place of the Holocaust in the Israeli psyche. The cinematic stories, dramatic characters, visual details, and other elements of artistic expression may reveal psychological undercurrents and ideological dissonances caused by the trauma, residing in the depths of the collective subconsciousness. The examination of the subject of the Holocaust in Israeli cinema suggests a historical narrative of national memory that has been dominated by two forceful psychological complexes and parallel ideological views: the anxieties of survival and the concerns of morality. On the one hand, the lesson of the Holocaust is the critical value of life and the defense of Jewish existence, what philosopher Emil Fackenheim called the 614th commandment.[1] On the other hand, the lesson from the Nazi crimes is also to banish all forms of evil and in the case of Israel a special determination to avoid any immoral acts in the conduct and struggles of the Jewish nation. These two lessons have become sources for pointed political conflicts, with evocations of the past and references to the Holocaust serving as proof or justification for different sides of the national debate.

Three underlying factors complicate the enunciation of the linkage between the Holocaust and the state of Israel. The first is the traumatic nature of the Holocaust. The second is the time factor and the dramatic history of modern Israel. The third is the existence of dual and conflicting visions of Jewish identity and Jewish history.

The Holocaust has been a historical trauma of monumental magnitude. Trauma entails critical tribulations of comprehension and representation, and the traumatic dimension of the Holocaust must be taken into consideration in any attempt to formulate a lesson, conclusion, or adequate response to the event. In the growing field of trauma studies, Dominick LaCapra states: "Trauma poses a limit to critical reason and—as wound, disaster, or catastrophe—eclipses thought itself."[2] Regarding Hitler's victims, Michael G. Levine notes that "the overwhelmingly immediate impact of the Holocaust on the first generation was such that it was not fully assimilated as it occurred."[3] Joshua Hirsch adds: "Trauma lingers in the psyche in the form of belated and repeated restructurings of the memory of the event as time passes and circumstances change."[4] Hence it is vital to offer a chronological examination of the historical narrative of the registration and inscription of the Holocaust in Israeli consciousness.

Contrary to popular views that see the establishment of Israel as a result of the Holocaust, the Zionists created a de facto state in Palestine before the Holocaust, a vibrant political entity of people with their own language, culture, national organizations, and distinct sense of identity.[5] During the war years Zionists were compelled to define their actions in relation to the special historical circumstances of the fight against Nazism. The recognition of the tragic predicament of the Jews in Europe eventually superseded the goals of achieving national independence in Israel. The anti-British activities were suspended and reversed as young people joined the British army in the Jewish brigade and special volunteers, like Hannah Senesh, were sent on dangerous missions to contribute to the war efforts and to try to save Jews under German occupation. In the aftermath of the Holocaust, the Zionist leadership engaged in diplomatic efforts and smuggling operations to bring the surviving victims—defined at the time as displaced refugees—to Israel.

The First Decade

The first Zionist film after the end of the war was *The Great Promise* (*Dim'at Hanekhamah Hagdolah*, 1947). The opening scene is calculated to underscore the pathetic condition of the survivor as victim. It features an old man, a refugee from the camps, whose physical wretchedness is magnified by his sorrowful confession about the loss of his home and his declaration that he wants to change his walking stick to a rifle. A handsome blond soldier of the Jewish brigade from Palestine enters the frame and states, "I have a home." The survivor asks: "And do you have a place for us under your roof?" The Zionist soldier replies: "We haven't forgotten you." This scene contrasts the blond, wholesome Sabra with the pitiful Jewish victim. It reflects an early strain of Zionist ideology known as *shlilat hagolah* (negation of exile), whose goal was to create new Jewish culture that would project national pride in contrast with diasporic powerlessness. This perspective "declared Holocaust survivors to be the representatives of the allegedly Diasporic passive and unheroic Jewry that the New Israeli Jew was trying to eradicate."[6]

The Great Promise is typical of other films made in Israel between 1946 and 1950, which usually featured Holocaust survivors arriving in Israel as traumatized victims and being transformed to healthy, happy people thanks to the adoption and cultivation of Zionist ideals such as farming, communal living, and defense, which are often demonstrated in the kibbutz lifestyle. Thus the manifest compassion toward the victims came with a patronizing attitude that sought to project a new identity onto them. In sum, the first cinematic expressions of the Holocaust featured resurrection narratives of victims along with thematic and visual contrasts between the misery of diasporic catastrophe and ideal life in Israel, conveying Israeli society's nationally confident patronization of Holocaust victims in the immediate aftermath of the Sho'ah.

The decade of the fifties is characterized by moral distance and harsh judgments. The reparations agreement with West Germany and the trial of Rudolf Kastner, an Israeli official who was accused of collaborating with the Nazis when he was one of the leaders of the Jewish community in Hungary, revealed deep rifts in Israeli society and set the tone for judgmental attitudes. Israeli dramas and literary works from these years are replete with references to survivors with questionable pasts in the Holocaust—women were associated with sexual exploitation, men were kapos in concentration camps or other types of collaborators, and survivors were accused of exploiting the past to turn a profit.[7] The national commemoration of the Holocaust was defined in terms of *Sho'ah ugvura* (Holocaust and heroism) as if to enable the assimilation of the Holocaust in Israel by stressing the heroics of partisans, ghetto fighters, and Zionist soldiers.

Curiously, the one important film made in the 1950s explores the traces of trauma in the struggle for the birth of Israel. *Hill 24 Doesn't Answer* (*Giv'a 24 Eina Ona*, 1955) chronicles Israel's War of Independence in three episodes framed by a story about the battle for a strategic hill near Jerusalem. The first episode features a valiant Holocaust survivor who commands clandestine operations to smuggle illegal refugees into Israel. But the episode focuses on the developing love affair between a British soldier and a local member of the Jewish underground, a dramatic narrative that marginalizes the Holocaust in favor of a transnational love story. The Holocaust appears again in the third episode of the film, against the unlikely background of the fierce fighting in the desert. The drama revolves around the capture of an Egyptian officer by an Israeli soldier. The young Sabra is a cheerful guy who keeps his sense of humor and light attitudes, unburdened by the risks of the moment or the critical stakes of the war. He undergoes a drastic change of mood, however, when he realizes that the officer he just captured is a German who served in the SS. The loquacious Sabra becomes speechless when the captive tries to talk his way out of the situation. The Nazi begins with words about the value of military honor and concludes with a hateful tirade against Jews. The scene ends as his shadow appears rising, hailing in the Nazi salute as he expires in a rigid fall to the ground. This scene includes one outstanding image when the confident, happy-go-lucky Sabra transforms for a brief moment into an Orthodox Jew, meekly facing his anti-Semitic adversary. This identification of the Israeli Sabra with the diasporic Jew reveals atavistic anxieties against transhistorical enemies personified by the Nazis and the mismatch in the battles of Jews with no military tradition against professional warriors driven by extreme ideology.

The 1960s–1970s

The decade of the sixties began for Israelis with intense exposure to the full scope of the Holocaust during the trial of Adolf Eichmann. Daily radio broadcasts and newspaper accounts of the horrific testimonies hypnotized the entire country. But the shattering details of history led only to qualified identification with the victims. After all, Eichmann was captured by daring and proactive Israeli secret agents who brought him to trial in Jerusalem, where he was subsequently indicted by an Israeli court and executed by Israeli police officers. In opposition to the wretched victims of the Holocaust, Israelis were placed in the role of the avenging victors. In the wake of the trial, Holocaust survivors Natan Gross and Shimon Yisraeli made a low-budget film called *The Cellar* (*Hamartef*, 1963). *The Cellar* explores the tortured life of the survivor in Israel. The protagonist goes on a revenge trip to Germany against an old school friend who became a Nazi and was responsible for the deportation of the survivor's family. This Nazi is shown only as a shadow, and the film is ambiguous about the actual reality of the revenge trip, suggesting that it is an expression of the survivor's tortured mind. In the last scene, however, the protagonist, back from his possibly imaginary journey, signals the end of lunch break to the workers at a construction site. He hits a metal box hanging from a pole, and the film's final image is of his shadow, like a person hanging from a gallows. The revenge narrative may be imaginary, but the final image is unambiguous—in the rebuilding of the new country loom shadows of the survivors' historical trauma.

For nearly two decades after the Eichmann trial Israeli cinema made only a few faint references to the Holocaust. The trauma was repressed. The amazing achievements of the young state, culminating in the great military victory of the Six Day War in 1967, instigated a mood of national triumphalism that was inimical to the massive victimization of the Holocaust. The critical turning point was the Yom Kippur War. The near defeat in 1973 raised fears of another national genocide. Israelis witnessed the impact of the Arab oil embargo as they were ostracized in world organizations and denounced in public media with imagery that recalled age-old anti-Semitism. The Jewish state became almost officially a pariah state with the United Nations decision in 1975 that equated Zionism and racism. The old Zionist view of the Diaspora as the site of Jewish suffering and grave risks was replaced by the realization that Israeli Jews were in more danger than Jews elsewhere in the world. Living in a modern ghetto surrounded by minefields and barbed wires, many Israeli Jews began to feel that they were subject to genocidal threats in a world whose politicians preferred to collaborate with the might of the Arabs and whose intellectuals developed anti-Zionist ideologies as a new type of anti-Semitism.

In addition to the Yom Kippur War, the rise of anti-Israeli terrorism, and other anti-Israel political warfare, the 1970s marked a new phase of coming to terms with the Holocaust from the distance and perspective of a generation after the event. The historical narrative of modern Israel, especially the new sense of national vulnerability, generated growing identification with the Jews' predicament under the Nazi menace. This process resolved the former conflict between the heroic Israeli and the victimized Jew of the Holocaust. Both official ceremonies and recollections indicated a marked shift from celebrating acts of heroism to narratives of loss and survival. New nostalgia for Jewish life in pre-Holocaust Europe, augmented by nostalgia for Jewish life in the Arab world prior to 1948,[8] reversed the earlier attitude of negation of exile .

In Menahem Golan's *Operation Jonathan* (aka *Operation Thunderbolt*; *Mivtza Yonatan*, 1977) the presentation of the daring rescue of hostages by Israeli commandos in 1976 is dominated by invocations of the Holocaust. The hijacking was carried out by a group of terrorists led by two Germans, consumed with radical hatred toward the Jewish state. In the plane an old man requests permission to go to the bathroom. As he raises his hand, the Auschwitz tattooed number is visible on his arm, and the German terrorist yells at him "schnell, schnell" ("quickly, quickly" in German), reminiscent of the manner in which Jews were hurried into the gas chambers. The initial diplomatic efforts to release the hostages suggest the impotence of the world to aid the victims. A nervous woman who has a relative in the plane complains to Israeli officials that the Jews in the camps also expected the world to help and nobody came to the rescue. When the terrorists separate Israeli and Jewish passengers from the others, the film clearly evokes the notorious selection scenes from the death camps. The orderly, loud calling of names in these moments also recalls deportation scenes from the Holocaust. This is why the Israeli commander of the rescue operation tells his soldiers that their mission is to save Jews who are victimized because they are Jews and because nobody else will help them, expressing the idea "never again."

The historic Israeli commando operation took place on July 4, 1976. Menahem Golan released his film in 1978, following two rushed productions of American TV dramas, *Victory at Entebbee* and *Raid on Entebbe*, made less than six months after the real event, to show U.S. viewers the sensational feat that took place on America's bicentennial Independence Day. The time lapse between the American productions and the Israeli movie is significant not only in terms of the better research and production values but also because of the ideological differences between them. In 1977 Menahem Begin was elected prime minister. Begin's worldview was shaped by the history of Jewish suffering in the Diaspora, as opposed to his Sabra predecessor, Yitzhak Rabin. Begin articulated what has become a prevalent sentiment in Israel, an existential Holocaust complex consisting of the fear of extermination by demonic enemies, the suspicion that no one will help the Jews but themselves, and the determination never again to be vulnerable and helpless. David K. Shipler, the *New York Times* correspondent during Begin's tenure, summarized this outlook by referring to Israel's "fierce sensation of vulnerability, the lusty devotion to military strength, the stubborn resistance to international criticism . . . the gnawing fear of powerlessness that grinds beneath the arsenal of tanks and planes, the lurking conviction that it can happen again, and that the rest of the world would look the other way."[9]

The deep psychological dimension of the Holocaust experience in the Israeli psyche is evident in the abundance of the imagery of shadows in Israeli films dealing with the subject. The early films from the forties contrasted the dark settings of Europe with the bright landscapes of Israel and employed visual images to suggest the shadowy past and the black holes of the traumatized victims. The looming shadow of the Nazi persecutor with its complex psychological and ethical implications appears in *Hill 24* and *The Cellar*. The few faint references to the Holocaust in the national heroic films of the sixties before the Yom Kippur War also employed the shadow element in the narrative or in the visual imagery.[10]

Ultimately, the obsession of Israeli culture with the trauma of genocide suggests the workings of a deep psychological Holocaust complex. Following Sigmund Freud and Carl Jung, the psychological complex indicates unconscious feelings and beliefs, often related to traumatic experience, whose manifestation is detectable through puzzling behavior or emotional stress. In Jung's theory, many complexes appear in complementary pairs. In Israel the Holocaust registered two different deep psychological complexes: the existential complex of survival and the moral complex of ethical conduct. The intense reactions provoked by any evocation of the Holocaust testify to a legacy of unhealed wounds in Israel's Jewish society. For some, the Holocaust is a force in the collective memory generating vital vigilance against genocidal enemies and a hostile world. Begin's order to destroy the Iraqi nuclear reactor in 1981 was regarded as a necessary action to prevent a second Holocaust against the Jewish state. For others, the Holocaust became a source for neurotic behavior that found expression in what some perceived as an aggressive overreaction to Palestinian terrorism or a paranoid mistrust of international organizations.

The political divisions in Israel are rooted in a profound and pervasive duality of Jewish identity. The alternative views of Jews and Judaism are enunciated in terms of national history and national destiny versus the terms of humanistic civilization and universal ethics. The differences between the visions of "a people that dwells alone" and the "light unto the nations" can be traced to the Bible, but they reemerged forcefully as primary categories of Jewish identity in modern times, especially in the past thirty to forty years. The numerous wars in Israel's short history, the continued existence of enemies who openly declare their desire to destroy the Jewish state, and the searing memories of the Holocaust mobilize Jews behind the national cause of Judaism. But Israel's military actions, which inevitably violate ideal moral values, alienate many who regard the national project of a Jewish state as a violation of Jewish universalist-humanistic ideals.[11]

The Holocaust also has been given two alternative interpretations along these ideological lines. The nationalist view of the Holocaust stresses the assault and attempted genocide against the Jewish people as a nation, the culmination of centuries of persecution and precarious diasporic existence that must be answered with a strong and viable Jewish state. The ethical humanistic approach stresses the manifest destiny of a civilization that has been in the forefront of struggles against evil. The inference of this metahistorical view is that the Jewish state must adhere to strict and exemplary ethical codes of social and political behavior. The conduct of an independent state in exercising its sovereignty or defending itself against its enemies inevitably poses ethical challenges. The intensive public debate in Israel over the proper conduct of the military, especially vis-à-vis the Palestinians, is replete with references to the Holocaust, expressed in newspaper articles, politicians' declarations, or supreme court rulings. The Holocaust is evoked as the ultimate yardstick for the dangers of immoral behavior.

While *Operation Jonathan* (*Mivtza Yonatan*) celebrates heroic military determination in the wake of the Holocaust, *The Wooden Gun* (*Roveh Khuliot*, dir. Ilan Moshenson, 1979), also featuring a protagonist named Yoni, deals with the moral dangers of military belligerence. The film is about children in the early years of the state who internalize adult narratives of military adventures by engaging in brutal gang wars. An encounter with a Holocaust survivor transforms the film's protagonist. As he flees the scene after shooting his rival, Yoni reaches a hut on the beach where an unstable Holocaust survivor lives with her memories and nightmares. She tenderly cares for him, and he sees inside her place numerous photographs and many candles, a kind of private Holocaust museum. He gazes at the famous picture of the child raising his hands before an SS man after the liquidation of the Warsaw ghetto. Suddenly the picture comes to life, the people in the frame are moving, and he sees the classmate that he shot in the figure of the child from the ghetto. Yoni begins to cry, and his tears reveal his lesson: the realization of the futility and evil of physical brutality.

The 1980s–1990s

In Israel's cultural history, *The Wooden Gun*'s delicate treatment of the ethical dilemmas of a war-burdened society has given way to extreme expressions against national ideals in Israeli culture.[12] The election victories of the right-wing Likud party have alienated most members of the artistic circles who profess leftist ideologies of postnational values. The 1982 war in Lebanon and the 1987 Intifada ignited intense political opposition. In the wake of the failure of the Oslo agreements and the assassination of Yitzhak Rabin, political positions have escalated to a critique of nearly all forms of Zionist nationalism, cultivating post-Zionist views and in extreme cases even anti-Zionist activities. Iconoclasm, historical revisionism, and willful withdrawal to private spheres advocating detachment from the national scene became rampant in museum exhibitions, theatrical drama, literary works, and cinema. In Israeli films the representative Iraeli protagonist has been replaced with marginal social figures whose perspective proposes a critique of national ideology.[13] The director of the landmark documentary *Because of That War* (*Biglal Hamilkhama Ha'Hi*, 1988), Orna Ben-Dor, claimed that she made her film about children of survivors to expropriate the Holocaust from what she defined as the ideological grip of the Right in Israel.[14] The film features two popular musicians, whose parents survived the death camps, struggling with the psychological predicament of children of traumatized survivors.

The Second Generation was a global phenomenon, starting in the United States in the early eighties; its political twist in Israel was the conscious stress on personal experience rather than national ethos. Consequently several powerful films were made, like the films based on Gila Alamagor's quasi-biographical *The Summer of Aviya* (*Hakayitz Shel Aviya*, 1988) and *Under the Domim Tree* (*Etz Hadomim Tafus*, 1995, both directed by Eli Cohen), which explored the predicament of survivors and their children in personal terms of family relationships and gender identity. Among the many documentaries made in a similar vein were the remarkable *Choice and Destiny* (*Habkhirah Vehagoral*, 1993), *Hugo* (1989, Yair Lev), and *Girlfriends* (*Habanot Melibau*, 1994, Yoel Kaminsky).[15] Although most personal films of children of survivors did not explicitly engage in political agenda, in exploring family roots their quest for identity often reclaimed a diasporic past in defiance of a Sabra Zionist identity. Other films transformed the image of the refugees from Olim (new immigrants) with hopeful national aspirations to desperate immigrants who display open longings for the German past, contrasting its alleged high art and cultural refinement with the sweaty reality and social vulgarity of contemporary Levantine Israel (*Transit*, Daniel Wachsmann,

1979; *Into the Night* [*Ad Sof Halayla*], Eitan Green, 1985; *Drifting* [*Nagu'a*], Amos Guttman, 1982; *Hide and Seek* [*Makhvo'im*], Dan Wolman, 1980; *Tel Aviv–Berlin*, Tzipi Trope, 1987; *Berlin–Jerusalem* [*Berlin-Yerushala'im*], Amos Gitai, 1989). Some films offered revisionist views of the absorption of the refugees after World War II. In *New Land* (*Eretz Khadashah*, 1994), Orna Ben-Dor attempts to show how the absorption of Holocaust survivors in a kibbutz subjugates them to brutal forms of victimization, including forcing the new Zionist identity on them. The concluding scene shows the young protagonists trying to escape at night from their host society, fantasizing that they will fly away from the literal and metaphorical garbage of their situation to a new land.

The efforts to denationalize the Holocaust were accompanied with denunciations of what some regarded as the excessive use of the Holocaust in the service of nationalist ideology. The critique claims that in the name of fears of genocide the country adopted military adventurism or brutal oppression of Israel's adversaries (for these critics, Israel's adversaries are often defined in the mild terms of neighbors or Israel's victims). Some argue that the Holocaust has become a religion in Israel, traumatizing the society and making it dispiritedly fearful and mistrusting.[16] Radical critics use the Holocaust to charge extreme expressions of anti-Zionism.[17] These include the comparison of the Israeli side in the political conflict with Nazi Germany and the equation of the Palestinians with the Jewish victims of the Holocaust or offering claims that the Holocaust accounts for deep national flaws. Some suggest that Israel is obsessed with death and destruction, for "in the case of Israel . . . the connection between nationalism and death is especially visceral. For the Jewish state is a nation that emerged from the ashes of a project of extermination."[18]

The 2000s

The moral anxieties of the Holocaust complex may account for some of the extreme anti-Zionist positions of many Jews, not only in Israel. Almost paradoxically, however, the existential burden of the trauma may also account for some weakening of national resolve in the Jewish state. The obsession with survival in the wake of the Holocaust is manifest in the supreme concern of Israelis for the loss of human life or the fate of Jews in captivity. Some prominent politicians and educators insist that nothing justifies the loss of life.[19] This categorical assertion had serious political implications for the way Israel conducted its wars and its fight against Arab terrorism. The withdrawal from Lebanon in 2001, the failed operation in Lebanon in

2006, and various agreements to bring home a handful of Israeli prisoners of war in exchange for the release of thousands of jailed Arab terrorists may indicate the roots of a deep traumatic complex. Curiously, the special anxiety about human loss is evident in *Operation Jonathan*. Despite the great success in the release of the hostages and the killing of the terrorists—and in significant contrast to the triumphant happy ending of the American networks' versions—viewers choke in tears in the end of Golan's film. The final sequence in the Israeli film contrasts the celebration of the liberated hostages and their families with the anguish of the returning somber soldiers who inform Yoni's girlfriend about his death, against the background of lush choral music accentuating the majesty of his death.

The rise of cultural forces critical of national ideology, the lingering mood of modernism in Israeli culture, with its dark vision of the human predicament, and the conditions of filmmaking based on low budgets and modest commercial ambitions all have shaped Israeli cinema, with stories of antiheroes in dramas of fall and defeat. In a curious contrast with this trend, the Holocaust has recently inspired new types of adventure dramas that revolve around narratives of revenge. These include Ari Folman's *Waltz with Bashir* (*Vals Im Bashir*, 2008) and *Made in Israel* (2001), Eytan Fox's *Walk on Water* (*Lalekhet Al Hamayim*, 2004), and Assaf Bernstein's *The Debt* (*Hakhov*, 2007), all of which deal with Israelis seeking to seize and punish Nazi war criminals.

Made in Israel was created in the tradition of the antinational political protest films from the 1980s,[20] rendering the Nazi hunt as a grotesque quest to kill old Nazis. The story takes place in the Golan Heights in an unspecified future on the occasion of signing a peace agreement between Israel and Syria. The political deal includes an old Nazi who had lived in Syria who is turned over to Israeli authorities. The plot involves the hiring of hired killers by an Israeli son of survivors to kidnap the Nazi so that he can personally execute the old man, defined as the last Nazi on earth. The area of the Golan, with its military history and political significance, features a stock of bizarre characters and ridiculous situations. All these elements become part of a plot characterized by digressions to episodic satirical moments. Reviewers who praised Ari Folman's visual achievements in the film also made the point that the initial narrative ploys, despite their obvious political charge, do not lead to any clear or even coherent message. Indeed, the postmodernist playfulness with narrative and character is primarily in the service of ideological subversion. Both state representatives and individual characters are obsessed with the "last Nazi," motivated by a grotesque desire for revenge, a grotesque quest for justice, or grotesque national commemoration.

The film does not explain why these drives are grotesque. In sum, the revenge narrative is deliberately used to confuse historical memory and dramatic motivation and is replete with iconoclasm of historical memory and mockery of identifiable national symbols and values.

In contrast, *The Debt* is a conventional narrative about Israeli agents who missed their Nazi target in the sixties and discover him in a home for the aged in the present. They reunite to complete their mission, compensating for their present limitations of age and skills with a strong sense of debt over their failed mission in the past. The film itself suffers from the limitations of a low budget and the expected flaws of a first feature by a young filmmaker. It includes the nearly standard antiheroic postures of Israeli cinema: the past story presents the failure of the Israeli agents as they clumsily lose the Nazi and then lie to their superiors; in the present they are visibly aged, physically weak, divided, and filled with hesitations, doubts, and guilt. The national implications of the story are downplayed in the present story, for the aging former agents choose to go on the mission without any official support. Overall, the revenge narrative suggests a nostalgic bridge to the heroic times of the Eichmann trial, but with a significant addition: the character of the female agent, as a young person in the past and the aging woman in the present (played by Gila Almagor). Her role introduces an intriguing gender perspective to the themes of victimization, the world of the secret agents, and the revenge action, ranging from recalling the pornographic cliché of sexual exploitation to echoing mythological heroines from the history of the Holocaust. The dramatic appeal of these themes led to the international production of another version of the story: *The Debt*, directed by John Madden (who directed *Shakespeare in Love*), featuring Sam Worthington (of *Avatar*) and Helen Mirren.

Walk on Water is a remarkable film, a polished secret agent drama that became the first Israeli movie in decades commercially distributed in the United States. The popular thriller features Eyal, a tough Mossad agent assigned to hunt down a former SS officer whose grandchildren are in Israel, a young girl living on a kibbutz, and her gay brother who comes to visit her. The film shows Israel as a multifaceted country, spanning its variegated geography from north to south and its rich history from biblical times to contemporary Tel Aviv. Daily life in Israel encompasses vibrant youth culture with occasional terror attacks in its cities and tranquil life on the kibbutz, punctuated by communal work and social dancing in the evenings. Made as a commercial film, *Walk on Water* still negotiates many polarities in Israel's identity. Eyal, the principal character, at first appears to be a model of Israeli heroism, a tough Mossad agent, who, like similar heroes in American popular cinema, is also burdened with personal problems af ter his wife commits suicide. His manifest masculine heroism is challenged when he befriends the gay German. After the initial shock of discovering his friend's sexual identity he develops a genuine affection for him. The arc of the narrative begins with an efficient assassination of an Arab terrorist and culminates when Eyal cannot carry out the final execution of the old Nazi. His initial toughness attributed to the destruction of his family in the Holo- caust has been replaced with sensitivity to human life and consciousness of the ubiquity of death that characterizes his profession and his identity.

Walk on Water explores a variety of themes central to Israeli culture, focusing on the confrontation with the legacy of the Holocaust through the actions and moral arc of the central character. The revenge theme invites a heroic narrative of determination and bold actions. In the course of the film, however, the strong motivation of revenge dissolves into paralysis and self-pity. The ending offers a Christian denouement: Eyal cannot kill the old Nazi, who is executed by his grandson. The Israeli agent falls into the arms of the young German, embraced in a posture that recalls the pietà scene in Christian art. The final scene shows Eyal happily married to the German woman, raising children on the kibbutz. Thus the film completely transpos- es revenge into reconciliation and love, possibly suggesting that the alleged Judaic concern with "an eye for an eye" should be replaced with values of mercy associated with Christianity, as may be indicated by the film's title.

The theme of revenge and the specific perspective offered by Israeli films should be evaluated by considering the special circumstances of Israel's his- tory and the specific psychological and moral legacies of the trauma that have led to a special "complicity in perpetrator-victim dynamics."[21] As de- scendants of the victims, Israelis are in a position to seek revenge against their victimizers. At the same time, Israelis are heirs of a rich Jewish culture that glorifies the values of human compassion and high ethical standards. The political entanglement in the Middle East and the human sacrifice of the national struggles further enhanced the desire for peace and nonviolent reconciliations. In May 2008 the president of Israel, Shimon Peres, gave a special articulation to the idea of the Holocaust and revenge in a commemo- ration ceremony in Poland:

> Revenge, surely we seek revenge. But a different kind of revenge, not a
> Nazi revenge but a Jewish revenge. And it came. . . . Kibbutz is the most
> righteous form of living in the world. This is revenge. A Jewish state was
> established, a leading state in the world in agriculture, in medicine, and in
> high tech. This is revenge. And even after the Sho'ah, when most countries
> in the world closed their gates to Holocaust survivors, the gates of Zion

opened. This is revenge. And when our neighbors attacked us seven times in sixty years and failed to defeat us. This is revenge.

And when, after the Holocaust, after the wars, after the intifadas, after the enriched uranium—we seek peace—this is revenge. This is the revenge of the sons of light against the sons of darkness.[22]

As the president of Israel, Shimon Peres attempted to negotiate differences and polarities in Israel's society, but his words offered no convergence for the conflicting narratives or the underlying dualities that define Jewish identity. The president's words played on both sides of the ideological debate, suggesting national achievements as one form of revenge but also mentioning general human achievements and the quest for peace as defining the revenge against genocide. The filmmakers of *Walk on Water* questioned the psychological motivation and moral value of revenge by resorting to Christian iconography. However, Jewish sources provide striking lessons. The Torah portion of Holocaust remembrance week in 2008 includes a warning against vengefulness, followed by one of the most famous and universal enunciations of Jewish heritage:

:בְּנֵי עַמֶּךָ, וְאָהַבְתָּ לְרֵעֲךָ כָּמוֹךָ-תִּטֹּר אֶת-תִּקֹּם וְלֹא-לֹא

(ויקרא פרק יט, פסוק יח, פרשת קדושים)

Seek not revenge, nor be mindful of the injury of thy citizens. Thou shalt love thy friend as thyself. I am the Lord. (Leviticus 19:18)

NOTES

1. Emil Fackenheim, a survivor of German concentration camps, became a distinguished Jewish philosopher. His famous argument was that after the Sho'ah Jews must add one more commandment to the traditional code of 613 commandments. The 614th commandment is to survive as Jews, lest the Jewish people perish. See *To Mend the World: Foundations of Future Jewish Thought* (New York: Schocken, 1982), 213.

2. Dominick LaCapra, *Writing History, Writing Trauma*, 21.

3. Michael G. Levine, "Necessary Stains: Art Spiegelman's *Maus* and the Bleeding History," in *Considering* Maus: *Approaches to Art Spiegelman's "Survivor Tale" of the Holocaust*, ed. Deborah R. Geis (Tuscaloosa and London: Alabama University Press, 2004), 64.

4. Joshua Hirsch, *Afterimage: Film, Trauma, and the Holocaust*, 10.

5. There is a striking gap between the popular notion of "Israel arising out of the ashes of Auschwitz" and the historical lack of any causal linkage between the genocide and the history of modern Zionism that led to the creation of Israel. The temporal proximity (Israel was established three years after the Holocaust) recalls the phrase *post hoc ergo propter hoc*—the logical fallacy of believing that temporal succession implies a causal relation. Obviously there is a profound connection between

the Holocaust and the Jewish state, and this chapter attempts to elucidate some of its aspects. But the Holocaust did not cause the establishment of Israel. See David Arnow, "The Holocaust and the Birth of Israel: Reassessing the Causal Relationship," *Journal of Israeli History* 15:3 (1994): 257–279.

6. Iris Milner, *Past Present: Biography, Identity and Memory in Second Generation Literature* (*Kirei Avar-Biografia, Zehut Vezikaron Besiporet Hador Hasheni*) (Tel Aviv University and Am Oved, 2003), 10.

7. See Ilan Avisar, "The Evolution of the Israelis' Attitude toward the Holocaust as Reflected in Modern Hebrew Drama," *Hebrew Annual Review* 9 (1985): 31–52.

8. See *Don't Touch My Holocaust* and discussion of the film in Yosefa Loshitzky, *Identity Politics on the Israeli Screen*, chapter 3.

9. David K. Shipler, *Arab and Jew: Wounded Spirits in a Promised Land* (New York: Penguin Books, 1986), 329.

10. Indeed, shadows are a prominent motif in many references to the Holocaust in Israeli films made until the mid-sixties. The survivors are haunted by the shadows of their suffering; their trauma is the shadow of the national project of modern Israel. But on the whole films made in Israel in its first two decades usually abstained from the subject of the Holocaust. The so-called national heroic films of the sixties and early seventies marginalized the Holocaust. *The Hero's Wife* is about a woman who survived a concentration camp, but the film focuses on her social situation and psychological predicament as a widow of an Israeli officer and hardly mentions her Holocaust past. The hero of *He Walked through the Fields*, Uri Kahana, falls in love with a girl who is one of a group of Tehran youngsters in the kibbutz. The story focuses on the Sabra fighter, with only some faint hints about the young woman's Holocaust experiences.

In 1974 notable poet and writer Haim Gouri collaborated with two filmmakers to create *The Eighty-first Blow*, a documentary on the Holocaust based solely on wartime footage and victims' testimonies. This film was followed by two more documentaries, *The Last Sea* and *Flames in the Ashes*, producing a trilogy that followed the traditional Zionist approach to the historical experience: the blow, the heroism of revolts and uprisings, and the road to Israel in the aftermath of the Holocaust.

In the late seventies more direct references to historical images became prevalent, in scenes that display the pervasive presence of memories of the Holocaust in Israeli consciousness. These include the selection scene in *Operation Jonathan*, the tableau vivant in *The Wooden Gun* (1979) of the child from the Warsaw ghetto raising his hands in front of SS soldiers, and the cutting of the girl's hair in *The Summer of Aviya* (1988) that recalls the shaved heads of the female victims in the camps. In films of the last twenty years, one can see literal trips to the sites of the past, establishing direct and concrete contacts between Israelis and the Holocaust. Thus the films show a consistent progress toward the reality of the trauma, from shadows to symbolic scenes and literal dramatizations. Curiously, the first Israeli Holocaust film whose plot takes place in Europe was made in 2008 as an Israeli/Polish coproduction, *Spring 1941* (dir. Uri Barbash).

11. See Ehud Luz, "The Moral Price of Sovereignty: The Dispute about the Use of Military Power within Zionism," *Modern Judaism* 7:1 (February 1987): 51–98. For a review of recent trends of the debate in radical Jewish circles, see Alvin Rosenfeld, "'Progressive' Jewish Thought and the New Anti-Semitism" (American Jewish Com-

mittee, December 2006, http://www.ajc.org/atf/cf/%7B42D75369-D582-4380-8395-D25925B85EAF%7D/PROGRESSIVE_JEWISH_THOUGHT.PDF).

12. See Yoram Hazoni, *The Jewish State: The Struggle for Israel's Soul*, chapter 1, "The Culture Makers Renounce the Idea of the Jewish State," 3–38, and chapter 2, "The Political Struggle for a Post-Jewish State," 39–73.

13. See Nurith Gertz, *Holocaust Survivors, Aliens, and Others in Israeli Cinema and Literature* (*Makhela Akheret: Nitzolei Sho'ah, Zarim Va'akherim Bakolno'a Uvasifrut Hayisra'elit*) (Tel Aviv: Am Oved, 2004).

14. Shaul Levanon "An Economic Disaster" ("Sho'ah Kalkalit"), *Ma'ariv*, May 1, 1989. The article also quotes Yaakov Gil'ad stating that the album *Dust and Ashes* (*Effer Ve'avak*) on Treblinka was designed to provoke reflections on the contemporary situation of Israel.

15. See Loshitzky, *Identity Politics on the Israeli Screen*, chapters 2 and 3.

16. Avraham Burg, former Knesset speaker and Jewish Agency chief, shocked many with harsh appraisals of the Zionist enterprise. In April 2008 he toured the United States, promoting his book *The Holocaust Is Over: We Must Rise from Its Ashes* (New York: Palgrave Macmillan, 2008). His main claim is that the Holocaust has become a religion in Israel, traumatizing the society and making it fearful and untrusting. An audio of Burg's speech is found at http://blogs.jta.org/telegraph/2008/04/03/the-burg-speaks-zionism-is-futile/.

17. See Elhanan Yakira and Michael Swirsky, *Post-Zionism, Post-Holocaust: Three Essays on Denial, Forgetting, and the Delegitimation of Israel* (Cambridge: Cambridge University Press, 2009).

18. Baruch Kimmerling, "Israel's Culture of Martyrdom," *Nation*, December 22, 2004. This article is a review of Idit Zertal's book *Nation and Death* (*Nation und Tod: Der Holocaust in der israelischen Öffentlichkeit* [Göttingen: Wallstein, 2003]).

19. Emphasis on the sanctity of life led to historical revisionism with respect to some exemplary events. For example, Daddi Zucker, a former member of the Israeli parliament, addressed the issue of the sanctity of life in praising a school principal who did not allow his students to take a trip to Masada (see *Ha'aretz*, March 26, 1997).

20. See Ilan Avisar, "Israeli Cinema and the Ending of Zionism," in *Israel in the Nineties*, ed. Fred Lazin and Greg Mahler (Gainesville: University Press of Florida, 1996), 153–168.

21. Mark Levene, *Genocide in the Age of the Nation State* (London: I. B. Tauris, 2005), 49.

22. Peres's speech was delivered at the site of the Warsaw ghetto in Poland on April 15, 2008 (my translation).

BIBLIOGRAPHY

Avisar, Ilan. *Screening the Holocaust: Cinema's Images of the Unimaginable*. Bloomington: Indiana University Press, 1988.

———. *Visions of Israel: Israeli Filmmakers and Images of the Jewish State*. New York: Charles Revson Foundation, 1997. http://www.jhvc.org/courses/index.php?url=visions.html.

Baron, Lawrence. *Projecting the Holocaust into the Present: The Changing Focus of Contemporary Holocaust Cinema*. Lanham, Md.: Rowman and Littlefield, 2005.

Hazoni, Yoram. *The Jewish State: The Struggle for Israel's Soul*. New York: Basic Books, 2000.

Hirsch, Joshua. *Afterimage: Film, Trauma, and the Holocaust*. Philadelphia: Temple University Press, 2004.

LaCapra, Dominick, *Writing History, Writing Trauma*. Baltimore: Johns Hopkins University Press, 2000.

Loshitzky, Yosefa. *Identity Politics on the Israeli Screen*. Austin: University of Texas Press, 2001.

Rosenfeld, Alvin, ed. *Thinking about the Holocaust: After Half a Century*. Bloomington: Indiana University Press, 1997.

FILMOGRAPHY

Because of That War (*Biglal Hamilkhama Ha'Hi*). Dir. Orna Ben-Dor, 1988.

Berlin–Jerusalem (*Berlin-Yerushala'im*). Dir. Amos Gitai, 1989.

The Cellar (*Hamartef*). Dir. Natan Gross, 1963.

Choice and Destiny (*Habkirah Vehagoral*). Dir. Tsipi Reibebach, 1993.

The Debt (*Hakhov*). Dir. Assaf Bernstein, 2007.

Don't Touch My Holocaust (*Al Ttig'u Li Basho'ah*). Dir. Asher Tlalim, 1994 (documentary).

Drifting (*Nagu'a*). Dir. Amos Guttman, 1982.

The Eighty-first Blow (*Hamakah Hashmonim Ve'akhat*). Dir. Haim Gouri, David Bergman, Jacques Ehrlich, 1974 (documentary).

Flames in the Ashes (*Pnei Hamered*). Dir. Haim Gouri, Jacques Ehrlich, 1985 (documentary).

Girlfriends (*Habanot Melibau*). Dir. Yoel Kaminsky, 1994 (documentary).

The Great Promise (*Dim'at Hanekhamah Hagdolah*). Dir. Joseph Lejtes, 1947.

The Hero's Wife (*Eshet Hagibor*). Dir. Peter Frye, 1963.

He Walked through the Fields (*Hu Halakh Basadot*). Dir. Yosef Millo, 1967.

Hide and Seek (*Makhvo'im*). Dir. Dan Wolman, 1980.

Hill 24 Doesn't Answer (*Giv'a 24 Eina Ona*). Dir. Thorold Dickinson, 1955.

Hugo. Dir. Yair Lev, 1989 (documentary).

Into the Night (*Ad Sof Halayla*). Dir. Eitan Green, 1985.

The Last Sea (*Hayam Ha'akharon*). Dir. Haim Gouri, David Bergman, Jacques Ehrlich, 1980 (documentary).

Made in Israel. Dir. Ari Folman, 2001.

New Land (aka *Newland*; *Eretz Khadashah*). Dir. Orna Ben-Dor, 1994.

Operation Jonathan (aka *Operation Thunderbolt*; *Mivtza Yonatan*). Dir. Menahem Golan, 1977.

Spring 1941. Dir. Uri Barbash, 2008.

The Summer of Aviya (*Hakayitz Shel Aviya*). Dir. Eli Cohen, 1988.

Tel Aviv–Berlin. Dir. Tzipi Trope, 1987.

Transit. Dir. Daniel Wachsmann, 1979.

Under the Domim Tree (*Etz Hadomim Tafus*). Dir. Eli Cohen, 1995.

Walk on Water (*Lalekhet Al Hamayim*). Dir. Eytan Fox, 2004.

Waltz with Bashir (*Vals Im Bashir*). Dir. Ari Folman, 2008.

The Wooden Gun (*Roveh Khuliot*). Dir. Ilan Moshenson, 1979.

I3   Near and Far

The Representation of Holocaust Survivors in Israeli Feature Films

LIAT STEIR-LIVNY

The immigration to Israel of approximately 500,000 Holocaust survivors in the aftermath of World War II has found ample expression in Israeli cinema throughout the years. Scholars of Israeli cinema maintain that the cinematic Zionist narrative of the 1940s and 1950s described the encounter between Holocaust survivors and Israelis in a stereotypical manner. Survivors were often portrayed as people broken in body and in spirit, who needed to be transformed from a "diasporic Jew" to a Hebrew "New Jew." These scholars further assert that over the years, especially since the late 1970s, the negative image of Holocaust survivors dissipated and was replaced by a more complex image.[1]

Contrary to these notions, I argue that the problematic image of Holocaust survivors in Israeli feature films has remained almost unchanged.[2] Instead of addressing the complexity of the Holocaust trauma and the varied facets of Holocaust survivors' identities, Israeli feature films from the late 1970s onward continue to replicate the same superficial imagery, portraying negative images of survivors, who are shown as collapsing under the burden of the past and losing their grip on reality. Moreover, in the Zionist narrative of the 1940s and 1950s the Holocaust survivors' representations were used to glorify the achievements of Zionism. Israeli feature films from the late 1970s onward still use Holocaust survivors, only now for an inverted purpose: to criticize the erosion of the Zionist ethos. Only in the last few years, alongside films that duplicate these stereotypes, do we find a very few films that offer a more complex image of the Holocaust survivor.

These persistent negative stereotypes stand in direct contradiction to the historical research on the subject. Despite having to cope with deep emotional scars, Holocaust survivors who immigrated to Israel left a profound mark on economics, politics, medicine, settlement, and the military.[3] Films do not reflect reality; however, they both influence and are influenced by public opinion. The nearly unaltered negative image of Holocaust survivors in Israeli fictional films indicates that, although the attitude toward the Holocaust has changed in Israel over the years, the attitude toward Holocaust survivors remains problematic and can be described as "near and far," complex, ambivalent, and fluctuating attitudes which empathize with the survivors and yet remain critically distant. They range widely from superficial to complex portrayals, from deepening stereotypes to shattering them, and from old, fixated perceptions to new, multicultural openness toward the "Other."

Negative Stereotypes and a Zionist Lesson: 1947–1960

The consolidation of every culture involves complex negotiations between the dominant group and various marginal groups within it—its "Others."[4] Jewish society in Eretz Israel was no exception. The metanarrative cultivated publicly during the 1940s and 1950s in the Yishuv (pre-state Israel) viewed the new Jewish society in the making in Palestine in opposition to the old, maligned Jewish society in the Diaspora.[5] Holocaust survivors who arrived in Israel were met with empathy but also with suspicion and often symbolized for Zionists the worst about the Diaspora; hence their encounter with Israelis was problematic. Many survivors preferred not to talk about their pasts, choosing instead to focus on building their new lives. Many others, however, wanted to tell their stories and share their pain. For various reasons some of them were encouraged to keep silent; others were accused of cowardice or of submitting to their fate "like lambs to the slaughter," or of committing "immoral acts" in order to survive.[6]

Israeli cinema in the 1940s and 1950s was dominated by ideological considerations. Films that distinctively propagated Zionist ideas served as an artistic platform for an ideological outlook through which the Zionist establishment sought to display its political, national, and economic achievements. Films focused on the Zionist struggle, donations to the Zionist movement, the establishment of a Jewish state in Eretz Israel, and support for the state after its founding. To this end, a number of films were produced in English and then translated into myriad languages and distributed throughout the world.

Such films necessarily presented a tendentious worldview. Like other aspects of Israeli culture during that era,[7] Israeli films did not deal directly with the Holocaust but rather with its Zionist "lesson": the importance of establishing a Jewish state in the Land of Israel. As part of this process, Holocaust survivors were reduced to a homogeneous entity that bore distinct negative connotations. The survivors were depicted as miserable and dejected figures, physically and mentally broken. Such films often focused on survivors' numerous problems, laying the blame on them for their difficult absorption and presenting them as stubborn, rebellious, introverted, and antisocial. These films also depicted the mental breakdown that survivors experienced during their absorption in Israel as a crisis that could only be solved with the help of the native Eretz Israeli Jews. The assimilation of survivors in these films is always linked to the erasure of their memories—they are required to leave their past behind in order to assimilate into Israeli life. This narrative clearly reflects and corroborates the Zionist narrative, which regards the Land of Israel as the only place where the survivors can heal and begin a new life.

Like most of the films that featured the survivors' inability to assimilate into their surroundings, The Great Promise (Dim'at Hanekhamah Hagdolah, Joseph Lejtes, 1947) tells the story of one child survivor, Tamar, who arrives in Palestine but refuses to integrate. She does not speak or communicate with the other children. She ignores their warm hospitality, steals everything within reach, and responds violently and runs away when the stolen goods are discovered under her bed. But because of the village children's warmth and kindness, she decides to come back and change. By the end of the film she has integrated herself so well that one cannot tell her from the other children. All of the children wear white and dance together in the warm Israeli sun as a homogeneous entity (extreme long shot). Only one sequence is dedicated to the group of survivors with whom Tamar arrived. The scant screen time dedicated to this latter sequence compresses the survivors' negative image into several short scenes, showing their behavior in their new surroundings. They violently refuse to have their bags taken from them; pounce on food that is intended to be shared by everyone, eating it greedily; steal food from the table and hide it in their coats; and steal soap and toothpaste in the shower.

In other films the survivors themselves testify about their unstable mental condition and describe themselves as mentally ill or unfit parents. My Father's House (Beit Avi, Herbert Klein 1947) follows David, an adolescent survivor, in his search for his father in Eretz Israel. Miriam, a beautiful young survivor, arrives with him. While the kibbutz members try to help them adjust to their new lives, Miriam decisively announces that every survivor should be treated like "a sick person." In *Yonatan and Tali* (*Yonatan VeTali*, Henry Schneider, 1953), a Holocaust survivor who is released from a mental institution gives up her two children, Yonatan and Tali, for adoption to a family of farmers that will raise them to be "proper" Israelis. The mother relinquishes her children of her own free will, exonerating the Israelis and magnifying the negative image of Holocaust survivors through their own self-incriminating testimony.

The female Holocaust survivors during those years are portrayed not only as unfit mothers and mental patients but also as women forced into prostitution (*My Father's House*; *The Sun Rises on the Horizon* [*Hashemesh Ola Ba'ofek*], Hervé Bromberger, 1960) or women who used their sexuality to survive (*The Faithful City* [*Kiryah Ne'emanah*], Joseph Lejtes, 1952). The women in these films undergo a process of purification, leaving them modest and asexual by the end of the films.

These negative images are aimed at glorifying the native Israeli New Jews, who are portrayed as the complete opposite. In most cases they are filmed outside in the countryside, in open and sun-filled frames, from low angles that elevate them as they dominate the land (*The Great Promise*), work it (*The Faithful City*), build new settlements (*My Father's House*), and cultivate the young generation (*Yonatan and Tali*). Many of the male figures symbolize the legendary Sabra as a handsome young Ashkenazi, intensively involved in working the land and fighting successfully against the Arabs.

1960–1980: Duplicated Stereotypes and a Slight Change in the Assimilation Process

The Adolf Eichmann trial (1961) changed the perception of the Holocaust in Israel. After years of repression, Israelis were exposed to numerous testimonies which made them understand the complexity of the Jewish predicament during the Holocaust, such as the difficulties in resisting the Nazis, grasping its mechanism of lies and deception, and clearly determining right from wrong. Following the trial, both the Holocaust and the Jewish past in the Diaspora began appearing more often in literature and theater.[8]

The films produced in the 1960s and 1970s, however, imply that the change was neither immediate nor particularly drastic. Only a few films that dealt with Holocaust survivors were produced during these decades, but some changes were made in the cinematic image of the absorption process. The notion that the memories of Holocaust survivors could be erased was replaced with an understanding that the traumatic past is part of the present. Likewise, the idea of total assimilation into Israeli society was replaced by an implied separation between the Holocaust survivors and the Israelis.

Such films include *The Cellar* (*Hamartef*, Natan Gross, 1963), in which the Holocaust survivor, Emmanuel Saraf, cannot free himself from his past. He is engrossed in prewar memories of his German girlfriend, of the war, and of the expulsion to the camps. He also dwells on postwar Europe and revenge against Hans, his former German friend, who became a Nazi and was responsible for the murder of his father. Contrasting lighting is used to emphasize Emmanuel's vacillation between the past and the present. This is a single-actor film (Shimon Yisraeli), so the characters he plays are filmed from behind or as silhouettes. The silhouettes dominate the screen just as they dominate Emmanuel's personality. *He Walked through the Fields* (*Hu Halakh Basadot*, Yosef Millo, 1967) tells the story of Uri, a young Sabra who returns to the kibbutz in 1947 to work and reunite with his family. Mika, the Holocaust survivor he meets, is haunted by her past in the refugee camp in Tehran (1942), where, it is implied, she had an abortion. In *The Wooden Gun* (*Roveh Khuliot*, Ilan Moshenson, 1979), a Holocaust survivor nicknamed Palestina lives in a deteriorating shack on the seashore. Pictures of her murdered family hang on the walls of her shack, and her vague references to "those who shall come from there," implying the sea, reveal that the past is blended with the present.

Contrary to films produced in the 1940s and 1950s, the Holocaust survivors in these later films do not undergo a change and are not assimilated into society. This modified portrayal of the assimilation process, however, did not alter the negative stereotypes of Holocaust survivors. For example, Emmanuel Saraf in *The Cellar* is a troubled and lonesome man living on the margins of society, unable to build a new life, and drowning in memories of the past. He is incapable of starting a family and maintaining a livelihood as a security guard at a construction site. Uri the Sabra in *He Walked through the Fields* is forced to work in the vineyard with Holocaust survivors absorbed by the kibbutz. The parallel editing highlights the unfathomable differences and clashes between the diasporic Jews and the New Jews that Uri represents. The survivors are filmed from a high angle that makes them look wretched, whereas Uri is filmed from a low angle that glorifies him. The survivors are idle, remain in one place, and fight with each other instead of working, while Uri is filmed riding through the vineyard, supervising the grape harvest (dolly). He reprimands them and tries to help them mend their ways. Negative stereotypes also appear in *The Wooden Gun:* Palestina, the Holocaust survivor, is a mentally ill, nonfunctioning woman who is abused by all. She lives on the margins of Tel Aviv (on the seashore) and spends her days staring at the sea and screaming endless delusional rants.

1980–2000: A Combination of a Shattered Zionist Narrative and Reconstruction of Negative Stereotypes

In the 1970s the hold of Zionist ideology gradually began to weaken for several reasons, including the 1973 Yom Kippur War and its harsh consequences; stagnation and corruption in the labor movement, which had been in power since the days of the Eretz Israeli Yishuv; the consequent ascent of the right-wing party Likud to power (1977); and the growing legitimacy of multicultural trends that replaced the dominant ideas about a homogeneous Israeli society. During these decades the Holocaust became an important part of the Israeli discourse. It was made a permanent feature of both the high school curriculum and matriculation examinations. Likewise, more and more Holocaust survivors began to publish their memoirs while the second generation, the children of Holocaust survivors, began to showcase their relationship with their parents through art.[9] Previously considered "Others," Mizrahi Jews, women, Palestinians, and Holocaust survivors became the protagonists in many feature films. The glorification of the Zionist ethos and the absorption process was replaced by a profound criticism of early Zionism and its attitude toward and treatment of marginal groups.[10]

Israeli cinema researchers suggest that these changes are also reflected in the image of the Holocaust survivors and claim that survivors are depicted in feature films from the late 1970s onward as being emotionally scarred but are treated with respect and empathy.[11] I argue, to the contrary, that most of the Israeli feature films from those decades continue to replicate the same negative images and portray the survivors as broken in body and spirit. Survivors are still attached to the Zionist ethos, but now (in contrast to the 1940s and 1950s) their representations are used to criticize it. There is nothing "respectable" in their depiction as passive, broken, and deviant people, and the "empathy" is still directed toward the weak, the broken, and the wretched, which actually deepens their negative image. Female survivors are still portrayed as sexual objects (*Alex in Love* [aka *Alex Is Lovesick*; *Alex Khole Ahava*], Boaz Davidson, 1986); *Newland* [aka *New Land*; *Eretz Khadashah*], Orna Ben-Dor, 1994) and as destructive mothers (*Blind Man's Bluff* [aka *Dummy in a Circle*; *Golem Bama'agal*], Anner Preminger, 1993, based on Lilly Amitai-Perry's novel). The men and children are portrayed as mentally troubled (*Hide and Seek* [*Makhvo'im*], Dan Wolman, 1980), as violent and wild (*Under the Domim Tree* [*Etz Hadomim Tafus*], Eli Cohen, 1995), or as a part of marginal groups (*Transit*, Daniel Wachsmann, 1979).

One of the most prominent Holocaust films of the period, *The Summer of Aviya* (*Hakayitz Shel Aviya*, Eli Cohen, 1988), describes the relationship between Henya, a Holocaust survivor, and Aviya, her ten-year-old daughter. Henya and Aviya live in a village at the beginning of the 1950s but are not an integral part of it. Their house, located at the edge of the village, reflects their geographic and symbolic exclusion from its center.[12] The village inhabitants treat Henya and Aviya like outcasts. Henya is referred to as "the crazy woman," and Aviya is banned from the local ballet class. The village children mock her and hit her. The image of the absorbing Israeli society has altered and Henya and Aviya are the protagonists, but that does not change the negative image of the survivors. Henya is hospitalized every few months in a mental institution. Alter, an Auschwitz survivor who enters their lives, is portrayed as someone who steals, hides food, and is unable to communicate. Henya starts to develop a close relationship with her daughter, but her mental condition deteriorates. In the final scenes she demands that Aviya close the shutters, mentally and physically severing any contact with the outside world as she slowly sinks into insane hallucinations.

The same ideas are found in *Tel Aviv–Berlin* (Tzipi Trope, 1987), which describes the life of Binyamin, a Holocaust survivor living in Tel Aviv in 1948. Like many other films of this era, *Tel Aviv–Berlin* criticizes the Israeli absorption process. Binyamin is completely detached from Israeli society and from the 1948 war. He spends most of his time in his house, turning it into a museum of German culture. Even when Binyamin leaves his house and goes outside, he continues his isolation. This is illustrated by the café he frequents: the patrons listen to music "from there," play chess, and speak German. The cinematography heightens the feeling that Tel Aviv is a continuation of the ghetto and the camps, highlighting Binyamin's estrangement and loneliness and the memories that engulf him. He is mostly filmed behind fences, framed within walls closing in on him, and in alleys, where he pursues the man he suspects was a kapo in Auschwitz.[13]

One of the places in which Binyamin secludes himself is the house of Gusty, a Holocaust survivor he met in Tel Aviv. Within the confines of this house, Gusty's friend reveals how they survived in Auschwitz. She attempts to engage Binyamin in the same seductive games that, according to her, they learned from Nazi officers when they were prostitutes in Auschwitz. Thus the film repeats the same accusation that appeared in earlier films: that the women survived because they prostituted themselves (a claim that is rejected by historians).[14] The imagery not only reconstructs this false accusation but deepens it. Women survivors who were presented as having been forced into prostitution are purified at the end of the films produced in the 1940s and 1950s. Alternatively, according to films from the 1980s and 1990s, the survivors who were sexual victims during the Holocaust retain this identity in the Israeli present and maintain the same behavior while hurting the people around them.

Family Secrets (*Sodot Mishpakha*, Nitza Gonen, 1998) reconstructs a destructive sexual link between the past and the present in a different way. The mental problems of the Holocaust survivor turn him into a demonic pedophile. In this film two cousins, Rivi and Shauli, meet during the summer at their grandmother's house. They develop an intimate relationship and try to make love. The Holocaust survivor Alfred, a family friend who is also staying at the house, discovers them together. He violently throws Rivi out into the yard and remains with Shauli in the room. The camera follows Rivi trying unsuccessfully to peep into the room. Rivi understands what has transpired only after Shauli comes out weeping, blood dripping from his pants. In an act of repentance, Alfred shuts himself in another room and hangs himself. It later becomes apparent that he was molested in the concentration camp and that this experience turned him into a pedophile. This link between the past and the present only worsens the image of the Holocaust survivor, by creating an analogy between abusers and victims.

The Third Millennium: Ambivalent Trends

In recent years the memory of the Holocaust has become an integral part of Israeli culture. Yet films that deal with the Holocaust still display ambivalent portraits of survivors. Some films continue to portray the basic, superficial stereotype of the Holocaust survivor as mentally troubled. Films like *Six Million Pieces* (*Shisha Million Ressissim*, Tzipi Trope, 2002) confine survivors to closed spaces indoors that exacerbate the sense of suffocation that characterizes their lives. The walls that close in on the survivors are a metaphor for the memories that haunt them and destabilize their mental health.[15] Set in 1969, the film features Ruth, a Holocaust survivor and mother, who is treated with sedatives and remains secluded in her home. She does not go out but spends her days wandering through the rooms of the house. As in earlier films, the Holocaust survivor is the one who criticizes the survivors. This serves to validate the stereotype in the sense that the individual is testifying against herself. For example, Ruth warns her daughter not to wander the streets because "they are filled with crazy Holocaust survivors."

Six Million Pieces not only replicates old stereotypes about survivors' mental health but exacerbates these stereotypes by claiming that Ruth transfers her mental illness to Maya, her daughter. Maya ultimately suffers a mental breakdown and is hospitalized in a mental institution because she sees visions from the Holocaust.

But other films represent Holocaust survivors in more nuanced ways that show their ability to rebuild new lives and become active members of society while coping with the dark shadows of the past. Amos Gitai's *Kedma* (2002), for instance, describes a few hours in the life of Holocaust survivors, who immediately after arriving in 1948 are asked to fight in Israel's War of Independence. The Holocaust survivors are not described as a homogeneous group but rather as individuals who differ from one another. Some argue that they should forget the past, while others tell and retell stories of ghettos and of persecutions. The camera offers a voyeuristic glance into their world, revealing strong yet scarred people, who live with trauma while trying to start a new life. Like many films in the 1980s and 1990s, *Kedma* does not glorify the Zionist ethos but rather confronts it. According to the film, the survivors are drawn unexpectedly into the 1948 war. Although many lack proper military training, some of them are eager to fight, and numerous survivors are killed. In contradistinction to earlier films, no positive future is presented as an option.

Another such prominent film is *Walk on Water* (*Lalekhet Al Hamayim*, Eytan Fox, 2004), about a "second-generation" ruthless and efficient Mossad agent, Eyal. Eyal is drafted by his supervisor Menakhem into a personal vendetta—to find Alfred Himmelman, a former Nazi officer who killed his family. Unlike the images of Holocaust survivors in the last sixty years of Israeli feature films, Menakhem is a respected man. He is a senior executive in the Mossad. His line of work demands mental strength, responsibility, and talent. His successes further emphasize these character traits. The numerous close-ups of his face depict a peaceful and serene man. He is not portrayed as a helpless victim or a mental patient but as a father figure and mentor to Eyal. When Eyal discovers that his wife has committed suicide, Menakhem is the first person he calls. Menakhem arrives immediately and enters Eyal's apartment with his own personal key. He is the one that pressures Eyal to see a therapist and refuses to let him carry on his regular duties.

In the films produced during the 1940s and 1950s Holocaust survivors who were absorbed into Israeli society had forgotten their traumatic past. *Walk on Water* confronts these notions. Menakhem is planted in the present but remembers the past. He is haunted by his past and hunts down the man responsible for his personal trauma. When Eyal tries to confront him, arguing that old Himmelman will probably die soon, Menakhem claims that he wants "to precede God." This expression is the title of a book that tells the story of Marek Edelman, one of the most significant fighters in the Warsaw ghetto revolt. Thus this expression strengthens Menakhem's active character and tells the story of delayed revenge for a survivor who wishes to change history rather than only be affected by it.

Menakhem is portrayed as a decisive, determined, and thorough man. He finds out about a birthday party that Himmelman's son is having, which might shed some light on the whereabouts of old Himmelman. Menakhem pressures Eyal to fly to Berlin to attend the party. His sharp instincts prove to be right: old Himmelman indeed reappears. Menakhem follows Eyal to Germany in order to make sure that the mission will be carried out and that Himmelman will die. Menakhem refuses to give him the right to be prosecuted in Israel and demands his execution in Germany, which eventually takes place. The executioner is not Eyal, however, but Axel, Himmelman's grandson, who by doing so compensates for his family's dark history.

Conclusion

Decades after Israeli cinema broke away from the Zionist dogma that informed it at an early stage, a majority of directors still portray Holocaust survivors negatively, as broken and deranged. The preponderance of this stereotypical imagery is surprising in light of the changes that Israeli films underwent and their increasing tendency toward social and ideological critique. Since the late 1970s Israeli cinema has been representing formerly marginal groups in increasingly complex and sophisticated ways. These include not only women, homosexuals, Mizrahi Jews, the Orthodox, Bedouins, Druze, and Palestinians, who enjoy in-depth cinematic representations, but also newer groups such as immigrants from the former USSR and foreign migrant workers. Holocaust survivors are the only group almost entirely unaffected by the changes that have taken place in this discourse. A change in this trend may be reflected in the few recent films that show a more mature and nuanced treatment of a very difficult and charged issue.

NOTES

1. See, for example, Nurith Gertz, *Holocaust Survivors, Aliens, and Others in Cinema and Literature*; Moshe Tzimmerman, *Don't Touch My Holocaust*; Meir Schnitzer, *Israeli Cinema*; Ilan Avisar, "National Anxieties, Personal Nightmares: The Holocaust Complex in Israeli Cinema."

2. This essay focuses on Israeli feature films and not on Israeli documentary films on this subject.

3. Hanna Yablonka, "Holocaust Survivors in Israel: At the Center of Action But at the Margins of Research."

4. For an expanded discussion of the "Other," see Laurence J. Silberstein, "Others Within and Others Without: Rethinking Jewish Identity and Culture."

5. See, for example, Yaron Peleg, *Derech Gever: Homoeroticism in Hebrew Literature, 1880–2000.*

6. Tom Segav, *The Seventh Million: The Israelis and the Holocaust*, 101–169.

7. See examples from literature, the educational system, and memorial pamphlets in Ruth Firrer, *Agents of a Zionist Lesson*; Gershon Shaked, *Israeli Literature, 1880–1980*; and Noa Amit, "Memorialization Patterns: Memorial Booklets for Soldiers."

8. Hanna Yablonka, *The State of Israel against Adolf Eichmann.*

9. For an expanded discussion on the "second generation," see Iris Milner, *Past Present: Biography, Identity and Memory in Second Generation Literature*, 19–35; Yosefa Loshitzky, *Identity Politics on the Israeli Screen*, 15–71.

10. Miri Talmon, *Israeli Graffiti: Nostalgia, Groups, and Collective Identity in Israeli Cinema*; Nurith Gertz, *Motion Fiction: Israeli Fiction in Films*; Ella Shohat, *Israeli Cinema: East/West and the Politics of Representation.*

11. See, for example, Gertz, *Holocaust Survivors*; Tzimmerman, *Don't Touch My Holocaust*; Schnitzer, *Israeli Cinema*; and Avisar, "National Anxieties, Personal Nightmares."

12. Gertz, *Holocaust Survivors.*

13. Ibid.

14. For example, see Iris Milner, *Narratives in Holocaust Literature*; *Stalags* (Ari Libsker, 2008).

15. Other such films include *Tonight: The Holocaust Survivor* (Gavriel Bibliovich, 2001), *PTSD* (Shmulik Calderon, 2004), *Forgiveness* (Udi Aloni, 2006), and *Letters to America* (Hanan Peled, 2006).

BIBLIOGRAPHY

Amit, Noa. "Memorialization Patterns: Memorial Booklets for Soldiers" ("Dfusei Hantzakha: Sifrei Zikaron Lekhayalim"). MA thesis, Tel Aviv University, 1995.

Avisar, Ilan. "National Anxieties, Personal Nightmares: The Holocaust Complex in Israeli Cinema" ("Kharadot Leumiot, Siyutim Ishi'im: Tasbikh Hasho'ah Bakolno'a Hayisra'eli"). In Nurith Gertz, Orly Lubin, and Judd Ne'eman (eds.), *Fictive Looks: On Israeli Cinema* (*Mabatim Fiktivi'im Al Kolno'a Yisra'eli*), 160–178. Tel Aviv: Open University Press, 1998.

Firrer, Ruth. *Agents of a Zionist Lesson* (*Sokhnim Shel Halekakh*). Tel Aviv: Hakibbutz Hameukhad and Haifa: Haifa University, 1989.

Gertz, Nurith. *Motion Fiction: Israeli Fiction in Films* (*Sipur Mehasratim: Siporet Yisra'elit Ve'ibudeihah Lakolno'a*). Tel-Aviv: Open University Press, 1993.

———. *Holocaust Survivors, Aliens, and Others in Cinema and Literature* (*Makhela Akheret: Nitzolei Sho'ah, Zarim Va'akherim Basiporet Hayisra'elit*). Tel Aviv: Am Oved, 2004.

Loshitzky, Yosefa. *Identity Politics on the Israeli Screen*. Austin: University of Texas Press, 2001.

Milner, Iris. *Past Present: Biography, Identity and Memory in Second Generation Literature* (*Kirei Avar-Biografia, Zehut Vezikaron Besiporet Hador Hasheni*). Tel Aviv: Tel Aviv University and Am Oved, 2003.

———. *Narratives in Holocaust Literature* (*Narativim Besifrut Hasho'ah*). Bnei-Brak: Hakibbutz Hameukhad, 2008.

Peleg, Yaron. *Derekh Gever: Homoeroticism in Hebrew Literature, 1880–2000* (*Derekh Gever: Homoerotika Basifrut Ha'ivrit 1880–2000*). Tel Aviv: Shufra, 2003.

Schnitzer, Meir. *Israeli Cinema* (*Hakolno'a Hayisra'eli: Kol Ha'uvdot, Kol Ha'alilot, Kol Habama'im Vegam Bikorot*). Tel Aviv: Kineret, 1994.

Segav, Tom. *The Seventh Million: The Israelis and the Holocaust* (*Hamilion Hasvi'i-Hayisra'elim Vehasho'ah*). Jerusalem: Keter, 1991.

Shaked, Gershon. *Israeli Literature, 1880–1980* (*Hasiporet Ha'iverit 1880–1980*). Tel Aviv: Hakibbutz Hameukhad, 1998.

Shohat, Ella. *Israeli Cinema: East/West and the Politics of Representation*. Austin: University of Texas Press, 1989.

Silberstein, Laurence J. "Others Within and Others Without: Rethinking Jewish Identity and Culture." In Laurence J. Silberstein and Robert L. Cohn (eds.), *The Other in Jewish Thought and History*, 1–34. New York: New York University Press, 1994.

Talmon, Miri. *Israeli Graffiti: Nostalgia, Groups, and Collective Identity in Israeli Cinema* (*Bluz Latzabar Ha'avud: Khavurot Venostalgia Bakolno'a Hayisra'eli*). Tel Aviv: Open University and Haifa: Haifa University Press, 2001.

Tzimmerman, Moshe. *Don't Touch My Holocaust* (*Al Tig'u Li Basho'ah*). Haifa: Haifa University Press, 2002.

Yablonka, Hanna. *The State of Israel against Adolf Eichmann* (*Medinat Israel Neged Adolf Aikhman*). Tel Aviv and Jerusalem: Yediot Akharonot, 2001

———. "Holocaust Survivors in Israel: At the Center of Action But at the Margins of Research" ("Nitzolei Hasho'ah Beisra'el: Bemerkaz Ha'asiya Akh Beshulei Hamekhkar"). *Mizkar* 16 (April 2002): 20–21.

FILMOGRAPHY

Alex in Love (aka *Alex Is Lovesick*; *Alex Khole Ahava*, dir. Boaz Davidson, 1986).

Blind Man's Bluff (aka *A Dummy in a Circle*; *Golem Bama'agal*, dir. Anner Preminger, 1993).

The Cellar (*Hamartef*, dir. Natan Gross, 1963).

The Faithful City (*Kiryah Ne'emanah*, dir. Joseph Lejtes, 1952).

Family Secrets (*Sodot Mishpakha*, dir. Nitza Gonen, 1998).

Forgiveness (*Mekhilot*, dir. Udi Aloni, 2006).

The Great Promise (*Dim'at Hanekhamah Hagdolah*, dir. Joseph Lejtes, 1947).

He Walked through the Fields (*Hu Halakh Basadot*, dir. Yosef Millo, 1967).

Hide and Seek (*Makhvo'im*, dir. Dan Wolman, 1980).

Kedma (dir. Amos Gitai, 2002).

Letters to America (dir. Hanan Peled, 2006).

My Father's House (*Beit Avi*, dir. Herbert Klein, Joseph Lejtes, and Ben Oyserman, 1947).

Newland (aka *New Land*; *Eretz Khadashah*, dir. Orna Ben-Dor, 1994).
PTSD (*Tguva Me'ukheret*, dir. Shmulik Calderon, 2004).
Six Million Pieces (*Shisha Million Ressissim*, dir. Tzipi Trope, 2002).
Stalags (dir. Ari Libsker, 2008).
The Summer of Aviya (*Hakayitz Shel Aviya*, dir. Eli Cohen, 1988).
The Sun Rises on the Horizon (*Hashmesh Ola Ba'ofek*, dir. Hervé Bromberger, 1960).
Tel Aviv–Berlin (dir. Tzipi Trope, 1987).
Tonight: The Holocaust Survivor (*Ha'erev: Hanitzol*, dir. Gavriel Bibliovich, 2001).
Transit (dir. Daniel Wachsmann, 1979).
Under the Domim Tree (*Etz Hadomim Tafus*, dir. Eli Cohen, 1995).
Walk on Water (*Lalekhet Al Hamayim*, Eytan Fox, 2004)
The Wooden Gun (*Roveh Khuliot*, dir. Ilan Moshenson, 1979).
Yonatan and Tali (*Yonatan VeTali*, dir. Henry Schneider, 1953).

14 Homonational Desires

Masculinity, Sexuality, and Trauma in the Cinema of Eytan Fox

RAZ YOSEF

Zionism's political project of liberating the Jewish people and creating a nation like all other nations was intertwined with a longing for the sexual redemption and normalization of the Jewish male body. In fin-de-siècle anti-Semitic scientific-medical discourse, the male Jewish body was associated with disease, madness, degeneracy, sexual perversity, and femininity as well as with homosexuality. This pathologization of Jewish male sexuality had also entered the writings of Jewish scientists and medical doctors, including Sigmund Freud.[1] Zionist thinkers such as Theodor Herzl and Max Nordau were convinced that the invention of a stronger, healthier heterosexual "Jewry of Muscles" not only would overcome the stereotype of the Jewish male as a homosexual but also would solve the economic, political, and national problems of the Jewish people. This notion of a new Jewish masculinity became the model for the militarized masculine Sabra (native-born Israeli). Unlike the passive, ugly, "feminine," diasporic Jewish male, the new Zionist Sabra man would engage in manual labor, athletics, and war, becoming the colonialist explorer in touch with the land and with his body. Israeli films expressed this national desire through various visual and narrative tropes, enforcing the image of the hypermasculine nation-builder—an image dependent on the repudiation of the "feminine" within men.[2]

These gender and sexual oppressive aspects of the Zionist project led to the (formal and nonformal) exclusion of gays and lesbians from Israeli society. The end of the 1980s and 1990s signified the growth of an Israeli gay and lesbian consciousness, which was related to the public and political activity of Aguda: The Association of Gay Men, Lesbians, Bisexuals and

Transgender in Israel. The association's members fought for the expansion of their civic rights and the right to represent sexual preference in culture and criticized the absence and marginality of gays and lesbians in Israeli society. A series of legal and social struggles led to the provision of a degree of civic legitimacy for gays and lesbians in the central institutions of Israeli society—the army, family, and motherhood—that define the limits of membership and participation in the Israeli collective.[3] The successes of these struggles also promoted the visibility of gay men and women in mainstream media as well as allowing the rise of an urban queer culture that confidently took its place within the heterosexual national consensus. Emphasis was placed on the "normality" of the community's members, being "good citizens," and being "like everybody else." As Lee Walzer writes: "the Aguda was pursuing a very mainstream strategy and image at that time—demonstrating that gays and lesbians are 'just like everyone else,' serving in the military, and living in committed long-term relationships."[4]

The cinematic work of Eytan Fox—the leading male gay filmmaker in Israel today—is responsible for the increasing visibility of gay people in Israeli culture. In his films such as *Yossi and Jagger* (2002), *Walk on Water* (2004), and *The Bubble* (2006), Fox tries to deconstruct Zionist national heterosexual masculinity and to offer new images of homosexual social existence that sometimes transgress national and ethnic boundaries. In *The Bubble*, for example, Fox places gay sexuality within the context of the Israeli-Palestinian conflict. The film focuses on the forbidden love between Noam (Ohad Knoller), a young Israeli man, and Ashraf (Yousef "Joe" Sweid), a handsome young Palestinian. Both men are entrapped in a national social reality of the violent conflict and occupation and are torn between love for each other, on the one hand, and familial and national loyalties, on the other.

The film begins at a checkpoint between Israel and the Palestinian Authority, depicting the degradation that Palestinians have to endure at the hands of the IDF. Noam is part of the patrol, and Ashraf and a dozen or so other Palestinians wait to cross the border. This setting becomes the opening for Noam and Ashraf's relationship. Checking for bombs, Israeli soldiers demand that the Palestinian men raise their shirts, and as Ashraf does so he catches Noam's queer gaze. The sexual subtext of the opening sequence continues as a pregnant Palestinian woman, also humiliated by the soldiers, goes into labor after the group is cleared. As the Palestinian men break into panic, Ashraf runs to Noam to get help. His immediate reaction is characterized by fear, and he shoots his machine gun in the air, but once he moves past this conditioning and realizes that human life is at stake he rushes to help. Noam stabilizes the woman until a doctor arrives to deliver the baby, but the effort is unsuccessful. The baby dies shortly after birth, leading to a near riot on the part of the Palestinian men, who blame the Israeli soldiers for the baby's death. In this scene Fox foregrounds the main idea of the film: the relation between sexuality and death, which also comes to dominate the relationship between Noam and Ashraf.

Sexuality and death converge in the climax of the film in an ever-widening spiral of violence. Ashraf's sister marries a member of a terror organization in the West Bank. After she is accidentally killed by Israeli soldiers in Nablus, Ashraf becomes a victim of fanaticism and bigotry. In his own community he is persecuted for being gay, while in Tel Aviv he is persecuted for being an illegal Palestinian resident who is often perceived as a threat to national security. Ashraf's attempts to find refuge in Tel Aviv are doomed to fail, particularly after his sister's tragic death. In the final episode of the film Ashraf arrives at a Tel Aviv shop with a bomb strapped on his body. His Israeli lover hugs him in greeting, and the camera moves in a circle around them—until the two men explode. As Gilad Padva and Miri Talmon argue in their discussion of this film, the two lovers die together like Romeo and Juliet, paying with their lives for challenging familial social

Figure 14.1. Noam (Ohad Knoller, right) and Ashraf (Yousef "Joe" Sweid, left) in *The Bubble* (Eytan Fox, 2006). Courtesy of United King Films.

boundaries as well as national, ethnic, and sexual borders between Israelis and Palestinians.[5]

In his films, however, Fox also represents an attempt by a man in the dominant Israeli gay culture to join the national heterosexual collectivity and to attach himself to the myths that constitute it at the price of normalizing and depoliticizing gay male identity. The film *Yossi and Jagger* demonstrates this notion. The film describes the "forbidden" love story of two Israeli army officers—Yossi (Ohad Knoller) and Lior, better known by his nickname, Jagger (Yehuda Levi)—serving in a snowy base on the Israeli-Lebanese border. The lovers' homosexuality ultimately remains secret. Jagger, who tries throughout the film to persuade Yossi to express their love publicly, dies in battle—a moment too late to hear Yossi succeed in saying the words "I love you."[6]

The film challenges the "natural" privilege of heterosexuals to participate in Israeli society's most dominant institution—the army—by homoeroticizing the male military group. In one of the episodes Jagger says to one of the soldiers nicknamed "Psycho" (Yuval Semo): "Say, Psycho, what would you do if I told you I'm a faggot?" Psycho replies: "Man, you are as pretty as a girl. Of course we'd fuck you." Psycho's use of the word "we" and not "I" hints that he thinks he is not the only one who could contemplate having sex with a man or even that he can imagine male group sex, with Jagger being penetrated. If Psycho can be suspected of homosexuality, then Adams (Hanan Savyon) most certainly can be too. Adams is a soldier who believes in Zen Buddhism and leaps to the defense of the "faggots from Tel Aviv" when he says to another soldier named Samocha (Yaniv Moyal): "You would kill to get laid like those faggots from Tel Aviv. They get laid like you guys won't all your life." Psycho replies by saying: "You've been man-drilled, huh? I noticed you walk funny." The film emphasizes the different and eccentric behavior of Adams; he seems to live in his own private and secret world, separated from the violent and macho military homosociality. This representation creates a signifying relation between Adams and Yossi and Jagger that allows the spectator to read Adams as a gay man in the closet.

The subversive and troublesome potential of homosexuality is embodied in the film by the character of Jagger. His captivating and challenging sexuality produces erotic ambivalence between the characters. He subverts sexual conservatism through his uncompromising demand that Yossi come out of the closet. In other words, Jagger is the queer who defines himself through resisting regimes of the normal. His death in the end of the film, however, demonstrates Fox's desire to join the collective national order.

During the scene of Jagger's death in battle we see Yossi bending over his lover's body in the same way he did when he was making love to Jagger in the snow in an earlier scene. As in the sex episode, Yossi opens the zipper of Jagger's snowsuit, revealing his muscular body; but now we see not a body lusting for gay sex but rather one covered in blood. In other words, Jagger's sexual body is cast aside for the sake of the powerful myth of dying for the nation.

The film associates itself with one of the central myths in national cultures: the "living dead." Within that myth, the ideal national body is that of the living dead: the fighter whose physical body is absent, dead, but present, alive, in the imagined national consciousness. The politics of national death ratifies and justifies the fighter's death by giving it a higher transcendental meaning. In his heroic death, Jagger becomes part of the imagined national community. He is absent yet present, dead yet alive, in the collective national memory. It is not by chance that the image of Yossi bending over Jagger's recumbent and bleeding body echoes the iconography of the pietà of Jesus. Like Christ, who in dying underwent a process of religious metaphysical transcendence, in death Jagger is also metamorphosed and comes to signify a national collective meaning. And again it is perhaps no coincidence that in one of the final scenes in the film we see a mourning notice that reveals Jagger's surname—Amichai (literally, "my nation lives"). The film dismisses Jagger's troubling presence while at the same time, through his representation as a "living dead" character, justifying his death by giving it a broader national meaning. Homosexuality, then, remains mute, silenced, and buried deep in the darkness of the closed space of the coffin—Jagger's coffin, the national coffin—or rather the national closet.

In the film *Walk on Water* Fox tries to undo and reinvent Zionist heteromasculinity by confronting the trauma of the Holocaust. The protagonist of the film is Eyal (Lior Ashkenazi), a cold and tough Israeli Mossad agent, who is sent on a special mission: to befriend the two grandchildren of a notorious Nazi criminal, Alfred Himmelman (Ernest Lenart), in the hope that information about their grandfather will be revealed through them. His commander in the Mossad, Menakhem (Gideon Shemer), insists on sending Eyal to this mission not only because he is fluent in German but also because of his family's past: Eyal's parents were Holocaust survivors from Germany. The German granddaughter, Pia (Caroline Peters), is a volunteer on a kibbutz in the north. The grandson, Axel (Knut Berger), who is gay, is traveling to Israel in order to convince his sister to visit their parents. Axel does not know that Pia has been avoiding contact with her family because they still maintain a relationship with the Nazi grandfather, who has returned to

Figure 14.2. Eyal (Lior Ashkenazi, left) and Axel (Knut Berger, right) in *Walk on Water* (Eytan Fox, 2004). Courtesy of United King Films.

Berlin after having escaped to South America in the aftermath of World War II. Masquerading as a tourist guide, Eyal joins Axel. On a long journey from Tel Aviv to Berlin, Israel to Germany, the Israeli male returns to the past, revealing and reconstructing the traumatic memories that have marked his identity.

According to Fox and his partner, the screenwriter Gal Uchovsky, *Walk on Water* is "a kind of a study of masculinity. We believe that the journey traveled by Eyal in order to connect to his feelings is a journey that many men still have not traveled through. Many of our close relatives and best friends are 'Eyals.' Furthermore, we believe that some of the best of Israel's men still grow up to become men like Eyal."[7] Eyal therefore is a prototypical character representing the desired change that heterosexual Israeli men are to experience. Through this cinematic fantasy, the filmmakers apparently wish to constitute a new Israeli agenda, more liberal and sensitive to the rights of sexual and national minorities.

I suggest that *Walk on Water* is a Holocaust second-generation male fantasy that endeavors to restage and repair the traumas that shaped the Israeli heterosexual male subjectivity by displacing them to a form of primal fantasy.[8] The phantasmatic restaging of the traumas enables the film to ensure their containment and imagined recovery and thus protect itself from the horror that these traumas evoke and from the present violence still being committed. In this sense, both the film and its protagonist are traumatized—both attempt to forget what must inevitably be remembered.

In contrast to Fox's and Uchovsky's "liberal" sexual agenda, I argue that the phantasmatic displacement of the trauma ultimately serves the film to reconstruct the normative Israeli masculinity and to reaffirm and perpetuate Zionist sexual and national norms. This version of Jewish militaristic masculinity had violent and discriminatory consequences, especially for the Palestinian population. The film attempts to tie up the traumatic story of the Holocaust second generation to the trauma of the Palestinian Other. This linkage created in Fox's film hence might lead to the encounter with the Other, through the very possibility of responding to the Other's trauma. The film does not take this challenge, however, and eventually appropriates and incorporates the Palestinian loss in favor of reconstruction of Israeli national heteronormative masculinity.

Restaging the Scene of Origin

In the opening sequence of *Walk on Water* Eyal is disguised as an innocent tourist aboard a ferry crossing the Bosphorus Strait in Turkey, which connects Europe and the Middle East. He is tracking the activity of a Hamas activist, Abu-Ibrahim (Mahir Tuocu), who is vacationing in Turkey with his wife (Nesrin Cevadzade) and young son (Ahmed Saydam). The Palestinian boy notices the foreigner observing him, turns around, and smiles at him. Eyal returns the smile. A bond is formed between the two. The mother scolds her son for his lack of manners, ordering him to look ahead. The boy's curiosity increases, however, and he gazes at Eyal once more. This time the father reprimands his son more harshly but not before turning his own suspicious gaze toward the uninvited voyeur. Eyal leaves them, enters the bathroom, and removes a hypodermic syringe from his pocket. He follows the family, which has disembarked from the ferry to the promenade, where the father buys his son a red balloon. Suddenly Eyal emerges from behind and plunges the needle into Abu-Ibrahim, who collapses and dies within a few seconds. His wife cries in vain for help. The boy looks helplessly at the traumatic sight of his dead father and lets go of the balloon, which drifts away in the wind. A getaway car awaits Eyal nearby, whisking him swiftly from the assassination scene. The camera returns to the Palestinian child, shown in close-up, with tears moistening his large eyes.

This opening sequence is a *mise-en-abîme* of the entire film: it presents the dilemma, the enigma, that the entire film attempts to work out. This dilemma, I claim, is the enigma of origin. The sequence is constructed as a fantasy: the cinematic cliché of the balloon drifting in the wind and the bold colors dominating the cinematic frame invest the scene with an unrealistic ambiance. This scene, which involves a narrative of voyeurism, investigation, and violence, is a symbolic version of the primal scene fantasy: the subject imagines himself within the traumatic Oedipal scene, fulfilling the child's fantasy of eliminating the father. These essential elements of the primal scene fantasy will be repeated throughout the film in different versions and will construct its course and meanings.

Upon returning to Israel, Eyal finds that his wife, Iris (Natali Shilman), has committed suicide. He refuses to seek therapy to help him work through the trauma and remains emotionally detached from the loss. Eyal not only refuses to confront the catastrophic event of his wife's death but also denies his parents' traumatic history. When Menakhem assigns him to this new mission to follow the grandchildren of the Nazi criminal Alfred Himmelman, Eyal doubts the relevancy of the operation. Furthermore, he criticizes his commander for his inability to forget the traumatic past. Unlike Eyal, Menakhem, a Holocaust survivor who survived World War II together with Eyal's mother, experiences the past as if it is occurring in the present. The restoration of his past takes the form of a vendetta against those who murdered his loved ones. In the absence of Eyal's biological parents (now dead) Menakhem serves as a substitute father figure. Menakhem also represents the paternal Zionist authority and its desire for revenge against the Nazi murderers as a way of finally being able to let go of the horror that afflicted the Jewish people and thus begin a new chapter in history.

The Zionist attitude toward the memory of the Holocaust has been ambivalent: on the one hand, in the 1940s the Israeli collective memory was quick to internalize and appropriate the Holocaust, granting it a central status in the process of establishing the state of Israel and in the formation of the myth of the creation of the New Jew; on the other hand, the individual stories of the survivors were not addressed or permitted to permeate the collective consciousness and as a result faded away almost entirely.[9] The heavy burden of the survivors' past was silenced because it did not suit the image of the new tough and brave Jewish masculinity that Zionism wished to create. The desire for a heterosexual Jewish manhood is an integral part of the Zionist effort to forget the traumatic "shameful" past of the Jews in the Holocaust. The desire expressed by Menakhem uncompromisingly to avenge the crimes perpetrated by the enemies of the Jewish people is an expression of Zionism's new perception of masculinity. Eyal, the Sabra, is an extension of this Israeli militant masculine heterosexual tradition. When Menakhem asks Eyal to go on the undercover mission, spying on the Germans, he presents photos of Himmelman, his son, and his two grandchildren. Eyal asks: "How do I get into this picture?" Eyal is caught in a sequence of images that will reactivate traumas that he did not experience when they actually happened but that have nevertheless defined his male identity.

These traumas are reactivated as soon as Eyal meets Pia and Axel. While the German siblings dance the Hora in the dining hall of the kibbutz where Pia lives, Eyal breaks into Pia's room and plants a listening device on her bedpost. He monitors their conversations from his own apartment through a computer on whose screen a wavy electronic graph of their voices is seen. At the beginning Eyal disregards the words, conceding no importance to the content of the things he hears: Axel attempting to persuade Pia to return to Germany. "And so, Hansel and Gretel fought for some fifteen minutes, he begged, sounding very dramatic," Eyal reports disparagingly to Menakhem.

The German conversation nonetheless takes Eyal back to an earlier experience that was not represented or comprehended while it was occurring, back to a traumatic childhood memory related to his parents. His parents never spoke of the Holocaust trauma, and Eyal grew up with lack of knowledge of their past. In another scene, he tells Axel: "I grew up without any German products in the house, without going to Germany, without speaking of it." And he adds: "When they were alone, believing that I was not listening, they spoke German." Listening in on Axel and Pia speaking in German constitutes a symbolic reenactment of the primal scene in which the child eavesdrops on his parents' intimate secret. In this retroactive reconstruction of the traumatic scene of origin, Eyal witnesses the process of his own creation, his muted history, the unspoken Holocaust past that has constituted his subjectivity. Moreover, like Freud's "Wolf Man," who disguised the primal scene in a children's fairy tale about wolves in order to facilitate a discussion of the event that had not been registered in his consciousness,[10] Eyal displaces the trauma of his Holocaust survivor parents to the legend of "Hansel and Gretel," the German children who survived a trauma of physical abuse, in order to represent the unrepresentable.

The phantasmatic retrieval of the past establishes and gives form to the second generation's desire to break the silence concerning the Holocaust, while revealing the coded secret that originated in the parents' trauma and has become an essential element in the protagonist's unconsciousness—all without directly discussing the trauma itself.

Multiple Identifications

Eyal's fantasy, however, goes beyond merely being present in the traumatic scene of origin, the forbidden past that he had never witnessed. He actually inserts himself into this traumatic past in an attempt to contain and correct it. In his fantasy Axel, the German homosexual, echoes Eyal's "feminine," diasporic, German Jewish origin. From their first encounter, the difference between Eyal's tough heterosexual native Israeli masculinity and Axel's "effeminate" one is apparent: during their joint trip across Israel, Eyal prefers to listen to "masculine" music by the "Boss," Bruce Springsteen, whereas Axel prefers the "feminine" music of the Italian female singer Gigliola Cinquetti.

Axel is silent about his homosexuality throughout these scenes. Gradually a close, intimate, even homoerotic relationship develops between the two.[11] Sitting around a bonfire at the Dead Sea, Eyal tells Axel: "I have always wondered how it was to grow up in Germany and then to realize what had happened during World War II." Both the German "effeminacy" and the historical recollection of the Holocaust are associated with the Jewish past that Eyal's culture has refused to acknowledge. Just like Axel, the German who does not speak of his sexual past, Eyal's father, the German Jew, never discussed the world he had left behind in Europe. It is somewhat odd that Axel hides his sexual preference from Eyal, as Pia comments later when recalling Axel's habit of shamelessly flaunting his gayness when he was a boy. But this contributes to the ability of the siblings to trigger Eyal's primal fantasy: the silence about his parents' history in Europe parallels Axel's silence regarding his sexual history.

Axel's sexual identity is eventually revealed to Eyal during a night out at a Tel Aviv gay nightclub. Eyal notices the German dancing with a waiter he had met at the restaurant and leaves the place in anger. The following morning, when he picks up the siblings from their hotel on the way to Jerusalem, Eyal discovers that the waiter with whom Axel has spent the night is still with them. He is an Arab from Jerusalem called Rafiq (Yousef "Joe" Sweid) and takes Axel to a clothing shop there, where his cousin works. Eyal angrily demands back the money that Axel pays the cousin for an apparently overpriced jacket. For Eyal, Axel is simultaneously the German homosexual sleeping with the enemy and the object of his rescue mission to save the "effeminate" innocent man from the scheming Arab. The rescue mission, however, is a failure: Axel does not want to be saved, and we later learn that he returned the money to the cousin.

Eyal complains to Pia that she and her brother have kept their familial and sexual history a secret: "He didn't tell me anything, and neither did you." The silence of Eyal's parents concerning their past reverberates in the silence of the Germans, who occupy in fantasy the positions of the father and the mother. "Why don't you go home for your father's birthday?" he asks Pia. "Did he tell you about that?" she wonders, and Eyal replies, "Is it a secret?" She says, "I just don't want to go, I don't want to go back there." Pia

Figure 14.3. Eyal (Lior Ashkenazi, front) and Axel (Knut Berger, back) in an underground station in Berlin in *Walk on Water* (Eytan Fox, 2004). Courtesy of United King Films.

is the German woman hiding her Nazi past while also, like Eyal's parents, refusing to return to Germany.

When Pia and Axel condemn Eyal for his behavior toward the Palestinian salesman, he retorts sarcastically: "How could I forget that you Germans were so humane. Suffering has always touched you." Pia and Axel are simultaneously and paradoxically both the victims and the victimizers, in the image of the German Jewish parents as well as that of the German Nazis. Axel and Pia's paradoxical double construction as both victims and the victimizers enables Eyal to identify with all possible positions in his fantasy: being both the Israeli savior and the Jewish victim, hence both the native Israeli child and his diasporic parents.

Indeed, only in the film fantasy can the Israeli male have his cake and eat it too. The film thus stages for the Israeli male subject an imaginary scene in which he appropriates and inhabits all positions. This effects a reconfiguration of the subject itself: Eyal appears and participates in a desubjectivized form in the phantasmatic scene. In other words, Eyal sees himself reflected in all of these positions: he is a traumatized male subject who narcissistically and repetitively appropriates and identifies with all the positions in the phantasmatic scenario. This enables him to dissimulate the trauma, recovering it in an imagined way in his fantasy.

Trauma and Repetition

According to Cathy Caruth, trauma is "a response, sometimes delayed, to an overwhelming event or events, which takes the form of repeated, intrusive hallucinations, dreams, thoughts or behaviors stemming from the event."[12] One of the main characteristics of trauma is belatedness: the trauma victim cannot grasp or represent the traumatic event at the time of its occurrence, and so the traumatic experience continues to haunt the victim and is repeatedly reenacted in his or her dreams or everyday life. The traumatic event is not repressed but returns in a deferred action to consciousness. In other words, trauma is established through a relationship between two events—a first event that is not initially necessarily traumatic because when it occurs it is still too soon to comprehend its full significance; and a second event that may not be inherently traumatic in itself but does trigger a memory of the earlier event, which is only then embedded with traumatic significance.

Walk on Water is characterized by a repetitive form—which is the symptom of the traumatic structure of the cinematic text itself. Events that occur in the first part of the film and are not registered in the protagonist's consciousness as having psychical significance are repeated in different variations and receive their meanings in a deferred relation to the events that take place in the second part. The return to the traumatic scene enables the film to ensure the imagined recovery of the loss in the fantasy.

In a key scene Eyal rescues Axel and his queer friends at an underground station in Berlin from two drunken German men who seem to be neo-Nazis. During the violent scuffle, Eyal draws his gun and calls out in fluent German to the neo-Nazi: "Get the hell out of here before I blow your head off." The German language—which for Eyal marks the muted Holocaust traumatic memory, the secret scene of origin—emerges again as an unintentional reconstruction of the event that could not be disowned. This scene revisits and repairs the earlier scene in which Eyal failed to "rescue" Axel from the "greedy" Palestinian salesman in Jerusalem. This time the Israeli man not only successfully saves the German homosexual but symbolically also rescues the German "effeminate father" from the "Nazi" enemy, thus completing the work of the past in the present and achieving the victory that the diasporic Jews, his parents' generation, never managed to accomplish. This is a manifestation of the son's Oedipal fantasy to reclaim the role of the failing diasporic father in order to make amends for his faults and heal his traumas, which have shaped the son's own identity. Like the sexual politics of the Zionist discourse, Eyal's assignment, and the mission of the film itself, is to redeem the "feminine" father from the position of the victim. This is done by Eyal when he assumes a paternal position in relation to his father, by reinventing him a second time by means of an appropriation narratively disguised as a last-minute rescue, so that the native Israeli son can be reborn this time, and finally, as a child.

At the end of the underground station incident Axel invites Eyal to his father's birthday party, which is taking place at the family villa that he calls his parents' "kibbutz." The villa itself is located near Lake Wannsee not far from the notorious Villa Wannsee where the "final solution" was conceived on January 20, 1942. In this traumatic space, reinvented as a kibbutz, Axel compels his family to dance a Zionist Hora dance. This scene repeats and repairs the Hora scene in the first part of the film, when Eyal refused to join Axel and Pia's dance in the kibbutz's dining hall. This time Eyal not only joins the dancers but has brought the Hebrew music for Axel from Israel. In other words, Zionism is restaged by the redeemed father and by the mediation of the savior son in the phantasmatic space in order to heal the trauma of the past.

This notion receives particular emphasis in the subsequent scene. During his stay at the villa, Eyal discovers that old Himmelman—the Nazi grandfather—is indeed alive. At the birthday celebration for Axel's father, the grandfather descends from his room, accompanied by a nurse and attached to an oxygen tank, to meet his family. Eyal leaves abruptly to meet Menakhem, who has suddenly materialized in Berlin. When Eyal suggests kidnapping Himmelman in order to bring him to trial in Israel, to his astonishment Menakhem tells him that he has never reported this mission to the Mossad. He hands Eyal a lethal hypodermic, asking the young man to assassinate the Nazi. The fact that Menakhem has emerged miraculously in Berlin and that Eyal's mission has never been officially registered in "reality" reiterates the notion that the film is actually the fantasy of the protagonist. Eyal returns to the villa. But, standing in front of the sleeping Himmelman's bed and holding the syringe, he finds that he is unable to complete the act. Axel, who on that same evening has discovered Eyal's true identity as a Mossad agent, suddenly appears; immediately after Eyal's departure from the room, Axel switches off his grandfather's oxygen supply. The Nazi grandfather suffocates and dies.[13]

Eyal has thus prepared the way for Axel, who has triggered the memory of Eyal's parents, to redeem himself: he is no longer the German effeminate victim and is now able to fight his own battle. Finally, after the "parents'" trauma has been healed—in other words, after the "feminine" threat that Axel represents has been lifted—Eyal can place himself in the position of the victimized child. Indeed, at the close of the dramatic scene the two are seen sitting on the edge of the bed. Eyal, the cold, macho Israeli man who was unable to cry (when he was fifteen physicians discovered that his tear ducts were dry), tells Axel about Iris's suicide and the note she left behind, while he weeps for the first time: "I cannot kill anymore. I don't want to kill anymore." He can now finally place himself in the role of the child.

Walk on Water is a perfect Oedipal fantasy that reenacts and repairs the father's trauma in the eyes of the son in order to reestablish Eyal's normative heterosexual masculinity. Now he can carry on a normal life in the community and raise a family, as he will indeed do with Pia at the end of the film. Like the official Israeli discourse, the film appropriates the Holocaust traumatic memory for the purpose of constructing Eyal's new masculinity. The reinvention of straight manhood as sensitive, open, and liberal is apparently achieved at the cost of the repudiation of the male "femininity."

This heteronormative sexual politics is emphasized at the end of the film. Two years after the earlier events, Eyal and Pia are newlyweds, living in a kibbutz in a house topped by a red tile roof, surrounded by a green garden. Eyal wakes up to the sound of his little son's crying. He picks him up gently and caresses the infant's blond hair. The child rests his head on his father's shoulder and calms down. After having lulled his baby back to sweet sleep, Eyal, now a former Israeli Mossad agent, e-mails Axel, inviting him and his new partner—"the loving uncles," as he calls them—to visit their "new family" in the kibbutz. He also tells him of a dream: both of them walking side by side, calmly and surely, like Jesus Christ, on the waters of the Sea of Galilee. They are smiling at each other, their arms spread wide, almost touching one another. This is a mystical fantasy of tenderness and love, understanding and identification, compassion and forgiveness, between the Jew and the Christian, the Israeli and the German, the straight and the gay, pacing together toward an infinite horizon, toward a better future of fulfillment and promise.

This futuristic fantasy seeks to rewrite and repair an earlier scene in the film: Axel failed in his attempt to walk on the Sea of Galilee and Eyal called out to him mockingly: "Hey, Jesus, they lied to you, you can't walk on water." Axel replied that in order to walk on water "you must purify yourself utterly. Your heart must be clean from the inside, without a negative attitude, free of bad thoughts." Now presumably cleansed of the personal and national traumas that shaped their identities, the two invite us to believe in the fantasy about a new future against all odds.

The representation of the child in the film reflects what Lee Edelman calls "reproductive futurism," which works to "*affirm* a structure, to *authenticate* social order, which it then intends to transmit to the future in the form of the Child."[14] Through the image of the innocent child—whose name in the film is not coincidentally Tom (in Hebrew: innocent)—that we all love and long to be like, who inspires nostalgic identification with what we once were but failed to become, the film reinforces the heteronormative social order. This is the child who is full of the promise of a better future; according to Edelman, he stands in opposition to the figure of the male homosexual, who is perceived as not caring about the future, as having no future, as defying the social decree for sexual reproduction.

At the beginning of the film it was Axel who was associated with children as a result of his work in a children's day-care facility, while Eyal was the one vehemently opposed to bringing offspring into the world. Now Eyal is the one siding with the fantasy of a reproductive futurism, asking his gay friend—and us, the gay viewers—to reproduce that which we do not follow, by speaking in the name of a future as an inheritance that we did not receive: we would try to be as straight as we could be, as if we would convert what we did not receive in a possession. This gay politics of the film asks gay and lesbian people to join the sexual-national hegemony and to be included in the straight space. This sexual agenda, however, contradicts the world of queer people who cannot, or will not, side with the consensus, who refuse to accept the future, and challenge the option to become enslaved to a fantasy of the future as a condition for our right to live.

The Wound of the Other

The phantasmatic recasting of the Holocaust trauma reactivates in the film one other trauma—that of the Israeli-Palestinian conflict, which is also connected to the role of the child that Eyal has entered. The film ostensibly criticizes the Israeli militant aggressive masculinity and presumably maintains that only the act of confronting the repressed Holocaust trauma can lead to an Israeli acknowledgment of the losses to both sides incurred by the bloody Israeli-Palestinian conflict. While Eyal is listening to the German siblings, the image of his dead wife reemerges together with an image of the traumatized Palestinian boy that Eyal left behind on the Turkish promenade, looking at him and weeping. This image of the child, however, does not represent only (if at all) a traumatic event that occurred in reality and that Eyal now recalls. Eyal, in fact, could not have seen the crying Palestinian boy: by the time that image appeared on the screen, Eyal was inside the getaway car and far from the assassination scene.[15] This event therefore is not referential: it does not refer directly to the reality. Rather, it alludes to the protagonist's psychical reality, to his fantasy. Eyal phantasmatically identifies with the weeping boy who approaches him in his fantasy, requesting to be seen and heard, asking that Eyal listen to *his* trauma. The boy beseeches him to be a witness to his traumatic wound, to take ethical responsibility for his trauma. The boy's appeal is the product of Eyal's fantasy, and thus his own male Israeli subjectivity becomes connected with and founded on the loss of the Other.

Nevertheless, the film does not acknowledge the structural implication of the Other's trauma for the construction of Israeli manhood. The end of the film, as a repetition of the essential elements of the fantasy of origin revealed in the opening scene (the assassination of the father by injection and seizing his place in relation to the mother and identification with the child), allows the correction of the Holocaust trauma and Eyal's rebirth. The film displaces and appropriates the Palestinian child's trauma in favor of the protagonist's Oedipal trauma in order to ensure its imagined recovery. This imagined recovery of the loss is achieved through the Israeli subject being able to inhabit all possible positions in *his* fantasy: he is both the child victim, through the phantasmatic identification with the Palestinian boy, and the father who was removed from the scene. The trauma of the Palestinian boy is thus appropriated and subjugated to the trauma that established Eyal's subjectivity. In other words, the Palestinian loss is detached from a specific space and time and projected onto the traumatic scene of origin of the Israeli subject.

Thus the film, like the dominant Israeli discourse, uses the Israeli traumatic memory of the Holocaust in order to expropriate the Israeli-Palestinian conflict from its regional, historical, and political context. In an earlier scene Rafiq tried to suggest to Eyal a different viewpoint concerning the Israeli-Palestinian conflict. He moved nearer toward Eyal's car and said: "You Jews are constantly occupied with what has and what hasn't been done to you. Maybe if you would relax about this past of yours, you could see." But Eyal does not allow Rafiq to finish his sentence and rolls the car window shut in his face. Indeed, like Eyal, the film itself refuses to deal with the tragic pain and loss on both sides of the national barrier. It shuts itself inside an insulated phantasmatic bubble, blind to the violent reality outside.

Walk on Water fails to listen to the trauma of the Other. The film does not take ethical responsibility for the Other's traumatic wound.[16] Instead, it channels the trauma of the Other in favor of reconstructing the Israeli male heterosexual subjectivity. In this film the Israeli subject indulges in a love affair with *himself*, dissimulating and recovering the lost object by identifying with him and inhabiting his place. This is an autoerotic fantasy of incorporation: thus it is no wonder that, immediately upon his return from Turkey, Eyal's fellow Mossad agent shows him a newspaper headline that hails the successful elimination operation, telling him: "Here, give yourself a blow job."

NOTES

1. On this topic, see, for example, Sander L. Gilman, *Freud, Race and Gender*; Daniel Boyarin, *Unheroic Conduct: The Rise of Heterosexuality and the Invention of the Jewish Man*; Michael Gluzman, "Longing for Heterosexuality: Zionism and Sexuality in Herzl's *Altneuland*."

2. Raz Yosef, *Beyond Flesh: Queer Masculinities and Nationalism in Israeli Cinema*.

3. For instance, the 1988 repeal of Israel's antisodomy law; forbidding discrimination in the workplace based on sexual orientation; the first sitting of the Knesset that dealt with homo-lesbian issues in 1993; and a Supreme Court of Justice decision in the case of Yonatan Danilowitz, an El Al air steward who demanded that the airline that employed him recognize his boyfriend as a partner. For a more detailed description, see Lee Walzer, *Between Sodom and Eden: A Gay Journey through Today's Changing Israel*.

4. Ibid., 41.

5. Gilad Padva and Miri Talmon, "Gotta Have an Effeminate Heart: The Politics of Effeminacy and Sissyness in a Nostalgic Israeli TV Musical." See also Jonathan C. Friedman, "The Problematic Ethnic and Sexual Discourses of Eytan Fox's *The Bubble*."

6. For a full analysis of this film, see Raz Yosef, "The National Closet: Gay Israel in *Yossi and Jagger*."

7. See the film's internet site: http:/www.walkonwater.co.il (accessed May 2007).

8. In a shorter analysis of this film with a different focus I discussed the role of the primal scene fantasy in Holocaust second-generation discourse. See Raz Yosef, "Phantasmatic Losses: National Traumas, Masculinity and Primal Scenes in Israeli Cinema—*Walk on Water*."

9. On this subject, see Anita Shapira, *New Jews, Old Jews*.

10. Sigmund Freud, "From the History of an Infantile Neurosis."

11. For example, at the Dead Sea Eyal introduces Axel to the Israeli military male homosocial ritual of a nocturnal bonfire and black coffee. Wrapped in a blanket, Axel complains about the extreme cold, and Eyal responds: "No, don't move away. The only way to get warm is to sit close to one another. Every Israeli soldier knows that." This male intimate camaraderie reaches a climax with an orgasmic outburst of collective urination.

12. Cathy Caruth, "Introduction," in *Trauma: Explorations in Memory*, 4.

13. The old Nazi's murder by suffocation is an ironic reversal of the way the Jews were suffocated by the Nazis' poison gases in the death camps.

14. Lee Edelman, *No Future: Queer Theory and the Death Drive*, 3.

15. On the weeping in this film, see Boaz Hagin, "Male Weeping as Performative: The Crying Mossad Assassin in *Walk on Water*."

16. On trauma and ethical responsibility, see Cathy Caruth, "Traumatic Awakenings (Freud, Lacan and the Ethics of Memory)," in *Unclaimed Experience: Trauma, Narrative, and History*, 91–112.

BIBLIOGRAPHY

Boyarin, Daniel. *Unheroic Conduct: The Rise of Heterosexuality and the Invention of the Jewish Man*. Berkeley: University of California Press, 1997.

Caruth, Cathy (ed.). *Trauma: Explorations in Memory*. Baltimore and London: Johns Hopkins University Press, 1995.

———. *Unclaimed Experience: Trauma, Narrative, and History*. Baltimore and London: Johns Hopkins University Press, 1996.

Edelman, Lee. *No Future: Queer Theory and the Death Drive*. Durham and London: Duke University Press, 2004.

Freud, Sigmund. "From the History of an Infantile Neurosis." In *Case Histories II*, trans. by James Stachey, 223–366. London: Penguin Books, 1991.

Friedman, Jonathan C. "The Problematic Ethnic and Sexual Discourses of Eytan Fox's *The Bubble*." In *Performing Difference: Representations of "the Other" in Film and Theater*, ed. Jonathan C. Friedman, 200–212. Lanham, Md.: University Press of America, 2009.

Gilman, Sander L. *Freud, Race and Gender*. Princeton, N.J.: Princeton University Press, 1993.

Gluzman, Michael. "Longing for Heterosexuality: Zionism and Sexuality in *Altneuland*" ("Hakmiha Leheterosexualiyut: Tziyonut Uminiyut Be'*Altneuland'*"). *Theory and Criticism* 11 Winter (1997): 145–163.

Hagin, Boaz. "Male Weeping as Performative: The Crying Mossad Assassin in *Walk on Water*." *Camera Obscura* 68:23.2 (2008): 103–139.

Padva, Gilad, and Miri Talmon. "Gotta Have an Effeminate Heart: The Politics of Effeminacy and Sissyness in a Nostalgic Israeli TV Musical." *Feminist Media Studies* 8: 1 (2008): 69–84.

Shapira, Anita, *New Jews, Old Jews* (*Yehudim Khadashim, Yehudim Yeshanim*). Tel Aviv: Am Oved, 1997.

Walzer, Lee, *Between Sodom and Eden: A Gay Journey through Today's Changing Israel*. New York: Columbia University Press, 2000.

Yosef, Raz. *Beyond Flesh: Queer Masculinities and Nationalism in Israeli Cinema*. New Brunswick, N.J.: Rutgers University Press, 2004.

———. "The National Closet: Gay Israel in *Yossi and Jagger*." *GLQ* 11:2 (2005): 283–300.

———. "Phantasmatic Losses: National Traumas, Masculinity and Primal Scenes in Israeli Cinema—*Walk on Water*." *Framework* 49: 1 (Spring 2008): 93–105.

FILMOGRAPHY

The Bubble (*Habu'ah*, Eytan Fox, Israel, 2006).
Walk on Water (*Lalekhet Al Hamayim*, Eytan Fox, Israel, 2004).
Yossi and Jagger (*Yossi VeJagger*, Eytan Fox, Israel, 2002).

* This research was supported by the Israel Foundation (grant no. 133/10).

PART V

Jewish Orthodoxy Revisited

15 Negotiating Judaism in Contemporary Israeli Cinema

The Spiritual Style of *My Father, My Lord*

DAN CHYUTIN

In reviewing the developing relationship between center and periphery within Israeli society of the past several decades, one cannot help but notice—and indeed be amazed by—a radical change in the stature of Jewish religion and religious devotion. During the nation's early stages of evolution, Zionist discourse established the secular-socialist Sabra identity as the norm, at the price of a relative marginalization of Jewish religious sentiment. As a result of the subsequent collapse of secular Zionism as a dominant ideology, however, religion gradually obtained a position of greater influence within Israel's sociocultural landscape. Looking back, it is possible to isolate the milestones of this transformation: the forming of the settlement movement in the 1970s, the emergence of the ultra-Orthodox Shas party as a political powerhouse during the 1980s, the explosion of spiritual celebrations and pilgrimages to holy sites, the rise to prominence of religious "miracle workers," and the growth in religious repentance (*khazara bitshuva*) since the 1990s. These manifestations have been singled out as formative phenomena and have accordingly been studied with great care in both academic and nonacademic literature.[1] Yet by no means do they encompass the turn toward religion in Israel, whose repercussions we are still far from fully grasping.

One of the most intriguing and least investigated symptoms of this state of religiosity has been the recent proliferation of representations of Jewish religious life in mainstream media.[2] In films such as Joseph Cedar's *Time of Favor* (*Hahesder*, 2000) and *Campfire* (*Medurat Hashevet*, 2004), Anat Zuria's *Purity* (*Tehora*, 2002) and *Sentenced to Marriage* (*Mekudeshet*, 2004), Giddi

Dar and Shuli Rand's *Ushpizin* (2004), Raphaël Nadjari's *Stones* (*Avanim*, 2004) and *Tehilim* (2007), Shmuel Hasfari's *Schwartz Dynasty* (*Shoshelet Schvartz*, 2005), Avi Nesher's *The Secrets* (*Hasodot*, 2007), Avraham Kushnir's *Bruriah* (2008), and Haim Tabakman's *Eyes Wide Open* (*Einayim Pkukhot*, 2009) as well as in television series like Udi Leon, Nissim Levy, and Jackie Levy's *Me'orav Yerushalmi* (2003–2009), Zafrir Kochanovsky, Ron Ninio, and Ronit Weiss-Berkowitz's *A Touch Away* (*Merkhak Negi'ah*, 2007), and Hava Divon and Eliezer Shapiro's *Srugim* (2008–2010), we find a rigorous attempt to negotiate present-day tensions between Israeli religious and secular identities and to explore their effects on larger issues of faith. Thus conceived, these texts offer a unique perspective on some of the preeminent questions troubling Israel's Jewish citizenry, believers and nonbelievers alike, at the dawn of a new millennium.

Of the current crop of religiously themed films and television shows, probably the most critically acclaimed work is David Volach's *My Father, My Lord* (*Khufshat Kayitz*, 2007).[3] Volach's film shares with several of the aforementioned media texts a preoccupation with a crisis of faith—a matter of growing concern for those religious circles that have increasingly come under the sway of secular culture in an attempt to become more involved in Israel's sociopolitical reality. Nevertheless, two important elements make *My Father, My Lord* an exceptional case. The first is the identity of the filmmaker: unlike the creators of these other texts—who are, by and large, recognized unequivocally as either observant or nonobservant—Volach grew up as an ultra-Orthodox Haredi Jew and then turned his back on religion. This liminal position provides him with privileged insight into the experience of a crisis of faith. This may also account for the second differentiating element: the choice to have *My Father, My Lord* present its themes through a "spiritual" cinematic style, thereby allowing it to function not only as a social document on religious identity within Israeli society but also, more importantly, as a theological essay on the value of religious belief. The film's spiritual style and its theological implications are at the heart of this essay.

Representing the Holy: *My Father, My Lord*

Although not widely theorized within the cinema studies field, the notion of a filmic spiritual style has succeeded in capturing the attention of numerous critics and scholars who have sought to explore—under diverse headings such as "devotional," "religious," or "sacramental" cinema—the medium's potential in representing the Holy. My understanding of the spiritual style is informed by a foundational text within this body of work: critic-cum-filmmaker Paul Schrader's *Transcendental Style in Film* (1972).[4] Schrader argues that filmmakers of different cultures use a general representative form in expressing the Transcendent. This "transcendental" style, which is an evolution of precinematic visual renderings of the Holy, may be found in its purest form in the works of filmmakers Robert Bresson and Yasujiro Ozu. As Schrader explains, both Ozu and Bresson perceive reality as, to an extent, masking divine presence; their films therefore interrogate everyday reality so as to position it as a tangible threshold onto the ineffable. In doing so, these filmmakers radically depart from classic cinematic traditions: instead of exploiting the medium's expressive means to create a plentiful image of the world, Ozu and Bresson choose to strip reality to its bare bones. It is a "stylization of elimination," where, in Schrader's words, "given a selection of inflections, the choice is monotone; a choice of sounds, the choice is silence; a choice of actions, the choice is stillness."[5]

Appropriately, the spectators' reaction to this unusual cinematic representation of reality differs from their response to the "reality effect" of a traditionally styled film. As Schrader notes in relation to Bresson's works: "[The representation of the] everyday blocks the emotional and intellectual exits, preparing the viewer for the moment when he must face the Unknown. The intractable form of the everyday will not allow the viewer to apply his natural interpretive devices. The viewer becomes aware that his feelings are being spurned . . . [gradually he] recognizes that there is more than the everyday, that Bresson has put a strangely suspicious quality into his day to-day living."[6] Schrader terms this form of reaction "schizoid"[7]—that is, it is an experience of imaged reality as simultaneously gesturing toward the concrete objects of our world and toward an entity or meaning which is not wholly reducible to these objects.

In commenting on *My Father, My Lord*, several critics have noted the similarity of its style to that of Bresson.[8] This similarity seems most evident in the approach to the function of narrative. As in Bresson's works, the basic tale which Volach's film depicts is very lean in nature: Jewish Orthodox parents prepare to go with their only son Menakhem on a trip to the Dead Sea; at the end of this trip, the child drowns, thereby prompting the parents to experience a crisis of faith. In adapting this unostentatious tale to the screen, Volach resisted the temptation to enhance its dramatic potentialities by adding action-oriented story lines. Instead he effectively stretched this fiction out over seventy minutes, thereby slowing down the pace of the film and allowing for spectatorial meditation on the texture of imaged reality and its hidden dimensions. In a telling interview, Volach explained this narrative approach through a distinction between "story" and "plot":

What is plot? In still images you get a story and you don't need any plot.
You see wrinkles, you see eyes. Every image is a story. Why can't cinema be
like that? . . . In cinema things need to happen to the character in order for
the spectator to become interested in its story, because the character cannot
reveal its story unless something happens to it. Plot is a condition, a tool for
telling the story. But it should not be mistaken for the story itself.[9]

Consequently, Volach, like Bresson, supports an aesthetic of elimination—
or, in his words, a "skimping on plot to flesh out the story."[10] In *My Father,
My Lord* we are not invited to skip over the fabric of reality in a hurried race
toward a cathartic ending; rather—through leisurely shots, blatantly mini-
malistic in action—we are given the opportunity to appreciate the coun-
tenance of the visible world not only for its physical attributes but for the
"story" which hides behind them, the meaning that transcends them.

Faced with this image of reality stylized through elimination, we are
then conditioned to perceive it as pointing to something else—as being referential. But to what does it refer? Principally, but not exclusively, to a set of
interconnected theological debates which form the basis of Jewish religious
law (Halakhah). Throughout his film, Volach inserts scenes which overtly
connote Halakhic discourses, thereby setting up the conceptual framework
for the appreciation of the symbolism of the narrative at large; this appreciation, in turn, unveils the narrative's goal of delegitimizing these discourses.

One prominent discourse which the film engages is that surrounding the
hierarchy of creation. Midway through the film we are shown a scene where
the father of the family, a rabbi and representative of religious law, is giving
a sermon on a common Halakhah wisdom: how only human beings have
souls, and how only human beings who spend their waking hours worshiping the Lord have superior souls. This axiom is undermined through other
moments in the film. For example, in one scene Menakhem is seen observing an old woman being carried into the back of an ambulance. He notices
the old woman's dog attempting to climb into the ambulance, only to be
unceremoniously thrown out by the paramedic. The dog's desire to stay at
its mistress's side, contrasted with the paramedic's heartless reaction, makes
us question why the former would be regarded as soulless by the Halakhah
simply due to its animality while the latter would be regarded as soulful
only by virtue of being human.

In another sequence Menakhem is shown trading picture cards with a
child who is apparently mentally disabled. In the Halakhah individuals with
mental disabilities are considered lesser souls because they are unable to
cope intellectually with the task of worshiping God; this understanding in

part prompted Halakhic authorities to put in place certain protective restrictions, such as the prohibition against trading with the mentally disabled.[11] In the film Menakhem not only breaks this Halakhic law regarding trading but also treats his friend not as a lesser soul but as an equal partner. Menakhem's behavior toward his friend is then contrasted with the behavior of the father toward Menakhem in the following scene. The father discovers that the card Menakhem obtained from his friend carries the image of a bare-chested African tribesman and thus may be considered an object of idolatry.[12] In handling this situation, the father, a superior soul in Halakhic terms, does not treat his son, a lesser soul, with the same respect and compassion that Menakhem extended to his friend; rather, he firmly orders Menakhem to rip up the card, reducing him to tears. The father's superiority is further undermined when his callous behavior is compared with the mother's affable demeanor. In the Halakhah women are considered to be inferior to men.[13] Yet in the film it is the mother who emerges as the favorable—and thus superior—character, counterbalancing the father's reserve toward Menakhem with acts of compassion and tender nurturing.

Another Halakhah discourse that is evoked by My Father, My Lord's symbolic narrative concerns divine providence, reward, and punishment. This discourse is called to mind through overt references to two noted stories within Jewish religious tradition. The first of these is the story of the binding of Isaac, which is explicitly referred to on two occasions in the film: initially when Menakhem and his friends recite the story of the binding in a classroom (heder) and later when the children, including Menakhem, pictorially re-create the binding scene on the blackboard in the same classroom. The second is the story of the notorious heretic Elisha Ben Avuyah and the bird's nest. This reference is made evident in a sequence where the father is seen performing the task of shiluakh haken, as is written in the Book of Deuteronomy: "If, along the road, you chance upon a bird's nest, in any tree or on the ground, with fledglings or eggs and the mother sitting over the fledglings or on the eggs, do not take the mother together with her young, let the mother go, and take only the young, in order that you may fare well and have a long life."[14] The Talmud tells us that the notorious heretic Elisha Ben Avuyah once walked by a tree with a bird's nest and met a man who, like the father in the film, was intent on performing the mitzvah spelled out in Deuteronomy. The man had sent his son up the tree; after expelling the mother bird, the son fell down and died. It was this event—in which following an important religious command resulted in punishment rather than reward—that persuaded Ben Avuyah to choose a life of heresy, according to the Talmud.

Both these stories parallel the narrative of *My Father, My Lord* and illuminate its theological stance in significant ways. The binding story, in which Isaac's life was spared because of Abraham's uncompromising belief, inspired the Halakhic maxim that those who trust in God and follow the Halakhah will be rewarded with divine protection. This form of providence, however, is absent in the film: the father, a devout believer, is not rewarded with the life of his son as in the case of Abraham. Rather, we find here a rendition of the story of Elisha Ben Avuyah and the bird's nest, in which a father's desire to abide by the Halakhah does not save him from suffering the worst punishment a parent can receive—the loss of a child.[15] In positioning these two intertexts within the film's narrative, it becomes evident that Volach wants the spectator to experience the family's tragic tale through Ben Avuyah's eyes and reach his foregone conclusion: the Halakhah is wrong and thus should be rejected.

Some would define this critique of the Halakhah as arguing against the existence of God. I would claim, however, that this is not what Volach attempts in *My Father, My Lord*. Volach's quarrel is with the interpretation of God by the Halakhah; his critique is aimed at invalidating this interpretation but not necessarily at invalidating the existence of a God that defies such an interpretation. In fact, Volach seems to go to great lengths to allow for the symbolic presence of the hidden God in his film. In making this presence known, we see the film's spiritual style, as a signifying system for the Divine, come to its fruition.

As previously described, this style conditions the spectator to perceive the imaged reality as being both object and symbol. Typically, Volach situates this reality as referring to—and subsequently invalidating—certain Halakhah discourses. Yet the film also contains a number of shots which escape this allegorical framework. These shots are beautifully crafted poetic close-ups of commonplace objects (water accumulating at the bottom of a saucer, a loose drape dancing in an afternoon breeze), which seem so utterly irrelevant to what little drama takes place in the film that they appear decisively aberrant. Within the style of the film we are impelled to read these lyrical images symbolically. But what do they symbolize? Although we acknowledge the existence of a referent, its exact nature remains undecipherable. A similar phenomenon may be found in Ozu's works. As Schrader explains, Ozu tends to puncture the dramatic flow of his films with seemingly irrelevant shots of everyday objects or outdoor landscapes. Each shot is paradoxically a disruption and an integrant of the natural order. It functions, according to Schrader, as a coda that "establishes an image of a second reality which can stand beside the ordinary reality; it represents the Wholly Other."[16] Through recognition of this duality, the still-life image invites us to transcend it—or rather to experience a connection with the Transcendent through it.[17]

Thus we can better understand why it was important for Volach to connect these spiritual codas to Menakhem, typically by designating them as his point of view shots. In making this association, Menakhem, and not his rabbi father, emerges as the one with greater access to God. (The only point of view coda shot assigned to the father—during the film's final scene, when he looks up at a darkened synagogue ceiling in a state of mourning—conspicuously lacks the other codas' poetic beauty, further underscoring this message.) Here the text again sides with Ben Avuyah, who allegedly believed that children stand closer to God since they have not yet been contaminated by years of studying religious law. God is present, the film seems to argue, and may be visible to a certain degree to those untainted by the Halakhah. The question which remains largely open at the end of My Father, My Lord, however, is whether the spectator should reach out to the God that allows for the death of Menakhem, its precious son. Perhaps it is better to ignore the presence of such a God than to attempt the insurmountable task of understanding it.

The Second Commandment and the Spiritual Style

Before bringing this discussion to a close, it seems necessary to mention an important concern that My Father, My Lord's invocation of a spiritual style unavoidably brings to the fore: the problem of visually signifying the Holy in light of the Second Commandment prohibition against the making of a graven image.[18] Schrader, for one, traces a shared spiritual style connecting Zen art to Byzantine iconography to the films of Ozu and Bresson and uses this common denominator to argue that "as much as the Transcendent is universal, the style which expresses it is universal too."[19] Yet this universality, for Schrader, encompasses only those cultures that allow for visual representations of the Holy; aniconic cultures like Judaism that prohibit such representations are left unexplored. Does this mean that examples of this shared style may not be found within Judaism? Or does Volach, as means and emblem of his heresy, intentionally borrow an artistic form that is radically foreign to Judaic tradition?

In fact, as recent studies have shown, the idea of Jewish aniconism was ostensibly an invention of nineteenth-century anti-Semitic and Jewish assimilationist discourses, meant to disavow the role of "Jewish art . . . [as] a significant constituent of Jewish thought and identity."[20] It seems true that adherence to the Second Commandment had traditionally limited Jewish artists in exploring the potentialities of an overt sacred art such as that found in Christianity. But this did not altogether prevent these artists from trying their hand at representing the Holy through art. To bypass the biblical prohibition, they utilized symbols excessively; the golden rule here, as historian Lionel Kochan phrased it, was that "if any material entity is to symbolize God, it must be of such a nature as both to disguise and reveal this relationship."[21] In fashioning these symbols, especially those of a figurative nature, an attempt was made to signify them as being to an extent immaterial, to avoid a situation where they are mistaken as "real" and thus as proper objects of idolatry. Consequently we may recognize in Jewish religious art a tendency toward a "negative aesthetic" of elimination that nevertheless does not eradicate the verisimilitude of the imaged object. This aesthetic, I would argue, connects Jewish art with the traditions discussed by Schrader and by extension with *My Father, My Lord*.[22]

To illustrate this point, a helpful analogy may be found between Volach's film and the Kabbalah's Sephirotic diagram, in light of their mutual tendency to evoke godly presence unabashedly through symbols. To the Kabbalists, the diagram was a concrete expression of God's mysteries: what seems a rather abstract structure connecting the ten *sephirot* (the divine qualities) also acts as a representation of the human body and of a tree, thereby symbolically fusing nature with the Holy in a fashion similar to Volach's candid codas.[23] Accordingly, meditation on this diagram—much like meditation on spiritual cinematic shots—is supposed to give the viewer some measure of transcendence. Yet my point in drawing this comparison is not only to indicate a stylistic connection but also to bring into the conversation, as a final note, the Kabbalistic notion of *tikkun olam:* the mending of a shattered world, "the restoration or integration of all things to their original condition."[24] In the Kabbalah the diagram represents this ideal unity of divine qualities, humankind, and nature, and reflecting on it is a way of enacting a repair. *My Father, My Lord* and to an extent many other religiously themed Israeli media texts are similarly preoccupied with the idea of *tikkun* from either an approving or a disapproving standpoint. As such, they attempt to address a period when Israelis have become increasingly torn between fundamentalism and liberalism, faith and material culture, the Transcendent and the worldly, offering up contemplations on the possibility of spiritual redemption or the lack thereof.

NOTES

This essay is part of a dissertation project dealing with the representations of Jewish religious identity in contemporary Israeli cinema. I would like to thank Lucy Fischer, Miri Talmon, Yaron Peleg, Ali Patterson, Nadav Hochman, Raz Schwartz, Mal Ahern, and Michael Chyutin for their insightful readings and invaluable research assistance.

1. See, for example, Oz Almog, *The Sabra: A Profile*; Yair Sheleg, *The New Religious Jews: Recent Developments among Observant Jews in Israel*; Baruch Kimmerling, *The Invention and Decline of Israeliness: State, Society, and the Military*; Yossi Yonah and Yehuda Goodman, eds., *Maelstrom of Identities: A Critical Look at Religion and Secularity in Israel*; Aviad Kleinberg, ed., *Hard to Believe: Rethinking Religion and Secularism in Israel*; and Avi Sagi, *The Jewish-Israeli Voyage: Culture and Identity*.

2. The few examples of studies focusing on the representation of Jewish religious identity in Israeli cinema include Ronie Parchak, "Beyond the Fence: Religious Sentiment in Israeli Cinema"; Yael Munk, "Le retour du cinéma israélien vers le judaïsme"; Nurith Gertz and Yael Munk, "Israeli Cinema: Hebrew Identity/Jewish Identity"; and Yuval Rivlin, *The Mouse That Roared: Jewish Identity in American and Israeli Cinema*.

3. *My Father, My Lord* was awarded the 2007 Best Narrative Feature Award at the Tribeca Film Festival and the Special Jury Award for Best Director at the Taormina Film Fest.

4. I use the term "spiritual" in part to indicate that my appropriation of Schrader's model of "transcendental style" is selective.

5. Paul Schrader, *Transcendental Style in Film: Ozu, Bresson, Dreyer*, 39.

6. Ibid., 70.

7. Ibid., 42.

8. See, for example, Meir Schnitzer, "Artistic Miracle."

9. Pablo Utin, *The New Israeli Cinema: Conversations with Filmmakers*, 62–63 (my translation).

10. Ibid., 63 (my translation).

11. Tzvi C. Marx, *Disability in Jewish Law*, 107–114.

12. The reference to idolatry here may be seen as the filmmaker's self-reflexive comment on his own "sin": that is, by creating a film within a spiritual style, he stood the risk of defying the Second Commandment prohibition against the making of a graven image (see the final section of the essay for more on this).

13. To cite one well-known example of this rule: "In pain shall you bear children. Yet your urge shall be for your husband, and he shall rule over you" (Gen. 3:16).

14. Deut. 22:6–7.

15. There is, of course, a double loss in the story of Elisha Ben Avuyah and the bird's nest: not only does the father lose his boy, but the female bird loses its offspring. This latter loss, like the former, is mapped in *My Father, My Lord* onto the figure of Menakhem. In the film the father takes Menakhem to the men's section of the beach because the child has grown too old to go to the women's section with his mother; subsequently, while the father is deep in prayer, the child wanders off to find his tragic end. Seen in relation to the Ben Avuyah story, the female bird's loss is analogous to the mother's, who is expelled, like the bird, from a position of protecting her child. As a result, the father's complicity in the loss is enhanced, because the death

came about not only due to his transferring parental responsibility to the Halakhic God but also due to his expulsion of the mother from the role of primary caregiver.

16. Schrader, *Transcendental Style in Film*, 49 (emphasis added).

17. It may be argued that on this occasion the spiritual style invites us to read the film as we would a Gothic stained-glass window: since light was traditionally equated with godly presence, the appropriate devotional response to such a window was "to look not at it but through it." See Roger Homan, *The Art of the Sublime: Principles of Christian Art and Architecture*, 65.

18. See also Parchak's extended discussion on this issue in "Beyond the Fence."

19. Schrader, *Transcendental Style in Film*, 10.

20. Melissa Raphael, *Judaism and the Visual Image: A Jewish Theology of Art*, 2. See also Kalman P. Bland, *The Artless Jew: Medieval and Modern Affirmations and Denials of the Visual*.

21. Lionel Kochan, *Beyond the Graven Image: A Jewish View*, 62.

22. Volach's words gain particular significance here: "[T]he whole religious world is a world of symbols. Think of God, isn't it a symbol for a father figure? We have a world here . . . whose power is in symbolism. . . . A man eats a matzo in Passover as a symbol for the exodus from Egypt, and I, who am making a film about religion, will ignore symbolism? It doesn't strike me as the right thing to do" (quoted in Utin, *The New Israeli Cinema*, 68; my translation).

23. See Leslie Atzmon, "A Visual Analysis of Anthropomorphism in the Kabbalah: Dissecting the Hebrew Alphabet and Sephirotic Diagram," 103–109.

24. Gershom Scholem, *On the Mystical Shape of the Godhead: Basic Concepts in the Kabbalah*, 242.

BIBLIOGRAPHY

Almog, Oz. *The Sabra: A Profile (HaTzabar—Dyokan)*. Tel Aviv: Am Oved, 1997.

Atzmon, Leslie. "A Visual Analysis of Anthropomorphism in the Kabbalah: Dissecting the Hebrew Alphabet and Sephirotic Diagram." *Visual Communication* 2, no. 1 (2003): 97–114.

Bland, Kalman P. *The Artless Jew: Medieval and Modern Affirmations and Denials of the Visual*. Princeton: Princeton University Press, 2000.

Gertz, Nurith, and Yael Munk. "Israeli Cinema: Hebrew Identity/Jewish Identity" ("Kolno'a Yisra'eli: Zehut Ivrit/Zehut Yehudit"). In *New Jewish Time: Jewish Culture in a Secular Age: An Encyclopedic View (Zman Yehudi Khadash: Tarbut Yehudit Be'idan Khiloni)*, vol. 3, edited by Dan Miron and Hannan Hever, 269–276. Jerusalem: Keter, 2007.

Homan, Roger. *The Art of the Sublime: Principles of Christian Art and Architecture*. Burlington: Ashgate, 2006.

Kimmerling, Baruch. *The Invention and Decline of Israeliness: State, Society, and the Military*. Berkeley: University of California Press, 2001.

Kleinberg, Aviad, ed. *Hard to Believe: Rethinking Religion and Secularism in Israel (Lo Leha'amin: Mabat Akher Al Datiyut Vekhiloniyut)*. Jerusalem and Ramat Aviv: Keter and Tel Aviv University Press, 2004.

Kochan, Lionel. *Beyond the Graven Image: A Jewish View*. New York: New York University Press, 1997.

Marx, Tzvi C. *Disability in Jewish Law*. London: Routledge, 2002.

Munk, Yael. "Le retour du cinéma israélien vers le judaïsme." *Cahiers du Judaïsme* 20 (2006): 4–10.

Parchak, Ronie. "Beyond the Fence: Religious Sentiment in Israeli Cinema" ("Me'ever Lagader: Haregesh Hadati Bakolno'a Hayisra'eli"). In *Fictive Looks: On Israeli Cinema* (*Mabatim Fiktivi'im: Al Kolno'a Yisra'eli*), edited by Nurith Gertz, Orly Lubin, and Judd Ne'eman, 328–341. Ramat Aviv: Open University Press, 1998.

Raphael, Melissa. *Judaism and the Visual Image: A Jewish Theology of Art*. London: Continuum, 2009.

Rivlin, Yuval. *The Mouse That Roared: Jewish Identity in American and Israeli Cinema* (*Ha'akhbar Shesha'ag: Zehut Yehudit Bakolno'a Ha'Amerikani Vehayisra'eli*). Jerusalem: Toby Press, 2009.

Sagi, Avi. *The Jewish-Israeli Voyage: Culture and Identity* (*Hamasa Hayehudi-Yisra'eli: She'elot Shel Zehut Veshel Tarbut*). Jerusalem: Shalom Hartman Institute, 2006.

Schnitzer, Meir. "Artistic Miracle" ("Nes Omanuti"). *NRG Ma'ariv* (August 24, 2007), http://www.nrg.co.il/online/5/ART1/626/947.html.

Scholem, Gershom. *On the Mystical Shape of the Godhead: Basic Concepts in the Kabbalah*. New York: Schocken Books, 1991.

Schrader, Paul. *Transcendental Style in Film: Ozu, Bresson, Dreyer*. Berkeley: University of California Press, 1972.

Sheleg, Yair. *The New Religious Jews: Recent Developments among Observant Jews in Israel* (*Hadatyim Hakhadashim: Mabat Akhshavi Al Hakhevra Hadatit Beyisra'el*). Jerusalem: Keter, 2000.

Utin, Pablo. *The New Israeli Cinema: Conversations with Filmmakers* (*Karkhonim Be'eretz Hakhamsinim: Hakolno'a Hayisra'eli HeKadash-Sikhot Im Bama'im*). Tel Aviv: Resling, 2008.

Yonah, Yossi, and Yehuda Goodman, eds. *Maelstrom of Identities: A Critical Look at Religion and Secularity in Israel* (*Ma'arbolet Hazehuyot: Diyun Bikorti Bedatiyut Vekhiloniyut Beyisra'el*). Jerusalem: Van Leer Jerusalem Institute and Hakibbutz Hameukhad, 2004.

FILMOGRAPHY

Avanim (Stones). DVD. Directed by Raphaël Nadjari. 2004. New York: Sisu Home Entertainment, 2005.

Bruriah. DVD. Directed by Avraham Kushnir. 2008. Ramat Hasharon: NMC United Entertainment, 2009.

Einayim Pkukhot (Eyes Wide Open). DVD. Directed by Haim Tabakman. 2009. Ramat Hasharon: NMC United Entertainment, 2010.

Hahesder (Time of Favor). DVD. Directed by Joseph Cedar. 2000. New York: Kino Video, 2001.

Hasodot (The Secrets). DVD. Directed by Avi Nesher. 2007. Netanya: Globus United, 2007.

Khufshat Kayitz (My Father, My Lord). DVD. Directed by David Volach. 2007. Or Yehuda: Hed Arzi, 2007.

Medurat Hashevet (Campfire). DVD. Directed by Joseph Cedar. 2004. Netanya: Globus United, 2004.

Mekudeshet (Sentenced to Marriage). DVD. Directed by Anat Zuria. 2004. Tel Aviv: Anat Zuria and Third Ear, 2004.

Me'orav Yerushalmi (Jerusalem Mix). Television series created by Udi Leon, Nissim Levy, and Jackie Levy. 2003–2009.

Merkhak Negi'ah (A Touch Away). DVD. Television series created by Zafrir Kochanovsky, Ron Ninio, and Ronit Weiss-Berkowitz. 2007. Netanya: Globus United, 2008.

Shoshelet Schvartz (Schwartz Dynasty). DVD. Directed by Shmuel Hasfari and Amir Hasfari. 2005. Netanya: Globus United, 2006.

Srugim. DVD. Television series created by Hava Divon and Eliezer Shapiro. 2008–2010. Ramat Hasharon: NMC United Entertainment, 2008.

Tehilim. DVD. Directed by Raphaël Nadjari. 2007. Ramat Hasharon: NMC United Entertainment, 2008.

Tehora (Purity). DVD. Directed by Anat Zuria. 2002. Tel Aviv: Amythos Films, 2002.

Ushpizin. DVD. Directed by Giddi Dar and Shuli Rand. 2004. New York: New Line Home Video, 2006.

16   Seeking the Local, Engaging the Global

Women and Religious Oppression in a Minor Film

NAVA DUSHI

Penetrating the intimacy of a world fixed in a religious time zone, otherwise hermetically sealed from its contemporary surroundings, the film *Kadosh* (Sacred; Amos Gitai, 1999) portrays the life of abstinence at the core of one of Jerusalem's religiously constituted enclaves. Much like the subject of his film, Gitai's gaze is committed to the exercise of restraint, reducing the cinematic form to the poverty of its language, to its desert, and as such rendering it barren and unfit for reproduction.[1] In this double play *Kadosh* never splits from that which is unique to its locality and at the same time sustains its freedom from the pervasive reign of any universal signifier, therein foregrounding the film's "minor" standing. But what do I mean by minor standing and what does it have to do with the production of meaning which is so critical for the interpretation of any film, regardless of its immediate context?

The interface between local cinematic texts and their foreign viewers is one of great intricacy. Members of juried committees in international film festivals, potential distributors, and general audiences worldwide perceive such films from some distance, outside of their local context. Still, in recent years a growing body of Israeli films has gained increasing international awareness. What qualities may be attributed to the ability of such texts to lend themselves to the derivation of meaning?

National Cinema in a Global Context

Analyzing the textual characteristics by which emerging national cinemas assume their mobility across cultural borders creates a new ordering scheme which positions such films as objects within a broader textual field. Similar to other human works (law, science, the fine arts, ethics, religion) observed by Pierre Bourdieu, cinema is produced in these "very peculiar social universes which are the fields of cultural production" in which competing agents fight for the monopoly over the universal.[2] Since the 1910s American narrative norms have occupied a central position of influence within the field by mounting a textual system which stands as a point of departure for international cinematic expression.[3] The term "films with legs" once used by the industry to describe films that endure is now related to their capacity to move easily in global markets,[4] implying a textual volatility detached from cultural particularity. It is this era of intensifying symbolic exchanges in which the very prospect of originating difference resurfaces and calls for reevaluation. The essay is thus concerned with the space of possibilities opened for emerging national cinemas, and Israeli cinema in particular, in the twenty-first century's global cinematic field.

As Zygmunt Bauman's account of mobility as the new power structure in *Globalization: The Human Consequences* suggests, "the freedom to move, perpetually a scarce and unequally distributed commodity, fast becomes the main stratifying factor of our late-modern or postmodern times."[5] In a world dominated by the massive movement of peoples, goods, images, and ideas the thinking of the nation demands the application of an adaptive imagination.[6] Stuart Hall posits that the erosion of the nation-state is spearheaded by Western-dominated media technologies and standards of representation which can no longer be limited by national borders. The free flow of cultural artifacts, forced by some of the largest transnational media conglomerates, takes on a powerful form of homogenization, undermining the mechanisms that centralized and mobilized national identity in the past—hence it is termed "globalization from above." Consequently, national identity undergoes a process of fragmentation from which a new kind of globalization emerges: a "globalization from below" the state, to use Hall's term,[7] or "grassroots globalization."[8] Grassroots globalization brings to the fore new voices that in past formations were marginalized or excluded from national discourse, such as new genders, new ethnicities, new regions, and new communities.[9] These voices presently counteract the homogenizing forces of the global through the local, as Ella Shohat suggests: "While the media can destroy community and fashion solitude by turning spectators into atomized consumers . . . they can also fashion community and alternative affiliations."[10]

Building on the notion of grassroots globalization, I suggest that over the past decade the emergence of local cinematic texts has formed a transnational web of themes upon which national cinemas thrive and assume their mobility across cultural borders. In this web, the fragmented national foregrounds local particularities that engage global audiences by way of association with similar localities in variable social contexts.[11] One of the prominent themes to surface from this emergence narrates the stories of women and their oppression. Films such as *Fire* (1996, India), *Two Women* (1999, Iran), *Kadosh* (1999, Israel), *The Circle* (2000, Iran), *The Day I Became a Woman* (2000, Iran), *Kandahar* (2001, Afghanistan), *The Magdalene Sisters* (2002, Ireland/UK), *Whale Rider* (2002, New Zealand), *Osama* (2003, Afghanistan), *Atash/Thirst* (2004, Palestine/Israel), *Water* (2005, India/Canada), and *Persepolis* (2007, France/USA) can be associated with this trend.

Minor Cinema

Gilles Deleuze and Félix Guattari find inspiration for their concept of minor literature in an extended diary entry of Franz Kafka, dated December 25, 1911, in which Kafka had begun reflecting on the dynamics of *kleine Literaturen* (small literatures) and in so doing engaged in an analysis of the sociology of literature.[12] Deleuze and Guattari read Kafka's approach as one of a very personal nature, from a particular point of view in the symbolic field: that of a Jewish writer at the dawn of the twentieth century, exposed to the consolidation of European nationalism and the emerging attempt of Zionism to form a self-contained Jewish entity in which the Hebrew language takes on a major formative role in its symbolic field. Kafka's reluctance to identify fully with either of the two gave way to the development of a body of work that Deleuze and Guattari rendered as minor literature,[13] based on a triptych of outlined characteristics which I consider adaptable to the discussion of cinema.

The first characteristic of minor literature is that it "doesn't come from a minor language; it is rather that which a minority constructs within a major language."[14] Minor literature is self-appropriated within a field dominated by a major language which the minor assumes to inhabit. Unlike a major literature, however, in which the social arena serves as a mere background to a foreground of an individual concern, in minor literature "its cramped space forces each individual intrigue to connect immediately to politics. The individual concern thus becomes all the more necessary, indispensable, magnified, because a whole other story is vibrating within it."[15] Hence minor literature is always political.

Furthermore, minor literature is charged with the role of collective enunciation: "it is literature that produces an active solidarity in spite of skepticism; and if the writer is in the margins or completely outside his or her fragile community, this situation allows the writer all the more the possibility to express another possible community and to forge the means for another consciousness and another sensibility."[16] This collectivity does not stem from the production of works that mirror an established representational model or a canon; minor literature invents itself by exposing the forces of difference and local particularity as an expression of a people to come. To stress the significance of this point, Deleuze and Guattari repeatedly insist that the distinction between minor and major is one of quality rather than quantity. The minoritarian is not understood in terms of its number value but as an entity that has no constitutive standard. For instance, despite their majority in numbers women form the world's largest minority group.[17] What then does the concept of minor literature hold for the discussion of contemporary Israeli cinema?

I conceive three patterns of enunciation by which Israeli cinema appears to operate in the context of the global field. The first group includes films that display complete submission to mainstream norms, emphasizing their difference only to render their perception as inferior instances of the same (major Israeli films designed for domestic consumption). The second group consists of films that reject the classical tradition, dealing with their local particularity in a rather introverted manner, and are often rendered unintelligible to foreign audiences. The third group contains films that act on their undecided positioning in the field, exhibiting a formal adherence to mainstream narrative norms while at the same time negotiating them by way of infusing intrinsic cultural elements of distinction. I suggest that films of the last group share the attribute of being minor films and, much like minor literature, are constructed within a field dominated by Western narrative norms and at the same time deconstruct them from within to enunciate that which is unique to their locality.

These departures from the representational model parallel their political standing, which seeks an expression that is creative rather than reflective of identity. The identity created is an identity in becoming, refuting the application of closed representational structures and the subordination of difference to sameness. Thus, in the lack of a model or a tradition, the enunciation of minor cinema takes on indefinite forms of appropriation, which can be accounted for only on the level of the individual text and as such must be read through a discourse unique to this individuality.

A Minor Film

The enunciation of the minor in *Kadosh* portrays a nested structure of three concentric circles in which the outer circle embodies the seclusion of an ultra-Orthodox community at the heart of the modern state's capital, the middle circle observes the status of women within the community, and the core circle contains the story of a barren woman. Each layer deepens the marginality of its subject in relation to its constitutive domain. Within the coordinates of this world, *Kadosh* inhabits the language of representation, if only to invoke its shortcomings.

We enter the world of a childless couple, united by a marriage of love. As they near their tenth anniversary, the religious procreative command condemns the continuation of their unfruitful communion as sinful. The devout husband, torn between his religious conviction and love of his wife, is pressured to divorce her and remarry. His father, the community rabbi who holds childbearing to be the epitome of the fulfillment of religious practice, argues the point with unrelenting recitation: "A man who dies without progeny rips a page from the Torah." Facing the father and son, we encounter the fate of the barren wife and her younger sister, who is in turn forced into an arranged marriage and denied communion with the man that she loves. The wife tells her sister about an anonymous letter that she received, citing from the Talmud: "A woman without a child is no better than dead." The younger sister responds: "The Talmud . . . women don't study the Talmud here, but our father said that the Talmud contains everything and its opposite." Willful and irrepressible, both women pose an impending threat to the community. Their route of escape from its suffocating oppression leads one to suicide and the other to abandon the community.

The film opens with a prolonged eight-minute shot, setting the pace of the film. Early morning: a man and a woman are sleeping in separate beds. The man wakes up and starts performing what appears to be his daily routine, wearing his *yarmulke*, blessing, washing his hands, getting dressed, covering himself with his prayer shawl, praying, waking his wife, and preparing to leave the house. The audiovisual field is thus saturated by what seems to be a meticulous performance of a repetitive daybreak ritual. All the while the wife remains in the foreground of the frame, silent and devoid of action. The stationary camera establishes a voyeuristic intentionality, that of an outsider looking in. At the same time, the denial of the cut withholds the viewer's ability to get closer and more involved with the characters. This minimalism entails the reduction of the representational field, stripping the text from the use of any cinematic convention. Moreover, *Kadosh* invites viewers to engage in a world whose unfamiliar religious praxis hinders their prospects of understanding its systems of signification. With this twofold reductionism the film lends itself to the viewer through the suspension of her/ his judgment, focusing solely on the appearance of pure cinematic phenomena, the unfolding of human action on the screen and in time. Hence the world of the film is reduced to the performance of mundane actions which determine the constitution of its protagonists: men study the Torah, worship, and procreate, and women bear children, raise children, and attend to their husbands' needs. Thus the nonaction of a barren woman can only amplify, by juxtaposition to the actions of her husband, her lack as nonbeing. But how are we to delineate meaning from nonaction and silence?

The cinematic experience involves the act of negotiating the space of meaning, which is never a void, thus eliminating the impassability or rather the impossibility inherent in the ideas of nonexistence or absence. The constitution of meaning entails the intentional act of delineating objects (social, textual, or critical), of extricating a unity from the phenomenal flux based on the notion of their essence. If essence is defined as the intrinsic nature of something without which it would not exist or be what it is, then what are the prospects of an infertile woman claiming any objective position and thereby her right to exist in a society in which women are essentially accounted for as child bearers? I argue that the intricacy embedded in the claim to existence of an object prior to or outside of its constitutive domain is a core enabler for the mobility of the minor in the symbolic field. As such, it is deeply rooted in the conflicting demands that *Kadosh* poses for its viewer—to constitute that which is becoming unconstituted.

In Edmund Husserl's theory of signs a distinction is made between two kinds of signs, the "indicative" and the "expressive." While indicative signs are conceived as "devoid of expressive intent and function as 'lifeless' tokens in a system of arbitrary sense," the expressive "represents the communicative purpose or intentional force which 'animates' language."[18] Jacques Derrida's deconstructive reading of Husserl provides a pathway to a reading of the minor in *Kadosh*: "Whenever the immediate and full presence of the signified is concealed, the signifier will be of an indicative nature."[19] Hence the religiously constituted actions that men perform in the film can only be perceived by viewers as indicative, given their unavoidable presuppositionless admission to the reality of the film. From this indicative plane emerges the expressive signifier of the film, that of nonaction and silence. The barren woman who implies the threat that such a nonconstituted object may impose is forced out of the community, out of her home, and ultimately out of her own body. Her expressive void raises the ultimate question: What is sacred?

Women who inhabit the religious community are seen as deprived of the use of a language that they can call their own and as such, Gitai suggests, resemble the historically marginal position of the Jews. This condition facilitated the upholding of an individualistic social consciousness and a unique point of view: that of coexistent belonging and lack of belonging.[20] This articulated duality, coupling the minoritarian position of women with that of the Jews, appears to have permeated the textual fabric of the film. It foregrounds a position by which one is able to create the aforementioned minor identity within the globalized culture by making possible or creating a process of becoming but never through ownership of a representative or static identity.[21] Man, says the rabbi to his son, was created to study the Torah and worship God. A woman can only play an indirect role in the fulfillment of religious commands by bearing his sons.

This role division is visualized in the second scene of the film. The first shot provides an objective wide view of the husband, among other men, praying in a synagogue. The second shot presents two women standing behind the partition which commonly divides the synagogue's space, between the main prayer area designated for men and the secondary area designated for women. While the image graphically implies a sense of imprisonment, the subsequent shots reveal the women's faces and their intimate gaze at the men (viewed through the partition's cracks), thus constituting an alternative realm of existence within the community—that of an outsider looking in.

The last two shots of the film present the sisters' ultimate deterritorialization. The wife enters her husband's apartment while he is sleeping and lies next to him. At daybreak he wakes up to find her by his side and attempts to wake her. As he holds her lifeless body in his arms, weeping and begging, the camera pans and moves toward the bookcase and his holy books. In the last shot of the film the younger sister is seen walking outside the community at daybreak. The camera follows her to reveal the old city of Jerusalem. She stands with her back to the camera and gazes at the city. The camera follows her as she goes out of the frame, then it pans left and remains fixed on the final image of film: the Temple Mount. Thus Gitai concludes his film with a modest mediation between the potentiality of becoming and icons of symbolic transcendence. Much like the barren woman who does not materialize the expectation of reproduction, *Kadosh* evidently refuses to uphold and thus accept the dominant language of representation; its lingering shots, meager montage, and minimalist sound design expose the process of becoming minor.

The Special Case of Contemporary Israeli Cinema

> How many people today live in a language that is not their own? Or no longer, or not yet, even know their own and know poorly the major language that they are forced to serve? This is the problem of immigrants, and especially of their children, the problem of minorities, the problem of a minor literature, but also a problem for all of us: how to tear a minor literature away from its own language, allowing it to challenge the language and making it follow a sober revolutionary path? How to become a nomad and an immigrant and a gypsy in relation to one's own language?[22]

Gilles Deleuze and Félix Guattari's reading of Kafka through the concept of minor literature brings to the fore issues and qualities of expression unique to the Jewish people and to Israeli society. Zionism's raison d'être—the reterritorialization of a historically deterritorialized people—persists in the comparatively recent constitution of the nation-state. Hence the dynamic relations between the major and the minor which mobilize the Israeli film animate a primal complex in the Jewish state: imagining itself between what we may call the creative freedom of the deterritorialized or exiled minoritarian Jew from a self-defining universal and the majoritarian desire to reterritorialize, to establish its own models and its own system of universals (expressed in the biblical reference of the people of Israel's demand to have a king like all other peoples). These competing movements are strongly linked yet play on the brink of mutual exclusion.

The unavoidable political enunciation of such ontological perplexity is thematically repeated in contemporary Israeli cinema.[23] This core property, I suggest, defines its minor role in the global cinematic field. Such minor tendencies actualize film language by originating duration that engages individual viewers with the singularity of character and event. Recent Israeli films stress the immanence of exile, not necessarily from the place itself as much as from the universal. Consequently, Israeli identity takes on new forms rendered not from a collective submission that either confirms or disputes a master narrative, which characterized much of twentieth-century Israeli culture (literature and cinema), but from the intensified appearance of distinctive life experiences that act as lines of escape through that narrative and its structure. It therefore seems fit that this minor sensibility would currently garner accolades, considering Deleuze's visionary observation that we are moving toward the age of minorities.[24] Over time, these works reconfigure the distinctive collective enunciation that Israeli national cinema embodies in both the local and the global context.

NOTES

1. Gilles Deleuze and Félix Guattari, *Kafka: Toward a Minor Literature*, 19. Deleuze and Guattari elaborate on the position of Franz Kafka, a Czech Jewish writer who chose to write in German. They suggest that his use of the German language of Prague in its very poverty enabled him to go "farther in the direction of deterritorialization, to the point of sobriety. Since the language is arid, make it vibrate with a new intensity," thus opposing it to "all symbolic or . . . simply signifying usages of it."

2. Pierre Bourdieu, *Practical Reason: On the Theory of Action*, 134–135. Bourdieu argues that the privilege of the universal cannot be dissociated from its historical and social conditions of possibility, as such aesthetic value is durably constituted rather than universally innate. His sociology of action seeks to expose the social and economic conditions in which the habitually conceived universals are engendered.

3. David Bordwell, *The Way Hollywood Tells It: Story and Style in Modern Movies*, 12–13.

4. Charles Acland, *Screen Traffic: Movies, Multiplexes, and Global Culture*, 23, 32–34. Acland's proposed argument rejects the prevalent assumption which correlates "degree zero" of cultural particularity (universality) with geographic mobility, as it fails to "account for the possibility that signs of cultural specificity may be precisely the qualities prized by international audiences" (34).

5. Zygmunt Bauman, *Globalization: The Human Consequences*, 2. Bauman's discussion of globalization's eroding effects on the nation-state points to the dual remapping and dissolving of cultural practices in space and time. The consequent elevated regime is that of mobility, freed from the regulating constraints of territoriality and charged with technological advancements of time compression, which perpetuate immediacy and in turn undermine cultural memory.

6. Arjun Appadurai, "Grassroots Globalization and the Research Imagination." Also see the relevance of Benedict Anderson's coined "imagined community" to discourses of national cinema, in Susan Hayward, *French National Cinema*, 2.

7. Stuart Hall, "The Local and the Global: Globalization and Ethnicity."

8. Appadurai, "Grassroots Globalization."

9. Baruch Kimmerling, *The End of Ashkenazi Hegemony*, 63–71. In a chapter titled "The Newest Israelis" Kimmerling outlines the characteristics of the 1990s massive Russian immigration. Kimmerling suggests that unlike prior immigrations, which met the hegemonic demand for assimilation, the new Israel is founded upon the model of ethic and cultural pluralism. The new Russian immigrants sought their professional and economic assimilation and sustained their strong lingual and cultural affiliations through the establishment of autonomic institutions which parallel state institutions, thus forming a subculture within Israeli society. This fashioning of a Russian subculture points to a greater process of national fragmentation which coincided with the rise of other subcultures within Israeli society.

See also Gershon Shafir and Yoav Peled, *Being Israeli: The Dynamics of Multiple Citizenship*, 213–334. In part three, titled "The Emergence of Civil Society," Shafir and Peled provide an account of what they term "agents of political change" by examining Israel's supreme court and constitutional system and its economy and business community as well as the immigration noted above.

10. Ella Shohat, "Post-Third-Worldist Culture: Gender, Nation, and the Cinema."

11. I therefore propose the label "Narratives of GloCalization," which includes but is not limited to emergent categories such as "women and religious oppression" (Gitai, *Kadosh*, 1999), "the imagiNation of queer sensibility" (Fox, *Yossi and Jagger*, 2002), "Ethnic Minorities in National Contexts" (Koshashvili, *Late Marriage*, 2001), and "urban networks, global migration, guest workers, and the local crossing of paths" (Geffen and Keret, *Jellyfish*, 2007).

12. Ronald Bogue, *Deleuze on Literature*, 92. Bogue cites Ritchi Robertson's understanding of Franz Kafka's envisaged literatures of small nations.

13. Iris Bruce, *Kafka and Cultural Zionism: Dates in Palestine*, 3–4. Bruce argues that Kafka's estranged existence was often wrongly interpreted by critics as an ambiguous or even hostile feeling toward his heritage. She favors Marthe Robert's insight: "Assimilated Jew, anti-Jewish Jew, anti-Zionist, Zionist, believer, atheist—Kafka was indeed all of these at different times in his development, sometimes all at once" (4).

14. Deleuze and Guattari, *Kafka*, 16. See also Gilles Deleuze and Félix Guattari, *A Thousand Plateaus: Capitalism and Schizophrenia*, 106. Here Deleuze and Guattari argue that the major and the minor "are two different treatments of language, one of which consists in extracting constants from it [major], the other in placing it in continuous variation [minor]."

15. Deleuze and Guattari, *Kafka*, 17.

16. Ibid., 17.

17. Adrian Parr, *The Deleuze Dictionary*, 164–165. Also see Deleuze and Guattari, *A Thousand Plateaus*, 105–106. Here Deleuze and Guattari insist that "all becoming is minoritarian," thus pointing to the inherent connection between the two concepts.

18. Christopher Norris, *Deconstruction*, 43–44.

19. Ibid.; and Jacques Derrida, *Speech and Phenomena*, 40.

20. Irma Klein, *Amos Gitai: Cinema, Politics, Aesthetics*, 296.

21. Parr, *The Deleuze Dictionary*, 164–165. Also see Deleuze and Guattari, *A Thousand Plateaus*, 106.

22. Deleuze and Guattari, *Kafka*, 19.

23. We encounter individuals breaking away from their constitutive environments, driven by the potentiality of becoming. In *Walk on Water* (Fox, 2004) the Mossad agent experiences a process of deterritorialization in his journey to a past that constitutes and informs his actions in the present. In *Sweet Mud* (Shaul, 2006) a fatherless boy in his liminal transition to adulthood is torn between his ill and alienated mother and the constitutive standards of the kibbutz, leading to his desired escape. In *Campfire* (Cedar, 2004) a widowed woman and her two daughters break away from their modern Orthodox environment and its stipulated social conduct. In *Late Marriage* (Koshashvili, 2001) the lead character, who seeks a relationship outside of his ethnic minority group, is forced by his family to deterritorialize. In many of the films a becoming coincides with suicide or death. In *Kadosh, Kippur* (Gitai, 2000), *Yossi and Jagger, Broken Wings* (Bergman, 2002), *Walk on Water, Campfire, Sweet Mud,*

The Bubble, and *My Father, My Lord* (Volach, 2007), their appearance either initiates a becoming or forges a minoritarian line of escape.

24. Parr, *The Deleuze Dictionary*, 164–165.

BIBLIOGRAPHY

Acland, Charles. *Screen Traffic: Movies, Multiplexes, and Global Culture*. Durham: Duke University Press, 2003.

Appadurai, Arjun. "Grassroots Globalization and the Research Imagination." In *Globalization*, ed. Arjun Appadurai, 1–21. Minneapolis: University of Minnesota Press, 2001.

Bauman, Zygmunt. *Globalization: The Human Consequences*. New York: Columbia University Press, 2000.

Bogue, Ronald. *Deleuze on Literature*. London: Routledge, 2003.

Bordwell, David. *The Way Hollywood Tells It: Story and Style in Modern Movies*. Berkeley: University of California Press, 2006.

Bourdieu, Pierre. *Practical Reason: On the Theory of Action*. Stanford: Stanford University Press, 1998.

Bruce, Iris. *Kafka and Cultural Zionism: Dates in Palestine*. Madison: University of Wisconsin Press, 2007.

———. *A Thousand Plateaus: Capitalism and Schizophrenia*. Minneapolis: University of Minnesota Press, 1987.

Deleuze, Gilles, and Félix Guattari. *Kafka: Toward a Minor Literature*. Minneapolis: University of Minnesota Press, 1986.

Derrida, Jacques. *Speech and Phenomena*. Evanston: Northwestern University Press, 1973.

Hall, Stuart. "The Local and the Global: Globalization and Ethnicity." In *Culture, Globalization and the World System: Contemporary Conditions for the Representation of Identity*, ed. Anthony King, 19–40. Minneapolis: University of Minnesota Press, 1997.

Hayward, Susan. *French National Cinema*. London: Routledge, 1993.

Kimmerling, Baruch. *The End of Ashkenazi Hegemony (Ketz Shilton Ha'akhusalim)*. Jerusalem: Keter Publishing House, 2001.

Klein, Irma. *Amos Gitai: Cinema, Politics, Aesthetics (Amos Gitai: Kolno'a, Politika, Estetika)*. Tel Aviv: Hakibbutz Hameukhad Publishing House, 2003.

Norris, Christopher. *Deconstruction*. London: Routledge, 1982.

Parr, Adrian. *The Deleuze Dictionary*. New York: Columbia University Press, 2005.

Shafir, Gershon, and Yoav Peled. *Being Israeli: The Dynamics of Multiple Citizenship*. New York: Cambridge University Press, 2002.

Shohat, Ella. "Post-Third-Worldist Culture: Gender, Nation, and the Cinema." In *Transnational Cinema: The Film Reader*, ed. Ezra Elizabeth and Terry Rowden, 39–56. London: Routledge, 2006.

FILMOGRAPHY

Broken Wings (Knafayim Shvurot). Nir Bergman. Norma Productions, 2002. DVD: Sony Pictures Classics.

The Bubble (*Habu'ah*). Eytan Fox. Metro Productions, 2006. DVD: Strand Releasing.

Campfire (*Medurat Hashevet*). Joseph Cedar. Cinema Post Production Ltd, 2004. DVD: Film Movement.

The Circle (*Dayereh*). Jafar Panahi. Jafar Panahi Film Productions, 2000. DVD: Win-Star Cinema.

The Day I Became a Woman (*Roozi Ke Zan Shodam*). Marzieh Makhmalbaf. Makhmalbaf Productions, 2000. DVD: Olive Films.

Fire. Deepa Mehta. Kaleidoscope Entertainment Pvt. Ltd, 1996. DVD: Zeitgeist Films.

Jellyfish (*Meduzot*). Shira Geffen and Etgar Keret. Lama Productions, 2007. DVD: Zeitgeist Films.

Kadosh. Amos Gitai. Agav Productions, 1999. DVD: Kino Video.

Kandahar. Mohsen Makhmalbaf. Bac Films, 2001. DVD: New Yorker Films.

Kippur. Amos Gitai. Agav Productions, 2000. DVD: Kino Video.

Late Marriage (*Khatuna Me'ukheret*). Dover Koshashvili. Morgane Productions, 2001. DVD: Magnolia Pictures.

The Magdalene Sisters. Peter Mullan. Scottish Screen, 2002. DVD: Miramax.

My Father, My Lord (*Khufshat Kayitz*). David Volach. Golden Cinema, 2007. DVD: Kino Video.

Osama. Siddiq Barmak. Makhmalbaf Productions, 2003. DVD: MGM Home Entertainment.

Persepolis. Marjane Satrapi and Vincent Paronnaud. 2.4.7. Films, 2007. DVD: Sony Pictures Home Entertainment.

Sweet Mud (*Adamah Meshuga'at*). Dror Shaul. Sirocco Productions, 2006.

Thirst (*Atash*). Tawfik Abu Wael. Ness Communications, 2004. DVD: Global Film Initiative.

Two Women (*Do Zan*). Tahmineh Milani. Arman Film, 1999. DVD: NEJ International Pictures.

Walk on Water (*Lalekhet Al Hamayim*). Eytan Fox. Lama Productions, 2004. DVD: Sony Pictures Home Entertainment.

Water. Deepa Mehta. Deepa Mehta Films, 2005. DVD: Fox Searchlight Pictures.

Whale Rider. Niki Caro. ApolloMedia, 2002. DVD: Columbia TriStar Home Entertainment.

Yossi and Jagger (*Yossi VeJagger*). Eytan Fox. Lama Productions, 2002. DVD: Strand Releasing.

17

Beaufort and
My Father, My Lord

Traces of the Binding Myth
and the Mother's Voice

ANAT ZANGER

It looks almost festive, excited, a huge procession, colorful and lively in its way: parents and brothers and friends, even grandparents, bringing their loved ones to the event of the season, she thinks, a closing down sale and in every car there is a young lad, the first fruits, a spring carnival with a human sacrifice at the end. And what about you, she digs at herself, look at you, how pretty and put together you are to bring your son, almost your only one, whom you loved so much, with Ishmael driving you in his taxi.

David Grossman, *Until the End of the Land*

Introduction

David Grossman uses indirect speech in order to describe the thoughts of his protagonist, Ora, as she accompanies her son to the meeting point before a military operation. Two levels of significance intertwine here. On one level, the narrative describes a common Israeli practice of parents driving their sons back to the army after a weekend at home. On another level, the father's name, Avr'am, and that of his son, Offer ("faun" in Hebrew), clearly allude to the mythical story of the binding of Isaac in Genesis.

Like most texts, *Until the End of the Land* employs what Gérard Genette calls "double writing" in his discussion of intertextuality and palimpsests.[1] I would like to subject two recent Israeli films to the same analysis: *Beaufort* (Joseph Cedar, 2007) and *My Father, My Lord* (*Khufshat Kayitz*, David Volach, 2007). At first glance, the two films have little in common. *Beaufort* takes place in a military outpost in southern Lebanon, Beaufort fortress, during the final days of Israel's eighteen-year occupation of the area. *My Father, My Lord* describes a short and fateful summer break that an ultra-Orthodox Jerusalem child takes with his parents at the Dead Sea. Yet both refer to the biblical myth of the binding of Isaac as well as to other Israeli films that deal with this myth directly or indirectly.

The story of the binding of Isaac (Genesis 22) has been transformed and transcribed in Jewish culture for centuries. Modern Israeli culture has made especially frequent use of it. Gidon Ofrat and Hillel Weiss both observe that it is rare to find Israeli literary texts or works of plastic art in which father-son relationships are not directly or indirectly related to the model of the biblical story.[2]

The texts I analyze here, which were created just before or immediately after the Second Lebanon War in the summer of 2006, are no different. What is noteworthy about them, however, is that all of them, including David Grossman's novel, deal with indifference in the face of society's ongoing demands for what appears to be futile and endless sacrifice. Furthermore, these texts express another voice that joins those of the father and the son in a new triangle: the desperate, sometimes protesting voice of the mother. Unlike Sarah, the biblical mother, who remained silent but died right after the event, in contemporary Israel of the 2000s the figure of the mother is present, either in the foreground (Grossman's text and *My Father, My Lord*) or in the background (*Beaufort*).

Transforming the Binding

The binding of Isaac in Jewish history is the myth of the sacrifice of the son told in conjunction with a theological account that elevates the son to the status of victim through an act of substitution. The sacrifice is thus transformed from being merely an arbitrary event into a religious trial, an intentional act of faith. Secular approaches, however, as noted by literary researcher Ruth Kerton-Bloom, replace "God, who commanded the trial of binding with another less clearly defined essence, whose beginning lies in what may be termed Jewish history, and whose end lies in total emptiness, as if the binding was never a commandment at all, but a wholly purposeless and meaningless existential act."[3] Zionism, which, like God, promised the Land to the people, has also in a way demanded the sacrifice of its sons. But there is a salient dissymmetry between the biblical binding myth and its analogues in modern Jewish history; from the pre-state Israel pogroms to the Holocaust and the Israeli-Arab wars, modern Isaacs are not always replaced by innocent rams. This old-new myth has functioned as the inner code of Israeli society throughout its relatively short history. Modern manifestations of the binding story, with its surface structure rearranged, engage in a constant dialogue with the model.[4]

Moshe Shamir's 1947 novel *He Walked through the Fields* (*Hu Halakh Basadot*) and its various incarnations in Israeli culture illustrate this process. Uri, the protagonist, sacrifices his own life in order to save his friends during a military operation. He thus becomes a symbol of the native-born Israeli, the Sabra, ready to die for the Zionist cause. In the late 1960s artist Yigal Toumarkin commented on the myth provocatively with a sculpture also titled *He Walked through the Fields* (1967). Toumarkin's walker does not move; his eyes are shaded with sunglasses, his upper limbs are missing, and his pants are down around his ankles. Toumarkin has redesigned Shamir's national hero as more dead than alive, with his innards exposed and an expression of pain on his face.[5]

In the cinematic adaptation of Shamir's novel, directed by Yosef Millo (1967), Assi Dayan, the youngest son of the famous military commander and government minister Moshe Dayan, plays the hero, Uri. After graduating from a prestigious high school, Uri finds it hard to integrate into the communal life of his kibbutz; nor is he entirely sure about joining the army. He has fallen in love with a woman who, unknown to him, is pregnant with his child. Ultimately he decides to join the Palmakh, the pre-state fighting force. The binding motif is conveyed through a dialectic between national symbolism and individual tragic destiny.[6] In the film version, Uri is killed in action and twenty-one years later his son, also named Uri, returns to the kibbutz from a battle on the West Bank to learn that one of his classmates, Eyal (literally "ram" in Hebrew), has been killed in action.

This dénouement can be interpreted as an ironic comment on the sanctity of the binding myth. In its reference to the cultural profile of the myth, the film harks back to the 1930s and 1940s. Officially it is part of the so-called national cinema: a conscripted cinema aimed at cultivating, preserving, and enhancing national identity and unity. Yet its fissures locate it in another phase of the myth, that of the 1950s and early 1960s, which depicted the trial of Abraham as an absurd command. As we shall see, in the first decade of the new millennium films like *Beaufort* and *My Father, My Lord* as well as *Until the End of the Land* express a new phase of despair, while relating to earlier versions of the myth such as *He Walked through the Fields* and *Three Days and a Child*.

My Father, My Lord: From a Theological to a Zionist Narrative

David Volach's film takes place at the end of summer in Jerusalem and at the Dead Sea. The film portrays three days in the life of Menakhem ("comforter" in Hebrew) and his family. Menakhemke, as he is called at home, is the beloved only child of older parents. The family home is modest to the point of being ascetic: its walls are lined with holy books, its rooms crowded with ceremonial prayers and religious prohibitions, leaving little space for the child's soul to breathe. The child's father, a rabbi of a local synagogue and yeshiva, is scrupulous in his observation of the Jewish commandments, large and small, never missing an opportunity to teach his son Torah. Menakhem enjoys secular conversation only with his mother. In the room in which Menakhem studies (*heder*), the rabbi is teaching the story of the binding of Isaac, but Menakhem's thoughts wander out of the window to the birds and trees outside. At the child's request, the family drives to the Dead Sea for a day out. Once there, the family observes the religious rule of separate bathing, and Menakhem stays with his father. While his father joins evening prayers by the seashore, Menakhem prefers casting small fish back into the sea. He gradually wades deeper and deeper, until another child notices that he has disappeared and alerts the praying men. His body is recovered by helicopter, after a long search. At the end of the film, when the seven days of mourning (*shiv'ah*) are over, the father tries to go on as before but cannot. The mother, however, expresses her bitterness by throwing prayer books one by one from the women's gallery of the synagogue to the men's prayer hall below, where a service is underway.

The film makes repeated reference to the binding of Isaac. The father's name is Abraham; the couple has had difficulty having children—Menakhem is their only child; Menakhem studies the story of the Akedah, the binding of Isaac, and fails to place the sacrificial lamb correctly in the picture on the board. The time sequence of the film, its season, and its place parallel those of the Akedah, which tradition holds took place during three days in the month of Ellul (late summer) on Mount Moriah, which according to legend is the location of the Temple Mount in Jerusalem.[7] Moreover, the film also corresponds with one of the few Israeli films which relate to the theological aspect of the myth: *Three Days and a Child* (*Shlosha Yamim Vayeled*), a 1967 adaptation of the eponymous short story by A. B. Yehoshua (dir. Uri Zohar). The opening sequence of this film is a voice-over spoken by the hero in direct reference to the beginning of the biblical story, which in fact constitutes a summary of the main events of the film's plot:

I had thought I would have to apologize; somehow it turned out the other way. The three-year-old son of the woman I had once loved was delivered into my charge in the last three days of the holiday, in the first days of autumn, in Jerusalem. First, I pondered over the child, then I wanted to kill him. I did not accomplish that, however. I must still discover what prevented me. Anyway, the time and place were ripe.[8]

Mordechai Shalev notes that the child's name, Yahli, is also an allusion to the biblical story, since Yahli is a diminutive of Eyal, alluding to the Ayil, the ram that was substituted for Isaac in the biblical story. Indeed, the entire scene is replete with connotations of the binding motif. In the film the act of binding is presented as a hallucination, hence as an option which is ultimately rejected. The protagonist's inner conflict is condensed in the swing scene. The hero ties the child Yahli to a swing as if it were an altar.[9] The symbolic signification of being thus suspended between heaven and earth is an ambivalence, charged with uncertainty and risk. The swing between horizontal and vertical, as Nicole Belmont has pointed out, is analogous to the Roman ritual of the *Levana*.[10] The vertical position of a newborn child, followed by laying the child at the father's feet, symbolizes the newborn's acceptance into society. The horizontal position, in contrast, is associated with submission, rejection, and death. Interestingly, the boy in *My Father, My Lord* is tied twice. The first time, on the way to the Dead Sea, his mother repeatedly takes hold of his head and neck, tying his skullcap in place with a string. Second, when he is taken out of the sea by the rescue helicopter he is first bound with ropes and then suspended between earth and sky in a manner reminiscent of the ancient Roman ritual described above.

At the same time, the film undergoes a significant transformation in that the act of substitution which is essential to the ongoing existence of the theological myth does not take place: the son remains a sacrifice on the altar of faith. The binding myth involves a familiar set of participants and their interrelationships, based on the principle of substitution. Each participant in the drama enacted in the symbolic setting of Mount Moriah may be substituted for another. All are in fact synonymous units with an identical function in the same system; each is bound in the central paradigm of binding. God, Abraham, Isaac, the ram, and Sarah are all victims of this trial of faith.[11]

No substitution occurs in David Volach's film, and in this sense it takes a secular approach. Since God who commands has been replaced by the state of Israel's recognition of binding as its ontology, however, the secular mythology tends to extract three cardinal motifs from the archetype: mar-

Figure 17.1. Menakhem casting small fish back into the sea in *My Father, My Lord,* by David Volach (2007). Courtesy of the director, David Volach.

tyrdom and the love of God; the covenant; and divine trial. By eliminating the substitutions, Volach's film suggests a unique alignment between martyrdom and the love of God. "I was wrapped up in my prayers, I was in the arms of God," explains the father after his son's death.

The Bible, together with all subsequent commentaries, emphasizes the binding myth as the antithesis of human sacrifice to the idol Moloch. *My Father, My Lord,* by tampering with the substitution at the core of the myth, is situated in opposition to the original archetypal binding story. Even before the binding episode itself, the film foreshadows or augments it with another episode in which the father and the *heder* teacher drive a hatching mother pigeon away from the *heder*'s window so that she does not distract the students. When Menakhem asks what will happen to the chicks, no real answer is forthcoming. Thus the film prefigures the event in which, in the name of Torah and observing the commandments, the mother is removed from the scene and her child is abandoned to his fate. During the search for Menakhem in the Dead Sea, Abraham, Esther (his wife), and an accompanying crowd gaze heavenward but receive no answer. Similarly, in the final sequence in the synagogue Abraham raises his eyes to meet only a cold, alienating neon light. Having been produced soon after the Second Lebanon War, the film records its "historical moment" (Anton Kaes's term) of despair and protest,[12] while pinpointing the figure of the mother as a present factor in the dynamics of the event. In this sense, it might be read as referring to both the theological and the Zionist narratives.

Beaufort: A Zionist and Post-Zionist Narrative

The helicopter hovering between heaven and earth toward the end of *My Father, My Lord* recurs in the opening sequence of *Beaufort*. The helicopter links the isolated world of the Beaufort stronghold with the outside world. It delivers supplies, evacuates casualties, and brings reinforcements. It is by helicopter that Ziv, a sapper, is sent to the unit to dismantle a mine, which kills him. The opening frames and titles of the film present Beaufort in three guises. First, the natural, in which the castle is perched on a hilltop overlooking the Lebanese mountains. Second, the historical, referring to the twelfth-century building, which served as a fort during the Crusades. Third, during the First Lebanon War, the fort was captured during a controversial battle which claimed many casualties. Eighteen years later, the fort awaits evacuation.

Two specific sequences in the film establish its course and its stance with regard to the events it portrays. The first is the sequence immediately following the credits, which describes the day-to-day battle for survival in the stronghold. The second, which follows it, depicts the sequence of events which leads to Ziv's death from his arrival in the stronghold to his attempt to dismantle the explosive charge. While the film deals with events in Lebanon and Israel at the end of the 1990s, it also seems to refer to at least three other texts beneath the narrative: Hollywoodian/American, Israeli, and mythological.

The American text is alluded to in the rabbit warren of tunnels in the stronghold, which create a claustrophobic maze through which the soldiers move between the narrow shelves assigned to each as a bed and the vulnerable, open territory of the stronghold that is under constant sniper attack. A computerized system broadcasts information about events in the outside world surrounding the stronghold, while a red telephone is used to communicate with the faceless line of command. Ziv the sapper, who is sent to the stronghold in order to dismantle the roadside bomb, suspects that this is an impossible task and expresses his objections, but his commanders insist that he must go ahead. When one of the soldiers in the stronghold asks why they do not use a robot to explode the booby-trapped mine, his friend answers that the army wants to exploit the rare opportunity of an enemy mine falling into their hands: "They want to examine the mine, not explode it."

The opening sequence as well as other parts of the film allude in various ways to Ridley Scott's *Alien* (1979). These include the way the stronghold's corrugated iron tunnels are filmed, the use of a computerized system to film events outside, and the anonymous chain of command, which sends soldiers to their deaths without considering their safety. Scott's film deals with the struggle for survival by a spaceship abandoned by its commanders. Central command's directive is discovered by all of the spaceship's team: the highest priority is to bring an alien to earth. The welfare of the team comes second. The central command is named "Mother," highlighting the unexpected and unnatural act of betrayal. In the context of *Beaufort* and the Zionist narrative, its possible connotation of "mother land" or "Imma adamah" (Hebrew for "mother" and "soil") has a specific meaning of betrayal. Later in *Beaufort* we see the preparations for withdrawal from the stronghold, in which a huge pile of flammable materials is stockpiled at great risk to the soldiers. The torching of the entire stronghold after evacuation also resonates with the burning of the spaceship *Nostromo* before it is abandoned.

With regard to the Israeli and mythological texts, the references to *Alien* in *Beaufort* both visually and narratively prefigure the story of betrayal and situate the story of survival in *Beaufort* in a critical position. The story of the soldiers' betrayal by the commanders they trust introduces the sacrificial Akedah (binding) story into the film and deconstructs it. At his first encounter with the inhabitants of the stronghold, Ziv the sapper says: "You know it was entirely unnecessary to capture this hill." The order to withdraw has been given, he adds, although it has not arrived yet. Later Ziv tells Liraz, the commanding officer, and Oshri, his right-hand man, that his uncle was killed there in 1982. He asked to be sent there because he had to see the place about which he had heard so much before it was evacuated.

The mission to dismantle the bomb is the only occasion in the film on which the soldiers are seen outside the territory of the stronghold. The area in which the soldiers are deployed is strewn with concrete pillars, mostly single, occasionally two or three together.[13] As Mordechai Omer observes, on the one hand pillars usually support buildings, and on the other pillars carry a large number of significances, including the pillar of smoke and the pillar of fire which protected and lit the way for the Jewish people on their exodus from Egypt. But the pillar, "with all of its violent and threatening erection," is also an altar on which sacrifices are brought: "like a post-primitive totem," says Omer, "this pillar arises as a remembrance of both the victim and the bringer of the sacrifice."[14] The tall pillars in *Beaufort*, next to each of which a soldier is positioned, recall Yitzhak Danziger's famous sculptures (*Altar* and *Ram*, 1940s) as well as the pillar-altar repeated several times in Uri Zohar's 1964 allegorical film *A Hole in the Moon*.

In *A Hole in the Moon* (*Khor Balevana*), a fragmentary and episodic parody, the triadic connections of the Land, Zionism, and Death constitute an undercurrent throughout. All the heroes' actions—either in the desert reality or in the film within the film—have to do with the Zionist cause, but these actions fail. Tzelnik and Mizrachi are two pioneers who compete with one another by opening two adjacent kiosks in the middle of the desert—an absolutely futile and useless pursuit. The frustrated heroes turn to film production instead. Ultimately they undertake a project aimed at encouraging population growth but are killed in the end by a disappointed and cheated public. Thus an analogy is created between Zionism and fictive cinema, suggesting that the Fata Morgana is the dominant metaphor of the film.[15]

Liberated from a rigid syntactic axis, the film's disconnected fragments foreground one motif which recurs again and again in various guises: death, whether by murder or suicide, on the one hand, and vertical pillar and obelisk, on the other. Like a displacement in the censored dream-work (Freud), this gesture appears in various disguises and reveals its meaning only retro-

Figure 17.2. Pillars and soldiers in *Beaufort,* by Joseph Cedar (2007). Photographed by Gil Sassover. Courtesy of the director, Joseph Cedar.

spectively. In this context, we may interpret the wild figure of a nomad on a horse, who, Hamlet-like, poses the question "to be or not to be," this time from a Zionist perspective. A few scenes later, this figure advances toward what seems to be an altar lifted from one of Shoshana Heiman's (1981, 1987, 2002) or Danziger's (1940s) sculptures of the Akedah and commits suicide in front of the altar. By means of both its plot and visual language, *A Hole in the Moon* refers symbolically to the lethal connection between Zionism and the land: the altar is everywhere across the country.[16]

Led by Liraz and Ziv, the stronghold's soldiers all take part in the operation to defuse the explosive charge. At first the team sends ahead a trained dog, which returns unharmed after a few tense moments. If the dog was ever meant as a substitute for the ram in the Akedah myth, the exchange is never realized. On the contrary, the unscathed dog appears as an undesired sacrifice. One of the soldiers then prepares Ziv to follow suit, binding his protective vest on him securely. The act of binding and Ziv's subsequent kneeling next to the bomb prepare him as an Akedah sacrifice. As they approach the bomb, Ziv says to Liraz: "Stay back, kid." Liraz replies, "Go for it, go for it young'un," reflecting both army slang and a reference to the young boy who is in fact the intended sacrifice in the Akedah. Which of them will be the next Isaac?

Like Uri in *He Walked through the Fields*, Ziv explodes the mine and himself along with it in order to ensure the safety of the army unit. At the same time, unlike Shamir and Millo's hero, Ziv expresses his doubts before going out on his mission. His comrades also cast doubt on the necessity of the operation: "Why was a person killed here? So we can have schnitzels?" asks Coris, one of the soldiers in the unit, after Ziv's death. Moreover, like the other soldiers, Ziv himself is portrayed as vulnerable: the camera lingers on his frozen face as the blood drains from it. Rather than reflecting the image of Uri in Shamir's book or Millo's film, then, the soldiers in *Beaufort* recall the living dead in Toumarkin's sculpture.

Beaufort confronts the binding directly, both in the soldiers' conversation as noted above and in the presence of the parents' generation. The senior officer of the unit (Alon Aboutbul) also talks about the battle for the fort in 1982 and about himself lying wounded while his friends were fighting and falling around then. During a television interview, viewed by Liraz, the commander of the fort, Ziv's father blames only himself. "I didn't bring him up right, I should have taught him to be afraid." But the film also draws the mother figure into the scene not only symbolically, by way of an allusion to *Alien* and its central command "Mother," but also by relating to the Four Mothers organization. Arba Imahot (Four Mothers, referring to the biblical matriarchs Sarah, Rebecca, Leah, and Rachel) was a group of peace activists, all mothers who had lost sons in Lebanon. As a grassroots civic organization, this group played a major role in the mobilization of Israeli public opinion in favor of the withdrawal from Lebanon.[17] During the days before the evacuation of the stronghold, the soldiers are discussing the incipient decision to withdraw. The Four Mothers organization is mentioned on various occasions in the film: "Four old whores won't tell us what to do," says one of the soldiers. When it becomes clear that the evacuation is imminent, Liraz says to his commanding officer: "Four old ladies have beaten us."

Toward a Conclusion

The two films discussed here create interesting and complex analogies between the theological and Zionist myths. As noted, modern Isaacs are not always replaced by rams. Religious interpretations tend to explain this dissymmetry between the binding myth and its analogues in Jewish history in terms of eternal choice. Death or martyrdom in the name of God (in Hebrew *kiddush ha-shem,* or sanctification of the name of the Lord), in their view, is the revitalizing force of the nation, given the eternal and closed circle of the Unity of God. Thus a paradoxical situation emerges in which refusing the principle of the binding would eradicate the nation's secret of existence.[18] In many Jewish and Israeli texts, the theme of the Akedah recurs, in regard to the complicated relationships between Zionism and its concomitant ethos of binding and sacrifice.

These films as well as other recent films, such as *Kippur* (Amos Gitai, 2000) and *Waltz with Bashir* (Ari Folman, 2008), include post-traumatic elements. Trauma, as Cathy Caruth writes, means a wound.[19] In *Beaufort* and *My Father, My Lord* the shriek of the open wound is written and heard through the mothers' voices: the terror, worry, and cry of Menachemke's mother but also her protest when she hurls the holy books to the synagogue floor after her son drowns in the Dead Sea; the central commander "Mother" in *Alien,* which *Beaufort* alludes to; the mother that Coris, one of the soldiers, calls immediately after his withdrawal from Lebanon; Liraz the commander's mother, who stopped asking what he was doing once he was nine years old because she was afraid to know; the Four Mothers movement, which appears in the film's background and in Israel's reality along with Women in Black. The shriek of dispute is heard also from Ora, the heroine of *Until the End of the Land,* whose son goes off on a military operation and who imagines, fears, and refuses to be present when the notifying officers knock on her door.

NOTES

This essay is part of a more extensive project supported by the Israel Science Foundation (fund #936/08)

1. Genette (1982).
2. Ofrat (1987); Weiss (1991).
3. Kerton-Bloom (1989: 10).
4. Following Kerton-Blum (1989), Ofrat (1987), and Weiss (1991), I describe the cultural profile of the myth in five main phases: from the binding as a collective, tragic myth (during the 1920s and 1930s) to protests against binding as a metaphor for existence (in the 1980s and 1990s). See Zanger (2003).
5. See Possek (2000: 57).
6. As Gertz (1993: 91) observes, Millo's film is based on the central ethos of the period of the Palmakh fighting force; although the hero ultimately becomes reconciled to the idea of national duty, the film also includes new individualistic components.
7. See Zohar (1974).
8. This monologue is based on the translation of Yehoshua (1968) by Miriam Arad, 35. Also cited in Hebrew in Zohar (1974: 34).
9. In his analysis of Yehoshua's story, Shalev (1988) mentions the similarity between the episode and language of the Akedah and the swing scene (Yehoshua 1968).
10. Belmont (1973).
11. See Spiegel (1964).
12. Anton Kaes, MA seminar on shell-shock cinema, Tel Aviv University, Film Studies (2007–2008).
13. In the Lebanese reality, these pillars have a protective function: they are protective slabs. In this film, however, and especially in this sequence, the visual cinematic framing presents them as pillars.
14. Omer (2006: 96, 102).
15. Various readings of Zohar's film emphasize its unusual language, its reflexivity, its fragmentary narrative, and its critique of the Zionist vision. See especially Schorr (1978), Ne'eman (1979), and Shohat (1991).
16. Paraphrasing Nathan Zach on Menashe Kadishman's work (Ofrat 1987).
17. For analysis of the media coverage of Arba Imahot and its framing within the maternal, see Lemish and Barzel (2000).
18. See also Sagi (1998).
19. Caruth (1996: 19).

REFERENCES

Belmont, Nicole. 1973. "*Levana* or How to Raise Up Children." *Annales E.S.C.* 28: 77–89.

Caruth, Cathy. 1996. *Unclaimed Experience: Trauma, Narrative and History*. Baltimore: Johns Hopkins University Press.

Genette, Gérard. *Palimpsestes: La littérature au second degré*. 1982. Collection Essais. Paris: Éditions du Seuil.

Gertz, Nurith. 1993. *Motion Fiction: Israeli Fiction in Films (Sipur Mehasratim: Siporet Yisra'elit Ve'ibudeihah Lakolno'a)*. Tel Aviv: Open University of Israel.

Grossman, David. 2008. *Until the End of the Land (Isha Borakhat Mibsorah)*. Tel Aviv: Hasifriyah Hakhadashah.

Kerton-Bloom, Ruth. 1989. "How Did I Get Hold of the Wood: The Binding as a Test Case for New Hebrew Poetry." *Mozna'im* 62 (9–10): 9–14.

Lemish, Dafna, and Inbal Barzel. 2000. "Four Mothers: The Womb in the Public Sphere." *European Journal of Communication* 15(2): 147–169.

Ne'eman, Judd. 1979. "Cinema Degree Zero" (Kolno'a Darga Effes). *Kolnoa: An Israeli Journal for Film & Television* 5: 20–23.

———. 1998. "The Moderns: Genealogical Tree of the New Sensibility" ("Hamodernim: Megilat Hayokhasin Shel Haregishut Hakhadasha"). In *Fictive Looks: On Israeli Cinema (Mabatim Fiktivi'im Al Kolno'a Yisra'eli)*, ed. Nurith Gertz, Orly Lubin, and Judd Ne'eman, pp. 9–32. Tel Aviv: Open University of Israel.

Ofrat, Gidon. 1987. *The Akedah in Israeli Art (Akeidat Yitzkhak Ba'omanut Hayisra'elit)*. Ramat Gan, Israel: Museum of Israeli Art.

Omer, Mordechai. 2006. "Fallen Coordinates and Broken Obliques: The Pillar in Israeli Art" ("Kariatidot Nefulot Ve'obeliskim Shvurim: He'amud Ba'omanut Hayisra'elit"). In *Contemporary Israeli Art: Sources and Affinities (Omanut Yisra'elit Bat Zmanenu: Mekorot Vezikot)*, pp. 95–121. Tel Aviv: Am Oved.

Possek, Avigdor. 2000. "Anatomy of Heroism" ("Anatomia Shel Gvurah"). *Muza: An Art Quarterly (Muza: Riv'on La'Omanuyot)* 2: 52–57.

Sagi, Avi. 1998. "The Meaning of the *Akedah* in Israeli Culture and Jewish Tradition." *Israel Studies* 3(1): 45–60.

Schorr, Renen. 1978. "The Cinematic Experience: The Reflection of the Sabra in Uri Zohar's Films" ("Hakhavaya Hakolno'it: Habavu'a Hatzabarit Bisratav Shel Uri Zohar"). *Kolnoa: An Israeli Journal for Film & Television* 15–16: 22–41.

Shalev, Mordechai. 1988. "Three Days and a Child of A. B. Yehushua (1968)" ("Shlosha Yamim Vayeled Le'Avraham. B. Yehoshu'a"). *Ha'aretz: Culture and Literature Supplement (Ha'aretz, Tarbut Vesifrut)* Nov. 8: 14, 19; Nov. 15: 16.

Shamir, Moshe. 1947. *He Walked through the Fields (Hu Halakh Basadot)*. Tel Aviv: Sifriat Hapo'alim.

Shohat, Ella. 1991. *Israeli Cinema: History and Ideology (Hakolno'a Hayisra'eli-Historia Veideologia)*. Trans. Anat Glickman. Tel Aviv: Breiroth.

Spiegel, Shalom. 1964. "A Scrap from the Binding Tales" ("Perur Me'agadot Ha'akedah"). In *Festschrift in Honor of A. Weiss (Sefer Hayovel Likhvod Avraham Veis)*, 553–566. New York: n.p.

Weiss, Hillel. 1991. "Remarks for Examination of 'Isaac's Binding' in Contemporary Hebrew Literature as Topos, Theme and Motive" ("He'arot Livkhinat Akedat Yitzkhak Basiporet Ha'ivrit Bat Zmanenu Ketopos, Tema Umotiv"). In *Fathers and Sons: Myth, Theme and Literary Topos (Ha'akedah Vehatokhekhah-Mitos, Tema Vetopos Basifrut)*, ed. H. Z. Levy, pp. 31–52. Jerusalem: Magnes Press and Hebrew University.

Yehoshua, Abraham B. 1968. "Three Days and a Child" ("Shlosha Yamim Vayeled"). In *Until the Winter of 1974 (Ad Khoref 1974)*, 198–253. Tel Aviv: Hakibbutz Hameukhad. English version in *The Continuing Silence of a Poet*, trans. Miriam Arad, 35–94. New York: Syracuse University Press, 1998.

Zanger, Anat. 2003. "Hole in the Moon: Transformations of the Binding Myth (H'akeda) in Israeli Cinema." *Shofar: An Interdisciplinary Journal of Jewish Studies* (special issue on Jewish Films, ed. Lawrence Baron) 22(1): 95–109.

Zohar, Orna. 1974. "Light Steps and Open Eyes: Three Days and a Child: The Story and the Film" ("Tze'adim Kalim Ve'einaim Pkukhot: Shlosha Yamim Vayeled—Hasipur Vehaseret"). *Close-Up* 2: 33–44.

FILMOGRAPHY

Alien. Dir. by Ridley Scott. USA, UK: 20th Century Fox, 1979.

Beaufort. Dir. by Joseph Cedar. Based on Ron Leshem's book *If There's a Heaven* (*Im Yesh Gan Eden*) (2005). Israel: United King, Metro Tikshoret, Muvi Plus, 2007.

He Walked through the Fields (*Hu Halakh Basadot*). Dir. by Yosef Millo. Based on Moshe Shamir's novel (1947). Israel: Yitzkhak Agadati and Yaakov Stiener, 1967.

A Hole in the Moon (*Hor Ba'levana*). Dir. by Uri Zohar. Written by Amos Ke'nan. Israel: Geva Films Ltd, 1964.

Kippur. Dir. By Amos Gitai. Israel: Agav Hafakot and M. P. Productions, 2000.

My Father, My Lord (*Khufshat Kayitz*). Dir. and written by David Volach. Israel: bCinema Project, 2007.

Three Days and a Child (*Shlosha Yamim Vayeled*). Dir. by Uri Zohar. Based on A. B. Yehoshua's book. Israel: A. Deshe, 1967.

Waltz with Bashir (*Vals Im Bashir*). Dir. by Ari Folman. Israel: Ari Folman, 2008.

PART VI

Filming the Palestinian Other

18

The Foreigner Within
and the Question of Identity
in *Fictitious Marriage*
and *Streets of Yesterday*

SANDRA MEIRI

Thou shalt not oppress a stranger: for ye know the heart
of a stranger, seeing ye were strangers in the land of Egypt.

Exodus 23:9 (King James Version)

The Foreigner Within

Haim Bouzaglo's *Fictitious Marriage* (1988) and Judd Ne'eman's *Streets of Yesterday* (1989) were made during a time when the violent events of the first Palestinian uprising (Intifada) had engendered a heightened sense of mistrust in Israel and the occupied Palestinian territories.[1] These two films compel us to reexamine the core aspects of the Hebraic Israeli identity in relation to the Palestinian Other by using one specific device—the impersonation of a Palestinian by an Israeli character, played by a Jewish actor. Dorit Naaman maintains that *Fictitious Marriage* reinforces and reaffirms ethnic boundaries, that the "passing . . . affirms existing . . . hierarchical social structures" and therefore that the film is not subversive.[2] I argue, however, that it is precisely the failure to escape the dominant ideology and stereotypes that renders *Fictitious Marriage* subversive and that the failure to contend with the Palestinian Other is conflated in both films with the repudiation of the Exilic Jew.

The phenomenon of "the negation of exile" was one of the fundamental elements in the construction of Zionist identity.[3] In developing this notion, since its inception at the end of the nineteenth century, Zionism severed Jewish identity from one of its fundamental theological and ethical aspects:

241

the memory and legacy of being "foreigners" in an alien country. I refer to this legacy as "the foreigner within." Among the repercussions of the exclusion of the element of alterity as an integral part of Jewish collective identity has been the difficulty of recognizing the rights of the Palestinian Other. I argue that this is the main theme that underlies both films discussed here.

Notwithstanding their pessimistic mood, *Fictitious Marriage* and *Streets of Yesterday* engage the question of identity by bringing together two entities—the Palestinian Other and the Exilic Jew—through the impersonation device. In *Fictitious Marriage* the protagonist assumes the mistaken identities of both a Palestinian worker and an Israeli expatriate (who emigrated to the United States). In *Streets of Yesterday* the protagonist impersonates a Palestinian refugee in West Berlin. While some of the actions of the protagonist of *Streets of Yesterday* are ingrained with a deep sense of guilt (he betrays his Palestinian friend), the protagonist of *Fictitious Marriage* cannot trace his bewildered and abstruse comportment to any specific event in the plot. But both films maintain that their melancholic, passive, drifting heroes are in this state because Israeli society has severed them from the ethical infrastructure that characterized the Jews in exile,[4] rendering them incapable of any moral treatment of the Other. Both *Streets of Yesterday* and *Fictitious Marriage* demonstrate the nihilism that followed the dissolution of the Zionist collective ideology that permeated every aspect of Israeli identity.[5] The aftermath of this dissolution has been a massive reliance on force and aggression, as portrayed in *Streets of Yesterday*, and the recourse to materialism, as emphasized in *Fictitious Marriage*.

Streets of Yesterday depicts the Israeli-Palestinian conflict as a protracted bloody, paranoiac vicious circle, within which two friends betray each other. Amin, a Palestinian and the best friend of the protagonist, Joseph, implicates him in a violent conspiracy. Joseph suspects Amin of murdering the Israeli foreign ambassador (the real murderer is Shalit—an Israeli Mossad agent who frames Amin) and contacts the Secret Service. Amin is killed by Shalit's subordinate, who is killed by Joseph in an act of rage and remorse. He then assumes the identity of a Palestinian refugee and flees to West Berlin. There he meets Konrad, a German archaeologist, who is a double agent trying to prevent bloodshed but who is murdered by Palestinian or Israeli extremists. The film does not specify which, thus diverting the emphasis from the identity of the killers to the act of killing, the continuous bloodshed on both sides. In the final scene, the arrogant Shalit is lynched by a group of enraged Palestinians.

Eldi, the protagonist of *Fictitious Marriage*, is a high school teacher living in a comfortable house in Jerusalem with his wife and two children.[6]

He plans to fly to New York but suddenly decides not to board the plane. He checks into a hotel in Tel Aviv, where he is mistakenly identified as an Israeli emigrant from the United States on a visit to his homeland by Judy, the hotel receptionist, and Bashir, the hotel's Arab worker (with whom he speaks literary Arabic). For no apparent reason, Eldi willingly assumes this role. This creates an eerie feeling in the spectator, which increases the next day when Palestinian workers mistake Eldi for one of their own. For the rest of the film he plays along with these two fake identities.[7] *Fictitious Marriage* reveals the materialism of Israeli society in almost every detail: we see a cab driver counting money; Eldi's children repeatedly remind him to bring them back presents from his planned trip abroad; his wife tells him not to forget "the Nike shoes"; the hotel receptionist Judy, Eldi's lover, dreams of emigrating to the United States; the hotel is called California; the American flag is printed on plastic shopping bags; a local shopping mall hosts an "American Week"; Judy and her helpful Israeli Arab assistant are happy to accept U.S. dollars; and so forth.

This Americanization of Israeli society signifies the shift from a collective ideology to individualism. The materialization indicates the complex mechanism behind the development of the notion of the negation of exile as an integral part of Israeli identity. As Anita Shapira emphasizes throughout her book, the Zionist ideology aspired to create a new Hebraic identity through a process of literalization and concretization of biblical (Hebraic) ancient myths as well as actualization of archaeological findings. Biblical narratives and heroes were appropriated to the consolidation of that identity, while the actualization of Jewish archeology "was intended to give credence to our historical succession in the land of Israel."[8] This process contributed to the gradual demise of the spiritual infrastructure that characterized the Jews in exile. The first two generations of Zionist settlers (before the declaration of the state of Israel in 1948 and after 1948) adhered to an ideology that disregarded the needs of the individual for the benefit of the collective, alongside the repudiation of the memory of the Exilic Jews. The dissolution of this Zionist ideology resulted in a longing for individualism and materialism—according to the film, the only form of exile conceivable to contemporary Israelis. Thus "America" became a fantasy for many Israelis who felt that they did not belong, especially for many male Israelis in the 1980s who could not identify themselves through the military apparatus. When Eldi decides not to board his flight to America, he leaves his suitcase at the airport, with his military reserve uniform packed in it.

While *Fictitious Marriage* depicts this longing for American materialism as a fantasy indicating nihilism and an attenuation of spirituality, *Streets of*

Yesterday emphasizes the need to revive the Jewish cultural and spiritual amnesia by reinstating the "foreigner within," the Exilic Jew that the Nazis set out to liquidate.[9] This ethical burden in the film is carried by Konrad, the German archaeologist. His digging up of the past signifies the need to go back and reintegrate the Exilic Jew in contemporary Israeli consciousness. According to Konrad, the failure to do so will result in more bloodshed, in perpetuating the negation of the rights of the Palestinian Other. Being a double agent is in fact an act of atonement. By helping both the Israelis and Palestinians in order to prevent bloodshed, he is trying to reconcile two "Others Within": the Jews of Germany and Europe at large before World War II, on the one hand, and the Palestinians today, on the other.

In one of the dialogues, Joseph asks Konrad if "digging up the dead" does not disturb him. "Not the ancient dead," Konrad replies. He shows Joseph two skulls that he found in an ancient cave in "the desert near Jerusalem." The skulls represent two types of Jews: "the European Jew" and the "Middle-Eastern, Jewish warrior, killed while fighting the Romans." He calls the latter a "fine specimen" but immediately states that finding both skulls in the same cave is his "proof for the dual origin of the Jewish people." By this he means that one type of Jew must not obliterate the other. While holding both skulls in his hands, he carefully balances one with the other. The warrior type clearly needs to be balanced with the Exilic European Jew that his own people tried to annihilate.

Hence Konrad associates Joseph with the "European Jew," with whom he himself identifies. He tells Joseph that they have "so much in common . . . Berlin was called 'the domain of the Jews,' the Nazi saw Jews everywhere, Jewish Catholics, Jewish Protestants, Jewish atheists, some Jewish Jews, of course." Konrad points to the inestimable contribution of the Jews to Germany and Europe at large and at the same time to the inability of the German people to contain the Jewish Other, which resulted in one of the greatest catastrophes in history. The extermination of six million Jews was a devastating loss not only for the Jewish people but for Germany and Europe as well.

"The Other Within"

Fictitious Marriage carefully designs the deceptive mechanism of identity at large: a series of ideal images with which we identify, in which we (mis)recognize ourselves. Almost all the signs in the films are misread and misinterpreted, and Eldi is constantly recognized and identified as someone he is not. Thus the film defines "identity" as "misrecognition," an illusion, a chain of such fleeting moments that reveal the emptiness of the subject.[10] Eldi is mistaken for both a Palestinian and an Israeli expatriate, however. This suggests that the historical events and psychological mechanisms behind the attempt to achieve a stable national identity were based on general misrecognition(s), historically involving the use of the indigenous Palestinian as an ideal mirror image in the process of (re-)creating an imaginary ancient type of Hebraic identity, including the bond with the land. This approach was succinctly manifested in the ideology of the Canaanites, who "wished to sever themselves entirely from historical Judaism and the Jewish people, which was also a severance from the Jewish system of moral norms."[11] The creation of this imaginary mythic ancient indigenous identity in "Canaan" was to a large extent modeled after the native Palestinians, inevitably and fatefully at their expense.

As Naaman notes, Eldi is mistaken for a Palestinian because he eats a traditional Arab bagel (*kaek*), grows a mustache, and "carries a plastic shopping bag rather than a briefcase."[12] This plastic bag signifies not merely the Palestinian as a representative of an ethnic group but also the specific status of being deprived of basic civil rights, reduced to "bare life," despite being a human being—*Homo Sacer* in Giorgio Agamben's term.[13] The plastic bags of the Palestinian workers—unlike those of Judy and Eldi after their shopping spree—contain basic foodstuffs, meant to sustain them for a whole working day.

It is helpful in this context to consider Jonathan Boyarin's distinction between two kinds of Otherness in his discussion of the constitution of Europe: "the Other Without," such as Muslims, whose otherness and exclusion were part of that constitution, and "the Other Within"—Europe's Jews.[14] Both *Fictitious Marriage* and *Streets of Yesterday* use the device of impersonating a Palestinian to engender a critical examination of the historical, ideological, and political processes within which the Jewish experience of being the Other Within in Europe (as well as in Mandatory Palestine and even before) was displaced onto the Palestinians, who became the major Other Within of Israeli society after 1948. The films offer many images of this diversion and of displacement, all stemming from the assumption of a false identity, in order to establish a connection between the notion of the Other Within and what I term "the foreigner within." The repudiation of the foreigner within as a substantial aspect of Jewish identity in Israel impedes the recognition of the human and civil rights of the Palestinian Other, erecting physical and psychological walls around what Israeli society experiences as the Other

Within. This is similar to Konrad's description of Germany's experience of the Jews as the Other Within (feeling threatened by this Jewish Other), in his conversation with Joseph quoted above.

I would like to focus first on instances in the films that create images of the Other Within and then discuss other instances of displacement, whose purpose is to (re)place the Israeli as the Other Within with the Palestinian. Thus a double effect is achieved: an awareness of the very mechanism of diversion (how the fate of the European Jews was diverted onto the fate of the Palestinian people) and, at the same time, a conflation of the notion of the Other Within with the foreigner within—the backbone of Jewish ethical consciousness. *Streets of Yesterday* contains two scenes in which a Jewish character is encircled by a Palestinian crowd. In the first one, we see Joseph arriving at Gaza, looking desperately for his Palestinian friend Amin in order to warn him that he has informed the Israeli Secret Service of his involvement in the assassination of the American diplomat. A crowd of suspicious Palestinians surrounds him. In this image, shot from a distance and from a high and side angle, the notion of the Other Within provokes an uncomfortable feeling both in Joseph and in the spectator, which foreshadows the final sequence of the film.

The other scene takes place in "Hitler's Olympic stadium," haunted by the six million Jews slaughtered by the Nazis. While looking at the empty seats in the stadium, Luria, a member of the Israeli Secret Service, tells Joseph: "There's my grandmother, my aunt, my uncle, you could fill this place up with slaughtered Jews . . . the moment we stop fighting back, it can happen again." The film tells us that this connection between Israel's inevitable destiny to "fight back" and the traumatic memory of the Holocaust is disastrous. The arrogant Shalit, who initiated the tragic chain of events by shooting the Israeli foreign minister (after having killed the Palestinian in charge of the assassination of the American diplomat), still believes in his own all-powerfulness. While Luria is conversing with Joseph, Shalit waves his revolver in the air and fires it in an attempt to intimidate the crowd of Palestinians who have also arrived at the stadium. But he is mistaken. The Palestinians slowly encircle him and an image of the inverted Other Within once more emerges. Shalit's disregard for the implications of his actions costs him his life: he is lynched by the Palestinians.

Shalit believes only in weapons, not unlike many of the Palestinian characters in the film. He is devoid of any moral considerations, expressed, inter alia, by his deep scorn for spiritual Judaism. "Go be a rabbi," he tells Luria in a scene in which he expresses his resistance to the idea of relinquishing any of the occupied territories. Herein lies the problem. Both Shalit and

Figure 18.1. "Hitler's Olympic Stadium": Shalit's lynching in *Streets of Yesterday*. (Judd Ne'eman, 1989). Courtesy of the director, Judd Ne'eman.

Luria represent the predilection for the literalization and concretization of the ancient Hebraic prototype (the warrior who had resisted the Romans) as well as the legacy of the Holocaust that emerged with the founding of the state of Israel. This legacy is epitomized by the slogan "Never again will Jews go like sheep to the slaughter," a widely accepted imperative that has become a justification for any form of injustice and oppression, according to historian Moshe Zuckerman.[15]

For many Israeli philosophers and historians who live in Israel, however, this is by no means the only imperative that came out of Auschwitz.[16] "The fumes of the furnaces in Auschwitz will never die out," writes Holocaust philosopher and critic Ephraim Meir. "But what is, or rather what should be, the content of our memory in relation to this traumatic event?"[17] Weaving through a Jewish theology as well as philosophies of dialogue based on that theology (by Martin Buber, Emmanuel Lévinas, and Franz Rosenzweig), Meir concludes that the fundamental content of the Israeli memory should protect equality among people without abolishing their differences, a form of humanism based on the acknowledgment of Otherness. The failure of such acknowledgment is astutely described in this last sequence of *Streets of Yesterday*.

The Olympic stadium as a site of trauma also reverberates with the "Munich massacre" that occurred during the 1972 Summer Olympics. Eleven

Israeli athletes and coaches were taken hostage and then killed by the militant group Black September. Israel responded to the massacre by a series of assassinations of those suspected of planning the killings. The film suggests that by insisting on a politics of power and intimidation ("an eye for an eye") the ones who are continuously forced to pay the price are not only the Palestinians who have been deprived of their home but also the Israelis themselves, who are doomed to live in a post-traumatic condition.[18]

Inspired by Bernardo Bertolucci's *The Conformist* (Italy, 1970), the film uses a nonlinear, fragmentary narrative, composed of flashbacks, which simulates the protagonist's post-traumatic state as well as a distorted historic consciousness that has no place for any moral judgment, akin to Clerici's in *The Conformist*. This distortion is evident in Luria's words too. After all, Israel's policy of power and aggression (represented in the film by the assassinations of the Israeli foreign minister and Amin) can hardly be described as "a destiny to fight back" in order to prevent a second Holocaust, although such behavior may be rooted in the Holocaust trauma. As even the title of the film suggests, another opportunity to revise the kind of historic memory represented by Luria and Shalit is missed. The chance to reintroduce the

Figure 18.2. "Hitler's Olympic Stadium": a post-traumatic distorted consciousness (Luria and Joseph in *Streets of Yesterday*) (Judd Neʾeman, 1989). Courtesy of the director, Judd Neʾeman.

moral backbone of the Jewish people—the memory of exile, the foreigner within—is forgone.

In *Fictitious Marriage* the failure of dialogue, of communication as a result of being unable to contain the Other Within, not only is conveyed in Eldi's pretending to be mute (he speaks only very little literary Arabic) but also is very successfully configured through the use of sound and image. In Eldi's first encounter with the group of Palestinian workers, he is sitting on a bench (the same one where he tells a foreigner that he feels terribly "confused"), eating a bagel. The camera focuses on him. Offscreen we hear voices speaking in Arabic. Slowly the camera withdraws from Eldi, a hand enters from the right side of the frame, then additional parts of other bodies appear on the bottom left of the frame, encircling Eldi. This creates an inverted image of the Other Within in reference to the present state of events. It conveys the idea that Eldi himself has now become the Other Within, while also reinstating the notion of inside alterity in regard to Jewish identity.

The image and its relationship to the ubiquitous offscreen voices provoke an eerie feeling pertaining to the realm of the "uncanny" in the Freudian sense, familiar and strange at the same time—the repressed.[19] Hence this scene simultaneously conveys both the notion of the repressed Exilic Jew diverted to the Palestinian Other and the very dynamics of the mechanism of displacement. After all, the Jews who immigrated to Palestine in the first half of the twentieth century were the Other Within vis-à-vis the native Arabs.

In another scene *Fictitious Marriage* shows how the Palestinians from the occupied territories have become a source of cheap labor that Israeli Jews use for building their homes, often treating the workers inhumanely. The film depicts the humiliation of the Palestinian workers by the Jewish bosses on the construction site. One day the little van that the workers use to get to the site and back home has a flat tire, so they are detained overnight. They sleep packed together on the floor of a dilapidated one-room house. But the film's textual politics does not aim to rectify this situation by suggesting a more humane treatment of the Palestinian workers. Rather, it calls for a renegotiation of the Israeli identity in relation to the very concept of nationality. We see Eldi lying on the floor, his body constricted between two Palestinians. This scene reinforces the idea of Eldi's self-positioning throughout the film as the Other Within. Together with his new Palestinian friends, he is reduced to "bare life," to a state that compels us to rethink the historical narratives and ideologies within which the concept of national identity was consolidated.

The Poetics and Politics of Displacement

In *Streets of Yesterday* the relationship between the two Others—the Exilic Jew (the foreigner within) and the Palestinian (the Other Within) is organized within three geographical spaces: Germany, Israel, and Palestine. The checkpoint through which Joseph passes from East Berlin to West Berlin looks like many Israeli checkpoints and roadblocks that separate Israel (as established after the 1948 war) from the Palestinian West Bank and the Gaza Strip.[20] The film is based on the novel *Under Western Eyes* (1911) by Joseph Conrad (whose name is given to two characters in the film: the Israeli who impersonates a Palestinian, Joseph/Youssouf; and the German double agent, Konrad the archaeologist). The camera slowly pans over a long line of Palestinian refugees waiting behind a high barbed-wire wall (later we see more such walls, which create long and narrow corridors, designed to monitor every movement). The following motto by Joseph Conrad appears on the screen: "All man can betray is his conscience." Who is the addressee of this motto? Does it reflect the protagonist's behavior? Konrad's? The spectator's? What is its meaning in a world full of violence, hatred, and paranoia?

Régine-Mihal Friedman maintains that by using historical sites in this film the fictional character is placed in a decisive historical context that compels him to take both a political stance and an ethical position. Berlin and Jerusalem are analogous cities (joined and divided), where yesterday's refugees and feelings of guilt are translocated to those of the present.[21] In other words, Friedman suggests that the use of these traumatic historical sites creates an analogy between the abode of the Jews in Europe during the 1930s and early 1940s (before the "final solution" was conceived and implemented by the Nazis) and the abode of the Palestinian refugees in order to render both Homines Sacri. By doing so, the film not only reinstates the notion of alterity (associated with the Exilic Jew, the foreigner within) but also provokes a crisis that compels us to assume an ethical stance, based on a reevaluation of the historical events that led to the consolidation of national identity.

After passing the checkpoint, Joseph/Youssouf embarks on a train to West Berlin. Upon arriving at the railway station he is forcefully apprehended by two German policemen. Konrad and his wife, Nidal (who is also Amin's sister), have been waiting for him. Konrad asks the policemen for an explanation, but they disappear, taking Joseph/Youssouf with them. The camera then focuses on an elderly woman who is passing by. Her reply to Konrad is unequivocal: "We have seen that before." This unknown character springing from nowhere evokes the generation of German Jewry that was forcibly taken to the railway stations, to the camps, never to return. The woman's words and Joseph's impersonation connect two historical narratives. But they also explain the tragic acceleration (due to the abode of the Jewish people in Nazi Germany) of the process whereby the suppression of one form of Otherness (the foreigner within) has led to the mis/nonrecognition of the Palestinian Other in Israel. This has resulted in turning the Palestinians into refugees—a condition that characterized Europe's Jews not even two generations ago.

The historic parallelism is reinforced by many additional meaningful spaces. The Palestinian refugees' hostel in West Berlin represents the abode of Palestinians who have been expelled from their land and homes, evoking simultaneously the expulsion of the German Jews from their homes and their transfer to the ghettos. After Joseph is released from the police station, we witness a Palestinian being forcibly removed by two German police officers. This image conveys both the dire fate of the German Jews and the inhuman way in which Palestinians are treated by the Israeli authorities. The high gridded walls and long corridors of the German checkpoint between East and West Berlin are evocative of the many checkpoints between Israel and the occupied territories that have become emblems of the continuous humiliating condition of the Palestinians. For some Jewish viewers, this may seem like a shocking comparison. We should keep in mind, however, that these analogies implying a historic sameness express a need to renounce hegemonic national discourse and psychological patterns by (re)introducing that which has been lost in the creation of Israeli identity and serve as a warning device.

Between Ideology and Ethics

The subversive power of *Fictitious Marriage* and *Streets of Yesterday* lies precisely in their failure to change the course of events in the narrative (which continues to conform to the hegemonic way of thinking) while undermining it through the use of imagery and space stemming from the impersonation device. Thus the position of the camera becomes an ethical burden for the spectator. We have seen how this works in *Streets of Yesterday* through the use of specific sites. The narrative adheres to a fatalistic chain of events not unlike the one characteristic of film noir. But here the images and the use of sites strive to shock the spectator into an ethical stance which the film conflates with the ethics associated with the experience of the Exilic Jew—the foreigner within.

In *Fictitious Marriage* this stance is provoked by the inability of the protagonist to distance himself from hegemonic ideology and prejudices. At the beginning of the film, Eldi plans to fly to New York but decides not to board the plane on an impulse. He leaves behind his briefcase—a signifier connoting his status (a middle-class Israeli Jew)—and seems amused when the airport security is alerted, in fear that it might be booby-trapped. Eldie's hoax makes fools of the security personnel, revealing the biased approach that Israelis employ in relation to Palestinians, as if interrogation is the only means of communication between the two. The tragic irony is that Eldi, who appears to be merely playing a joke on the system, ends up being duped by the very same inescapable system.

In the end, it is not Eldi's suitcase game that makes the audience aware of the limitations of the hegemonic political discourse in Israel but the shock of his being a victim of it. It is precisely the failure to escape the dominant ideology and stereotypes that renders *Fictitious Marriage* subversive. The film ends with Eldi suspecting, through a series of misread signifiers, that the Palestinian workers he has befriended are terrorists planning to blow up a playground. This ending implies that no distancing from the dominant ideology is possible, overturning Eldi's apparent ability to play with the system, as hinted at the beginning of the film.

Clearly, the joke is on Eldi and the audience, who are initially led to believe that such a distance is possible. The ending should be read, therefore, as a meeting of the two Others Within, the Exilic Jew and the Palestinian Other. The repudiation of the first has led to the incapability of establishing a real dialogue with the second. No wonder, then, that in order to join the group of Palestinian workers Eldi must first "become mute" so that his real identity is not revealed. The disintegration of the experience of the "foreigner within" of Jewish identity is what makes it impossible for Eldi to trust what he knows in his heart—that his Palestinian friends are incapable of blowing up a playground. His muteness symbolizes his moral paralysis, the impossibility of rendering himself to dialogue, the 1980s young generation's association of Jewish life in exile only with materialism and consumerism rather than with spiritual values.

Both *Fictitious Marriage* and *Streets of Yesterday* echo, to a large extent, the post-Zionist debates that emerged in the late 1980s.[22] They constitute an attempt to revive the forgotten notion of Jewish Otherness as a means of altering the ways in which the notion of the Other has been explored in cultural and postcolonial studies. Rather than maintaining that any construction of identity is inevitably achieved through the exclusion and at the expense of an Other, these films thrust their protagonists into the experience of the Other Within. By so doing they not only address a specific problem in the constitution of Israeli identity—the repudiation of the Exilic Jew that resulted in a failure to acknowledge the Palestinian Other—but also suggest that a revival of the foreigner within Israeli Jewish identity in contemporary Israel is mandatory.

NOTES

1. The First Intifada broke out in 1987 and lasted until 1993, demonstrating a united Palestinian front: the PLO, Hamas (founded in 1988), and Islamic Jihad. It involved all the occupied territories in the Gaza Strip and the West Bank. The stoning of armed Israeli forces by children and young men became its emblem.

2. Naaman, "Orientalism as Alerity," 51.

3. The concept of "the negation of exile" refers to the repression of the Jewish culture of exile and its cultivation in the Diaspora. The term "Diaspora" denotes a collective noun for Jews living in different countries, while "exile" was defined by Zionists as an abnormal condition whereby Jews, as a minority, were subjected to oppressive political, economic, and social constraints. The exilic condition was hence seen by Zionists as the root of a "Jewish problem," whose solution was the establishment of a sovereign state in the Land of Israel (Eretz Israel) through organized emigration. See Aviva Halamish, "Finished—But Not Completed," 168. The concept of "the negation of exile" has been discussed and debated by many Israeli historians. For a partial account, see Anita Shapira, "Where Has 'the Negation of Exile' Gone," in *Jews, Zionists and In Between,* 63. Worth noting, in particular, is Amnon Raz-Krakotzkin, "Exile within Sovereignty: A Critique of 'the Negation of Exile' in Israeli Culture."

4. On the notion of exile as a necessary condition for Judaism's ethical and cultural importance, see, for example, Assaf Sagiv, "George Steiner's Jewish Problem." The traditional image of the Jew as perpetual foreigner was praised by many thinkers, such as Hannah Arendt, Edmond Jabes, Jean-François Lyotard, Zygmunt Bauman, and George Steiner (Sagiv, "George Steiner's Jewish Problem," 138), as well as by Jewish philosophers such as Hermann Cohen and Franz Rosenzweig, who opposed the emerging Zionist movement (ibid.). Sigmund Freud, too, was concerned about Palestine being a national center for the Jews and expressed his apprehensions regarding the conflation of Judaism with nationalism/nationality. In his last essay, "Moses and Monotheism," aptly written when he himself was forced to flee his home and become a foreigner, Freud perceives the Jewish people as a "prototype of intellectuality . . . deriv[ing] its name from . . . the Hebrew 'ruakh' [spirit]" and contends that Moses was an Egyptian prince (a "foreigner") who was compelled to leave Egypt because he had practiced monotheism (Freud, "Moses," 361). See also Said, *Freud and the Non-European.*

5. This mood is expressed very strongly in the New Sensibility films of the 1960s and 1970s. See Judd Ne'eman, "The Death Mask of the Moderns: A Genealogy of New Sensibility: Cinema in Israel"; see also Sandra Meiri, "Masquerade and Bad Faith in *Peeping Toms.*"

6. By the look of the house it might have belonged to an Arab family that fled Jerusalem or was forced out in 1948.

7. In 2006 Bouzaglo made a remake of *Fictitious Marriage,* titled *Janem Janem.* The Palestinian workers from the occupied territories are replaced in this film by foreign migrant workers. Its protagonist is also a high school history teacher. Disillusioned with the social and political life in Israel as well as his childless marriage and having lost a friend during his army reserve duty, he decides to take a break and go to Paris. But he never boards the plane. Instead, he joins a group of Romanian and Turkish workers. Like Eldi in *Fictitious Marriage,* he hides his identity, pretending to be mute.

8. Anita Shapira, "The Bible and Israeli Identity." In *Jews, Zionists and In Between,* 294.

9. On the cinematic expression of the tragic coincidence of the Zionist project to liquidate the Jews of the Diaspora by transferring millions of Jews to British Palestine and the actual physical liquidation of six million Jews by the Nazis, see Judd Ne'eman, "The Tragic Sense of Zionism: Shadow Cinema and the Holocaust."

10. Jacques Lacan, "The Mirror Stage as Formative of the I Function as Revealed in Psychoanalytic Experience."

11. Shapira, "The Bible and the Israeli Identity," 182.

12. Naaman, "Orientalism as Alterity," 49.

13. Giorgio Agamben, *Homo Sacer: Sovereign Power and Bare Life.*

14. Jonathan Boyarin, "The Other Within and the Other Without"; see also Raz-Krakotzkin, "Exile within Sovereignty," 43.

15. Moshe Zuckerman, *Sho'ah in the Sealed Room.*

16. See also Idith Zertal, *Death and the Nation: History, Memory, Politics.*

17. Ephraim Meir, *Toward an Active Memory: Society, Man, and God after Auschwitz,* 11.

18. The same theme is explored in Steven Spielberg's treatment of the Munich massacre and the events that followed in *Munich* (2005).

19. According to Michel Chion, there is always an element of eeriness in the use of the offscreen voice, "the *acousmêtre,*" because it pertains to a primordial stage in the life of the subject, dominated by the dialectics of absence (lack) and presence. See Michel Chion, "The *Acousmêtre,*" in *The Voice in the Cinema,* 17–29.

20. These two discontiguous regions were originally contained in the British Mandate of Palestine and later seized by Jordan (the West Bank) and Egypt (the Gaza Strip) in the late 1940s. Israel captured and occupied these territories in the 1967 Six Day War. In 1980 Israel unilaterally annexed East Jerusalem. At the time the films were made the West Bank and the Gaza Strip were still under full Israeli occupation and military administration. The only Palestinians who were recognized as citizens (they were given Israeli identity cards in the wake of the annexation) were those living in East Jerusalem. Israel built many Jewish settlements in both regions, which are considered in the world at large to be a violation of international law. While the twenty-one settlements in the Gaza Strip were abandoned as part of Israeli withdrawal from this area in 2005 (the disengagement), the ones established in the West Bank after 1967 are still expanding and, alongside the problem of Palestinian refugees (created during the 1940s and 1950s), continue to be a major impediment to reaching a peaceful agreement.

21. Régine-Mihal Friedman, "Espaces du cinéma et labyrinthes de l'histoire."

22. Among the most prominent "new historians" associated with these debates are Ilan Pappé, Benny Morris, Avi Shlaim, Tom Segev, Amnon Raz-Krakotzkin, and Idit Zertal. For an illustration of post-Zionist discourse and ideology (not just from historical perspectives but also from sociological and cultural ones), see Laurence Silberstein (ed.), *Postzionism: A Reader.*

BIBLIOGRAPHY

Agamben, Giorgio. *Homo Sacer: Sovereign Power and Bare Life.* Palo Alto: Stanford University Press, 1998.

Boyarin, Jonathan. "The Other Within and the Other Without." In *Storm from Paradise: The Politics of Jewish Memory*, 77–98. Minneapolis: University of Minnesota Press, 1992.

Chion, Michel. *The Voice in the Cinema.* Trans. Claudia Gorbman. New York: Columbia University Press, 1999.

Freud, Sigmund, "Moses and Monotheism: Three Essays" (1939). In *The Origins of Religion*, ed. Albert Dickenson, trans. James Strachey, 239–386. London: Penguin Books, 1990.

Friedman, Régine-Mihal. "Espaces du cinéma et labyrinthes de l'histoire." *Études Littéraires* 21, no. 3 (1988–1989): 129–140.

Halamish, Aviva. "Finished—But Not Completed" ("Tam Velo Nishlam"). *Cathedra* 94 (1999): 155–172.

Lacan, Jacques. "The Mirror Stage as Formative of the I Function as Revealed in Psychoanalytic Experience" (1949). In *Écrits*, trans. Bruce Fink, 75–81. New York: Norton, 2006.

Meir, Ephraim. *Toward an Active Memory: Society, Man, and God after Auschwitz (Ma'ase Zikaron: Khevra, Adam Ve'Elohim Le'akhar Auschwitz).* Tel Aviv: Resling, 2008.

Meiri, Sandra, "Masquerade and Bad Faith in *Peeping Toms.*" *Shofar* 24, no. 1 (2005): 107–124.

Naaman, Dorit. "Orientalism as Alterity in Israeli Cinema." *Cinema Journal* 40, no. 4 (Summer 2001): 36–54.

Ne'eman, Judd. "The Death Mask of the Moderns: A Genealogy of New Sensibility Cinema in Israel." *Israel Studies* 4, no. 1 (1999): 100–128.

———. "The Tragic Sense of Zionism: Shadow Cinema and the Holocaust." *Shofar* 24, no. 1 (2005): 22–36.

Raz-Krakotzkin, Amnon. "Exile within Sovereignty: A Critique of 'the Negation of Exile' in Israeli Culture" ("Galut Mitokh Ribonut: Leibikoret Shlilat Hagalut"). *Theory and Criticism* 3 (1993): 23–55.

Sagiv, Assaf. "George Steiner's Jewish Problem." *Azure* 15 (2003): 130–154.

Said, Edward W. *Freud and the Non-European.* London: Freud Museum, 2003.

Shapira, Anita, *Jews, Zionists and In Between (Yehudim, Tzionim Uma Shebenehem).* Tel Aviv: Am Oved, 2007.

Silberstein, Laurence (ed.). *Postzionism: A Reader.* New Brunswick, N.J.: Rutgers University Press, 2008.

Zertal, Idith. *Death and the Nation: History, Memory, Politics (Ha'uma Vehamavet: Historia, Zikaron, Politika).* Or Yehuda: Dvir, 2002.

Zuckerman, Moshe. *Sho'ah in the Sealed Room* (*Sho'ah Bakheder Ha'atum*). Tel Aviv: Published by the author, 1993.

FILMOGRAPHY

Bertolucci, Bernardo. *The Conformist* (Italy, 1970).
Bouzaglo, Haim. *Fictitious Marriage* (*Nisu'im Fiktivi'im*, Israel, 1988).
———. *Janem Janem* (Israel, 2006)
Ne'eman, Judd. *Streets of Yesterday* (*Rekhovot Ha'etmol*, Israel, 1989).
Spielberg, Steven. *Munich* (USA, 2005).

19   A Rave against the Occupation?

Speaking for the Self and Excluding the Other in Contemporary Israeli Political Cinema

DORIT NAAMAN

Introduction

In an early scene in *The Bubble* (Eytan Fox, 2006) we see Yahlli, a flamboy-ant Tel Aviv gay waiter, trying to dress Ashraf, a Palestinian from Nablus, to fit in at the trendy café where Ashraf has just been hired under the assump-tion that he is an Israeli. Yahlli is choosing colorful clothes from his own wardrobe, while his roommates No'am (who is Ashraf's lover) and Lulu are sitting on the bed joking. From the lighthearted argument between No'am and Yahlli, it becomes clear that the point of the scene is how "gay" rather than how "Israeli" Ashraf should look. Soon afterward, however, when they need to find Ashraf a Hebrew name, they converse about his lack of Arabic accent. The question of his hidden identity pops up in numerous puns and eventually in a narrative twist, when his identity is revealed. In this film Ashraf is passing for an Israeli: he assumes the body language, linguistic, and fashion markers of Israelis in order to hide his Palestinian identity. Audiences know that Ashraf is a Palestinian passing as an Israeli, so this dramatic device is used to encourage them to ask questions about both the ontology and utility of the binary categories "Israeli" and "Palestinian." The assumption that the two people are not just enemies but inherently and radically different from one another is challenged and mocked in the film, at least temporarily. The passing device could be seen to highlight the tensions and demarcations between belonging and exclusion in the Israeli social fabric, and as such the film addresses some of the burning political

issues Israel faces today. Ultimately, by the end of the film Ashraf is marked
as an external Other, who cannot belong in Israeli society.[1]

The Bubble is reminiscent of much of the 1970s and 1980s Israeli po-
litical cinema, a dominant genre which Ella Shohat dubbed "The Palestin-
ian Wave," alluding to the liberal politics of Israeli filmmakers engaged
cinematically with the occupation.[2] With very few exceptions (including
Yellow Asphalt and *Lemon Tree*), during the 1990s and 2000s the external
Other Palestinian has been replaced by the migrant foreign worker (*James'
Journey to Jerusalem, Janem Janem, Free Zone, Noodle*). Films that deal with
Israel's wars altogether lack any images of Lebanese or Syrian enemies
(*Beaufort, Kippur, Yossi and Jagger*). Films that have narrative segments in
the occupied West Bank (*Walk on Water, Time of Favor*) do not actually show
the West Bank and its Palestinian population. But the majority of highly acclaimed films avoid the Palestinian-Israeli conflict altogether (*Sweet Mud,
Broken Wings, Jellyfish, Turn Left at the End of the World, Campfire, Late Marriage, Or, Desperado Square, The Secrets*). This very partial list of films that
in recent years won the Ophir Awards (Israeli Oscars) consists of those that
focus on domestic dramas (often melodrama) and sometimes on interethnic
relations within Israel's Jewish social periphery.

In 2008 Pablo Utin published *The New Israeli Cinema: Conversations with
Filmmakers* (in Hebrew, Icebergs in the Land of Heatwaves). In the introduction he argues that contemporary Israeli cinema can be characterized by
an aesthetic of disengagement, a withdrawal from direct political content.[3]
Utin claims that even those films that deal with social and political issues
choose a minimalist aesthetics (hence we do not see the enemy), a subtle
look inward, as if we are exposing the tip of an iceberg, knowing full well
that the mass is lying just underneath the surface.[4] Indeed, to follow the
metaphor of disengagement, even the few films that overtly deal with the
Israeli-Palestinian conflict, like *The Bubble*, do so more as a backdrop for an
investigation of internal social issues, thus placing the Other as a marker of
the social border of inclusion and exclusion.

In this essay I analyze the representation of Otherness, mostly the Palestinian and Arab Other but also the migrant worker of the new global economy. I use the theoretical formulation of Edward Said's *Orientalism*, which
provides a useful language to discuss how a Self represents the Other. More
specifically, I look at films that engage in the phenomenon of "passing,"
both in the film's plot and in the casting decisions of the filmmakers. I argue
that passing in these films destabilizes ideological formations within Israeli
society. Ultimately, however, contemporary Israeli films that represent Otherness (be it Palestinians, Egyptians, or foreign migrant workers) cannot

imagine those groups as belonging to Israeli society or even as partaking in a debate about what Israeli society should be.[5] To that extent, these films affirm Benedict Anderson's claim that the nation is an imagined community and is imagined as both limited and sovereign. By "limited" Anderson means that the nation is inherently at odds with the idea of universalism.[6] A nation needs to mark its Others not so much by means of citizenship, which alludes to state institutions rather than to the nation per se, but by shared cultural texts such as films. Thus when Israeli cinema tackles the issue (which is rare) it imagines the nation as a Jewish nation, even when it represents the fissures and problematics of that assertion.

Representing Otherness

Orientalism examines the Eurocentric field of study of the Near and Middle East as well as representations of the region in European art and literature. At a theoretical level the book provides an invaluable model to address the geopolitical power relations embedded in representation (be it academic or artistic), especially when the representer is external to the culture discussed. Said showed that the work produced by Euro/Caucasian Orientalists did not simply represent the Middle East but actually produced a view of the region reflected through the fantasies, assumptions, and anxieties of the Euro/Caucasian self. As a body of work, those representations produced a version of the Middle East that was inferior in political agency and lacking both culturally and socially. Those representations had negative political ramifications far beyond academia or art, especially inasmuch as they were used as political and ideological justifications in the region's colonial subordination.

Israel was established as a result of the efforts of the Zionist movement, a European Jewish national movement, much in the spirit of other European national movements of the nineteenth century. The reliance of Zionism on its European cultural heritage and its consequent disassociation from Middle Eastern culture are evident in the writings of Benyamin Ze'ev Herzel, Ze'ev Jabotinsky, Ahad Ha'am, and other leaders of the movement at the time.[7] The early Zionist settlers in Ottoman Palestine had a twofold goal: (1) to create a new Jewish identity based on agriculture, self-defense, and a return to the Hebrew language; and (2) to be missionaries of European ideology (nationalism), European culture, and the advancers of technology and modernism. The role as ambassadors of Europe in the Levant, while secondary to the Zionist project of settlement, had substantial repercussions for Middle Easterners, Jews as well as Arabs.[8] In effect it positioned all Middle

Easterners as internal Others (if Jewish) and external Others (if Palestinian) in relation to the Zionist project.

Until the 1990s the complex relationship between Zionism and the Levant was manifested in the representation of both Middle Eastern Jews and Arabs by the hegemonic Ashkenazi filmmaking community.[9] Significantly, the geopolitics of Israeli cinematic representations work quite differently from the European colonial ones. There is no territorial division with an emporium-center and a far, unfamiliar colonized periphery, so "self" and "Other" share the same space. At the same time, hegemonic Zionist discourse did postulate a cultured, advanced Euro-Jewish self as distinct from, even exclusionary of, a backward Middle Eastern Other.[10]

Until the early 1980s the external Others were included in Israeli cinema only as minor characters, always Arabs.[11] As such they rarely had lines to deliver; they were mostly seen in groups, through long shots, deprived of any individuation. Almost all characters could fall into one of three categories of stereotypes: (1) the good-hearted, harmless, and primitive Arab; (2) the evil Arab (spy, thief, liar); (3) the sexually exotic but forbidden Arab.[12] In *Orientalism* Said notes that the hegemonic culture tends to read and represent the ethnic Other as a projection of the kinds of impulses the culture itself is afraid of acknowledging but fascinated by.[13] All of the stereotypes of Arabs in early Israeli films can be seen as standing in opposition to the new Zionist ideal mentioned above: a secular, rational, productive member of a Western society. But this opposition is not simply exclusionary; it actually represents aspects of the society that it is reluctant to deal with overtly.[14]

During the 1980s, however, following the continuation of the oppression in the occupied territories and the Israeli invasions of Lebanon, filmmakers started to produce a body of overt and complex political films. These films create a three-dimensional Palestinian character: Arabic is spoken, Middle Eastern music is incorporated, and the camera sometimes shows things from the point of view of Palestinians. While a significant improvement over the stereotypical representation of Arabs in previous decades, these films are not without their problems. Except for *Avanti Popolo*, all of the films are focalized through an Israeli male (as the main character). He is the one around which the drama evolves, the person who has to face the ethnic/national conflict and bring it to a resolution. *Beyond the Walls* (Uri Barbash, 1984) takes place in a prison, and we see Issam (the Palestinian leader) mostly through the eyes of Uri (the leader of the Israeli prisoners). When seen by himself, Issam speaks Arabic to his fellow Palestinian prisoners, which is sometimes but not always translated into subtitles in Hebrew. We can literally understand Issam and accept him only after Uri accepts him as a partner for a shared fight for prisoners' rights.

It is interesting to note that the Israeli prisoners are mostly Mizrahi criminals who unite forces with the Palestinian prisoners (who are all political prisoners) against the Ashkenazi jail authorities. This structure can be read as a metaphor for the region's need to unite against the larger imperialistic powers (the United States and the USSR at that time). But whether the film is read as a local or a global allegory, it is important to note the hierarchical structure through which (at least in this fictional world) the Mizrahim have more dramatic power than their Palestinian counterparts. In the hierarchical structure of Zionist hegemony the internal Other, the Mizrahi, has a better position with regard to power (even if only in terms of dramatic control) than the external Other, the Palestinian.

Hamsin (aka *Eastern Wind*; Daniel Wachsmann, 1982) provides a more complicated point of view than *Beyond the Walls*. The film follows the relationship between Gedaliah, a Jewish farmer and landowner, and Khaled, his Palestinian worker, in the explosive context of land confiscation by the Israeli government for the purpose of a Jewish resettlement. Gedaliah is trying to buy Palestinian-owned land before it is confiscated by the government; the owners of the land are interested in selling, but the deal is canceled after Palestinian nationalists threaten them. Khaled is caught between his Jewish employer and his Palestinian friends. He is often seen on his own, with other Palestinian workers, in the neighboring Palestinian village, and at a watermelon vendor's. But his shots are often framed through doors, through windows, or from a distance. This creates a strong voyeuristic feeling, as if Khaled is never by himself, never fully independent. He is always followed by some Israeli shadow—subject to a controlling Israeli gaze—either Gedaliah's or the filmmaker's. Khaled refuses to participate in Palestinian retaliation against the land confiscation and is generally apolitical, an Arabic version of Uncle Tom.[15] Barely managing to walk the fine political line between his Palestinian friends and his Jewish employer, Khaled fails at maintaining the taboo of interethnic romance. The filmic time that has been granted to him without "supervision" proves to be destructive: Khaled and Khava (Gedaliah's sister) embark on an affair, which eventually leads to Khaled's death.[16]

Gedaliah sees himself as liberal, offering to purchase his Palestinian neighbors' land before the government confiscates it. He trusts Khaled and shares intimate moments with him (the two even shower together) and feels utterly betrayed by Khaled's affair with Khava. While much more fully fleshed out than Issam's in *Beyond the Walls*, Khaled's presence on the screen is allowed only in order to enhance the conflict of the main Israeli character and therefore is subordinated to the main character's dramatic needs. As a result, Israeli audiences are still exposed to a view of the external Other through the perspective of the (usually) Ashkenazi Israeli male. In an article about multiculturalism in American cinema, Ella Shohat claims that "[t]his concept [focalization] facilitates the analysis of liberal films . . . which foster the 'positive' images, granting the 'other' literal point of view shots and dialogues, yet focalized through Anglo-American protagonists who represent hegemonic cultural norms."[17] The presence of the Other in films like *Hamsin* is an indication of a need in Israeli society to deal with its own political/ethnic prejudices rather than an attempt to let the Other have an independent voice with which to express a Palestinian agenda.

A few films, however, try to bypass the Israeli hegemonic view in different ways. *Avanti Popolo* (Rafi Bukai, 1986) tells the story of two lost Egyptian soldiers, wandering through the Sinai desert after a cease-fire has been declared at the end of the 1967 war. An encounter with Israeli soldiers toward the end of the film exemplifies how much we have come to identify with the Egyptian soldiers during the course of the narrative. The film is in Arabic and had Hebrew subtitles when it was screened in Israel, thus increasing its authentic feel.[18] But more importantly the film gives the Arabs a voice, this voice is in Arabic, and it is not mediated through the Hebrew voice (and literal point of view) of an Israeli protagonist. The main achievement of *Avanti Popolo* is in placing the Israeli audience in the shoes of the Egyptian soldiers, showing the futility and the horror of war quite literally from the other side of the fence. But the film was released in the mid-1980s, after the peace agreement with Egypt had acquired a relatively stable status in Israel, resulting in massive Israeli tourism to Egypt and a sense that Egypt was no longer an enemy. In other words, without discounting the film's value, it is not a coincidence that this film is about Egyptian soldiers of the 1967 war and not about Syrian or PLO soldiers of the much more recent Lebanon war.[19]

Similarly, *The Band's Visit* (Eran Kolirin, 2007) is a minimalist comedy about an Egyptian band coming to perform in Israel but accidentally arriving in a desert development town.[20] The main story focuses on the affectionate flirtation between Dinah (an Israeli restaurant owner) and lieutenant colonel Tawfiq Zacharya, the Egyptian leader of the band. While the story is focalized primarily through Tawfiq's gaze, we actually learn little about him; our identification is not as strong as in *Avanti Popolo*. In addition, Tawfiq and Dinah communicate in broken English. Their plot line is the most developed and dialogue in the film is minimal in general, so little Arabic is heard. The characters in the film never discuss politics, which is somewhat understandable since they are all disenfranchised and may care little about governments that do not seem to represent them.

Twice in the film Dinah initiates a sense of cultural sharing: when she selects Arabic music in the restaurant and when she tells Tawfiq about her fond childhood memories of the Egyptian films shown on TV every Friday afternoon. The film then cautiously suggests a new category: the Arab Jew who transcends the binary of Jewish/Arab so prevalent in political discourse as well as in Israeli cinema. But in both instances Tawfiq does not respond (and in fact when his band members play music it is never Arabic music until their final concert).[21] In the economy of the film the affinity that Dinah suggests is not reciprocated or even recognized by the band's members. But it does function in tandem with other Israeli films that include Arabic, Moroccan, French, Russian, and Yiddish as part of the acceptable Israeli/Jewish fabric.[22] Going back to Anderson's critical formulation, contemporary Israeli cinema imagines the nation to be much more multicultural than it ever did before; and the films that address previously marginalized Jewish communities tend to be both popular and highly acclaimed.[23]

Still, Kolirin's choice to avoid Israeli/Arab politics overtly is somewhat curious,[24] especially as the Arab world is boycotting cultural projects with Israel (such as this film) in an attempt to avoid normalizing relations until the plight of the occupied Palestinians is addressed. While such a visit is impossible at the current historical moment, Kolirin chose not to address those circumstances, and the genre of the film is a surreal comedy, all leading to escapist aesthetics and not to an engaged political or even cultural drama.

Passing: Crossing to the Other Side?

Passing is a phenomenon in which characters pass for another ethnicity/nationality within the film's plot or in which casting decisions allow a member of one ethnic/national group to play another. Passing is a main essence of the traditional carnival, which permits the poor to be rich, the man to be a woman, the whore to be a nun—for a day.[25] The carnival allows chaos and confusion and temporarily creates a nonhierarchical society. While the carnival is doomed to end, and the hierarchical order to be restored, the carnival still offers the marginalized as well as the mainstream a view of each other from within the other's shoes. In cinema the ability to pass for the Other and its many twists and turns in the plots create a utopian multicultural world in which alterity does not designate the boundaries of (ethnic) group identity but the lack of (personal or group) identity altogether. Such passings create a Brechtian effect of alienation (or defamiliarization),[26] and the audience's pleasure at the recognition of passing is, or at least can be, harnessed to problematize the pleasure itself.

Fictitious Marriage (Haim Bouzaglo, 1988) portrays the most complex relationship between ethnic representation and identity yet discussed. Eldi is a high school teacher from Jerusalem who misses a flight to New York due to a personal crisis (possibly as a result of his last military reserve tour of duty during the first Intifada). He checks into a hotel in Tel Aviv, where he is mistakenly identified by Judy, the hotel receptionist, as a *yored* (an Israeli émigré to the United States) who has returned for a homeland visit. Eldi immediately assumes the role of the *yored*, which creates a set of other passings and lies at the core of the film's drama. From a short exchange with Bashir, the hotel's Arab worker, we learn that Eldi speaks literary Arabic.[27] Later, as he sits on a bench one morning eating a traditional Palestinian bagel (*kaek*), some construction workers mistake him for an Arab. He soon finds himself encouraged by the workers to join them in a street-side selection for temporary work. The Palestinians' mistake is encouraged by Eldi's mustache, the bagel, and the fact that he carries a plastic shopping bag rather than a briefcase. While understanding everything that is being said, Eldi cannot speak his literary Arabic (which would betray his passing), so he pretends to be dumb. Curious but helpless, Eldi is adopted by an older worker, Kamel, who not only teaches him how to build but also completes his transition to looking the part of a stereotypical Palestinian worker by placing a wool hat (*tuk*) and a scarf (*kaffiya*) on Eldi's head and shoulders.

Passing for a Palestinian in *Fictitious Marriage* requires an elaborate visual transformation and the loss of voice. Although Mizrahi people in Israel are routinely ethnically profiled as Palestinians,[28] the film goes to great length to mark Eldi's transformation from an Israeli to a Palestinian, as if to indicate that the transformation cannot easily happen and is not a result of lack of ethnic/national differences. The film's choice of allowing the transformation to happen but marking it very clearly is particularly important for dramatic reasons (see the discussion below). Eldi spends the next few days (and the rest of the film) with the Palestinian workers, once even sleeping with them at a locked storage space. The audience's knowledge that Eldi is faking the two identities (the *yored* at the hotel and the Palestinian worker during the day) creates a comic effect but also forces the audience to keep a critical distance. The twofold passing structure enables the film to expose some of the failures of the Zionist project. On the one hand, almost everyone in Tel Aviv (as Judy so well exemplifies) wants to be American. On the other hand, the work of constructing and redeeming the holy land is being carried out not by pioneering productive Jews but by the Palestinians who were deprived of the same land. The audience follows Eldi's bafflement at the two discoveries, which is comic, poignant, and at times painful.

The construction site where Eldi and his new friends work is in a yuppie suburb of Tel Aviv, where the next-door neighbor is a painter (Avigail) who often exposes herself in lingerie, to the joy of the construction workers. One day Avigail asks for a worker to come and fix a "crack in my wall." Eldi wins a lottery among the workers, goes over to fix the wall, and ends up having sex with her. Avigail is very excited about having an affair with a Palestinian, but the audience knows that the interethnic taboo has not been broken. Sami Smooha asserts that "[a]s long as Israel is a Jewish-Zionist state, the Jews have a strong interest in maintaining the Arab population in the status of an ethnic minority, in order to reduce the chances of assimilation and mixed marriages, and in order to prevent Israel from becoming a truly pluralistic society."[29] Smooha points out the underlying ideology of the Jewish state, which explains why the audience may feel a sense of relief at knowing the "forbidden" act was actually not across ethnic boundaries (therefore only adulterous but not tabooed). At the same time, the scene exposes the hypocrisy of the taboo and its aura. Avigail's excitement over having sex with the unknown Other is stripped of its romanticization, and her failure to recognize the mistaken identity raises the question of the validity or meaningfulness of the taboo in the first place.

The film uses the audience's knowledge of both passing and true identities to create a humorous defamiliarization and as a result a critical look. While these challenges are valuable to the reflexive process of self-examination of the Israeli conscience and to the goal of emptying Otherness from the stereotype of the "sexually unattainable Other," they do not serve as a positive construction of Palestinian identity. For the few potential Palestinian viewers, the fake interethnic romance actually strengthens the notion of the power of the taboo. From their perspective the taboo is never seriously challenged, as the dozen other Arab workers have not won the lottery or had the opportunity to "fill in Avigail's crack." The narrative enables Eldi an access to sex precisely because he is not an Arab, thus confirming the suspicion that the Palestinians have gained nothing as far as the possibility of breaking the taboo. After all, if Avigail had random sex with an Arab worker, the power relations of both gender and nationality would play out quite differently between them. The joke of the film is played both on Avigail (a woman who is fooled) and on the Palestinian men, whose lack of access to sex and the Israeli society is strongly reasserted.

Another interesting aspect of passing in *Fictitious Marriage* occurs toward the end of the film when Eldi visits Kamel's home in Gaza. At first Eldi freezes when an Israeli soldier bypasses him in an alley, invoking the traumatic memory of his own reserve duty. But while Eldi and the audience through his point of view are privileged to get a glimpse of the occupation from the Palestinian perspective, the visit ultimately reconfirms Eldi's identity as an Israeli. After he and Kamel return to the construction site, Eldi suspects that they have brought back a bomb hidden in a tire designated to be a swing at the local playground. After the workers who install the swing quickly leave the site, Eldi, who is watching from Avigail's house, screams in Hebrew: "A bomb!"

Passing in this case placed Eldi in what he thought to be an epistemically privileged position, potentially enabling him to save lives. And the Israeli audience has no doubt that Eldi's suspicion and subsequent action were justified. While the filmmaker chose a narrative ending in which Eldi was mistaken and the workers were innocent of terrorism, the scene exposes the prejudices of the Israeli collective psyche and the limitations of an attempt to challenge these prejudices. The audience, together with Eldi, cannot go beyond the threshold of fear of Palestinians. While Bouzaglo could have privileged the audience to know what Eldi does not (that in fact there was no bomb in the tire), thus encouraging a critical perspective, he instead chose to subordinate the audience's knowledge to Eldi's. As a result, in its climax the film refrains from a moral judgment of Israeli prejudices against Palestinians and claims that ethnic boundaries cannot be overcome. Thus passing, as an attempt to understand the Other, is doomed to end with suspicion and tragedy.

Moreover, the relative (even though eventually mistaken) epistemic privilege of Eldi and the audience is not shared by the Palestinian workers. At the sound of his scream, they appear in the windows of the building in which they are working. They seem utterly disappointed to realize that Eldi is actually Israeli and that he could suspect them of terrorism. From a Palestinian perspective, despite the goodwill (of Eldi or the filmmaker), the film still manifests enormous biases. Not only is the gap between the Palestinian characters and Eldi finally reestablished, but they must also realize their location at the bottom of the epistemic totem pole. They turn out to be the ones who are duped in the film. Thus the film reinforces ethnic boundaries: Eldi is an Israeli, and they are potential terrorists because they are Palestinians. Eldi does not talk or apologize to his fellow workers. He collects his stuff at the hotel and returns home to his forgiving wife in Jerusalem. Eldi never manages to squat like the Palestinian workers, but it is interesting to note that during the end credits of the film we see Eldi's son successfully playing while squatting down. Here Bouzaglo may be suggesting that the historical trajectory of marked differences is being slowly erased for future generations.

Bouzaglo remade the film in 2006, with a nearly identical plot. But this time Eldi is passing as a migrant foreign worker. In *Janem Janem* he integrates into a community of Romanian and Turkish workers in Tel Aviv and develops a relationship with a Russian runaway mail bride, Yelena, who is assumed by everyone to be a prostitute. This time Eldi speaks English, the lingua franca of a globalized world, and no one really cares where he is from: everyone is from somewhere else. The film, much like its predecessor *James' Journey to Jerusalem* (Ra'anan Alexandrowicz, 2003), shows Israeli society from the perspective of its foreign workers: it is opportunistic, full of lies, deceit, and abuse of power. While this sobering look may be uncomfortable, it is nonetheless presented as a reality that could be neither conquered nor changed. At the end of *Janem Janem* Eldi is a victim of a Palestinian suicide attack. This time he did not suspect a thing, and his wounds send him back to the arms of his loving wife. In the last shot of the film we see Eldi in the hospital, his wife next to him, and Yelena arriving but stopping at the door, then leaving once she realizes that her relationship with him is over. This last scene is shot from inside the hospital room, where everyone is Israeli. Yelena is framed by the door, which is physically open but metaphorically closed for her.

The Limits of Progressive Films

In *Janem Janem* the Palestinian does not exist as a political or narrative counterpart of the land. The only manifestation of Palestinianness is in the sheer (and narratively unexplainable) power of destruction (ironically targeting primarily foreign migrant workers). The migrant workers, too, have little power over their fate and, as Yelena's character symbolizes, do not have access into the mainstream of Israeli society.

The Bubble (Eytan Fox, 2006) presents an interesting double set of passings. In the main plot Ashraf, a Palestinian from Nablus, arrives in Tel Aviv (despite having no permit) to return the lost ID of an Israeli soldier, No'am. The two fall in love. When in the cosmopolitan and gay-friendly Tel Aviv Ashraf can outwardly live his sexuality, but he is forced to hide his nationality lest he be deported. He stays with No'am, Lulu, and Yahlli in a trendy part of town and participates in leftist anti-occupation parties, passing as an Israeli. As mentioned earlier, as in *Fictitious Marriage*, Ashraf's visual transformation is marked. But the scene is coded more as part of a gay subculture than as an ethnic/national visual transformation. When he is "outed" as a Palestinian, Ashraf returns to Nablus, hiding his homosexuality there. At home his brother-in-law Jehad discovers Ashraf's sexual orientation, threatening to "out" him unless Ashraf marries Jehad's sister. After Ashraf's sister Rana is shot dead by Israeli fire, Ashraf decides to go on a suicide bombing mission.

In a subset of passings, the Israeli lover No'am and his friend Lulu pass as a French TV crew, in order to enter Nablus in search of Ashraf. From the outset, though, the two sets of passings do not operate in reciprocal relations. No'am and Lulu have to pretend to be French in order not to expose their heavy Israeli accents when they speak English. Their interlude in Nablus is short, full of anxiety that they will be exposed, and ends in a disaster (as No'am and Ashraf are caught kissing). Ashraf's passing is much more subtle and complex. First, he can speak perfect Hebrew and Arabic, both without any accent, and his fair looks do not mark him as a Palestinian.[30] Furthermore, while the audience knows from the beginning that he is a Palestinian, his body language and manners fit right in with the trendy environment of No'am, Yahlli, and Lulu's neighborhood. Finally, until the film's twist toward the end, Ashraf is seen as harmless, so the epistemic privilege of the audience is used for entertainment. In other words, we (the audience) know more than most other characters (both in Tel Aviv and in Nablus); thus we feel superior and engaged. Even the suicide mission itself is pitched—in the logic of the film—as motivated not by political conviction but by the trap of his homosexuality.[31] As a result, the audience members pity Ashraf because of his repressive society and so are encouraged to forgive him and his act of passing while still feeling liberal (at least in terms of their sexual politics).[32]

Passing does not occur solely within the plots of the films. Some casting decisions as well as characters' history and background draw attention to the political context in which these narrative choices were made. In *Beyond the Walls* director Uri Barbash made an interesting casting decision: he cast Arnon Tzadok, a dark-skinned actor, in the role of the Israeli prisoners' leader and cast Mohammed Bakri, a blue-eyed and blond Palestinian actor, in the role of the Palestinian leader. Within the context of the film there is no confusion about who is who, but in international film festivals the pictures of the two were often transposed (alongside the opposite name captions) because the editors of publicity materials thought that a mistake had occurred. Barbash admits that he wanted to challenge the notions of visual stereotypes, which fits well with his presumed agenda of portraying a shared Palestinian-Mizrahi interest against the jail authorities. But, as noted, this challenge to visual stereotypes is not carried through in terms of the distribution of narrative power in the film.

A different safety net around interracial romance and casting occurs in *The Band's Visit*. Dinah is trying unsuccessfully to seduce Tawfiq, who is played by Sasson Gabai, a Mizrahi Israeli Jew. Within the film's narrative frame Dinah is attracted to an Egyptian (and ends up having sex with another). But the audience knows that her affections are for a Jewish Israeli actor passing as an Egyptian, so the loaded potential of the attraction is dulled. The choice to cast a Mizrahi Jew for the role of the main Egyptian character is particularly striking because the rest of the band is played by Palestinian citizens of Israel and Gabai's own voice is dubbed by a Palestinian when singing.[33] While it was common for Mizrahim to play the roles of Palestinians and for Ashkenazi Jews to play Mizrahim in the early days of Israeli cinema, this practice has largely disappeared: more often than not actors play characters of their own ethnic/national origin. For that reason, Kolirin's decision to cast Gabai for the main role can be considered reactionary.

Avanti Popolo plays with notions of casting and identity in a playful/layered manner. Salim Dau, a famous Palestinian actor, plays one of the Egyptian soldiers, who worked as an actor before he was drafted into the army. In a painful confession to his fellow soldier, he admits that he has been classified as "the Jew" since he played the role of Shylock onstage in Cairo. Here a stage persona transcended the performance in the play and infiltrated the life of the in-film actor, who, ironically, is now fighting the Jews. The scene foregrounds the cinematic and theatrical tension between acting and casting and reminds the audience members that they are watching an Israeli citizen, who is a Palestinian actor, performing the role of an Egyptian soldier/actor who is called "the Jew" in Cairo. This series of identity displacements (or alienations) expands the boundaries of the film and reminds the audience of the political/historical context of the text. Once the viewers become aware of this extratextual context, they inevitably obtain a critical distance from the text, which exposes them to possible perspectival manipulations of the film.

Moreover, as Carol Bardenstein shows, the Palestinian actors make no attempt to speak colloquial Egyptian Arabic, so any viewer who speaks Arabic experiences another level of defamiliarization.[34] In *The Band's Visit* Kolirin solves the problem of colloquial language by minimizing the dialogue. With the exception of three characters (Tawfiq, his deputy Simon, and Khaled), the rest of the band is nearly mute for the duration of the film. Whether intentional or accidental, these linguistic decisions overlie casting decisions, creating a complex web of identity displacements and destabilizations.

In *The Bubble* Eytan Fox chose to cast an actor who embodies passing physically. Yousef "Joe" Sweid, a Palestinian with Israeli citizenship, plays Ashraf. Sweid has a light complexion, has almost no Arabic accent, and thus represents a possible bridge between the two nationalities or an antidote to the ethnic dichotomy that most of the films discussed here worked so hard to assert. This casting advantage, however, is used only as a dramatic asset within the narrative of the film, not for a critical engagement with the politics of ethnic segregation so common in Israeli culture and society.[35]

Summary

In her 2005 article Bardenstein speculates that cinematic passings in Israeli and Palestinian films are likely to disappear in favor of "circumscribed, univocalizing, and reified categories of ethnic, social, and religious identity."[36] She attributes this predicted change to the political climate in which passing serves both sides in the conflict for destructive ends (in the form of Palestinian suicide operations and Israeli extrajudicial assassinations).

But films like *The Bubble, The Band's Visit,* and *Janem Janem* seem to prove her wrong. Despite the challenges of passings in the political reality of the region, films still employ this device for numerous narrative and political ends. The question that remains open is whether those identity displacements achieve Brechtian-style alienation and as a result a critical distance from the text (and perhaps from political reality as well). When discussing passing in American cinema, Mark Winokur notes that "[i]n an attempt at equal opportunity, Hollywood portrays passing on a two-way street: white men can also pass as black. This is another attempt at configuration in which distinctions between black and white collapse without any real injury to representations of a benign, patriarchal capitalism."[37] Passing for the Other in Israeli cinema enables a liberal outlook on the Other as well as a fresh and critical look at Israeli society. But the narrative structure of the Israeli films ends up positioning the Israeli viewer back in a comfortable place within mainstream Zionist ideology, one that imagines the nation as Jewish although no longer only Ashkenazi. Passing and defamiliarization fall short of empowering Palestinians/Others to think that they can participate in or be full members of Israeli society. To that extent the Palestinian/Other serves as a prop in the Israeli cultural psyche rather than as an equal social (and narrative) agent and is therefore, as in past Israeli films, objectified and Orientalized.

NOTES

1. Here I am following Franz Fanon's discussion about nationalism and exclusion in *The Wretched of the Earth*. In the case of Fanon and the French colonial project, the exclusion was based on race; but his formulation becomes the basis for other postcolonial theorists in discussions of national struggle and inclusion/exclusion. Homi K. Bhabha works this idea further in his article "DissemiNation: Time Narrative and the Margins of the Modern Nation."

2. Ella Shohat, *Israeli Cinema: East/West and the Politics of Representation*, chapter 5, 237–274. A few of the titles belonging to that genre are *On a Narrow Bridge, Hamsin* (aka *Eastern Wind*), *Beyond the Walls, The Smile of the Lamb, Fictitious Marriage*, and *Fellow Travelers*.

3. Pablo Utin, *The New Israeli Cinema: Conversations with Filmmakers*, 13–27. "Disengagement" here is a metaphor referencing Israel's 2005 dismantling of settlements in the Gaza Strip.

4. Ibid., 13–14. Utin focuses on the stark contrast between the films' subtleties and the 1980s cinema that addressed politics in a direct way. Interestingly enough, in his interviews he takes the same approach, refraining from asking direct questions about the politics of this aesthetic choice.

5. In 2001 I published an article about the representation of both Middle Eastern Jews (Mizrahim, in contrast with Ashkenazim or European Jews) and Palestinians in the cinema of the 1970s and 1980s. I argued that passing, in particular, was used to empower the Mizrahim socially, while the same device excluded the Palestinians. The current chapter relies in part on the 2001 version. See Dorit Naaman, "Orientalism as Alterity in Israeli Cinema."

6. Benedict Anderson, *Imagined Communities*, 6.

7. See Joseph Massad, "Zionism's Internal Others: Israel and the Oriental Jews."

8. Early Zionist pioneers had a fascination with Arab (particularly Bedouin) culture, including the art of sword fighting and horse riding. Sociologist Oz Almog shows, however, that Middle Eastern elements that were adopted into Israeli culture were generally subordinated into a European framework. As one example, Almog argues that the "Mizrahi tradition was never honestly adopted by the Zionist settlers, but served as 'spicing' in the new popular-national recipe. The Israeli music was never Middle Eastern. The Israeli composers did not use Mizrahi scales, but added a slight Middle Eastern tone to the European structure of half tones" (*The Sabra: A Profile*, 290). The whole section shows colonialist and Orientalist ambivalence that sees Others as exotic, romanticizes their culture, but ultimately views them as inferior (ibid., 289–309).

9. Part of the 1990s change in Israeli cinema and TV production was a move toward self-representation by groups that until then had been almost entirely disenfranchised. Not only Mizrahim but also Russian Jews, Orthodox Jews, and settlers started producing self-representations, exposing the heterogeneous nature of Israeli society. This move was facilitated by the global movement of identity politics but more importantly by the establishment of a second TV channel, the regulation of cable TV in Israel and legislation regulating original Hebrew language content, and the changing modes of financing for feature films.

10. For an extensive discussion of the representation of Mizrahim, see Shohat, *Israeli Cinema*, chapter 3, 115–178.

11. Until the 1980s Arab characters had no national identity but were represented as diffused Arabs.

12. Examples of the first two types can be seen in films like *Hill 24 Doesn't Answer* (1955) and *They Were Ten* (1960). An example of the sexually forbidden Arab can be seen in *My Michael* (1976), where Hannah, the introverted main character, is attracted to Arab twins she grew up with. As a result of this attraction, the twins come to signify a generalized, impersonal, exotic but tabooed Other. A detailed analysis of the film, also tying it to colonialist cinematic practices and Said's *Orientalism*, can be found in Yosefa Loshitzky, *Identity Politics on the Israeli Screen*, chapter 5, 90–111.

13. Said, *Orientalism*, chapter 1.

14. This tension is particularly paramount with the representation of Mizrahim, whereby they are presented as Others, but the possibility of mixing (through passing, intermarriage, or upward mobility) is not only hinted at but actually celebrated. See Naaman, "Orientalism as Alterity in Israeli Cinema."

15. This derogative term refers to the African American character Uncle Tom in *Uncle Tom's Cabin* (Harriet Beecher Stowe, 1852), who is subservient and servile to his white owners.

16. Loshitzky provides a thorough analysis of the sexual economy of the conflict, with its taboos, desires, and transgressions. In addition to *Hamsin* she discusses films such as *The Lover, On a Narrow Bridge, Nadia, Streets of Yesterday, Crossfire*, and others. See *Identity Politics on the Israeli Screen*, chapters 6–7.

17. Ella Shohat, "Ethnicities in Relation: Toward a Multicultural Reading of American Cinema," 226. Shohat discusses films such as *The King of Jazz* (1930) and *High Society* (1956): films "involving allusions to 'subaltern' communities address themselves to a presumably 'nonethnic' spectator, claiming to initiate him or her into an 'alien' culture" (226).

18. The actors are Palestinians, however, so the dialect is not Egyptian.

19. In contrast, Carol Bardenstein argues that the film is very much about the Palestinian-Israeli conflict because the actors are Palestinian citizens of Israel and no attempt was made to speak Egyptian dialect. See "Cross/Cast: Passing in Israeli and Palestinian Cinema," in *Palestine, Israel and the Politics of Popular Culture*, 113–115.

20. The mistake itself is based on a racializing joke: Arabs have difficulty pronouncing *p* and it sounds like *b* (so instead of asking for Petah Tikva, the information attendant thinks they ask for Bet Hatikva).

21. Khaled sings and plays a Chet Baker song, and Simon plays a clarinet "overture to a concerto" he composed, which sounds similar to klezmer music.

22. See, for instance, *The Seven Days/Shiv'ah, Turn Left at the End of the World, My Father, My Lord*, and *Paper Snow*, to name just a few.

23. Ilan Avisar celebrates this collision of the national with the popular, arguing that it yields a "representation of national identity less narrow and more open to alternative types, thereby suggesting new vistas of national culture and promising an exciting future for Israeli cinema" ("The National and the Popular in Israeli Cinema," 143).

24. There are subtle moments in the film, as when the Egyptians smirk at a picture of former prime minister and war hero Yitzhak Rabin and cover another picture of Israeli soldiers, but these are hardly ever developed to a narrative critique.

25. The carnival and passing are thoroughly discussed by literary critic Mikhail

Bakhtin in *Rabelais and His World* and applied to cinema by Robert Stam in *Subversive Pleasures: Bakhtin Cultural Criticism and Film.*

26. Bertolt Brecht promoted a theater that defamiliarizes the familiar or alienates audiences from what they consider to be a natural, even neutral reality in order to provide them with critical distance from their ideological position. Passing and the carnival can serve as tools toward such defamiliarization.

27. The Arabic that Israelis are able to learn in schools is not the spoken dialect but a classic literary form not used in everyday speech.

28. Ethnic/national profiling is very common in Israeli streets, whereby police pull aside a person who looks like a Palestinian and ask for an ID card. For the most part, the Mizrahim accept this humiliating practice as a necessity because of the forms of Palestinian political violence.

29. Sami Smooha, "Class, Ethnic, and National Cleavages and Democracy in Israel," 191.

30. The recent Israeli TV series *Arab Labor* (2006, written by Sayed Qashua and directed by Ron Ninio) quite often takes aim at such ethnic/national profiling so commonly experienced by the Palestinians, including citizens of Israel and, as noted, Mizrahi Jews who look Middle Eastern. In the first episode Amjad, the main character, begs his wife to talk to the police at a checkpoint, because she is fair skinned and can speak without an accent.

31. The film uses the same logic that Israeli and Western media use in explaining female suicide bombings: as a response to a repressive patriarchal society rather than as a sophisticated political choice. For a fuller critique, see Dorit Naaman, "Brides of Palestine/Angels of Death: Media, Gender and Performance in the Case of the Palestinian Female Suicide Bombers."

32. Furthermore, the film slightly mocks the well-intentioned but completely impotent "Rave against the occupation" that the protagonists are organizing. The characters themselves admit that they never went to see what the occupation really looks like. But when No'am and Lulu pass at the checkpoint, the focus is on No'am, who fears that the soldiers will recognize him. There is no commentary on the long lines of humiliated Palestinians.

33. Eran Kolirin interview in Utin, *The New Israeli Cinema*, 86.

34. Bardenstein, "Cross/Cast," 113–114.

35. A counterexample can be seen in Deepa Mehta's *Bollywood/Hollywood* (2002), where the "true" ethnic identity of one of the main characters (Sunita) is at play for both the main male character and the audience, in a clear attempt to challenge the premise of ethnic purity altogether (albeit for comic purposes).

36. Bardenstein, "Cross/Cast," 120.

37. Mark Winokur, "Black Is White/White Is Black: 'Passing' as a Strategy of Racial Compatibility in Contemporary Hollywood Comedy," 201.

BIBLIOGRAPHY

Almog, Oz. *The Sabra: A Profile (HaTzabar—Dyokan)*. Tel Aviv: Am Oved, 2004.

Anderson, Benedict. *Imagined Communities*. London: Verso, 1983.

Avisar, Ilan. "The National and the Popular in Israeli Cinema." *Shofar* 24, no 1 (2005): 125–143.

Bakhtin, Mikhail. *Rabelais and His World*. Cambridge, Mass.: MIT Press, 1968.

Bardenstein, Carol. "Cross/Cast: Passing in Israeli and Palestinian Cinema." In *Palestine, Israel and the Politics of Popular Culture*, ed. Rebecca L. Stein and Ted Swedenburg, 99–125. Durham: Duke University Press, 2005.

Bhabha, Homi K. "DissemiNation: Time, Narrative and the Margins of the Modern Nation." In *Nation and Narration*, ed. Homi Bhabha, 291–320. New York: Routledge, 1990.

Fanon, Franz. *The Wretched of the Earth*. New York: Grove, 1991 (first published in French, 1961).

Loshitzky, Yosefa. *Identity Politics on the Israeli Screen*. Austin: University of Texas Press, 2001.

Massad, Joseph. "Zionism's Internal Others: Israel and the Oriental Jews." *Journal of Palestine Studies* 25, no. 4 (Summer 1996): 53–68.

Naaman, Dorit. "Orientalism as Alterity in Israeli Cinema." *Cinema Journal* 40, no. 4 (2001): 36–54.

———. "Brides of Palestine/Angels of Death: Media, Gender and Performance in the Case of the Palestinian Female Suicide Bombers." *Signs* 32, no. 4 (Summer 2007): 933–955.

Said, Edward. *Orientalism*. New York: Random House, 1978.

Shohat, Ella. *Israeli Cinema: East/West and the Politics of Representation*. Austin: University of Texas Press, 1987.

———. "Ethnicities in Relation: Toward a Multicultural Reading of American Cinema." In *Unspeakable Images, Ethnicity and the American Cinema*, ed. Lester Friedman, 215–250. Urbana and Chicago: University of Illinois Press, 1991.

Smooha, Sami. "Class, Ethnic, and National Cleavages and Democracy in Israel." In *Israeli Democracy under Stress*, ed. Larry Diamond and Ehud Sprinzak, 389–413. Boulder, Colo.: Larry Rienner Publishers, 1993.

Stam, Robert. *Subversive Pleasures: Bakhtin Cultural Criticism and Film*. Baltimore: Johns Hopkins University Press, 1989.

Utin, Pablo. *The New Israeli Cinema: Conversations with Filmmakers* (*Karkhonim Be'eretz Hakhamsinim*). Tel Aviv: Resling Publishing, 2008.

Winokur, Mark. "Black Is White/White Is Black: 'Passing' as a Strategy of Racial Compatibility in Contemporary Hollywood Comedy." In *Unspeakable Images, Ethnicity and the American Cinema*, ed. Lester Friedman, 190–213. Urbana and Chicago: University of Illinois Press, 1991.

FILMOGRAPHY

Avanti Popolo (Rafi Bukai, 1986).
The Band's Visit (*Bikur Hatizmoret*, Eran Kolirin, 2007).
Beaufort (Joseph Cedar, 2007).
Beyond the Walls (*Me'akhorei Hasoragim*, Uri Barbash, 1984).
Bollywood/Hollywood (Deepa Mehta, 2002)
Broken Wings (*Knafayim Shvurot*, Nir Bergman, 2002).
The Bubble (*Habu'ah*, Eytan Fox, 2006).
Campfire (*Medurat Hashevet*, Joseph Cedar, 2004).
Desperado Square (*Kikar Hakhalomot*, Benny Torati, 2001).

Fellow Travelers (*Magash Hakesef*, Yehuda Judd Neʾeman, 1983).

Fictitious Marriage (*Nisuʾim Fictiviʾim*, Haim Bouzaglo, 1988).

Free Zone (*Ezor Khofshi*, Amos Gitai, 2005).

Hamsin (aka *Eastern Wind*; *Khamsin*, Daniel Wachsmann, 1982).

Hill 24 Doesn't Answer (*Givʾa 24 Eina Ona*, Thorold Dickinson, 1955).

James' Journey to Jerusalem (*Masʾot James Beʾeretz Hakodesh*, Raʾanan Alexandrowicz, 2003).

Janem Janem (Haim Bouzaglo, 2006).

Jellyfish (*Meduzot*, Shira Geffen and Etgar Keret, 2007).

Kippur (Amos Gitai, 2000).

Late Marriage (*Khatuna Meʾukheret*, Dover Koshashvili, 2001).

Lemon Tree (*Etz Limon*, Eran Riklis, 2008).

My Father, My Lord (*Khufshat Kayitz*, David Volach, 2007).

My Michael (*Mikhaʾel Sheli*, Dan Wolman, 1976).

Noodle (Ayelet Menahemi, 2007).

On a Narrow Bridge (*Gesher Tzar Meʾod*, Nissim Dayan, 1985).

Or (Keren Yedaya, 2004).

Paper Snow (*Haya O Lo Haya*, Lena Chaplin and Slava Chaplin, 2003).

The Secrets (*Hasodot*, Avi Nesher, 2007).

The Seven Days (*Shivʾah*, Ronit Elkabetz and Shlomi Elkabetz, 2008).

The Smile of the Lamb (*Khiyukh Hagdi*, Shimon Dotan, 1986).

Sweet Mud (*Adamah Meshugaʾat*, Dror Shaul, 2006).

They Were Ten (*Hem Hayu Asarah*, Baruch Dienar, 1960).

Time of Favor (*Hahesder*, Joseph Cedar, 2000).

Turn Left at the End of the World (*Sof Haʾolam Smolah*, Avi Nesher, 2004).

Walk on Water (*Lalekhet Al Hamayim*, Eytan Fox, 2004).

Yellow Asphalt (*Asfalt Tzahov*, Dan Verete, 2001).

Yossi and Jagger (*Yossi VeJagger*, Eytan Fox, 2002).

20 Borders in Motion

The Evolution of the Portrayal of the Israeli-Palestinian Conflict in Contemporary Israeli Cinema

YAEL BEN-ZVI-MORAD

During the 1980s a remarkable phenomenon occurred in Israeli cinema. The main genre attracted leading directors who chose to identify with Israel's most entrenched enemy—the Palestinian people. The major films of the decade addressed Palestinians suffering from the occupation, depicted Palestinian activists as freedom fighters, gave voice to the Arabic language and Arab worldview, and evoked positive feelings toward those who were perceived by the general public as threatening. The leading films of the 1980s were generally referred to as left-wing movies. In the 1990s these films gave way to a more personal and sectoral cinema. The 1990s dealt primarily with social circles in Tel Aviv, reexamined the absorption of immigrants in Israel, and looked at the relations between different Jewish groups such as Mizrahim and Ashkenazim.[1]

In the first decade of the twenty-first century, however, the Israeli-Palestinian conflict returned to Israeli movie screens. But this time movies about the conflict became just one of a broad spectrum of issues, and the treatment of the conflict combined the activist leanings of the 1980s with the hedonism of the 1990s. In other words, the depiction of the conflict is interwoven with the personal narratives of pleasure-loving young people. This has created films such as *The Bubble* (*Habuʾah*, Eytan Fox, 2006), which centers on a Tel Aviv crowd of young straight and homosexual men and women that for the first time contains a young Palestinian as well. The portrayal of the hedonistic Tel Aviv lifestyle, a frequent theme in the 1990s, is combined here with the depiction of the Israeli occupation in the territories.

Over the course of Israeli cinematic history, the division into genres has reflected an inability to combine normal, routine life with life in the shadow of the conflict. Almost every genre of Israeli cinema has wrestled with the conflict separately from its treatment of universal personal themes and its portrayal of sectoral problems in Israeli society. Films made after 2000 combine the topics for the first time. If in the past the difficulty of combining routine life with life in the shadow of the conflict took the form of a split between genres, Israeli cinema in the first decade of the twenty-first century addresses this difficulty directly by juxtaposing the bourgeois Tel Aviv lifestyle with the conflict. In this sense Israeli cinema is grappling for the first time with a problem that it eschewed in previous decades.

The portrayal of the Israeli-Palestinian conflict is now interwoven with a broad spectrum of personal and sectoral issues addressed by contemporary Israeli cinema. Often the issues are integrated into the films themselves, which present Israeli reality in all its complexity. For instance, *Walk on Water* (*Lalekhet Al Hamayim*, Eytan Fox, 2004) points out the links between the Holocaust, the negation of exile, and the occupation. The protagonist is a security officer who fights Palestinian terror. He represents the ultimate Sabra (native-born Israeli). He has always avoided setting foot on German soil because of the Holocaust, but a trip to Berlin on security business changes his worldview. According to Amnon Raz-Krakotzkin, the negation of exile is a central factor in the Zionist metanarrative.[2] He argues that the Holocaust is taken to prove the need for a Jewish state and for the negation of the Diaspora; the monumental memory of the Holocaust justifies Israel's quest for security. The movie *Walk on Water* returns to the exile in general and to Germany in particular. Along with the persecution trauma that the protagonist experiences there, he also longs for the Diaspora and for the diasporic language while discovering a human and social complexity that is not dichotomous. His acceptance of the Diaspora and his struggles with the sense of persecution evoked by the trip to Germany reduce his impulse to see everything in terms of security and make it possible for him to see Palestinians not only as enemies but also as human beings. This process deconstructs the male rigidity of the Sabra and allows feminine and homosexual traits to penetrate the Israeli scene.

Only Dogs Run Free (aka *Wild Dogs*; *Rak Kluvim Ratzim Khofshi*, Arnon Zadok, 2007) focuses on the linkage of poverty, crime, violence against women, violence against Palestinians, and the disintegration of Israeli masculine identity.

As noted, in the first decade of the twenty-first century Israeli cinema again took up the issue of the Israeli-Palestinian conflict from a left-wing vantage point similar to that articulated in the films of the 1980s. Like the movies of the 1980s, films of the first decade of the twenty-first century depict Palestinians as belonging to the space and the soil. The Palestinians' views, lives, culture, and language find expression. Today, as in the 1980s, the cinema conveys pessimism, guilt, and the impotence of the left-wing activists in the face of a militant reality.

Films in the 2000s raise a complex self-criticism, however, when they portray the left-wing activists as militant. The worldview rendered by the movies of the 1980s was based on a dichotomy between peace lovers and militant forces. The core narrative of the films depicts an Israeli leftist who strives for peaceful relations with moderate Palestinians but is stymied by a show of force on the part of the Israeli security forces. The Palestinians who join up with the leftists are attacked by militants from their own side. The movies embrace the aspiration for coexistence through the eyes of the peace-loving protagonist. The criticism leveled against the conflict by 1980s movies focuses on the considerable power of the militarist forces on both sides of the barricades and the weakness of Israeli and Palestinian peace activists.

While the films of the 1980s draw a clear distinction between moderates and extremists on the Israeli and Palestinian sides, those of the first decade of the twenty-first century make this distinction only in order to dissolve it and to highlight its artificiality. At the denouement of the works, it transpires that there is no significant difference between left-wing activists and military personnel. Both suffer from a sense of persecution that blinds them to the suffering of the Palestinians and leads them to use violence against them. Such a state of affairs whereby even peace lovers are inclined to barricade themselves in violent positions excludes any possibility of dialogue and coexistence.

The critiques of 1980s films find conscious and reflexive expression in films made after 2000. For example, Ella Shohat and Nurith Gertz argue that, despite the identification with the Palestinians, the films of the 1980s ultimately deal with the soul searching by the Israeli Left, whose members are portrayed as victims.[3] Numerous films conclude with the death of the Israeli peace activist rather than focusing on the concrete reality of Palestinian life or political processes. In comparison, some of the works of the first decade of the twenty-first century are aware of the left-wing activists' preoccupation with themselves. *Lemon Tree*, which is the subject of the following discussion, creates a reflexive awareness that left-wing cinema, while aspiring to a dialogue with the Palestinians, is capable only of reflecting itself, like the peace activists themselves.

Some critiques of films of 1980s cinema also find conscious expression in movies of the first decade of the twenty-first century. Gertz and Nitzan

Ben Shaul reason that while the films of the 1980s admittedly express leftist positions, their hidden narrative structure and their cinematic expression charge the works with a right-wing, separatist worldview.[4] Gertz points out that the circular form of the narrative reflects despair and the impossibility of change. This narrative structure mirrors a circular worldview—of history repeating itself. This outlook is identified, in her view, with the Right, which regards Jewish history as a succession of attacks that threaten to annihilate Israel and the Jews. Such a historical conception reinforces the need for Jews to arm themselves and to separate themselves from others. Thus, while on the surface the films convey a desire to exploit an unprecedented opportunity for dialogue, they present reality as blocking change and as a sequence of catastrophes that compel Israelis to rely only on themselves and on their military might.

Ben Shaul identifies manifestations of a "siege syndrome" in both the narrative structure and the cinematic expression of 1980s films. This syndrome is particular to a social group that is imprisoned within a separatist worldview and interprets any approach as a threat. According to Ben Shaul, although this worldview typifies the Israeli Right, it paradoxically emerges in 1980s movies that express left-wing positions. The claustrophobic buildings, the gloomy lighting, the narrative that is impervious to change, and the isolation of the hero do not allow the innocence of dialogue to grow out of the dovish films.

The reference to a "siege syndrome" is a criticism of the films of the 1980s. It is a hidden current that emerges from the cinematic expression and narrative structure of the works and contradicts their overall dovish creed. In contrast, some films made after 2000 such as *Lemon Tree* and *Zirkus Palestina* (aka *Circus Palestina*; *Kirkas Palestina*, Eyal Halfon, 1998) themselves cultivate an awareness of siege syndrome, portraying it as a society-wide problem with which the Left is also afflicted. The protagonist, who represents the Israeli Left, suffers from two conflicting inclinations: the pacifist inclination on the one hand and the siege mentality that leads him to barricade himself and act violently on the other. This conflict leads David, the main character of *Forgiveness* (*Mekhilot*, Udi Aloni, 2006), to shoot innocent Palestinians and to commit suicide. It is this duality of the heroes of the contemporary films that leads to the failure of the Left, rather than the security forces as depicted in the films of the 1980s.

In this sense movies of the first decade of the twenty-first century represent a more complex form of self-scrutiny, in which the Left accepts some of the responsibility for the absence of peace. While the films of the 1980s depict a nightmarish takeover of Israeli society by militant forces, thus expressing the sentiments of the Left after the Likud's ascent to power,[5] the movies of the first decade of the twenty-first century subsist in a daily reality in which violence has become a routine shared by Israeli society in its entirety, including peace activists.

The Violent Occupier within the Humane Leftist in *Forgiveness*

Forgiveness (*Mekhilot*, Udi Aloni, 2006) depicts the experiences of David, an American Zionist and the son of a Holocaust survivor, who has enlisted in the Israeli army. During the course of his service, David treats the occupied Palestinian population humanely, but fear of armed Palestinians causes him to fire on an innocent Palestinian woman and her daughter. The incident sends him into shock, which leads to his subsequent hospitalization in a mental institution. Because the shooting incident is not treated but merely repressed with tranquilizers, when he returns to New York David reenacts the trauma and threatens to shoot another Palestinian woman with whom he is in love. He demands that the woman's child give him the key to the family's abandoned home in Palestine. When she refuses, he kills himself in front of them. The Israeli occupier is unable to get the key to Palestine/

Figure 20.1. David (Itai Tiran) suffers in *Forgiveness* (Udi Aloni, 2006). Courtesy of the director, Udi Aloni, and United King Films.

Israel, which remains in the hands of the Palestinian as a symbol of her moral ownership of the land.

Forgiveness presents a link between the Holocaust and the occupation. Each situation—being a persecuted people or being an occupying people—is now portrayed as a trauma that feeds the other situation. Holocaust fears of persecution impel David to enlist in the Israel Defense Forces. The shooting of the Palestinians is also presented as a trauma rather than a crime. The trauma drives David to commit other insane acts. In the mental institution Holocaust survivors are hospitalized along with him. Having the soldier and Holocaust survivors hospitalized together renders the occupation the moral equivalent of the Holocaust from the standpoint of the occupier, as a trauma that requires healing. The hospitalized Holocaust survivors are called Muselmann—a name that points to an ideological connection between the terms used for Jewish prisoners in the death camps and Muslims in Israel. In other words, the film suggests a similarity between the Jews in the Holocaust and Palestinians in Israel. The mental hospital is located on the ruins of Deir Yassin, a Palestinian village where a massacre was committed in 1948. "With this act—which has something perverted about it—the young Zionist state intended to hide the traces of one destruction (Deir Yassin) by covering it with the traces of the survivors of another destruction (the Holocaust)."[6]

The attempt to cover up the traces fails, as the Holocaust survivors hospitalized there burrow into the ground and discover the remains of the Palestinians and the traces of the massacre. In a similar fashion, the attempt to blur the traces of the shooting trauma in David's psyche also fails. Through the fog of the sedatives the memory of the shooting surfaces, and David is driven to reenact it and then to end his life. The film presents the burial of the evidence of the killing of innocent Jews and Palestinians as an act of psychological repression carried out by Israeli society. The repressed material that erupts afresh feeds further acts of killing and lunacy. It is impossible to burrow through the mounds of earth burying the near and distant past to reach the Palestinian Other and the future. The burrow—the passageway to the Palestinian Other—cannot come into being until the perpetrators face their crime and request forgiveness. The Hebrew word for "forgiveness," articulated in the film's Hebrew title (in the plural: *mekhilot*), is phonetically identical to the Hebrew word for "burrows" (*mekhilot*). Hence the film's title in Hebrew deals with the association of self-forgiveness, memory, and reaching out for the Other. Moreover, the film's Hebrew title connotes the concept of "Gilgul Mekhilot": the belief that all Jewish people who died in the Diaspora will return to the holy land and be revived when the Messiah

Figure 20.2.
"Muselmann" (Moni
Moshonov) talks to
"Abed" in *Forgive-
ness* (Udi Aloni,
2006). Courtesy of
the director, Udi
Aloni, and United
King Films.

comes. Thus the film and its title deal not only with the past and with guilt
but also with the future and with Salvation.

The animated film *Waltz with Bashir* (*Vals Im Bashir*, Ari Folman, 2008)
addresses director Ari Folman himself, who repressed the trauma of being
present at the massacre of Sabra and Shatila during the First Lebanon War.
Like David (the main character of *Forgiveness*), Ari, the protagonist of *Waltz
with Bashir*, is the son of Holocaust survivors and cannot come to terms with
the fact that as an Israeli soldier he witnessed the Christian Militia commit
the massacre. The repressed trauma disturbs him, and he delves into it until
he recovers his memory of the event. The discovery of the violent warrior
who resides in every Israeli male against his will is one of the insights that

seems to distress Israeli filmmakers most in the first decade of the twenty-first century.

The seeds of this insight are planted in the film *The Wooden Gun* (*Roveh Khuliot*, Ilan Moshenson, 1979). Yoni, the son of a Holocaust survivor, discovers that the battles he fights in his neighborhood render him a violent perpetrator along the lines of a Nazi soldier. The fights of the neighborhood boys in the film mirror the wars that the adults fight against Arabs. According to the film, the native Israeli is required to be a hero, the antithesis of the persecuted Jew in the Holocaust. The fear of resembling Holocaust Jews almost turns Israelis into violent persecutors similar to the Nazis. These messages are examined in this early film as part of the treatment of internal

Figure 20.3. Amal (Tamara Mansour), the Arab girl, represents both guilt and forgiveness in *Forgiveness*. (Udi Aloni, 2006). Courtesy of the director, Udi Aloni, and United King Films.

problems in Israeli society, and its conclusions can only implicitly be projected onto the occupation. In contrast, in films made after 2000 the portrayal of internal problems and the direct engagement with the conflict are clearly intertwined. The movies present the destructive consequences of the occupation to the moral fiber of Israeli society and its inability to continue functioning in view of leftists' horror at their own violent deeds.

A Conscious Expression of the Limitations of Films Dealing with the Conflict: The Case of *Lemon Tree*

Lemon Tree (*Etz Limon*, Eran Riklis, 2008) addresses the failure of an Israeli dialogue with the Palestinians. As in *Forgiveness*, in *Lemon Tree* the failure to connect and converse stems from the barriers that the Israeli protagonist, Mirah, erects around herself. Mirah, the wife of defense minister Israel Navon, designed their new home that was built not long ago on the Israeli-Palestinian border. Salmah, a Palestinian woman who owns a lemon orchard, lives on the other side of the fence. Out of fear for the minister's security, her trees are cut down and a high concrete wall is erected between the two houses. Mirah, exposed to the injustice of the occupation for the first time, identifies with Salmah and publicly denounces her husband. The relations between husband and wife deteriorate when she criticizes him for the gap between his humane public stance and the predatory practices that prevail under his command. Ultimately Mirah leaves her home and her spouse.

The conflicting positions of Mirah and Israel ostensibly render them the representatives of two opposing streams in Israeli society. On the face of things, Mirah represents the moderate Left, while the fictional defense minister represents the militant Israeli stream. This dichotomy resembles the pattern of 1980s films about the conflict, which portray peace activists as helpless vis-à-vis the powerful security forces. Similarly, in the film *Crossfire* (*Esh Tzolevet*, Gideon Ganani, 1989) the central female character is engaged in a romance with a Palestinian man and is ready for an Israeli-Palestinian connection, while Israeli men represent the militants who forcibly prevent coexistence. But this dichotomy is established in *Lemon Tree* only on the surface. The film dissolves it and adopts a more complex interpretation, whereby the walls exist at the very core of the moderate Left.

Mirah and Israel are not opposites. They both represent Israeli hegemony. Mirah is an architect, shapely and stylish, and they are friendly with other high society members. Israel, as his name implies, represents the entirety of Israeli society. Although Israel is the defense minister, the positions he adopts toward Palestinians in the media are humane. The dual nature of his personality also finds expression in his name. His given name, Israel, symbolizes patriotism, while his surname, Navon (wise), resembles in sound and sense the word *na'or* (enlightened). In other words, he has progressive opinions. *Na'or* has taken on an additional meaning in Israel: a humane attitude toward Arabs. The word *na'or* is part of the term "enlightened occupation," which is used in connection with the Israeli occupation of the territories and signifies a humane administration of the Palestinian population. The idea of an enlightened occupation has been criticized in various venues, including the 1983 book *The Smile of the Lamb* (*Khiyukh Hagdi*, David Grossman) and the film based on the book by the same title (Shimon Dotan, 1986). The criticism focuses on the impossibility of maintaining an occupation that is also enlightened, as this is an oxymoron. The contradiction between occupation and enlightenment is exemplified by the character of Israel Navon, who comes across as humane in public but is also in charge of security, including the occupation.[7] Israel represents the Zionist hegemony enjoyed by the center-left parties, which champion the paradoxical combination of peace and security.

Mirah, like Israel, embodies the contradiction between humanism and aggressive jingoism. As the person responsible for planning and designing her home, she plants an olive tree in the garden, which evidently was uprooted from a Palestinian orchard. She subsequently criticizes her husband for cutting down Salmah's trees, oblivious that she herself is responsible for uprooting a Palestinian tree. Throughout most of the movie Mirah neglects to hold a dialogue with her neighbor, talking only to the Israeli press and to her husband about the neighbor's trees. Even when she eventually decides to speak with Salmah and walks over to her house, she does not meet the neighbor, who is inside her home. The door to Salmah's house is closed; Mirah, peeping inside, sees only her own reflection in the glass.

The poster for the movie shows Mirah with her eyes closed juxtaposed against the resolute gaze of Salmah, who is fighting for her land. The film does not address the possibility for dialogue offered by women on both sides of the barricades but the blindness of the Israelis, who unwittingly imprison themselves. Even when Mirah leaves her home it does not signify a turning point in the film. It ends with Israel relaxing by the wall that blocks the view from his garden, juxtaposed with Salmah continuing to tend to her cut trees.

The reflection of Mirah in the window is one of the most powerful statements in the movie. In this scene Riklis reflects the Israeli Left's inability to foster a dialogue with the Palestinians due to its obsessive preoccupation with itself. Moreover, the character of Mirah represents a self-criticism of Israeli cinema, which aspires to see the Palestinian Other but actually reflects only itself. The glass window resembles a movie screen onto which left-wing artists project themselves when they try to see the Palestinians.[8]

The character of Mirah, as a creative person who creates an expanse in which human beings function, reflexively represents Israeli film directors. The dualism of Mirah's character expresses the self-criticism of Riklis as a movie director vis-à-vis the traditional representation of the conflict in Israeli cinema. The wish to perceive the Palestinians that ends with a reflection of self is present in films of the 1980s on an unconscious level. It emerges in the reviews written about these films. *Lemon Tree* is an implicit expression of this critique of itself and of the cinematic tradition that preceded it.

It is important to note that such a critique was also voiced in the past in Dina Zvi-Riklis's film *Look Out* (*Nekudat Tatzpit*, 1990), which directly addresses the limitations of the Israeli view of Palestinians and reflexively presents the limits to the power of left-wing cinema in the preceding decade.[9]

Cinematic Coexistence

The narrative and cinematic expression of *Lemon Tree* depict the wall that Israeli leftists erect between themselves and Palestinians. Nevertheless, the production of the film made it possible for an Israeli-Palestinian dialogue to be reflected in the work. Jewish-Israeli director Eran Riklis wrote the screenplay together with Suhah Arraf, a Palestinian Israeli director and screenwriter. Both voices, Israeli and Palestinian, are present in the work, which paradoxically deals with the inability to create coexistence. In other words, in contrast with the characters in the film, the directors conducted a dialogue that led to the coexistence of Israeli and Palestinian cinematic traditions.

Lemon Tree expresses the Palestinian view of the conflict, relying on the Palestinian cinematic tradition. One of the prominent characteristics of Palestinian cinema, which is seen in *Lemon Tree*, is the focus on an older woman who bears the national struggle on her back. In many Palestinian films the maternal figure is depicted as strong, sometimes physically big, and in some movies is the leader for her sons, daughters, and grandchildren. This figure of the strong mother fights for her land through her familial activities.[10] Palestinian women, and especially mothers, unite the family, restore it to the homeland, and cling tightly to the soil. The films (whether feature films or documentaries) that trace such mothers' actions indeed deal with a particular woman and a particular family; however, they use the family narrative to articulate the national narrative. Thus, allegorically, the mothers are portrayed as being responsible for recovering and steadfastly holding onto the land. This theme is explicit in the films *Legend* (Nizar Hassan, 1998) and *Three Centimeters Less* (Azza El-Hassan, 2002).

In the great majority of Palestinian movies, the father of the family is missing, sick, weak, or physically and mentally unwell, and his disability symbolizes his surrender to the Israeli regime.[11] Areen Hawari argues that during previous periods in Palestinian society the mother would take the father's place as the head of the family when he was absent or dead.[12] In many senses the national wound damages the authority of the father, whose masculinity is symbolically and practically undermined by the occupation.[13]

In *Lemon Tree* the father of the family is missing, and the mother fights on behalf of the homeland. She does this through nonviolent means, by her stubborn insistence on continuing to live and perpetuate the family dynasty on her soil. As in many Palestinian films, women grab hold of the homeland by holding fast to their roots in the full sense of the word—they continue to grow crops, struggle to attain possession of the home and fields, and use the crops they raise to prepare traditional Palestinian food.[14] The pickling of the lemons in *Lemon Tree*, like the preparation of traditional food in numerous Palestinian films, has a national-cultural significance. In many Palestinian films, such as *Wedding in Galilee* (Michel Khleifi, 1987), *The Tale of the Three Lost Jewels* (Michel Khleifi, 1995), and *Waiting for Salah-Eddin* (Tawfik Abu Wael, 2001), traditional Palestinian cuisine receives extensive treatment on the screen because it is a repetitive daily activity by means of which Palestinian women preserve and renew the national culture. One Palestinian short film, *Makluba* (Rashid Masharawi, 2000), is entirely devoted to a description of the preparation of a dish known as *makluba*. Women in Palestinian cinema thereby validate Homi K. Bhabha's argument that nationalism is preserved and renewed through daily rituals.[15]

Lemon Tree reduces Palestinian cuisine, with its wide variety of dishes, to the single act of pickling lemons, which symbolically expresses the preservation of Palestinian tradition in jars. In other words, live Palestinian culture is compressed into exotic symbols. The symbolic compression admittedly detracts from the vitality of daily customs but still leaves something for Palestinian cinematic modalities. The Palestinian woman who fights for her land is also condensed in this movie: she is not the big mother who leads the family in *Three Centimeters Less* or *Legend*. She lives alone; her grown children are far away and hardly figure in the plot. Yet it is still the woman

Figure 20.4. Salmah (Hiam Abbass) and Abu Husam (Tarek Copti) in the lemon orchard in *Lemon Tree* (Eran Riklis, 2008). Courtesy of United King Films.

who holds fast to her land, even if her life and customs have undergone individualization.

In Palestinian cinema the woman, the home, and the homeland are three intertwined symbols. *Makluba* depicts a woman who prepares a chicken dish with rice and vegetables (*makluba*) in an abandoned Palestinian house. At every stage in the movie assorted views of Palestine are shown through the windows: a refugee camp, the sea off the coast of Gaza, Jerusalem, mountains and holy places, until finally the *makluba* flies up in a superimposition above the skies of Jerusalem and al-Aqsa. Thus the spaces of the divided homeland are unified through cinematic devices. All of Palestine can be glimpsed through the windows of the home, and ultimately it is unified in an excursion above Jerusalem, with the mosques on Temple Mount serving as the crown of the united expanse. The woman, the home, and the dish redeem Palestine.

In *Lemon Tree* as well the homeland is unified around the woman, the home, and pickled lemons. Palestine unites before our eyes in Salmah's journey through the land, as she travels from house to house, from office to office, and from court to court in a quest for justice. At every stage there are checkpoints, and then another part of the country is shown, with its name and location appearing in captions on the screen. This technique of interspersing photographs from various parts of the country identified with captions is employed in many Palestinian films and makes it possible to unify the disconnected expanses in a single cinematic work. Salmah ultimately arrives in Jerusalem, and there, in the Supreme Court, her struggle reaches its climax. In order to emphasize the importance of Jerusalem and of the struggle over territory in this city, Salmah is filmed climbing up a bridge. Mirah, in contrast, who has come to support Salmah, is shown in the full glory of her stylish suit, descending steps in order to reach the courthouse.

The graphic conflict whereby the ascent of the Palestinian is juxtaposed against the descent of the Israeli conveys a sense of the deterioration of Israeli society. With this visual device the film affiliates itself with the Israeli cinematic tradition that developed in 1980s movies about the conflict. For instance, at the conclusion of the film *The Smile of the Lamb* (*Khiyukh Hagdi*, Shimon Dotan, 1986) the military governor descends a slope, while Khilmi, the Arab who is in possession of the land, climbs up. A new dawn breaks in the space that belongs to the Palestinian, while the Israeli leaves the site after sustaining defeat.[16] In similar fashion, at the outset of *One of Ours* (*Ekhad*

Figure 20.5. Salmah (Hiam Abbass) and Lawyer Daud (Ali Suliman) interviewed by news reporters in *Lemon Tree* (Eran Riklis, 2008). Courtesy of United King Films.

Mishelanu, Uri Barbash, 1989) the open spaces and the soundtrack belong to the Palestinians. After speeding past an Arab man and child riding on a donkey, an Israeli military jeep spins out of control farther down the lane. This opening, which corresponds to the patriotic film *He Walked through the Fields* (Yosef Millo, 1967), points to a loss of the sense of control over space as well as technological and cultural superiority over the Palestinians. The Palestinians are portrayed as the moral landowners and the ones who enjoy generational continuity on the land, while the Israelis are in decline, trudging down the slippery slope of military rule after invading a domain that is not their own.

The Israeli conclusion of *Lemon Tree* conveys a sense of decline and despair. Israeli society is felt to be nearing its end. The dysfunctional family has fallen apart. Mirah and Israel did not produce offspring, and the mature girl they adopted late in life lives in the United States. While Israel imprisons himself between defensive walls, the Palestinian woman Salmah holds fast to the land and to her familial dynasty. The Palestinian ending of the work communicates the spirit of hope coming from Palestinian cinema.

Lemon Tree fosters a sense of pessimism due to the blockage of any kind of national dialogue and the disruption of the Israelis' lives by virtue of their attitude toward the Palestinians. It conducts a moral stocktaking of left-wing activists and of leftist cinema itself and depicts the blockage of dialogue and the impediment to normal life as the fault of the Israeli Left and center rather than of militant forces. Despite the worldview that emerges from the work, according to which there is no room for discussion, the film makes possible the coexistence of two cinematic traditions, the Israeli and the Palestinian. In so doing it raises the possibility of a fruitful dialogue and the dissolution of barriers between the peoples by means of joint artistic endeavors.

....

Israeli cinema in the first decade of the twenty-first century has returned to the Israeli-Palestinian conflict after a decade devoted to addressing personal and social problems. Contemporary cinema presents a more complex worldview than that of previous decades and is clearly aware of the limitations of the cinematic tradition that preceded it.

Contemporary film does not create a separation between its treatment of different social and personal issues in Israeli life. Thus it addresses the gap between the routine of normal life in Israeli cities and the nightmarish reality in the territories. The gap between these two forms of life is the focal point for Israeli cinema in the 2000s.

While the films of the 1980s drew a distinction between the militant Right and the moderate Left, films of the first decade of the twenty-first century shatter this dichotomy by portraying the violent side of the leftists themselves. The worldview presented by the films is bleak: not only is the Israeli Left held responsible for the occupation but the guilt that plagues it as a result prevents it from functioning and from leading a normal life and effecting change on the national level.

NOTES

1. See Ben-Zvi (2006).
2. Raz-Krakotzkin (1993).
3. Shohat (1989); Gertz (1993).
4. Gertz (1993); Ben Shaul (1989).
5. See Gertz (1993); Shohat (1989).
6. Munk (2007: 59).
7. According to Nimrod Buso (2008), the character of Israel is based on Shaul Mofaz, a former chief of staff who went on to become a senior member of the center-left Kadima party.
8. See Ben-Zvi (2008).
9. See Lubin (2003) for an analysis of the movie.
10. Ben-Zvi-Morad (forthcoming).
11. Pinhasi (1999); Gertz and Khleifi (2008); Ben-Zvi-Morad (forthcoming).
12. Hawari (2004).
13. See Monterescu (1998); Gertz and Khleifi (2008); Ben-Zvi-Morad (forthcoming).
14. Ben Zvi-Morad (forthcoming).
15. See Bhabha (1999).
16. See Gertz (1993).

REFERENCES

Hebrew

Ben Shaul, Nitzan. 1989. "Siege" ("Matzor"). *Sratim: Ktav Et Lakolno'a Vetelevizia* 4 (Winter): 2–9.

Ben-Zvi, Yael. 2006. "Center and Periphery in Israeli Cinema of the 1990s" ("Merkaz Uperiferiya Bakolno'a Hayisra'eli Shel Shnot Hatish'im") *Alpayim* 30: 248–256.

———. 2008. "A Lemon Tree Is Planted beyond the Fence" ("*Etz Limon* Shatul Me'ever Lagadder"). In Erez Perry (ed.), *The Curator's Book (Seffer Ha'otzrut Shel Festival Kolno'a Darom 2008)*, 87–101. Sderot: Sapir College.

Ben-Zvi Morad, Yael. Forthcoming. *Patricide: Family and Nationalism in Contemporary Palestinian Cinema (Retzakh-Av: Mishpakha ULe'umiyut Bakolno'a HaFalastini)*. Tel Aviv: Resling.

Buso, Nimrod. 2008. "The Neighbors: Mofaz, Zuharia and All That Is between Them" ("Hashakhen: Mofaz, Hashkhena Zuharia Vekhol Ma Shebeynehem"). *Yediot Nathanya*, April 4: 98–100.

Gertz, Nurith. 1993. *Motion Fiction: Israeli Fiction on Film* (*Sipur Mehasratim: Siporet Yisraʾelit Veʾibudeihah Lakolnoʾa*). Tel Aviv: Open University Press.

Lubin, Orly. 2003. *Women Reading Women* (*Isha Koret Isha*). Haifa: University of Haifa Press.

Monterescu, Daniel. 1998. "Identity within Foreignness: The Cultural Structuring of Arab Masculinity in Jaffa" ("Zehut Mitokh Zarut: Hahavnaya Hatarbutit Shel Gavriyut Arvit BeYaffo"). Master's thesis, Tel Aviv University.

Munk, Yael. 2007. "Land, Man, Blood: On *Forgiveness* (Udi Aloni, 2006)" ("Adamah, Adam, Dam: Al *Mehilot* [Udi Aloni, 2006]"). *South Cinema Notebook No. 2: On Destruction, Trauma & Cinema* (*Makhbarot Kolnoa Darom 2: Al Khurban, Trauma VeKolnoʾa*): 59–65.

Pinhasi, Maya. 1999. "The 'Other' of the 'Other': On the Portrayal of Israelis in the Palestinian Cinema of Masharawi and Khleifi" ("'Haʾakher' shel 'Haʾakher': Al Yitzug Hayisraʾelim Bakolnoʾa Hafalastini Shel Masharawi UKhleifi"). Seminar paper for the course "Israeli Cinema as Masculine Geography," taught by Professor Nurith Gertz, Tel Aviv University.

Raz-Krakotzkin, Amnon. 1993. "Exile within Sovereignty: A Critique of 'the Negation of the Diaspora' in Israeli Culture" ("Galut Betokh Ribonut: Levikoret 'Shlilat Hagalut' Batarbut Hayisraʾelit"). *Theory and Criticism* (*Teʾoriah Uvikoret*) 3: 23–55, part 1.

English

Bhabha, Homi K. 1999. "DissemiNation: Time, Narrative, and the Margins of the Modern Nation." In Homi K. Bhabha (ed.), *Nation and Narration* (1993), 291–322. London and New York: Routledge.

Gertz, Nurith, and George Khleifi. 2008. *Palestinian Cinema: Landscape, Trauma and Memory* (2006). Bloomington: Indiana University Press.

Grossman, David. 1991. *The Smile of the Lamb* (1983). Trans. Betsy Rosenberg. London: Cape.

Hawari, Areen. 2004. "Men under the Military Regime." *Adala's Review* 4 (Spring): 33–44.

Shohat, Ella. 1989. *Israeli Cinema: East/West and the Politics of Representation*. Austin: University of Texas Press.

FILMOGRAPHY
Israeli Films

Aloni, Udi. 2006. *Forgiveness* (*Mekhilot*).

Barbash, Uri. 1989. *One of Ours* (*Ekhad Mishelanu*).

Dotan, Shimon. 1986. *The Smile of the Lamb* (*Khiyukh Hagdi*).

Folman, Ari. 2008. *Waltz with Bashir* (*Vals Im Bashir*).

Fox, Eytan, 2004. *Walk on Water* (*Lalekhet Al Hamayim*).

———. 2006. *The Bubble* (*Habuʾah*).

Ganani, Gideon. 1989. *Crossfire* (*Esh Tzolevet*).

Halfon, Eyal. 1998. *Zirkus Palestina* (aka *Circus Palestina*; *Kirkas Palestina*).

Millo, Yosef. 1967. *He Walked through the Fields* (*Hu Halakh Basadot*).

Moshenson, Ilan. 1979. *The Wooden Gun* (*Roveh Khuliot*).

Riklis, Eran. 2008. *Lemon Tree* (*Etz Limon*).

Zadok, Arnon. 2007. *Only Dogs Run Free* (aka *Wild Dogs*; *Rak Klavim Ratzim Khofshi*).

Zvi-Riklis, Dina. 1990. *Look Out* (*Nekudat Tatzpit*).

Palestinian Films Produced in Israel and the Palestinian Authority

Abu Wael, Tawfik. 2001. *Waiting for Salah-Eddin* (*Fintithar Salah-Eddin*).

El-Hassan, Azza. 2002. *Three Centimeters Less* (*Thalathato Centimetratin Akall*).

Hassan, Nizar. 1998. *Legend* (*Ostura*).

Khleifi, Michel. 1987. *Wedding in Galilee* (*Urs al-Jalil*; Hebrew title *Khatuna Bagalil*).

———. 1995. *The Tale of the Three Lost Jewels* (*Hikayatol Jawahiri-th-Thalath*).

Masharawi, Rashid. 2000. *Makluba* (*Upside Down*).

21   Smashing Up the Face of History

Trauma and Subversion in *Kedma* and *Atash*

NURITH GETZ

GAL HERMONI

Introduction

Find the differences:

Scene 1:

Long shot. A ship's deck. A crowd of people fills the frame, winding like streams toward the little boats tied to the ship's side. They are moving along, across the frame, from top to bottom, from bottom to top, from the foreground of the frame to its background, from background to foreground. They are uncountable. Cut. Long shot. A seashore. The camera moves slowly, tracking the horde of people settling on the shore, in all directions—the screen's width, length, and depth. Extreme long shot. The camera moves slowly, every moment discovering more and more people, uncountable. Some are sitting on the shore, around them baggage, suitcases, packages, objects. Adults hold children, a couple walks back and forth. The British are armed and uniformed. The Palmakh soldiers are not uniformly dressed; they are in khaki but do not appear to be an organized armed army like the British in the scene before. Soldiers are leading men and women. A human pandemonium. In the nondiegetic musical soundtrack a string section plays lush, slightly dissonant harmonies, in a low register and minor scale, legato.

Scene 2:

Long shot. Exterior. A gray, peeling concrete structure, set in yellow sand. In the background is the ridge of a hill, gray too. Two teenagers—a boy and a girl—are seated in the bottom of the frame, leaning against the concrete wall, looking straight ahead. A gloomy stringed instrument plays a repetitive melody in the soundtrack, with short, clipped, and monotonous phrases. The music's source is unidentified. Cut. Close-up on a stringed instrument, with the girl's hand plucking it: the music is being revealed as diegetic. Cut. Back to a long shot. The teenagers are still leaning against the wall, in the lower left side of the frame, almost "glued" to it. A truck drives up out of the background, filling the frame as it comes closer. Rooted to their spot, the teenagers watch the truck as it goes past. It leaves the frame. Boy to girl: "Go on." Cut. Close-up on the girl as she resumes playing the same tune on the stringed instrument.

The first scene is taken from Amos Gitai's film *Kedma* (Israel, 2002) and the second from Tawfik Abu Wael's film *Atash* (*Thirst*, Israel, 2004).

Kedma is a sort of epic road movie that describes the journey taken by Holocaust survivors from their arrival in Israel until they take part in the harsh, violent battle waged on Jerusalem's outskirts. Their journey is in fact a rite of passage during which they are transformed from "ghetto Jews" into New Jews. The film presents that ritual as an eternal, irresolvable conflict that will foster antagonism between the incoming Jewish refugees and the Palestinian refugees who are leaving their homes and between the two Jewish identities—the former exilic identity and the newly acquired one.

Atash, in contrast, is a small-scale film concerning a Palestinian family whose lives are overshadowed by a tyrannical father. He forces his family to leave their ancestral village and leads them to a desolate place where they confront both intolerable conditions and a domineering father.

What do the two films have in common, and where do they differ? As we can see from the two scenes depicted above, the first visible difference is quantitative: multiplicity and congestion in *Kedma*, lack and emptiness in *Atash*. It is simple math; to find the result, just count the objects in the various frames. Beyond the quantitative difference, the films also differ in the nature of movement and space. In *Kedma* movement is multiple, intensive, and multidirectional, while *Atash* is almost static. Space in *Kedma* seems to spill out of the frame, which appears too small to encompass it. The spectator can clearly see that the incident continues developing outside of it. The musical soundtrack assists that sense of vast space. In contrast, space is demarcated in *Atash*, its boundaries clearly marked even within the cinematic frame by the concrete wall and the ridge of the hill. Accordingly, the monotone diegetic musical soundtrack evokes a sense of restriction and confinement.

But what if those differences are exactly what the two films share? What if the minimalism of *Atash* and the excess of *Kedma* are actually two different reactions to the same problem? This is precisely what we would like to

argue: that the problem expressed in *Atash* and *Kedma* is the narrative paralysis linked to the incapacitated referentiality of language that both films
articulate.

Both *Kedma* and *Atash* lock horns with the dominant language of the
mainstream cinema, which creates causal plot and national narratives leading to clear definite goals.

Both films immobilize this structure of movement and thus subvert it,
each using a different principle of the dichotomy noted above. *Kedma* applies a "flooding" technique, while *Atash* displays a "drying up" technique.[1]
Seemingly embodying opposite aesthetics, the films use two ostensibly antithetical practices against a joint "occupier"—the major narrative—be it
cinematic or ideological. With pincer movements from each side, *Kedma* and
Atash launch an assault on this narrative to "smash up its face."

Both films disrupt the causal movement of events, unravel the ties between signifier and signified, and use types of dismantling and disruption
in order to undermine the hegemonic, teleological narrative that leads lin-
early from objectives to their attainment.[2] We attempt to attribute those
types of disruption to a post-traumatic condition and in that sense read the
post-traumatic condition that both films articulate as a historical-political
resistance.

The two films engage with national traumas undergone by the societies
where both films were made. In the case of *Kedma*, the trauma of the Holocaust and the encounter with the Arab inhabitants of the country; and in the
case of *Atash*, the trauma of the Nakba (literally, "catastrophe," referring to
the defeat of the Palestinian Arabs in the war of 1948) and expulsion. Com-
pounding those national traumas are the individual traumas related in the
film—the loss of family and loved ones in *Kedma* and abuse by a tyrannical
father in *Atash*. The traumas are discernible not only in the films' content
but also in their structure and style. Arguably, both films engage with ap-
palling events that were repressed because they were so difficult to cope
with and rise to the surface in various forms in the present. Both films, then,
express post-traumatic situations.

The condition identified by Sigmund Freud as "post-traumatic stress dis-
order" is characterized by symptoms that recur long after the traumatic
event took place. That gap between the time of the traumatic experience
and the time of its belated effect as well as the displacement of the former
to a different place and time—into another experience that signifies it—dis-
rupts the causal progression of events, on one hand, and generates a system of signs detached from their referents, on the other.[3] Thomas Elsaesser
maintains that the postmodern condition, which is experienced as a condi-

tion lacking a referent and a signified, is in fact a delayed post-traumatic effect of the historical event of the Holocaust.[4] Drawing on Cathy Caruth's work, he assumes that it is not a matter of an absent reality but of a reality that was shifted away from its location in the past and concealed by other events and types of reality. Based on the work of Elsaesser and Caruth, we identify the referential and causal detachment as a post-traumatic severance. We assume that, in order to produce new accessibility to the reality, to the referent, one must understand it as such and be able to read through it the past as a historical situation of trauma that has escaped from its original location on the narrative continuum and returned as a disrupted present. We attempt to explore how that severance serves as the tool of an ideological struggle in the two films examined here.

Kedma

Spatial and Temporal Flooding

Structurally Kedma belongs to the "road movie" genre and as such is fundamentally based on movement. As noted above, it follows the movement of the refugees from the Holocaust of European Jewry, from the ship to the shores of the Land of Israel, and from there toward Jerusalem. Along that trajectory, the refugees participate in a cinematic plot embodying the Zionist narrative: they must forget the traumatic events of the past, overcome their memories of the Diaspora, shed traits of their Jewish identity, join the battle with Arabs, and be transformed from passive Jews into Hebrews waging an active war for their lives and destiny.

But this is a broken journey, lacking direction, occupied by figures moving back and forth, devoid of a goal. The journey disintegrates and is stopped by the flooding of cinematic language at all levels. It includes a clash between movement toward the future, adopting the Zionist narrative, and the inability to do so because of the unprocessed post-traumatic condition that cannot be worked through as long as the survivor protagonists move on, leaving their past behind them.[5]

The film Kedma creates a congestion of objects and movements in the cinematic frame, presenting an excess of citations, bookmarks, ideological slogans, and reminders of historical events. It fills a single cinematic moment with an assortment of temporalities, movements, and objects. This congestion entails clashes between antithetical forces—between past and future, movement and stasis, progress and regression—and thus creates a flooding that paralyzes the movement of the film's plot and simultaneously reveals and conceals the reality it addresses. The missing traces of that reality are covered and concealed, like the traces of a trauma that still defies resolution and inclusion in a coherent narrative.

Immobilization usually results from two opposed, mutually incapacitating forces. It is signified already at the aesthetic level, at the film's opening, by the crowded shot flooded with movement in opposite directions. This is a sequence-shot in which the camera follows a protagonist coming up from the ship's hold to its deck,[6] where he is swallowed up in the mass of immigrants, who are sitting, standing, or lying motionless. The contrast created between the movement of the camera depicting the space and the stasis of the figures filling it creates the impression of formal paralysis. The shot swells until it is burst apart by the immobile objects that cram it to overflowing, thus neutralizing the camera movement which contains it.

Throughout the entire film, flooding the frame and space has parallels in the flooding of historical periods. In 1948, when the battle described in the film was fought, the war's outcome was still unknown. The flight of Palestinians from the country en masse had not yet occurred, the British Mandate was still in effect, and the great triumph of the Jews lay ahead. Nevertheless, the film gives the unknown future a presence in the happenings of the past, via elements in the filmed landscape—ruins, terraces, and abandoned prickly pear bushes. In 1948, when the filmed events occurred, the Arab villages, even those already abandoned, were still intact and surrounded by prickly pear cactus hedges. In 2004, when the film was shot, only ruins and a few prickly pear bushes were left as reminders of the existence of the abandoned villages.[7] In 1948 a prickly pear bush and an Arab stone house signify the existence of a village. In 2004 the same elements signify its destruction. As the camera lingers on them, it injects the future, the results of the battle and the expulsion, to the point in the past before it happened. This sort of temporal flooding is what mixes up the succession of time, halts its movement, paralyzes it, transforms past, present, and future into a conflated time frame, and thus prevents the linear progress of the "Zionist" plot from the Diaspora to the Land of Israel.

Ideological Flooding of Signifiers

The film contains an array of literary, essayist, and cinematic citations, taken from different sources, some Jewish, some Arab. It reduces the citations to cinematic clichés, detaches them from their original context and their original signifieds, and transplants them into a new context that grants them a new signified and a new meaning. Detaching signifier from signified allows signifiers from various sources to be juxtaposed and scattered throughout a fabric of concealments, contradictions, and clashes between ideological and historical narratives as well as between trajectories of movement in space and time. That scattering of contradictions also paralyzes the plot of the film, which moves toward the Zionist redemption.

The debate over the Jewish victims who became aggressors in their country is signified by two juxtaposed episodes. In the first, a survivor describes his wartime tribulations and the events through which he became an orphan. In the second, he hurls curses and threats at an Arab, an expelled refugee. The historical arguments about the Israeli public's unwillingness to listen to the stories of Holocaust survivors, which appeared in countless books and films, are expressed in an episode where a survivor is asked to sing a song but becomes silent after it is revealed that his song is not an Israeli one. (They ask "the cantor" to sing a Purim song instead, a happier song, but it is still in Yiddish and is far from being Israeli.) Historical and literary analyses have described how the righting of a wrong done to one people, the Jewish Holocaust, caused a wrong to another people, the Palestinian Naqba. In the film they are described in an encounter between a convoy of Jewish refugees going to their new homes and the convoy of Arab refugees leaving their old homes. Here and in other cases, myths, historical narratives, and texts are crammed into one or two signifying episodes, with no attempt to establish causality between them or historical logic. The cinematic text is accordingly flooded with detached and intersected signifiers, creating overload and density, which halt the film's ideological and cinematic narrative movement.

Kedma: The Post-Traumatic Condition

We have described practices of flooding and clashes that subvert the historical narrative, which Kedma addresses as a coherent, unified, linear narrative, and strip it of its authority as a hegemonic major narrative. At this point it is worth discussing the flooding and subversion from another theoretical perspective: as trauma.

As noted, the post-traumatic condition is typified by recurring experiences of symptoms deriving from a traumatic event that surface a long time afterward. Thus the original event is displaced into another experience that both signifies and conceals it. The post-traumatic condition is one of narrative failure: deconstructing the movement of events in time, on the one hand, and concealing them, on the other: one event dresses up as another, so it can "say its piece."[8] We might say, then, that the rhetoric of the narrative failure discussed so far is a post-traumatic one—displacing signs of events from their referents and also from the temporal continuum where they occurred. In doing so, this rhetoric paralyzes the cinematic plot and the Zionist narrative to which it relates.

Here, though, a question emerges: the film *Kedma* ostensibly works through the trauma of the Holocaust of European Jewry by relating it, talking about it, making it part of the narrative, and thus paving the way to overcoming it. It also broadens the narrative and brings into it the stories of Palestinian refugees. By doing so, it creates a multiplicity of stories, which is an essential part of coming to terms with trauma. The way to cope with trauma is to tell it, introduce it into a narrative, turn it into part of a continuum of past and future, part of a story that makes it possible to acknowledge the lost object and to free oneself from it.[9] Indeed, the stories assembled in *Kedma* are meant to take that route and work through the trauma. But if this is the case, why does the film's rhetoric remain a post-traumatic rhetoric of detachment and paralysis? The answer is that the Holocaust in *Kedma* is only the tip of an iceberg that conceals other traumas beneath it.

Freud argued that traumatic memory is structured as a chain of traumas, so that each overt trauma can be discovered as a symptom of another, a covert one. Thus each traumatic event should be seen as signifying another trauma, which is expressed through it.[10]

In this sense we can consider the trauma of the Holocaust as it emerges in the film *Kedma* as only one trauma out of scores that occurred in the Diaspora and later in Israel: they include the trauma of the battle for Latrun, in which the Israelis were defeated, and other battles concealed behind and reflected in it: battles in which the Israelis were victorious and which resulted in the expulsion and banishment of Palestinian peasant families and entire towns. Those facts are hinted at in the film itself. This tapestry of traumas entails the paradox of Jewish/Israeli existence with which Gitai engages: the unwillingness to be a victim versus the impossibility of accepting the role of the aggressor and the lack of a solution for those who find themselves trapped between those two options.

That chain of traumas—some still not worked through and unresolved—may provide an explanation for *Kedma*'s preserving of the post-traumatic structure that severs the linear chain and the connection between signifiers and signified, shaping what Caruth calls "non-referential history."[11] The film engages with the overt trauma, addresses and discusses it, but its post-traumatic structure indicates that other traumas can be found under the overt trauma that was identified and processed.

It is those traumas that flood the film with signifiers that mask their signs and paralyze its movement. *Kedma* dismantles the cinematic narrative and, in doing so, signals the failure of the historical-ideological narrative, under whose shadow we live. Beyond that failure, we can read the post-traumatic rhetoric that paralyzes it and signals us to halt, look back, and try to work through the events that engendered it.

Atash

Drying Up Space

In one of the final scenes of *Kedma* a Palestinian refugee yells to Israeli soldiers: "We will remain here, in spite of you, like a wall . . ." At that point, where the film *Kedma* is about to end, we can start a discussion of Tawfik Abu Wael's film *Atash* (Thirst). In fact, it fulfills the prophecy of that refugee, embodies the resistance that he called for, and engenders incessant clashes with the Zionist narrative as well as with the Palestinian one. This is achieved via an aesthetic of narrative detachment and paralysis anchored in a post-traumatic rhetoric, as in *Kedma*. This time the trauma is Palestinian, and the paralysis is created by drying up, not flooding.

Atash tells the story of a Palestinian family of five, living in an abandoned Israeli army training installation outside its native village, cut off from all social contact with civilization. The family's life is conducted under the tyranny of a stern, cruel father who refuses to return to the village and to civilization. To maintain his family in this forsaken place, he taps illegally into the state's water supply. The father's refusal to leave that space where he and his family live can be read as resistance to time and space "out there": the time and space of the Israeli state where he used to live and even the time and space of the Arab village that he abandoned. The relationship between the autarchic space where the family lives and the hegemonic space located "out there" calls attention to and problematizes historical temporality.

Unlike *Kedma*, which is conducted within history and in touch with its narratives, *Atash* positions itself beyond them, in a sort of enclave. And unlike historical time and the concrete geographic space to which *Kedma* relates, *Atash* unfolds "out of time" and "out of space." In that sense, it is extrahistorical and extraterritorial, despite a few hints as to concrete time and space in the form of the water infrastructure and the land that the family uses. The space in which the story takes place is closed, unified. The protagonists hardly move beyond the restrictions of the small, cramped area they inhabit. It is an arid waste: although it is small and constrained, it is almost completely empty. Even the few objects it contains are minimalist: it certainly does not spill over with the baroqueness that characterizes *Kedma*.

The *Atash* space is monolithic, wall-like: piles of sand that demarcate it and signify its boundaries; the destroyed concrete building that is the family's home; recurring shots of people and objects trapped between symmetrical lintels and doorways; the burning sun; dust rising in the air; the fire and smoke spiraling up. Scenes are often filmed through monochromatic filters that make it hard to distinguish between the background and the figures moving in it (figure-ground), who are swallowed up in it. They imbue that space with a visually "yellowing" impression, which is extremely arid in physical and sensory terms.

Aridity is also embodied in the protagonists' silence, the silence prevailing around them, and the film's soundtrack, consisting mostly of diegetic sounds of friction between objects or friction of hands with coarse, heavy, or rough items such as pickaxes, logs, shovels, rusting metal pipes, and concrete. Even the minimalist musical soundtrack is largely produced by the female protagonist's hands playing on an untuned metallic stringed instrument, as previously described. The aridity, the contracted and restricted nature of the space, is also manifest at the level of the plot: in the passivity of the family members, who feel trapped and buried in the desolate place that the father dragged them to.

In comparison with that arid, closed prison, other spaces in the film are not so limited, such as the village that the family left and the forests and fields under the state's control. This is where water flows, where trees grow, which the family uses illegally. But the space of the village hardly appears in the film, and the fields and forests that hold the family's source of livelihood are also dangerous and harbor patrolling forest wardens who threaten the trespassing family. Thus the static, desiccated space where the family lives becomes a form of resistance to the surrounding space of life and movement, where historical changes occur.

From Sign to Object

The motif of water in the film is another metaphor for resistance. The title *Kedma*, which means "eastward" in Hebrew, denotes movement. *Atash*, which means "thirst" in Arabic, suggests stasis, the unending situation of lack and deficiency. By choosing to live in a waterless wasteland, the father enforces that aridity on his family, defying both his Palestinian culture and Israeli culture.[12]

Aridity is not found solely in the portrayed content but also in how the film's cinematic language signifies that content: more precisely, the way it refuses the option of imparting meaning and detaches signified from signifier. That mechanism, which appeared in *Kedma*, functions in *Atash* in several different forms. One of them is the use of sequence shots focusing on static objects, particularly figures in a situation of stasis. These long shots and long takes, accompanied by slow camera movements, seem to insist on penetrating the still landscape and the static figures trapped in it, to extract from it some meaning that refuses to be extracted.

This is in opposition to the flooding of meaning created by cinematic signs in *Kedma*. In *Atash* the long observations of objects and figures only emphasize their physical presence or existence, their "suchness," their "intensive material expression," as Gilles Deleuze and Félix Guattari define it.[13] In this manner the divide between the two "members" of the sign, between the signifier (the objects and the figures observed on the screen) and what they are intended to signify (the meaning they bear), is intensified. In *Atash* we are ostensibly left with the object itself, without being able to convert it to meanings it may stand for, with no attempt to fulfill its potential to become a symbol and metaphor.[14] In other words, while *Atash* wages war by "drying up," *Kedma* does so by flooding signifiers. In both films the sign refuses to be an "actor" in the signifying process. It says "I am a signifier and nothing more" in one film and "I am an object and nothing more" in the other.

The detachment between signifier and signified finds a parallel in the fragmented plot, in the recurring, cyclical, Sisyphean actions of the protagonists. The film has no coherent, linear, causal, or analogical sequence that constitutes meaning or narrative. The causal continuum is interrupted in various ways: by starting the shot after the action has been launched and cutting it before the action ends or by breaking the causal Hollywood editing style of "shot/reverse shot" and replacing it with additive successions of silent gazes. As noted, it also uses recurring Sisyphean actions—digging in the ground, chopping wood, loading heavy objects, and moving them from one place to another. The repetition of these actions, which recall a caged lion pacing back and forth, underscores the limits of space and again proves the impossibility of change created by movement.

The connection between the breach in cinematic causality and the disrupted historical narratives is discernible in the presentation of objects and things that have lost their original purpose and have been severed from the causal procedure that they originally belonged to: a concrete structure used for military training, where a family now lives; rifle bullet shells left on the ground and now used as play blocks; safety catches of hand grenades now fashioned into a decorative curtain. What once served military purposes has lost that function and has been severed from the causal chain to which it belongs. Israeli history, in a linear progression toward the future, left behind empty husks lacking a function or purpose. The family's insistence on collecting and preserving them attests to the insistence on remaining outside the course of that particular history, thus sabotaging its movement, halting it, and transforming its past into present.

The family does not make do only with subverting Israeli history: it sabotages Palestinian history as well. The land where the father brought his wife and children was his family's land until 1948. Without taking into account the historical changes that have taken place, without bearing in mind the conditions of the current reality, the father settles on that land. As if history had stopped progressing, in a sense he establishes a new settlement in a desolate place where water is drawn from the ground. He maintains a now largely extinct Palestinian Arab way of life on that site. The film is cast with local nonactors who speak with the accent of the Palestinian villages that is no longer preserved in contemporary Palestinian cinema and who work as charcoal burners, the traditional occupation in their abandoned village Umm al-Fahm (Arabic: the source of charcoal). The film expresses the position of resistance to the histories of both peoples and their narratives, in that it stops their movement and freezes their past.

Atash: A Post-traumatic Situation

In the case of *Atash,* as in *Kedma,* we can stop the discussion at this stage in order to examine the rhetoric of resistance as a type of post-traumatic rhetoric. As noted, trauma is a grave event that is not grasped by consciousness and so ostensibly leaves no record or at any rate exists as a repressed memory that would later resurface.[15] Such a return to the traumatic event is a return to the moment of loss—the traumatic moment—but also a return to what was lost.[16] Time comes to a stop because the lost object lives in the consciousness as if it still exists: the events of the past recur in the present, seeming to happen again and again. The past replaces the present, and the future is considered a return to the lost past. Hence the detachment between signifier and signified and the impossibility of relating to the traumatic history as a causal, chronological narrative.[17]

Because the traumatic incident that caused the father's decision to leave the village has been repressed and distanced from memory, it is not completely defined, not totally clear. Perhaps the oldest daughter had a love relationship with a man before marriage, when the family still lived in the village, or maybe someone molested or even raped her.

In any event, the family's good name was stained. Instead of fighting for his honor, the father decides to leave the village and forces his family to resurrect the village's lost way of life in the "wrong" places and times.[18] Outside civilization, without water, with no school, no radio, and no people around, the exhausting, repetitive movements and actions typify post-traumatic fixedness.

As in *Kedma*, the overt trauma in *Atash* conceals other traumas beneath it. The hidden, paralyzed relations of abusive and suppressed love between father and daughter hide the trauma of 1948, which "bursts into" the present in the very form of the housing the family occupies: a military training installation that simulates an Arab village, containing the memory of the villages that were destroyed in 1948 as well as the destroying army.[19] As such, the father's decision to leave the village results not only from the mortifying event that happened to his daughter but also from the trauma of 1948: the need to live on the land seized in the past and again experience life before the loss. Many Palestinian films that were made in the 1980s and 1990s similarly revitalized the past before the calamity and presented it as a mythic, idealized past, a fantasy of the lost paradise.[20] Like other films made at that time, among them Elia Suleiman's *Chronicle of a Disappearance* (1996) and *Divine Intervention* (2002), *Atash* demystifies that past. Holding onto the land does not open up the spaces of the country to the protagonists. Water and trees do not create ties to the land. Moreover, the traditional patriarchal family, which in all the other films is a source of stability, here constitutes a source of oppression and violence that generates new traumas on top of the old ones. This time it is not only the trauma of the victims but also the trauma of the aggressor: the violent father who subjects his family to the same terror and oppression that the Israeli authorities used against him.[21]

The national history of the seized land, the destroyed villages, the army takeover, and the disintegration of the fabric of rural life are completely absent from the plot. This history has no place in the protagonists' awareness or memory. But it does appear and is embodied, like any traumatic event, in the wrong place and at the wrong time—in the landscape, the space, the objects that signify and conceal at the same time the traumatic event itself and the lost life that preceded it. That life and those events are hidden beyond the family trauma that halts and paralyzes the film's plot.

The film's adherence to the post-traumatic structure is in fact a declaration of a preference for paralysis. This is its aesthetic/political statement that has affirmative validity—the world continues to turn, but I refuse to move with it. The post-traumatic situation is preferable to an ethical and aesthetic bowing of the head.

Summary

The two practices of "drying up" and "flooding" are allegedly antithetical, but both frustrate and disrupt the movement of the two films discussed here, as bearers of narrative. We have read disruption as a post-traumatic rhetoric that finds various methods for expression in each film. *Kedma* levels its gaze at the Zionist narrative of Holocaust and revival, simultaneously adopting and paralyzing it, and floods it with sections of texts, clichés, and other narratives that are antithetical and contradictory as well as parallel and analogous. In this way it engenders an eclectic multivoiced narrative that can encompass contradictions and does not insist on enforcing their reconciliation. *Atash*, in contrast, prefers to "dry up" the hegemonic languages in which Palestinian film exists, to disregard them, to remain outside the narrative—and thus outside the perimeters of history.

The two films describe a traumatic history. In both of them those histories contain the trauma of the victim and, beyond it, the adversities of the victim who assails the figure of the aggressor and remains trapped in it. Both films use the traumatic structure as an act of resistance against history and the narrative it enforces on them. But if *Kedma* chooses to locate the traumatic event in the new polyphonic narrative and thus to express the act of refusal, *Atash* expresses that act by welcoming the post-traumatic rhetoric with open arms. We can say that *Kedma* takes diverging historical paths that delay and dismantle movement, paths that *Atash* avoids from the outset.

NOTES

This essay is based on research funded by the Israel Science Foundation (no. 637/08). We thank George Khleifi for assisting in its writing and Sharon Forgash for helping in its preparation.

1. Here we use the terminology of Gilles Deleuze and Félix Guattari, *Kafka: Toward a Minor Literature*. See also Gilles Deleuze, *Cinema 1: The Movement-Image*; *Cinema 2: The Time Image*; and Frederic Jameson, *The Political Unconscious: Narrative as a Socially Symbolic Act*. For a further discussion of the dismantling of narrative in the work of Amos Gitai, see Nitzan Ben-Shaul, *Israeli Persecution Films*.

2. Homi K. Bhabha, "DissemiNation: Time, Narrative and the Margins of the Modern Nation." See Bhabha's discussion of linear, teleological, and causal narrative movement as an ideological instrument of the hegemony.

3. Sigmund Freud, *The Psychopathology of Everyday Life*; idem, "Remembering, Repeating and Working Through"; idem, "Mourning and Melancholia."

4. Thomas Elsaesser, "Postmodernism as Mourning Work."

5. For an extensive discussion of cinematic representations of the Zionist narrative as a hegemonic narrative, see Nurith Gertz, *Holocaust Survivors, Aliens, and Others in Israeli Cinema and Literature*; Ilan Avisar, "Israeli Cinema and the Ending of Zionism"; Judd Ne'eman, "The Tragic Sense of Zionism: Shadow Cinema and the Holocaust"; Nitzan Ben-Shaul, *Mythical Expressions of Siege in Israeli Films*; Raz Yosef, *Beyond Flesh: Queer Masculinities and Nationalism in Israeli Cinema*; Yosefa Lushitzky, *Identity Politics on the Israeli Screen*; Ella Shohat, *Israeli Cinema: East/West and the Politics of Representation*; Irma Klein, *Amos Gitai: Cinema, Politics, Aesthetics* (*Amos Gitai: Kolno'a, Politika, Estetika*) (Tel Aviv: Hakibbutz Hameukhad, 2003); Paul Willemen, "Bangkok-Bahrain-Berlin-Jerusalem."

6. For a recent discussion on the long-take, see Aharon Kashels and Eran Sagi, "On the PCS or the Fear of the Cut."

7. On ruins as allegory, see Walter Benjamin, *The Origins of German Tragic Drama*; for a discussion of landscape in Israeli cinema, see Yael Munk, "The Space of the City of Accre as the Space of a Sick Body: On Judd Ne'eman's Film *Looking at Acre*"; Anat Zanger, "Blind Spaces: Roadblock Movies in Contemporary Israeli Film"; idem, "Zionism and the Detective: Imaginary Territories in Israeli Popular Cinema."

8. See also Thomas Elsaesser, "One Train May Be Hiding Another: Private History, Memory and National Identity." Elsaesser used the term "parapraxis" to describe trauma; the term was coined by Freud in *The Psychopathology of Everyday Life*, to define a situation in which the absent (something forgotten, distanced, hidden) appears as present but not fully present—and in the wrong place, at the wrong time.

9. See Cathy Caruth, *Unclaimed Experience: Trauma, Narrative, and History*; Freud, "Mourning and Melancholia" and "Remembering, Repeating and Working Through"; Dominick LaCapra, *Rethinking Intellectual History: Texts, Contexts, Language*; Lawrence L. Langer, *Holocaust Testimonies: The Ruins of Memory*; Shoshana Felman and Dori Laub, *Testimony: Crises of Witnessing in Literature, Psychoanalysis, and History*. See also Anton Keas, *Shell Shock Cinema: Weimar Culture and the Wounds of War*. The depiction of trauma in this essay is very much based on this seminal book, which deals with post-traumatic experience regarding World War I and its representation in Weimar cinema.

10. Caruth: *Unclaimed Experience*; Freud, "Mourning and Melancholia."

11. Cathy Caruth (ed.), *Trauma: Explorations in Memory*.

12. On the place of this film in Palestinian culture and in the framework of Palestinian film, see Nurith Gertz and George Khleifi, *Palestinian Cinema: Landscape, Trauma and Memory*, 197.

13. Deleuze and Guattari, *Kafka*, 50.

14. On this practice and its effect, see ibid., 53–54. See also the discussion of Roland Barthes on the "punctum" and camera lucida in *Reflections on Photography*; at the same time, it is noteworthy that the observer is granted freedom of interpretation to search for different meanings. These meanings have been widely discussed by critics. See, for example, Uri Klein: "Atash—Thirst"; Matan Aharoni, "Atash-Thirst: Call for an Arab Revolution"; Uri Breitman, "Atash-Thirst."

15. On this point, see LaCapra's discussion in "Acting Out," in LaCapra, *Rethinking Intellectual History*.

16. Freud, "Mourning and Melancholia."

17. Caruth, *Unclaimed Experience*, p. 12.

18. See Elsaesser, "One Train May Be Hiding Another," drawing on Freud on the displacement of a symptom from the original time and space that created it. See also Régine-Mihal Friedman, "The Double Legacy of Arbeit Macht Frei."

19. It is customary in Palestinian literature and culture to link failure to conserve women's honor with failure to retain the land—the recurring accusations leveled at the generation that failed in the 1948 war. In those terms, the trauma of failing to safeguard his daughter's honor is connected to the trauma of losing the land in that war. Caruth, following Freud and Lacan, describes the return to the traumatic event as an attempt to return to the moment when it was still possible to change things, to prevent the terrible event. Caruth, *Unclaimed Experience*, p. 13.

20. For a broad discussion of the historiography of Palestinian film, see Gertz and Khleifi, *Palestinian Cinema*.

21. This is expressed in the dream where the father identifies himself with the Israeli soldier. The connection between the patriarchal father and the Israeli occupier is dealt with in many Palestinian films, the most renowned of them being *Wedding in Galilee* (Michel Khleifi, 1987). For an analysis of the phenomenon, see Gertz and Khleifi, *Palestinian Cinema*.

BIBLIOGRAPHY

Aharoni, Matan. "Atash-Thirst: A Call for an Arab Revolution" ("Atash-Tzimaʾon: Kriʾa Lemahapekha Arvit"), http://www.tv-il.com/cinema-208.htm.

Avisar, Ilan. "Israeli Cinema and the Ending of Zionism." In *Israel in the Nineties*, edited by Fred Lazin and Greg Mahler, 153–168. Gainesville: University of Florida Press, 1996.

Barthes, Roland. *Reflections on Photography*. New York: Hill and Wang, 1981.

Benjamin, Walter. *The Origins of German Tragic Drama*. London: Verso, 1988.

Ben-Shaul, Nitzan. *Mythical Expressions of Siege in Israeli Films*. Lewiston, N.Y.: Edwin Mellen Press, 1997.

———. *Israeli Persecution Films*. Forthcoming.

Bhabha, Homi K. "DissemiNation: Time, Narrative and the Margins of the Modern Nation." In *Nation and Narration*, edited by Homi K. Bhabha, 291–323. London/New York: Routledge, 1990.

Breitman, Uri. "Atash-Thirst." In *Criticism Doesn't Build Anything* (*Bikoret Lo Bona Klum*), http://breitman.homestead.com/films/atash.html.

Caruth, Cathy (ed.). *Trauma: Explorations in Memory*. Baltimore: Johns Hopkins University Press, 1995.

———. *Unclaimed Experience: Trauma, Narrative, and History*. London: John Hopkins University Press, 1996.

Deleuze, Gilles. *Cinema 1: The Movement-Image; Cinema 2: The Time Image*. Paris: Éditions de Minuit, 1983–1985.

Deleuze, Gilles, and Félix Guattari. *Kafka: Toward a Minor Literature* (1975). Translated by Dana Polan. Minnesota: University of Minnesota Press, 1986.

Elsaesser, Thomas. "Postmodernism as Mourning Work." In *Screen* 42 (2001): 193–201.

———. "One Train May Be Hiding Another: Private History, Memory and National Identity." In *Topologies of Trauma: Essays on the Limit of Knowledge and Memory*, edited by Linda Belau and Petar Ramadanovic, 61–74. New York: Other Press, LLC, 2002.

Felman, Shoshana, and Dori Laub. *Testimony: Crises of Witnessing in Literature, Psycho-analysis, and History*. New York: Routledge, 1992.

Freud, Sigmund. "Mourning and Melancholia" (1909). In *The Second Edition of the Complete Psychological Works, Vol. 12*, 243–258. London: Hogarth Press and Institute of Psychoanalysis, 1974.

———. "Remembering, Repeating and Working Through." In *The Standard Edition of the Complete Psychological Works, Vol. 12* (1909), 147–156. London: W. W. Norton and Company, 1974.

———. *The Psychopathology of Everyday Life* (1901). London, W. W. Norton and Company, 1990.

Friedman, Régine-Mihal. "The Double Legacy of Arbeit Macht Frei." *Prooftexts* 22, nos. 1–2 (Winter/Spring 2002): 200–220.

Gertz, Nurith. *Holocaust Survivors, Aliens, and Others in Israeli Cinema and Literature (Makhela Akheret: Nitzolei Sho'ah Zarim Va'akherim Bakolno'a Uvasifrut Hayisra'elit)*. Tel Aviv: Am Oved/Open University, 2004.

Gertz, Nurith, and George Khleifi. *Palestinian Cinema: Landscape, Trauma and Memory*. Edinburgh: Edinburgh University Press, 2008.

Jameson, Frederic. *The Political Unconscious: Narrative as a Socially Symbolic Act*. Ithaca, N.Y.: Cornell University Press, 1981.

Kashels, Aharon, and Eran Sagi. "On the PCS or the Fear of the Cut." In *New Views on Film Philosophy (Thesis, the Academic Periodical of the Bauhaus University)*. Forthcoming.

Keas, Anton. *Shell Shock Cinema: Weimar Culture and the Wounds of War*. Princeton: Princeton University Press, 2009.

Klein, Uri. "Atash—Thirst." *Ha'aretz*, June 16, 2005.

LaCapra, Dominick. *Rethinking Intellectual History: Texts, Contexts, Language*. Ithaca, N.Y.: Cornell University Press, 1983.

Langer, Lawrence, L. *Holocaust Testimonies: The Ruins of Memory*. New Haven and London: Yale University Press, 1991.

Lushitzky, Yosefa. *Identity Politics on the Israeli Screen*. Austin: University of Texas Press, 2001.

Munk, Yael. "The Space of the City of Accre as the Space of a Sick Body: On Judd Ne'eman's Film *Looking at Acre*" ("Merkhav Hair Akko Kemerkhav Haguf Hakhole: Al Sirto Shal Judd Ne'eman 'Histaklut Al Akko'"). *Southern Cinema Notebooks* (Sapir College) (*Makhbarot Kolnoa Darom*) 1 (2006): 85–90.

Ne'eman, Judd. "The Tragic Sense of Zionism: Shadow Cinema and the Holocaust." *Shofar* (special issue, edited by Nurith Gertz) 24 (2005): 22–36.

Shohat, Ella. *Israeli Cinema: East/West and the Politics of Representation*. Austin: University of Texas Press, 1989.

Willemen, Paul. "Bangkok-Bahrain-Berlin-Jerusalem." In *The Films of Amos Gitai: A Montage*, 5–16. London: BFI Publishing, 1993.

Yosef, Raz. *Beyond Flesh: Queer Masculinities and Nationalism in Israeli Cinema*. New Brunswick, N.J.: Rutgers University Press, 2004.

Zanger, Anat. "Zionism and the Detective: Imaginary Territories in Israeli Popular Cinema." *Journal of Modern Jewish Studies* 3, no. 3 (2004): 307–318.

————. "Blind Spaces: Roadblock Movies in Contemporary Israeli Film." *Shofar* (special issue on Israeli cinema) 24 (2005): 4–37.

FILMOGRAPHY

Kedma. Amos Gitai. 2002.
Thirst (Atash). Tawfik Abu Wael. 2004.
Wedding in Galilee (Urs al-Jalil; Hebrew title *Khatuna Bagalil)*. Michel Khleifi, 1987.

PART VII

New Cinematic Discourses

22 Discursive Identities in the (R)evolution of the New Israeli Queer Cinema

GILAD PADVA

Contemporary Israeli Queer Cinema is inspired by the North American and West European New Queer Cinema. It is mostly known for Eytan Fox's melodramatic films *Yossi and Jagger* (2002), a love story between two Israeli soldiers, and *Walk on Water* (2004), about the intense relationship of a macho Mossad agent with the gay grandson of a Nazi war criminal and the young man's sister. Early Israeli Queer Cinema in the late 1970s, however, was not melodramatic and was inspired rather by the French Nouvelle Vague (New Wave) cinema and its modernistic, often nonemotional, alienated, and existential approach. The changes in the cinematic articulation of queer subjectivities reflect the complicated Israeli politics of identities and (homo) sexualities and relate to significant changes in the social, political, and cultural spheres in Israel over decades.

Until the mid-1960s most Israeli films glorified the male body of the heroic Sabra (native Israeli), inspired by Westerns and Hollywood war films. But although the Sabra was represented as stronger, healthier, and more hetero-masculine than the Jew of the Diaspora, these images contained a homoerotic subtext: images of muscular Zionist farmers, builders, and soldiers and their male bonding and close friendships. In contrast, the Palestinian (Arab) body, whether female or male, evoked both anxiety and passion in Jewish characters, as shown in Alexander Ford's *Sabra* (*Tzabar*, 1933) and in later radical films like Dan Wolman's *Hide and Seek* (*Makhvo'im*, 1980), the tragic love story of a Jewish teacher and his Arab male lover in Jerusalem in the 1940s; Dan Wachsmann's *Eastern Wind* (*Khamsin*, 1982), about a suggested love triangle involving a Jewish farmer, his sister, and their Arab farmhand; Amos Guttman's *Drifting* (*Nagu'a*, the long version, 1982), in which the male protagonist is penetrated by a Palestinian fugitive;[1] and Eytan Fox's *The Bubble* (*Ha'buah*, 2006), which portrays the intimate relationship between a Jewish Israeli man from Tel Aviv and a Palestinian man from Nablus.

Early Israeli cinema was characterized by nationalist films. This Zionist cinema was critically examined and extensively analyzed by Israeli academia.[2] In the 1960s and 1970s they were gradually replaced by populist Bourekas (slapstick) ethnic comedies and melodramas as well as by intellectual dramas inspired by the French New Wave cinema.[3] In the 1980s a new political cinema criticized the Israeli occupation in the West Bank, Gaza Strip, and south Lebanon. During the 1990s and 2000s the Israeli mainstream cinema mostly focused on family melodramas in both central and peripheral Israel and reexamined local ethnicities and diverse subaltern communities inside and outside Tel Aviv.

The Israeli Queer Cinema, from the late 1970s to the late 2000s, is interconnected with most of these significant cinematic trends. The New Israeli Queer Cinema of the 1990s and 2000s, in particular, is interwoven with the deconstruction of Israeli machismo, the growing acceptance of nontraditional masculinities, and the global diffusion of queer subcultures into mainstream popular cultures. This dynamic process reflects the (r)evolutionary queer identifications of Israeli filmmakers, who challenge the powerful Israeli collectivism and its sexual imperatives and practically reshape the Israeli public perception of sexual dissidence and erotic transgression.

Identification, according to Stuart Hall's discursive approach, is a construction, a process never completed but always "in process. It is not determined, in the sense that it can always be 'won' or 'lost,' sustained or abandoned. Identification is in the end conditional, lodged in contingency, and the total merging it suggests is, in fact, a fantasy of incorporation."[4] This essay, inspired by Hall's conceptualization of the politics of identity, reevaluates the journey of the Israeli Queer Cinema from its "closeted" days of the 1970s and 1980s to the dramatic changes in the 1990s and the new challenges of the 2000s.

Agonized Martyrs: The Late 1970s and the 1980s

Amos Guttman, born in 1954, is the pioneer of Israeli gay filmmaking. He began his brief filmic career with three black-and-white short films: *Safe Place* (*Makom Batu'akh*, 1977), about a closeted adolescent and his attempts to come to terms with his homosexuality; *Repeat Premieres* (*Premyerot Khozrot*, 1977), which focuses on a campy young puppetry artist and his homoerotic fantasies; and *Drifting* (*Nagu'a*, the short version, 1979), which focuses on a rough closeted young man and his relationship with an effeminate male dancer in a Tel Aviv cabaret.

Most of Guttman's films, inspired by the New Wave and the emerging Israeli genre of "personal cinema" and its intellectual dramas, were made between the establishment of the Gay, Lesbian, Bisexual, and Transgender (GLBT) Association (previously known as the Society for the Protection of Personal Rights) in 1975 and the rescinding of the law against intermale intercourse by the Knesset in 1988.[5] The public hostility toward sexual minorities in Israel at that time is strongly reflected in this cinema's politics of martyrdom. Guttman's *Safe Place*, for instance, is an adolescence film about Kleinman (Doron Nesher), a high school student who comes to terms with his attraction to men. Significantly, the protagonist is lonely, without friends. He lives in a nice house in Tel Aviv with his mother, a frustrated unemployed actress, and his beloved younger sister. His father is absent. He cannot talk to them about his homosexuality.

This film integrates a queer youth melodrama and an existentialist drama inspired by the style of Jean-Luc Godard and the French New Wave cinema: continuous, lingering shots accompanied by dramatic silence, stylized composition, melancholic atmosphere, and a desperate search for the meaning of life. The young protagonist is doomed to live a double life, wandering between home and school, and attempts to cope with his desire on the promenade of Tel Aviv's beach.

Another gay martyr is Doron (Ze'ev Shimshoni), the closeted protagonist in Guttman's *Drifting* (the short version). He tries to confront his sexual identity in a different liminal site—a cabaret where effeminate seminaked young men are performing. Doron often visits this place with his girlfriend. The term "liminality" here is borrowed from the field of anthropology, where it refers mainly to processes, rites of passage, states, and cultural forms existing "betwixt and between."[6] According to Victor Turner, liminality is a temporal interface whose properties partially invert those of the already consolidated order, which constitutes any specific cultural cosmos.[7]

In his visit to the cabaret, which is a sort of countercultural cosmos, (dis)located between the mundane and the extraordinary, Doron accepts the gay dancer Effi's offer to meet after work. Later, in bed, Doron tells Effi (Boaz Turjeman) that he lives with a woman. When the dancer remarks that Doron is fully aroused, Doron quickly dresses and leaves. The insulted dancer follows him to the stairs, shouting that he should pay for the time he wasted. Both films nonetheless end more optimistically. The boy in *Safe Place* returns to the dark cinema, reaching out his arm to the seat near him, ready and willing to touch another man. Likewise, *Drifting* ends when the protagonist returns to the dancer's dressing room, smiling at him. In other words, both protagonists have come to terms with their homosexuality.[8]

Guttman's first feature film, also titled *Drifting* (1982) but very different from the short version, portrays the story of Rubi (Jonathan Segal), a frustrated young gay filmmaker in Tel Aviv, and his relationship with his absent parents, his aging grandmother (with whom he lives), and several marginalized Israeli and Palestinian characters. Historically, this feature film reflects the melancholic, closeted days of the Israeli GLBT community, characterized by individual and collective despair and loneliness, five years before the official law against homosexuality was canceled by the Knesset.

Guttman's long version of *Drifting* was followed by three more feature films: *Bar 51—Sister of Love* (1985), a tragic love story between Thomas (Juliano Mer) and Marianna (Smadar Kilchinsky), a brother and sister act in a decadent cabaret in downtown Tel Aviv; *Himmo, King of Jerusalem* (*Khimmo Melekh Yerushalayim*, 1987), which reflects a genuine, surprising queer perspective on Israel's 1948 War of Independence and homoerotic comradeship based on Yoram Kaniuk's novel; and *Amazing Grace* (*Hessed Mufla*, 1992).[9]

According to Yosefa Loshitzky, Guttman's exaggerated style and theatrical set in this film (associated with Hollywood melodramas) politically challenge the dominant Israeli ideology. Loshitzky adds that Guttman's campiness, emphasizing aesthetic values, is contrasted to the "realist Zionist" style of most Israeli films.[10] Guttman's significant film *Amazing Grace* (*Hessed Mufla*, 1992) focuses on the unfulfilled love between young Jonathan (Gal Hoyberger) and Thomas (Sharon Alexander), an older man who lives with AIDS. Guttman died of an AIDS-related disease in February 1993, at the age of thirty-nine. *Amazing Grace*, the first Israeli film about an AIDS victim, reflects not only the filmmaker's coping with his own disease but also the Israeli gay community's AIDS crisis and its consequent feelings of helplessness, loneliness, isolation, victimization, and devastation. *Amazing Grace* does not politicize the AIDS crisis. Significantly, the word "AIDS" is not mentioned even once (until the mid-2000s not a single Israeli feature showed a gay character explicitly living with AIDS).[11] Raz Yosef notes that representations of (homo)sexuality in Guttman's films offer no redemptive vision. "The protagonists are hopelessly caught in vicious circles of sexual and emotional exploitation," he adds. "They are oppressed, manipulated, and betrayed, but at the same time they exercise power and domination over others."[12]

Melodramas, in contrast, usually concentrate on the viewpoint of the victim, sometimes managing convincingly to present all the characters as victims.[13] This is certainly the case in Ayelet Menahemi's *Crows* (*Orvim*,

1987), a 45-minute film in which almost all the characters are glorified as martyrs. Maggie (Gilli Ben-Ozillio), the female protagonist, is a country girl who moves to Tel Aviv after her mother's suicide. There she meets a group of queer young men who are marginalized by urban society, living outside the heteronormative sexual order. The queer commune members are dominated by Yuval (Boaz Turjeman), Eli (Doron Barbi), and Daniel (Itzik Nini), a male-to-female transgender who is initially hostile to Maggie but gradually befriends her.

This queer youth's solidarity is scrutinized in a violent scene in which Yuval humiliates Daniel, who stabs at him with broken glass. This melodramatic, emotional crisis reflects the destructive rather than affirmative power of melodramas. Barbara Klinger notes that melodramas are usually characterized by the psychic destructiveness of social institutions, often centering on a (heterosexual) couple and resulting in a rampageous representation of ambition and a romantic love disquieted through expressions of nymphomania, impotence, suicidal tendencies, obsessions with paternity, and so forth.[14] This destructiveness, as manifested by American melodramas, echoes in the films discussed here, which depict remarkable social transgressions and spectacular violations of bourgeois codes, particularly suicidal tendencies and glorification of the (gay) martyr.[15]

Flamboyant Queens and Passionate Soldiers: The 1990s and the 2000s

The New Israeli Queer Cinema, created by openly gay filmmakers, first emerged in the early 1990s, a few years after the cancellation of the law against homosexuality in 1988 and the emergence of a second generation of committed GLBT activists in Tel Aviv, Haifa, and Jerusalem, with the films of Eytan Fox, a mainstream filmmaker. His debut film, *After* (1990), portrays unfulfilled desire between a closeted gay officer and his cadet.

Following *Song of the Siren* (*Shirat Hasirena*, 1994), a straight romance between a female advertiser and a male food engineer in Tel Aviv, Fox directed the first season of the TV series *Florentine* (1997–2001), scripted by his partner, Gal Uchovsky. This series signifies a new phase in the perception of sissiness and homosexuality in Israeli society. One of the protagonists is Iggy (Uri Banai), an effeminate and openly gay man of Eastern origins. Iggy is a colorful avid fan of Eurovision song contests, drag shows, and flamboyant outfits, who earns his living by baking cakes for coffeeshops. He has a romantic relationship with the straight-acting Tomer (Avshalom Polack), a gay man of Ashkenazi (Western) origins, who is gradually coming out to his friends and family. *Florentine* is the first Israeli TV program that included explicitly gay sex scenes and a gay kiss on prime time.[16]

Fox's film *Yossi and Jagger* (2002) focuses on a relationship between a closeted officer, Yossi (Ohad Knoller), and his deputy, Jagger (Yehuda Levy), on a remote army base. Yossi keeps the affair secret, however, even after Jagger is killed in a military action. *Yossi and Jagger* is located in the heart of the Israeli consensus: the IDF. Although this film is often criticized for its mainstream attitude and the death of one of the gay protagonists, the portrayal of gay love inside the army is a significant contribution for greater acceptance of homosexuality among its many straight viewers.[17]

Fox's international debut film *Walk on Water* (*Lalekhet Al Hamayim*, 2004) deals with the relationship of Eyal (Lior Ashkenazi), an Israeli Mossad agent, with Axel, a gay German whose grandfather was an infamous Nazi officer, and his sister, who lives in an Israeli kibbutz. This film emphasizes the developing friendship between Eyal and Axel (Knut Berger), who encourages Eyal to sublimate his chauvinistic masculinity and become more tolerant and gay friendly. The end of this film, however, follows the heterocentric, commercial imperative: Eyal does not get married to Axel but rather to Axel's sister Pia (Caroline Peters).[18]

Fox's latest film, *The Bubble* (*Habu'ah*, 2006), scripted with Uchovsky, demonstrates a more politicized, critical perspective of the leftist part of the Israeli gay community on the Israeli-Palestinian conflict and the continuous Israeli occupation in the West Bank. *The Bubble* focuses on a forbidden love between Noam (Ohad Knoller), a young Israeli man, and Ashraf (Yousef "Joe" Sweid), a handsome young Palestinian. Both men are entrapped in a national social reality of conflict, occupation, and terror and are torn between love and devotion to each other, on the one hand, and familial and national loyalties, on the other.

The dramatic conflict peaks as the Palestinian's sister Rana (Roba Blal) is accidentally killed by Israeli soldiers in Nablus, and the Palestinian gay protagonist becomes a suicide bomber. He explodes together with his Jewish lover in a horrifying dance scene.[19] Like Romeo and Juliet, both lovers die together, paying with their lives for challenging not only the familial and social but also the national, ethnic, and sexual borders between two tribes.

Unlike Guttman and Menahemi, who created their films in the 1980s, focusing on gays in the margins of cinematic creations about the margins of Israeli society, Eytan Fox creates at the center of Israeli prime-time and mainstream discourse in the more pluralistic Israeli society of the 1990s and 2000s. His films challenge tenets of Israeli society beyond sexuality. He has paved the road for a lively production of Israeli gay feature films of the

2000s, including Nir Ne'eman's *Send Me an Angel* (*Shlakh Li Mal'akh*, 2003), about an unexpected relationship between a thirty-something gay man and a young rent boy; Yair Hochner's *Good Boys* (*Yeladim Tovim*, 2005), a violent and often sadistic portrayal of the sordid life of two young rent boys in Tel Aviv; Chaim Elbaum's groundbreaking short film *And Thou Shalt Love* (*Veahavta*, 2008), in which he initially deals with an unrequited gay love between two young, religious Orthodox Jewish men in a yeshiva in Jerusalem; and Tamar Glezerman's lesbian drama *The Other War* (*Hamilkhama Hashniya*, 2008), which features the story of two young women in love in Tel Aviv during the Second Lebanon War.

The win by the Israeli transgender singer Dana International in the Eurovision song contest in 1998, political and legal advancements in the late 1990s and 2000s, the increasing popularity of the annual Pride Marches and the growing gay scene in Tel Aviv, and the greater acceptance of sexual minorities by the Israeli mainstream media have stimulated a new phase in the Israeli Queer Cinema and television: Itzik Cohen and Jonathan Koniak created their anarchistic, campy TV sitcom *Mommy Queerest—Johnny* (2002–2003).[20] This carnivalesque comedy focuses on Doris, a flamboyant drama queen of Jewish Iraqi origins, and her gay son, Johnny. Although this prime-time sitcom is based on ethnic, ageist, gender, and sexual stereotypes, it consistently confronts homophobia and celebrates the seminaked male body, focusing on Yakov, Johnny's muscular boyfriend.[21]

Notably, dozens of queer documentaries have been produced in Israel in the 1990s and 2000s, dealing with diverse issues such as queer culture, coming out, love and partnership, gender identification, ethnicities, and homophobia. Erez Laufer's *Don't Cry for Me, Edinburgh* (*Edinburgh Lo Mekhaka Li*, 1996), for example, documented an Israeli gay show at the Edinburgh Festival. Ran Kotzer made several documentaries, including *Positive Story* (*Sipur Khiyuvi*, 1996), about young Israeli gay men who live with AIDS; *Amos Guttman, Filmmaker* (*Amos Guttman, Bamai Kolno'a*, 1997); *The Gay Games* (*Miskhakim Alizim*, 1999); and *Cause of Death: Homophobia* (*Sibat Hamavet—Homofobia*, 2004).

The Israeli cinema has come a long way since Amos Guttman, the very first pioneer of Gay Israeli filmmaking, made his student films about his life as a young gay man in a hidden, marginal gay community in Tel Aviv. Fox followed his path, yet managed to take his student filmmaking all the way to the center of the mainstream. He is a popular Israeli filmmaker known worldwide, who places the gay experience within the Israeli center, on prime-time small screen and global silver screen.

In recent filmmaking, the personal experience of gays living in diverse

Israeli environments is portrayed in documentary films which capture the authentic experience of Israeli gays from a uniquely personal perspective. Rather than being commodities for mass consumption, these documentaries reflect the filmmakers' own world as queers or the real lives of gay persons in their real settings.[22]

For example, Orna Ben-Dor's film *Mommy, I Didn't Kill Your Daughter* (*Imma, Lo Haragti et Habat Shelakh*, 2007) portrays the loving relationship of two Israeli female-to-male transgender people and their confrontation with the Israeli Ministry of the Interior, which refuses to change the sex registration on their identity cards. In Yair Qedar's *Gay Days* (*Hazman Havarod*, 2009) the filmmaker, who established the Hebrew GLBT monthly magazine *Hazman Havarod* (Pink Time) in the mid-1990s, integrates his personal memories and the local GLBT community's history, from the closeted days of the 1970s and the 1980s to the flamboyant 1990s and early "mainstreaming" 2000s.

Conclusion: Erotics, Politics, and a Multicultural Society

Israeli Queer Cinema, from its beginnings in the late 1970s to the new queer films of the 1990s and 2000s, has made tremendous progress. This independent, countercultural cinema is influenced and encouraged by the significant commercial and artistic success of the New Queer Cinema in Europe, America, Australia, and parts of Asia and Africa since the early 1990s.[23] The Israeli version of the global New Queer Cinema began in the closet days of the Israeli GLBT community, reflecting the fear, angst, marginality, and despair of prosecuted queer subjectivities, offscreen and on.

Over the decades many parts of the Israeli (straight) society became more tolerant and liberal toward sexual minorities. The increasing visibility of GLBT activists, filmmakers, singers, artists, and politicians in the Israeli public spheres enables a significant development of queer filmmaking.

Further, diverse subcultures both outside and inside the mainstream queer community (e.g., Orthodox gays and lesbians, transgender people, Asian and Arab GLBT people) that were often secluded and mistreated are currently represented in more and more features and documentaries. This increasing visibility is an essential contribution to the multiculturalism and pluralism of the Israeli society.[24] It reverses processes of symbolic annihilation of gays in Israeli media that have persisted for many decades.

A greater acceptance and understanding of sexual differences, orientations, preferences, and identification benefits the Israeli public and domestic spheres. Cinema, as powerful persuasive communication, explores and exposes Israeli subaltern sexual communities to broad audiences inside and outside Israel.[25]

The journey of the local queer cinema is a never-ending one. In a divided and conflicted society, in which almost all progress is countered by fanatic politicians and their nationalist and ultra-Orthodox supporters, a queer cinema is not only an entertainment but also an important instrument for social change and cultural advancement.

NOTES

1. See Gilad Padva, "Israel, Filmmaking," 312–313.

2. The term "Israeli Heroic Nationalist Cinema" was coined by Ella Shohat in *Israeli Cinema: East/West and the Politics of Representation* in relation to hegemonic Zionist films in the 1950s and 1960s that glorified the Jewish settlers in Palestine/Eretz Israel, before and after the establishment of the state. For example, *Hill 24 Doesn't Answer* (*Giv'a 24 Eina Ona*; Thorold Dickinson, 1955) mythologizes the efforts of four Zionist fighters in 1948 to maintain a strategic hill that controls the way to Jerusalem. Heroic Zionist films also emerged after military operations, including the Six Day War in 1967. For example, *He Walked through the Fields* (*Hu Halakh Basadot*; Yosef Millo, 1967) is about a mythic Zionist soldier who fought the British Mandate soldiers and helped Holocaust survivors to land on the shore of Palestine, and Menahem Golan's 1977 film *Operation Jonathan* (aka *Operation Thunderbolt*; *Mivtsa Yonatan*) is a dramatization of the heroic liberation of citizens who were kidnapped by Palestinian terrorists and forced to land in Entebbe, Uganda.

3. See Shohat, *Israeli Cinema*; Nurith Gertz, *Motion Fiction: Israeli Fiction in Film*; Amy Kronish, *World Cinema: Israel*; Nitzan S. Ben-Shaul's *Mythical Expressions of Siege in Israeli Films*; Dorit Naaman, "Orientalism as Alterity in Israeli Cinema"; Miri Talmon, *Israeli Graffiti: Nostalgia, Groups, and Collective Identity in Israeli Cinema*; Yosefa Loshitzky, *Identity Politics on the Israeli Screen*; Moshe Tzimmerman, *A Hall in the Camera: Studies in Israeli Cinema*; Raz Yosef, *Beyond Flesh: Queer Masculinities and Nationalism in Israeli Cinema*; and Padva, "Israel, Filmmaking."

4. Stuart Hall, "Introduction: Who Needs 'Identity'?" 3.

5. Amit Kama, "From *Terra Incognita* to *Terra Firma*: The Logbook of the Voyage of Gay Men's Community into the Israeli Public Sphere."

6. Madeleine Schechter, "Defining the Grotesque: An Aesthetics of Liminality," 363.

7. Victor Turner, *From Ritual to Theatre: The Human Seriousness of Play*.

8. The real martyr in *Drifting*, however, is not the protagonist Doron or the effeminate cabaret dancer (and hustler?) Effi, but Rammi (Yossi Yablonka), who owns the apartment where Doron and Effi go for sex. Rammi is an aging gay man who lives with his elderly mother. This melancholic landlord comforts himself with heavy drinking and listening to opera. He provides the young dancer with a place for sex encounters, hoping for something in return. Rammi does not hide his attraction to Doron, questioning him on how he met the young dancer and whether Doron's girlfriend knows about his sex with other men. Whereas Doron eventually makes peace with Effi, Rammi remains with his old mother, lonely, neglected, bitter and cynical, and doomed to suffer, after his gay days have long passed.

9. The film is set in a hospital located in a Gothic monastery in Jerusalem, where the patients are traumatized by their comrade Himmo, who has lost all his limbs in battle, and their complicated relationship with Hamutal (Alona Kimchi), an attractive female nurse resembling the glorious Hollywood divas of the 1940s.

10. Yosefa Loshitzky, "The Bride of the Dead Man: Phallocentrism and War in *Himmo, King of Jerusalem*," 254.

11. Only in 2006 did Dan Wolman release his feature film *Tied Hands* (*Yadayim Kshurot*) about a gay male dancer (played by the Israeli openly gay dancer Ido Tadmor) who is clearly living with AIDS.

12. Yosef, *Beyond Flesh*, 144.

13. Martha Vicinus, "Helpless and Unfriended: Nineteenth-Century Domestic Melodrama."

14. Barbara Klinger, "'Cinema/Ideology/Criticism' Revisited: The Progressive Text," 36.

15. A different portrayal of queer subjectivities in the 1970s is embodied in Michal Bat-Adam's film *Moments de la vie d'une femme* (*Rega'im*, 1979), featuring the intimate relationship between a (presumably) bisexual female author (played by Bat-Adam) and a French female tourist in Jerusalem. The climax of this film is a ménage-à-trois scene in which the two women are having sex together with the partner of the Israeli author. This film was initially censored by the Israeli authorities, but the Israeli Supreme Court approved it. *Moments*, inspired by the existentialist philosophy and stylized aesthetics of the New Wave, is a rare reference to (female) bisexuality in Israeli cinema.

16. Padva, "Cinema."

17. Whereas *Yossi and Jagger* does not criticize the Israeli occupation in Lebanon and the militaristic imperatives, it does challenge the heterocentricity of most of the comrades. In particular, this film criticizes straight-acting Yossi's attempts to hide his sexual identity and celebrates Jagger's flamboyancy. The tragic end of the film does not "punish" the queer subjectivity for its deviancy. Rather, this ending enhances the viewers' identification with Yossi and Jagger's gay love and provokes a greater empathy for Yossi, who has lost his male lover and cannot even mourn his loved one openly. In this manner, *Yossi and Jagger* criticizes the intolerant and often homophobic Israeli society for its oppressive sexual regime.

18. In this manner, *Walk on Water* embodies Fox and Uchovsky's controversial (cinematic) mainstreaming of the Israeli gay community.

19. This overwhelming resolution offers a negative, devastating version of Nohav and Guri's dreamlike dancing scene in *Gotta Have Heart* (Fox's romantic TV musical), in which they fantasize about a long-term relationship, growing older in one another's arms until they are two old lovers, to the sounds of Frieda Boccara's nostalgic Eurovision hit song "Un jour, un enfant." While Nohav and Guri's dance is an optimistic sweet dream, the all-male dance scene at the climax of *The Bubble* is definitely a nightmare, a deterministic, fatal *danse macabre* that reflects Fox and Uchovsky's angst and despair over the tragic political situation in the Middle East. When this lethal dance ends—with the couple's explosion—the Tel Aviv bubble and its dreams of peace, solidarity, and equality are blown away too (Gilad Padva and Miri Talmon, "Gotta Have an Effeminate Heart: The Politics of Effeminacy and Sissyness in a Nostalgic Israeli TV Musical").

20. Itzik Cohen is a former member of the successful Israeli drag group Pessia's

Daughters, named after a famous bra shop in King George Street in Tel Aviv. Jonathan Koniak played gay characters in several Israeli TV series.

21. Another arguable manifestation of the growing self-confidence of the Israeli gay community is the emergence of a genuine local gay pornography, such as Motti Banana and Roy Raz's *Too Hot in Tel Aviv* (*Tel Aviv Lohetet*, 2006) and Roy Raz's *My Israeli Platoon* (*Hayekhida Hatzvai't Sheli*, 2009).

22. Among the most popular Israeli queer documentaries of this period are Tomer Heymann's *It Kinda Scares Me* (*Tomer Vehasrutim*, 2001), in which he recounts his coming out to rough kids for whom he was a counselor, and his personal and intimate documentary series *On My Way Home* (*Baderekh Habayta*, 2010). Ronit Fox and Tamar Barkai's *Yellow Peppers* (*Pilpelim Tzhubim*, 2001) documents the developing romance of the lesbian owners of a Jerusalem soup restaurant. Ruthie Schatz and Adi Barash's documentary *The Garden* (*Gan*, 2003) politicizes the sexual and ethnic oppression of young gay Palestinians by following the friendship of two hustlers in Tel Aviv, a Palestinian and an Israeli Arab, their desperate search for a home, and their complicated relations with the Israeli and Palestinian authorities.

23. See, for example, B. Rubi Rich's "A Queer Sensation"; Emanuel Levy's *Cinema of Outsiders: The Rise of American Independent Film*; and Alexander Doty's "Film: New Queer Cinema."

24. A significant advance in the representation of GLBT people in the local media is the 1997 episode of the Israeli Educational Television's talk show *Open Cards* (*Klafim Ptukhim*, hosted by Nattiv Robinson), which featured queer youth. This episode was banned by the Orthodox politician Zvulun Hammer, Israel's education minister, until the Supreme Court issued a countervailing decision (Kama, "From *Terra Incognita* to *Terra Firma*").

25. See Amit Kama, *The Newspaper and the Closet: Israeli Gay Men's Communication Patterns*.

BIBLIOGRAPHY

Ben-Shaul, Nitzan S. 1997. *Mythical Expressions of Siege in Israeli Films*. Lewiston, N.Y., and Ceredigion, UK: Edwin Mellen Press.

Doty, Alexander. 2000. "Film: New Queer Cinema." In George G. Haggerty (ed.), *Gay Histories and Cultures: An Encyclopedia*, 321–323. New York: Garland.

Gertz, Nurith. 1993. *Motion Fiction: Israeli Fiction in Film* (*Sipur Mehasratim: Siporet Yisra'elit Ve'ibudeihah Lakolno'a*). Tel Aviv: Open University of Israel Press.

Hall, Stuart. 1996. "Introduction: Who Needs 'Identity'?" In Stuart Hall and Paul Gay (eds.), *Questions of Cultural Identity*, 1–17. London: Sage.

Kama, Amit. 2000. "From *Terra Incognita* to *Terra Firma*: The Logbook of the Voyage of Gay Men's Community into the Israeli Public Sphere." *Journal of Homosexuality* 38(4): 133–162.

———. 2003. *The Newspaper and the Closet: Israeli Gay Men's Communication Patterns* (*Ha'iton Veha'aron: Dfusei Tikshoret Shel Homo'im*). Tel Aviv: Hakibbutz Hameukhad.

Klinger, Barbara. 1984. "'Cinema/Ideology/Criticism' Revisited: The Progressive Text." *Screen* 25(1): 30–44.

Kronish, Amy. 1996. *World Cinema: Israel*. Madison, N.J.: Fairleigh Dickinson University Press.

Levy, Emanuel. 1999. *Cinema of Outsiders: The Rise of American Independent Film*. New York and London: New York University Press.

Loshitzky, Yosefa. 1998. "The Bride of the Dead: Phallocentrism and War in *Himmo, King of Jerusalem*" (*Kalat Hamet: Phallocentrism Umilkhama BeKhimmo Melekh Yerushalayim*). In Nurith Gertz, Orly Lubin, and Judd Ne'eman (eds.), *Fictive Looks: On Israeli Cinema* (*Mabatim Fiktivi'im Al Kolno'a Yisra'eli*), 247–260. Tel Aviv: Open University of Israel Press.

———. 2002. *Identity Politics on the Israeli Screen*. Austin: University of Texas Press.

Naaman, Dorit. 2001. "Orientalism as Alterity in Israeli Cinema." *Cinema Journal* 40(4): 36–54.

Padva, Gilad. 2005a. "Films, Youth and Educators." In James T. Sears (ed.), *Youth, Education, and Sexualities: An International Encyclopedia*, vol. 1, 321–328. 2 vols. Westport, Conn.: Greenwood Press.

———. 2005b. "Israel, Filmmaking." In David Gerstner (ed.), *Routledge International Encyclopedia of Queer Culture: Gay, Lesbian, Bisexual and Transsexual Contemporary Cultures*, 312–313. New York and London: Routledge.

———. 2008. "Cinema." In James T. Sears (ed.), *The Greenwood Encyclopedia of Love, Courtship, and Sexuality through History*, vol. 6: *The Modern World*, 42–46. Westport, Conn.: Greenwood Press.

Padva, Gilad, and Miri Talmon. 2008. "Gotta Have an Effeminate Heart: The Politics of Effeminacy and Sissyness in a Nostalgic Israeli TV Musical." *Feminist Media Studies* 8(1): 69–84.

Rich, B. Rubi. 1992. "A Queer Sensation." *Village Voice*, March 24, 4–41.

Schechter, Madeleine. 1994. "Defining the Grotesque: An Aesthetics of Liminality." PhD dissertation. Tel Aviv University.

Shohat, Ella. 1989. *Israeli Cinema: East/West and the Politics of Representation*. Austin: University of Texas Press.

Talmon, Miri. 2001. *Israeli Graffiti: Nostalgia, Groups, and Collective Identity in Israeli Cinema* (*Bluz Latzabar Ha'avud: Khavurot Venostalgia Bakolno'a Hayisra'eli*). Tel Aviv and Haifa: Open University of Israel Press and Haifa University Press.

Turner, Victor. 1982. *From Ritual to Theatre: The Human Seriousness of Play*. New York: Performing Arts Journal Publications.

Tzimmerman, Moshe. 2003. *A Hole in the Camera: Studies in Israeli Cinema* (*Khor Bamatzlema: Iyunim Bakolno'a Hayisra'eli*). Tel Aviv: Resling.

Vicinus, Martha. 1981. "Helpless and Unfriended: Nineteenth-Century Domestic Melodrama." *New Literary History* 13(1): 127–143.

Yosef, Raz. 2004. *Beyond Flesh: Queer Masculinities and Nationalism in Israeli Cinema*. New Brunswick, N.J.: Rutgers University Press.

FILMOGRAPHY

After (Israel, 1990). Director: Eytan Fox.

Amazing Grace (*Hessed Mufla*, Israel, 1992). Director: Amos Guttman.

Amos Guttman, Filmmaker (*Amos Guttman, Bamai Kolno'a*, Israel, 1997). Director: Ran Kozer.

And Thou Shalt Love (*Veahavta*, Israel, 2008). Director: Chaim Elbaum.

Bar 51—Sister of Love (*Bar 51*, Israel, 1985). Director: Amos Guttman.

The Bubble (*Habu'ah*, Israel, 2006). Director: Eytan Fox.

Cause of Death: Homophobia (*Sibat Hamavet—Homofobia*, Israel, 2004). Director: Ran Kozer.

Crows (*Orvim*, Israel, 1987). Director: Ayelet Menahemi.

Don't Cry For Me, Edinburgh (*Edinboro Lo Mekhaka Li*, Israel, 1996). Director: Erez Laufer.

Drifting (the short version) (*Nagu'a*, Israel, 1979). Director: Amos Guttman.

Drifting (the long version) (*Nagu'a*, Israel, 1982). Director: Amos Guttman.

Eastern Wind (aka: *Hamsin*; *Khamsin*, Israel, 1982). Director: Dan Wachsmann.

Florentine (TV series) (Israel, 1997–2001). Director: Eytan Fox.

The Garden (*Gan*, Israel, 2003). Directors: Ruthie Schatz and Adi Barash.

Gay Days (*Hazman Havarod*, Israel, 2009). Director: Yair Qedar.

The Gay Games (*Miskhakim Alizim*, Israel, 1999). Director: Ran Kozer.

Good Boys (*Yeladim Tovim*, Israel, 2005). Director: Yair Hochner.

Gotta Have Heart (TV musical) (*Ba'al Ba'al Lev*, Israel, 1997). Director: Eytan Fox.

He Walked through the Fields (*Hu Halakh Basadot*, Israel, 1967). Director: Yosef Millo.

Hide and Seek (*Makhvo'im*, Israel, 1980). Director: Dan Wolman.

Hill 24 Doesn't Answer (*Giv'a 24 Eina Ona*, Israel, 1955). Director: Thorold Dickinson.

Himmo, King of Jerusalem (*Khimmo Melekh Yerushaluyim*, Israel, 1987). Director: Amos Guttman.

It Kinda Scares Me (*Tomer Vehasrutim*, Israel, 2001). Director: Tomer Heymann.

Moments de la vie d'une femme (*Rega'im*, Israel/France, 1979). Director: Michal Bat-Adam.

Mommy, I Didn't Kill Your Daughter (*Imma, Lo Haragti Et Habat Shelakh*, Israel, 2007). Director: Orna Ben-Dor.

Mommy Queerest—Johnny (TV series) (*Johnny*, Israel, 2002–2003). Creators: Itzik Cohen and Jonathan Koniak.

My Israeli Platoon (*Hayekhida Hatzvai't Sheli*, Israel, 2009). Director: Roy Raz

On My Way Home (*Baderekh Habayta*, Israel, 2010). Director: Tomer Heymann.

Open Cards (TV talk show) (*Klafim Ptukhim*, Israel, 1997). Editor: Sary Amiram. Director: Shabtai Kaminer.

Operation Jonathan (aka *Operation Thunderbolt*; *Mivtza Yonatan*, Israel, 1977). Director: Menahem Golan.

The Other War (*Hamilkhama Hashniya*, Israel, 2008). Director: Tamar Glezerman.

Positive Story (*Sipur Khiyuvi*, Israel, 1996). Director: Ran Kotzer.

Repeat Premieres (*Premyerot Khozrot*, Israel, 1977). Director: Amos Guttman.

Sabra (*Tzabar*, Palestine/Eretz Israel, 1933). Director: Alexander Ford.

Safe Place (*Makom Batu'akh*, Israel, 1977). Director: Amos Guttman.

Send Me an Angel (*Shlakh Li Mal'akh*, Israel, 2003). Director: Nir Ne'eman.

Song of the Siren (*Shirat Hasirena*, Israel, 1994). Director: Eytan Fox.

Tied Hands (*Yadayim Kshurot*, Israel, 2006). Director: Dan Wolman.

Too Hot in Tel Aviv (*Tel Aviv Lohetet*, Israel, 2006). Directors: Motti Banana and Roy Raz.

Walk on Water (*Lalekhet Al Hamayim*, Israel/Sweden, 2004). Director: Eytan Fox.

Yellow Peppers (*Pilpelim Tzhubim*, Israel, 2001). Directors: Ronit Fox and Tamar Barkai.

Yossi and Jagger (*Yossi VeJagger*, Israel, 2002). Director: Eytan Fox.

23 Kibbutz Films in Transition

From Morality to Ethics

ELDAD KEDEM

The question is not: is it true? But: does it work?
What new thoughts does it make possible to think?
What new emotions does it make possible to feel?
What new sensations and perception does it open in the body?
Massumi (2003: 10)

What does Israeli cinema say about kibbutz life? Does it try to tell the "truth," reveal untold stories of conflicts, tensions, and violence behind the kibbutz myth, as for example many films from the 1980s do?[1] Or does it criticize kibbutz ideology but at the same time also make possible another mode of thinking about it, as do some films from the late 1990s on? What are some of the trends in the representation of kibbutz life on film? Do Israeli films repeat many of the same stories, characters, and social conflicts or do they go beyond them to transform the way we understand the kibbutz idea, past and present?

This essay examines the transition from the former group of films to the latter and charts a shift in the treatment of the idea of kibbutz on the screen, a transition from what I would call "morality" to "ethics." Morality, according to Gilles Deleuze, is a way of judging life, whereas ethics is a way of assessing what we do in terms of existing in the world.[2] Morality implies that we judge ourselves and others on the basis of what we are and should be, whereas ethics implies that we do not yet know what we might become. Ethics, as used by Deleuze and his longtime collaborator Félix Guattari, is a term that refers to a different way of thinking about the connections between social production and conceptual production. The opening citation reflects this ethical mode of thinking, in which spirit I ask: can recent kibbutz films pave the way for new thoughts, new sensations and emotions, regarding cinema as well as concerning the kibbutz?

A "Moral" Reading of Kibbutz Films, 1980s–2000s

From the beginning of the 1980s kibbutz films were strongly influenced by screenwriters' and directors' liberal-humanist agenda, evident in films such as *Noa at 17* (*No'a Bat 17*, Yeshurun, 1982), *Atalia* (Tevet, 1984), *Stalin's Disciples* (*Yaldei Stalin*, Levitan, 1987), and *Once We Were Dreamers* (*Hakholmim*, Barbash, 1987). The historical backdrop was the reaction to and disillusionment with the 1982 Lebanon War, the continued occupation of the West Bank and Gaza, and a profound disappointment with the Labor party and with outdated Zionist values. All of these films return to the distant or recent past to criticize kibbutz society, values, and ideology. The reexamination of the past embodies the filmmakers' dissatisfaction with the moral decline and nationalistic trends of the times. The symbolic place that the kibbutz had in Zionist history made it an obvious focus for criticizing and deconstructing Zionist ideology.

The most dominant theme in these films is the clash between kibbutz values and ideology and the desires and needs of the individual—the oppression of the "other," as Nurith Gertz argues: "The cinema of the outcast and the alien recurred, then, in national cinema, confronted it, criticized it, and in this way attempted to build a new model out of its doctrines and content."[3] In the kibbutz films mentioned above, ideological collectivism and a totalitarian approach to equality are presented as the cause of the individual's oppression, especially of those who are different. The uncompromising idealism and group pressure are shown as the cause of destructive personal distress.

For example: *Noa at 17* is a drama that revisits the early 1950s and the political storms that resulted in a rift in the kibbutz movement.[4] Noa is a young girl who along with her friends plans the educational program for their youth group. The group also prepares to join a kibbutz. Noa is aware of the falsity of the political slogans that her friends repeat and searches for a way to express herself in the face of her friends' conformity. Meanwhile, a distraught uncle arrives from the kibbutz for a visit and draws Noa's parents into political discussions and to the brink of a family rift. Noa chooses to rebel against her friends from the youth movement, thus losing her boyfriend as well as her best friend, and remains alone, adhering to her own personal beliefs.[5]

Atalia's distinctive way of dressing in *Atalia* is perceived as sexually pro-vocative in her kibbutz. Her affair with a young soldier results in angry looks and poisonous gossip. Members of the kibbutz think of her as the kibbutz harlot, which prompts one of them to abuse her sexually. In *Once We Were Dreamers* the harsh demand to turn over all private property to the collective, even intimate belongings, is one of the reasons for a com-mune member's suicide. As Miri Talmon writes, the film "makes a clear intergenerational connection between the 'pioneers' and the shattering of the dream, which is the experience that the audience and the individual filmgoer faced at the end of the eighties."[6]

In *Stalin's Disciples* the choice given to the Holocaust survivor—to refuse to take the reparations money from Germany or to put it into the collective kibbutz fund—is presented as abusive cruelty toward an ailing survivor.[7] These and other problems create negative, intrusive dynamics within the closed community. They highlight the negative side of communal life, the hypocrisy, insularity, and arbitrariness. The ideological rigidity is depicted as causing intolerance, blindness, and emotional indifference toward the individual.

Directors and critics in these films judge and evaluate the past through the prism of morality, determining through that particular lens whether kibbutz life was good or evil, right or wrong, just or unjust, positive or nega-tive. Their subjectivity can be gleaned from the subjugation of the fictional world to the judgment of a single perspective, from reflexive categories and binary oppositions. In *Noa at 17* it is the triumph of the individual over the collective. In *Once We Were Dreamers* it is life against death. In *Stalin's Dis-ciples* it is the choice between complete harmony and madness. And in *Atalia* it is perfect solidarity as opposed to estrangement from the community and alienation. Morality in those films emerges as criticism of and resentment toward kibbutz life on the basis of what it should have been and has failed to become and in a more general context what the Zionist enterprise did not succeed in accomplishing and maintaining.

During the 1990s very few films focused on the kibbutz. While new the-matic trends were developing in the Israeli film industry, films relating to the kibbutz did not differ much from the discontented fare of the previous decade. In fact, the kibbutz was represented in even harsher terms than be-fore, as being an antisocial place in a state of conflict and degeneration and with no prospects of improvement. The notion of an ultimate social and ide-ological crisis is evident in films such as *No Names on the Doors* (*Ein Shemot Al Hadlatot*, Levitan, 1996), *No Longer 17* (*Kvar Lo Bat 17*, Yeshurun, 2003), *The Galilee Eskimos* (*Eskimosim Bagalil*, Paz, 2006), and in a more modest and implicit manner also in *Operation Grandma* (*Mivtza Savta*, Shaul, 1999), *Sweet Mud* (*Adamah Meshuga'at*, Shaul, 2006), and the documentaries *Mother of the Gevatron* (*Imma Shel Hagevatron*, Magen and Gil, 2003), *Children of the Sun* (*Yaldei Hashemesh*, Tal, 2007), and *Eight Twenty-eight* (*Shmone-Esrim Ushmone*, Ben Gal, 2007).

Most of these films also echo the crisis in the kibbutz movement, which erupted in the mid-1980s and has continued to unfold ever since. Among many other causes, the crisis was a result of deflated financial resources, new free market policies, inflation, bad investments, and the collapse of Israeli banks in 1983.[8] Many kibbutzim discovered that they owed billions of shekels in debts that they could not repay. As a result, they lowered living standards, which prompted many members to leave and find a better future elsewhere.

Toward the end of the 1980s some predicted the end of the kibbutz in its historic cooperative form and recommended radical structural changes in order to save it, especially privatization.[9] This involved transferring the responsibility for earning money from the kibbutz to individual members, separating the business side of the kibbutz from the community, minimizing the members' dependency on the kibbutz, and drastically cutting the kibbutz movement's bureaucracy. The previous system of mutual assistance still applies, but only regarding guarantees to the elderly founding members, who receive a pension from the cooperative's treasury, and the guarantee of a minimal wage for weaker populations.[10]

The body of films from the 1990s forward that relate to the kibbutz should be considered in this context as well. Some of the films relate to the kibbutz crisis directly, while others are associated with it indirectly. But echoes of the failure of the Zionist-socialist hegemony and the collapse of one of the chief symbols of this hegemony, the kibbutz, can be found in various modes in all these films. In *No Longer 17* the kibbutz secretary announces that the kibbutz has found itself with a debt of 40 million dollars. The only way out of this disaster is to absorb young members and transfer the older members to another kibbutz or a retirement home in the city. The film deals with generational conflicts, betrayal, death, and exile. As one film journalist wrote, "ideas of solidarity and self-realization were distorted into lies, deceit, and wickedness. On the personal and social level . . . the subject of the film is treachery and betrayal of faith."[11]

Other films from the last decade seem to highlight similar themes and ideas. In *The Galilee Eskimos* the eighty-year-old ailing kibbutz founders wake up one morning and find out that all the other members and families have left the kibbutz. They later realize that the kibbutz has been sold to a real estate tycoon and try unsuccessfully to fight back. *No Names on the Doors* portrays the loneliness, alienation, and despair of a widow, an elderly sick father and his retarded son, and two bachelors living in a kibbutz. In similar ways, *Sweet Mud* describes the hostility and oppression against the weak and the outsider, the sick mother and her Swiss lover. *Operation Grandma* is a short comedy that describes the ridiculous efforts of three brothers, ex-kibbutz members, to bring their grandmother to rest in the kibbutz cemetery. The film parodies and mocks kibbutz authorities, norms, and rituals. *Mother of the Gevatron* is a documentary film whose subject matter and themes resemble those of the dramatic films of the era. The film delineates the rise and fall of the Gevatron, a vocal ensemble made up entirely of Kibbutz Geva members (the ensemble was founded in 1948 and remained very popular until the end of the 1970s). Another documentary, *Children of the Sun*, is a nostalgic and traumatic gesture toward the outdated and disappearing culture of the traditional kibbutz.

No Longer 17 focuses on two major crises in the kibbutz society: the economic and ideological predicaments facing kibbutzim and the fact that young people abandon the kibbutz and sometimes settle abroad. The first issue is already presented in the film's opening scene, when it is announced in the general assembly that the kibbutz has gone bankrupt. The second focus is presented through the demise of a local dynasty and the scattering of its offspring in the Diaspora. The second generation has left the country to make a living abroad, while the third generation backpacks around India and South America. These themes converge to create a sense of alienation in a place that was once the symbol of the Zionist national homeland. Similar themes of disappointment, betrayal, and transience can be found in *Sweet Mud*, *No Names on the Doors*, *The Galilee Eskimos*, *Operation Grandma*, and *Children of the Sun*.

The stories in all of these films are organized around binary oppositions that generally depict the shattered dream. If in the past the kibbutz symbolized a dynamic, developing entity facing a secure future, these films convey a sense of dead end, decline, and death. Alienation is expressed through an inability to integrate into the geographical place and through motifs of wandering and exile. All of these constitute an antithesis to the classic Zionist vision of building both a private and a national home. They are represented in an amplified manner in the films through references to death, suicide, exile, and abandonment as well as an atmosphere of detachment and transience. Past experience seems to be disconnected and insignificant, while the future seems unclear or hidden from view.

In various ways, all of these films deconstruct myths, ideals, and symbols identified with the kibbutz, including solidarity, harmony, and equality. Egalitarian ideals of helping the old and the infirm are replaced by capitalist considerations of a market economy, such as efficiency, expediency, profit, and loss. These coalesce into an inverted binary construction, which corresponds with Israeli and kibbutz films produced from the 1930s to the 1960s. This polar structure is summarized in Table 23.1.

All of these films rebel against the kibbutz as an ideological "father figure" and especially against the founders of kibbutzim as a metonym for Zionism and the state. Their Oedipal focalization revolves around the question of how to reject, dishonor, and disavow the Zionist ideology as condensed in the idea of the kibbutz and how to become free of it. Aptly enough, the rebellion against the Zionist symbolic father in these "morally critical" films is signified by images of flawed masculinity connected with madness, illness, cruelty, and deviant sexuality.[12]

Table 23.1. The Kibbutz in Past and Present Films

1930–1960s	1980–2010
Utopia/the dream	Dystopia/the shattered dream
Socialism	Capitalism
Agricultural labor	Commercial enterprises
Innovativeness	Anachronism
Social justice	Discrimination
Harmony/solidarity	Competition/conflict
Productivity/fertility	Sterility
Honesty and mutual respect	Hypocrisy and exploitation
A "sanctified" place	A "secularized" place

As Deleuze and Guattari state, however, "the question of the father isn't how to become free in relation to him, an Oedipal question, but how to find a path where he didn't find any."[13] In light of this observation, I would like to suggest that a few of the films, especially those made by younger filmmakers, such as *Operation Grandma, Mother of the Gevatron, Sweet Mud, Children of the Sun,* and *Eight Twenty-eight,* have found a path and a way out in relation to the symbolic father—the kibbutz. More importantly, they allow a different approach, considering our understanding and engagement with these images. The next section focuses on the notion of transition from morality to ethics, from judgment and the burden of higher and transcendent values to experimentation and affirmation.

An Ethical Turn: Thinking with—Not about—Contemporary Kibbutz Films

I suggest that a few of these recent kibbutz films, produced in an era of social and cultural transformation in Israel, allow for a different approach, an alternative methodology, and a new way of thinking about them. It is possible and legitimate to consider questions such as: What do films reflect and represent? What are the filmmaker's positions and beliefs or the veiled meanings and overall structure that they contain? Do films actually express the truth, or do they manipulate it? How do films reproduce and disseminate one ideology or another?

Yet we can also engage with film in other ways and raise a different set of questions, problems, and ethics, such as: What does a movie do? What kinds of links does it enable us to create? Is it possible to suggest a political interpretation that not only deals with the macro-political level (the ideology and mythology of the nation or large groups in society) but offers an interpretation on the micro-political level as well—politics that take place in a complex of lines, planes, forces, and relationships? For example, can these films be considered not representations of reality with ideological significance but experimentations that make it possible to rethink the connection to place, time, and space, without organizing them into a coherent arrangement or an organized spatial representation? Such a methodological shift reflects significant political and ethical issues as well as aspects of film theory.

Sweet Mud takes place on a kibbutz in 1974 and describes the coming of age of twelve-year-old Dvir.[14] In the course of his bar mitzvah year, the boy has to perform various coming-of-age ceremonies, which mark the transition from childhood to adulthood. Since Dvir's father committed suicide, he has been reared by his mother, an eccentric woman who gradually loses her mind after her elderly Swiss lover is expelled from the kibbutz over an incident with one of its prominent members.

In terms of morality it seems as though *Sweet Mud* articulates meanings and ideologies represented in the 1980s films discussed above. The film revisits the past in order to describe the harsh clash between alleged kibbutz values and individual weak members. The choice between right and wrong, good and evil, proper and improper, seems to be very clear. As one critic wrote: "Something is rotten in the Zionist endeavor. . . . Shaul created this film in order to examine once and for all what went wrong with such a promising project."[15] Another reviewer argued that the author "burns alive the kibbutz collective of the 1970s, an idealistic way of life, [that is represented as] irrational and inhuman, [and] that represses the individual."[16]

I suggest that *Sweet Mud* can also provide an escape and a way out of judgment and morality. The film fractures the macro-politics of the individual versus the collective and creates multiple micro-relations, subcoalitions, and subspaces within the kibbutz and its surroundings. It suggests proximity between very different situations and experiences and a zigzag between various states of desire.

Certain elements express deterritorialization, in the sense of movement that creates a change, forcing disarticulation, freeing up fixed relations that contain a body, and all the while exposing it to new organizations. The term "body" here refers to the protagonist as well as to the film or the kibbutz. Deterritorialization is thus tied to the possibility of change immanent in a given territory or any given body, but this change often implies new fixed connections and rigid limitations—that is, reterritorialization. Deleuze and Guattari suggest, for example, that memory yields reterritorialization of childhood.[17]

At least seven scenes in the film feature a solitary tree on a hill, for instance, in the background or foreground of the mise-en-scène. The tree serves Dvir as a hiding place and a refuge from personal and social chaos in some scenes and as a lookout post and a spy hole in others. Sometimes the tree is a place of forbidden pleasures, and on other occasions it is a secret meeting place for Dvir and his mother. In addition, the tree is an intersection between inside and outside, like a border marking the end of the known world, and a launching pad for sensation, experimentations, imagination, and intuition. But the tree, framed and shot against the horizon, is also an interface between earth and sky, between the infinite universe and the microscopic mineral composition of the earth. In addition, the tree changes its texture and vibrations according to the seasons into which the film is divided.

The tree scenes are movement-images that recur each time with different qualities and intensities, as an action-image, a perception-image, and an affection-image.[18] As an action-image or index, it folds and unfolds milieus and modes of behavior, inhabited and territorialized space and time. As a perception-image, it unfolds a mental landscape of disconnected and disorganized space, a sensation of a boundless territory and a space of potentials and choices. As an affection-image, it renders visible sensations of adolescence, affecting and augmenting the power of the protagonist to act, to create, or to connect with human and nonhuman bodies. Thus the audience can share with Dvir the sensation of a sonorous landscape. We can sense the tree as a refrain and a developing variation as well as a melodic landscape and a soothing lullaby in the face of personal-familial chaos. The tree returns like a refrain and a loop that disarticulates or deterritorializes hierarchical values or a fully constructed signifier, whether it is a kibbutz or a subject. Hence all these possibilities and sensual qualities act in proximity and precede representation and manifestation of institutional power.

The film establishes the protagonist's desire as one based on lack and on loss, the absence of the father and the silence and madness of the mother. At the same time, the initiation ceremonies as well as the tree scenes suggest that desire is not pregiven or blocked but is produced and proliferates through connections and encounters that break through the boundaries of the subject or territorialized functions. Desire as a process is produced via encounters with impersonal prereflexive forces and intensities of mineral, topographical, and meteorological sensations. Desire is produced and transferred as the protagonist-film-viewer comes into contact with day and night, sunrise and sunset, earth and water, light and darkness, plants and animals, and the whole wide spectrum that relates to perception of colors, smells, voices, and rhythms (some are human and some are not). Those encounters affirm the powers of love as expressed through the forces of the seasons, temperatures, soil, and multiplicitous molecular connections—the topography of life being lived.

I would argue, in conclusion, that experimentation and affirmation emerge as the film swings between the surfaces that stratify a subject or a territory and the plane that sets them free. Another example: in one scene, the grandmother gives Dvir jars of homemade jam and a list of names, after deleting a hostile member from the list. Nevertheless, this act of territorialization, imposing limits, authority, and social order—an act that blocks desire—is immediately deterritorialized. We see Dvir riding his bike with his dog through a boundless space, where the line between inside and outside is being blurred and the excitement of movement and speed emerges.

The "blacklist" as a reactive force is transformed into an affective and active force depicted through the bodily experimentation and sensations of movement, speed, rhythms, and the potential to move in multiple directions.

This multiple and simultaneous movement, of stratifying and setting free, of territorialization and deterritorialization, is evident in other films of the last decade, like the award-winning documentary *Eight Twenty-eight*. The film narrativizes, telling about the director's departure from his kibbutz. After living a few years in Tel Aviv and graduating from film school, twenty-eight-year-old Lavi received a letter asking him to decide whether he wanted to return to the kibbutz or leave it and lose his rights in the community. The film becomes his farewell to his childhood home, containing a mixture of interviews with old kibbutz members and a portrait of places that are gone or disappearing, like the local synagogue and the empty children's houses. It also presents nostalgic archival footage of childhood and holiday ceremonies on the kibbutz.

The palpable sense of a paradise lost in the film, where the dismal kibbutz in the present is compared with its idyllic past and is laced with the longing and melancholy of the departure, is relatively expected and common (as in *Children of the Sun*, for instance). Nevertheless, the film also transcends that through the irony and self-reflexive tone of the voice-over commentator and several experimental scenes. In one of them, "nine paths," the narrator, Lavi, observes: "Between my house and my parents' house there are nine paths: the path to the library, the path to the soccer field, the path to the swimming pool, the path to the new neighborhood, the path to the dining room, . . . but I like to cross in-between paths." We see a montage of nine shots, each conveying a different path with its unique texture, materiality, direction, composition, atmosphere, rhythm, and intensity. In the next shots a dog literally speaks, asking Lavi why he left the kibbutz. The scene expresses sensations and experimentation: sensations of the human body as it encounters other bodies, human and nonhuman, as well as cinematic experimentation with space, movement, and variations—a motionless journey.

Again I would point to the coexistence or convergence of stratifying and setting free at one and the same time. A childhood memory of an absent home and fantasies of a lost paradise, and of blocked and oppressed desire, are met with a gesture of improvisation, creativity, and experimentation and with an emerging desire that proliferates its connections. Each path gives out a sensation of texture, materiality, noise, rhythm, direction, composition, and atmosphere; these are reminiscent of the developing variation and the melodic landscape mentioned earlier. What seems to be a familiar representation—the same kibbutz, the same paths, and the same losses—becomes a new beginning, affirming the power of the new and the unforeseeable.

As argued earlier, these representations involve different movement-images. The paths function as an action-image of milieus, territorialized space, and social functions, a perception-image that expresses a mental landscape of boundless territory, disconnected from its everyday use, and an affection-image, the sensation of the human body as it encounters other bodies, as it affects and is being affected and thus becoming-other. As Laura Marks explains: "In the affection-image, a becoming-other occurs; for as soon as we have sensation or feeling, we change. Thus, in the affection-image there is an enfolding of perceiving self into perceived world."[19]

The question that arises, then, is how can these sensations and becoming-other be attributed to *Sweet Mud* and *Eight Twenty-eight?* Perhaps it is the sensation of being lost and found, or the sensation of fusing with the world, the sensation of a fresh beginning, the excitement of exploring unknown territories, the magic of appearance, or traveling without moving: "but I like to cross in-between paths": that is, I intervene, I create a change, I become active, I become imperceptible—catch me if you can!

These films are also an experimentation of filmic articulation concerning the kibbutz space, as they intervene and thus deterritorialize the "dogmatic" image of the kibbutz as a social institution into a network of relations and forces. It becomes an ethical gesture through the affirmation of the productive and creative forces of life being lived. Instead of just seeing these films as judging, preaching, or patronizing their subject matter (the kibbutz), they can also restore our belief in the world and in our experience of it, even when it seems to be falling apart.

Epilogue

"There is always a place, a tree or grove, in the territory, where the forces come together in a hand-to-hand combat of energies."[20] The kibbutz is such a place, with its trees and paths, as I mentioned above. In kibbutz films there is always a grove, or at least a grave or a cemetery, expressing the forces of life and death. The combat of energies might be evolving around staying or leaving, the ideal past versus the fallen present, ideology and its aftermath. But, as I have suggested, we should also consider the forces and movements of thought, release thinking from the obvious and commonsense (morality), and expose it to new organizations, new sensations, and new applications concerning subject, concepts, and being.

NOTES

The term "kibbutz films" refers mostly to feature or drama films such as *Atalia* or *Sweet Mud*, which take place in a kibbutz, but also to films such as *Sallah, He Walked through the Fields*, and *Noa at 17*, where kibbutz characters and images play a significant role. I also include under this heading films about the first communes in Palestine, such as *Once We Were Dreamers*.

1. At that time Israeli cinema was preoccupied with politics. Gertz (1993: 176).

2. Marks (2005: 85).

3. Gertz (1993: 17 and a wider discussion, 175–217).

4. The split in the kibbutzim was known as "Ha-pilug," 1951–1954.

5. As Miri Talmon (2001: 152) writes: "*Noa at 17* reflects the struggle with the decline of collectivism and socialism as ideological and social norms. . . . Kibbutz society and the workers' settlements began to be exposed as crumbling frameworks holding onto ideals that have lost their strength in Israeli society."

6. Ibid., 99.

7. After World War II and the Holocaust, some of the survivors were absorbed in kibbutzim. According to the egalitarian ideals of the kibbutz, the reparation money had to be deposited into the communal fund.

8. See detailed discussions of this matter in Ben-Rafael, Ya'ar, and Soker (2000).

9. For example, see Harel (1993: 165–241).

10. A small number of kibbutzim remain whose members support the retention of the old cooperative structure.

11. Fuchs (2003). *No Longer 17* (2003) is a film sequel to *Noa at 17* (1982). The director, Yitzhak Yeshurun, wished to revisit the characters from the previous film after twenty years. The same actors play the chief roles—Noa, her mother, and her uncle from the kibbutz.

12. See, for instance, the bestiality scene in the opening of *Sweet Mud* that involves one of the leaders of the community.

13. Deleuze and Guattari (1986: 7–8).

14. *Sweet Mud* won the Israel Film Academy's prize for best film of 2006. It was chosen to represent Israel at the Academy Awards competition in Hollywood. In January 2007 the film won first prize in the foreign film category at the Sundance Film Festival.

15. Shavit (2006: 13).

16. Mokhiakh (2006: 1).

17. Deleuze and Guattari (1986: 70–78). Generally speaking, any organism or body is subjected to a constant process of territorialization, deterritorialization, and reterritorialization. For example, the debts of the kibbutzim that I mentioned earlier caused a significant deterritorialization of the social and economic structures of the kibbutzim. The outcome is a necessity to reterritorialize various functions, such as new occupations for some of the members. The process might end in a new arrangement of the kibbutz topography, a new distribution of the land—that is, a different kind of territorialization. Obviously, this process affects personal issues and private bodies.

18. Following Henri Bergson, Deleuze finds three specialized images: the "perception-image," whereby the living image senses the world outside; the "action-

image," which structures the space surrounding the living image; and the "affection-image," which connects the living image's outer perception, inner feelings, and motor responses to other images. Cited in Bogue (2003: 4).
   19. Marks (2000: 197).
   20. Deleuze and Guattari (2003: 321).

BIBLIOGRAPHY

Ben-Rafael, Eliezer, Ephraim Ya'ar, and Ze'ev Soker. 2000. *The Kibbutz and Israeli Society: Continuity and Change (Hakibbutz Vehakhevra Hayisra'elit: Hemshekhiut Veshinui)*. Tel Aviv: Open University Press.
Bogue, Ronald. 2003. *Deleuze on Cinema*. New York: Routledge.
Deleuze, Gilles. 1986. *Cinema 1: The Movement-Image* (1983). London: Athlone Press.
Deleuze, Gilles, and Félix Guattari. 1986. *Kafka: Toward a Minor Literature* (1975). Minneapolis: University of Minnesota Press.
———. 2003. *A Thousand Plateaus: Capitalism and Schizophrenia*. Minneapolis: University of Minnesota Press.
Fuchs, Sarit. 2003. "The Main Thing Is the Exercise" (*Ha'ikar Hatarguil*). *Ma'ariv*, Culture Supplement, October 31.
Gertz, Nurith. 1993. *Motion Fiction: Israeli Fiction in Film (Sipur Mehasratim: Siporet Yisra'elit Ve'ibudeihah Lakolno'a)*. Tel Aviv: Open University Press.
Harel, Yehuda. 1993. *The New Kibbutz (Hakibbutz Hekhadash)*. Jerusalem: Keter Press.
Kedem, Eldad. 2007. "The Kibbutz and Israeli Cinema: Deterritorializing Representation and Ideology." PhD diss. University of Amsterdam.
Marks, John. 2005. "Ethics." In *The Deleuze Dictionary*, ed. Adrian Parr, 85–86. New York: Columbia University Press.
Marks, U. Laura. 2000. "Signs of Time: Deleuze, Peirce, and the Documentary Image." In *The Brain Is the Screen: Deleuze and the Philosophy of Cinema*, ed. Gregory Flaxman, 193–214. Minneapolis: University of Minnesota Press.
Massumi, Brian. 2003. "Introduction." In *A Thousand Plateaus: Capitalism and Schizophrenia* by Gilles Deleuze and Félix Guattari, ix–xv. Minneapolis: University of Minnesota Press.
Mokhiakh, Nakhum. 2006. "Sweet Mud" (*Adamah Meshuga'at*). *Habama*, September 17. www.habama.co.il/newscomplete.
Shavit, Avner. 2006. "Something Is Rotten in the Zionist Enterprise" (*Mashehu Rakuv Bamifal Hatzioni*). *Ha'ir*, September 28.
Stivale, J. Charles (ed.). 2005. *Gilles Deleuze, Key Concepts*. Stocksfield: Acumen Publishing.
Talmon, Miri. 2001. *Israeli Graffiti: Nostalgia, Groups, and Collective Identity in Israeli Cinema (Bluz Latzabar Ha'avud: Khavurot Venostalgia Bakolno'a Hayisra'eli)*. Tel Aviv: Open University and Haifa: University of Haifa Press.

FILMOGRAPHY

Atalia. DVD. Directed by Akiva Tevet. 1984. Jerusalem, Israel: Ulpanei Habira, Golan-Globus.

Children of the Sun (Yaldei Hashemesh). DVD. Directed by Ran Tal. 2007. Or Yehuda, Israel: Hed Artzi.

Eight Twenty-eight (Shmone-Esrim Ushmone). DVD. Directed by Lavi Ben Gal. 2007. Tel Aviv, Israel: Claudius Films.

The Galilee Eskimos (Eskimosim Bagalil). Directed by Jonathan Paz. 2006. Israel.

Mother of the Gevatron (Imma Shel Hagevatron). Video. Directed by Shahar Magen and Ayelet Gil. 2003. Tel Aviv, Israel: Third Ear.

Noa at 17 (No'a Bat 17). DVD. Directed by Yitzhak Yeshurun. 1982. Netania, Israel: Globus United Ltd.

No Longer 17 (Kvar Lo Bat 17). DVD. Directed by Yitzhak Yeshurun. 2003. Netania, Israel: Globus United Ltd.

No Names on the Doors (Ein Shemot Al Hadlatot). DVD. Directed by Nadav Levitan. 1996. Tel Aviv, Israel: Paralite, Hed Artzi.

Once We Were Dreamers. (aka *Unsettled Land*; *Hakholmim*). DVD. Directed by Uri Barbash. 1987. Israel, a Belbo Film Production, Hemdale Film Corporation.

Operation Grandma (Mivtza Savta). DVD. Directed by Dror Shaul. 1999. Tel Aviv, Israel: Paralite.

Stalin's Disciples (Yaldei Stalin). DVD. Directed by Nadav Levitan. 1987. Ramat Hasharon, Israel: NMC United.

Sweet Mud (Adamah Meshuga'at). DVD. Directed by Dror Shaul. 2006. Netania, Israel: Globus United Ltd.

24 The End of a World, the Beginning of a New World

The New Discourse of Authenticity and New Versions of Collective Memory in Israeli Cinema

MIRI TALMON

Introduction: Cultural Identity, Immigration, and Israeli Cinema

Stuart Hall has argued that cultural identity is about both "being" and "becoming."[1] We constitute ourselves not only as "what we really are" but also in terms of "what we have become," as history intervenes and subjects individuals and communities to traumas of war, immigration, exile, and transition. Cultural identities are those unstable constructs of identification which are made within the discourses of history and culture. They are not essences but positionings, constituted not outside but within representations. Cinema, in this context, is not a mirror held up to our faces, both as individuals and as imagined communities, to reflect our identities as they already exist but a form of representation that enables us to negotiate our identities, discover who we have become, constitute ourselves as new kinds of subjects, and rediscover hidden histories. Discussing how Caribbean cinema negotiates cultural identity by relating to the past, Hall argues:

> It is because this New World is constituted for us as place, a narrative of displacement, that it gives rise so profoundly to a certain imaginary plenitude, recreating the endless desire to return to "lost origins," to be one again with the mother, to go back to the beginning. . . . And yet, this return to "the beginning" is like the "Imaginary" in Lacan—it can neither be fulfilled nor requited, and hence is the beginning of the symbolic, of representation, the infinitely renewable source of desire, memory, myth, search, discovery—in short, the reservoir of our cinematic narratives.[2]

Israel's history and nation-building processes are inextricably bound with traumas of displacement and immigration. In early mythologies constructed in the culture, including Hebrew cinema, such traumas were part of the pre-Zionist exilic phase in the indigenous nation's "prehistory." These traumas are now becoming a constitutive part of Israelis' histories. Their self-consciousness and self-definition are constantly evolving. They are constantly in a state of becoming, still negotiating not only their future but their past as well. This negotiation of the past is no longer collectively generalized as it used to be but is becoming more individualized and in many senses privatized. It is this yearning that Hall describes, to return to an imaginary lost plenitude of an original, stable identity in the past in order to resolve the pains of immigration, indeterminacy, and multilayered identities that feed Israeli cinema's retro and nostalgia imageries and narratives.[3] It is the second generation's quest for severed roots that feeds the narratives of Israeli cinema with personal biographies and Israeli culture with rituals of root searching as well as pilgrimage to original places in the Diaspora.[4] This essay is about the articulation of these trends and the negotiation of Israeli identity and history in Avi Nesher's film *Turn Left at the End of the World* (*Sof Haʾolam Smolah*, 2004).

Authenticity, Take One: Whose Story, Whose History?

The film *Turn Left at the End of the World* was surrounded by debates, which reverberated with past controversies. These past controversies are associated with the popular Israeli genre of the Bourekas films;[5] the film *Shkhur* (Azoulai-Hasfari and Hasfari, 1994) was also controversial.[6] Questions of cinematic quality versus commercialism as well as questions concerning the authenticity of representations—both of ethnic identity and of authorship— are at the core of these debates. In the case of the Bourekas films it had been argued that Mizrahim (Israelis of Middle Eastern/Sephardic heritage) were represented stereotypically and falsely in films mostly created and directed by Ashkenazim (Israelis of European/Western heritage); therefore, it was argued, the films offered an Orientalist, unauthentic perspective of Mizrahim.[7] Furthermore, critics viewed Bourekas films as vulgar commercial products aimed at the lowest common denominator within Israeli audiences and thus both too formulaic to be authentic and not representative of any authentic experience, biography, or collective history of Mizrahim in Israel.

Associated with the Bourekas and criticized for such challenged authenticity was *Sallah* (*Sallah Shabbati*, 1964), a film about a Mizrahi protagonist made by Ephraim Kishon, an immigrant to Israel from Hungary. It achieved both phenomenal success with Israeli audiences when released in 1964 (1,184,000 viewers) and international recognition as well. *Sallah* ran six months in New York's Little Carnegie Theater, was nominated for the Oscar, and won both the Hollywood foreign press Golden Globe Award for best foreign film and the 1964 San Francisco Film Festival awards for best actor (Haim Topol) and best screenplay (Ephraim Kishon).[8] Yet Israeli critics and film scholars, as part of a well-established elitist tradition in academe and cinema institutions of criticism and authorship, dismissed *Sallah* as an example of the debased Bourekas popular genre.[9] They failed to appreciate its subversive, satirical, antihegemonic criticism and the unique elements of Kishon's authorship expressed in the film.

Unlike *Sallah*, the film *Shkhur* was embraced by Israeli critics and by the Israeli Film Academy. It was awarded six Israeli Academy Awards in 1994, including film of the year.[10] Nevertheless, *Shkhur* was bitterly criticized for misrepresenting Mizrahim and their traditions and for distorting the images of the Jewish Moroccan community and its practices—in particular those associated with family, warmth in interpersonal relations, and hospitality on the one hand and with violence, superstition, and primitiveness on the other. Critics claimed that the film confirmed prejudiced images and perpetuated degrading stereotypes that inscribed the backwardness and inferiority of Mizrahim in Israeli society, symbolically extending this backwardness to the third generation.[11] Moreover, they found this confirmation of such distorted prejudices even more problematic because it originated in the Mizrahi intellectual elite itself. The author of the screenplay, Hannah Azoulai-Hasfari, whose family came to Israel from Morocco, links the (distorting) fictional reality in the film with her own biography.

The debates around *Turn Left at the End of the World* focused on similar issues. In spite of the film's phenomenal success at the Israeli box office,[12] the film was not nominated for the significant awards (best film, best director) of the Israeli Film Academy in the 2004 ceremony. Eyebrows as well as printed protests were raised against the academy's denial of the film's qualities and enthusiastic reception by Israeli audiences. In their published protests public figures associated with the Israeli press, entertainment, and politics, some with Mizrahi heritage, echoed the quality/commerciality debate in the film institutions' attitudes toward *Sallah* in particular and the Bourekas genre at large.[13] The Israeli journalists Amnon Dankner and Avi Bettleheim, for example, speculated that the Israeli Film Academy members or a significant number of them might have "decided to disqualify the film because they can not handle the problematic issue that the film raises. As far as they are concerned, the past should be dead and buried and in no way brought to bear upon the current Israeli agenda. They exempt themselves, by saying to themselves or among themselves that this is a Bourekas film and therefore is not worthy of their nominations."[14]

Criticism was directed at the Israeli Film Academy for ignoring not only the film's cinematic quality but its cultural, social, and historical value as well. The narrative of *Turn Left at the End of the World* focused on the traumatic history of the immigration of Mizrahim to Israel and their expulsion to the margins, to development towns in the "Wild South." Supporters of the film claimed that it put this chapter in Israeli history on the screen in a courageous manner and touched open wounds in collective Israeli memory yet was treated as a popular, lightweight film and that its significance in the sociocultural discourse was overlooked.

Along with the debates surrounding the representations of Mizrahim and their history in the film, questions of authenticity related to agency and authorship were raised as well. As in the cases of *Sallah* and *Shkhur*, the question of "who tells the story" of the traumatic absorption of Mizrahim in Israel, and not only "what kind of story" is told, was of great concern. In the case of *Sallah*, it was the Ashkenazi director Kishon's moral authority that was questioned, regarding his ability to reproduce authentic cinematic fictional Mizrahi protagonists, histories, and stories.[15] Such heated debates abounded in regard to the film *Shkhur* as well. In this case, however, criticism was directed at the authenticity of Mizrahi experiences, traditions, and histories in a film created by an autobiographically authentic Mizrahi woman, telling her own story and still blamed for distorted representations of ethnicity and communal history.[16]

In the case of *Turn Left at the End of the World* the public controversy concerned crucial questions of agency and collective memory as well: whose story it was telling and whose traumatic history it was inscribing as a chapter in collective Israeli memory. The director, Avi Nesher, one of the three authors of the script, dedicated this film about two Mizrahi girls coming of age in a southern Israeli small town in the 1960s to his father, Aryeh Nesher, originally Leon Ratter, who passed away in New York on the eve of the production of the film. On the face of it, Nesher's father's own biography, as an Ashkenazi man who immigrated to Israel from Europe, was remote from the film's story about Mizrahi (women's) history. Moreover, the film ends as Sara (one of the female protagonists and the diegetic narrator in the film) concludes in a first-person voice-over that the film's story has to be told so "the world never forgets those lost people who loved us so much."

Who are the "lost people" the film is about? Undoubtedly they are the immigrants whose story is told in the film, lost in the Negev desert in that desolated southern territory that was alien to them. They were lost because they were uprooted from their homelands, their cultures, and struggled as foreign implants to assimilate into the Israeli melting pot, foreign culture, and alienated space. The feminine first-person voice can easily be associated with the voices and biographies of the female authors of the screenplay.[17] Yet, in journalistic interviews and in the director's commentary for the film's DVD, Nesher articulates his creative credo.[18] He comments that the film is about the whole lost generation of immigrants to Israel, parents like his own, who had sacrificed their lives hoping to secure a better future for their children. Those lost people that his film depicts are immigrants like his own father, who immigrated to Israel in the 1940s rather than in the time that the film depicts, the summer of 1968. The Sabra (native-born Israeli) generation, Nesher argues, had no empathy for their helpless, culturally foreign parents and were ashamed of them. The native-born Israeli generation had no real communication with their immigrant parents and could not empathize with the traumatic shattering of their parents' lives that immigration to Israel inevitably entailed.

Nesher's interpretation of his own film universalizes the experience of immigration in the Israeli and global context and also insists upon a new discourse, according to which the trauma of immigration and absorption in Israeli history is not necessarily ethnically bound or exclusively associated with the history of Mizrahim. Moreover, Nesher privatizes or personalizes the collective, national endeavor of immigration and absorption as well as the ethnic experience associated with it; he depicts it from a personal point of view both within the diegesis (fictional world) and as an authorial starting point. In this, Nesher's film becomes another instance of the "second-generation" discourse so characteristic of current Israeli cinema, produced in the 1990s and first decade of the 2000s. The first-person point of view and narration hence offer a personalized version of collective histories.

Israeli films, typically since the 1980s, negotiate Israeli history and specific issues within Israeli culture from a privatized "second-generation" positioning and authorial agency. For example, *The Summer of Aviya* (*Hakayitz Shel Aviya*, dir. Eli Cohen, 1988), which renegotiates 1951, is based on the prominent Israeli actress Gila Almagor's autobiographical story, play, and script. The traumatic immigration of Jews from the Middle East to Israel is cinematically negotiated by authors of the second generation, who invest their biography in their retrospective stories. Hannah Azoulai-Hasfari in *Shkhur* (1994) goes back to her southern development town childhood. Ronit Elkabetz and Shlomi Elkabetz (*To Take a Wife* [*Velakakhta Lekha Isha*], 2004) return to their childhood home in an immigrant neighborhood near

Haifa, where the shattered patriarchal authority of their father and their mother's yearnings to assimilate in a modern, secular Israeli society tore their childhood home apart.

In a similar way, second-generation sons and daughters of the communal experience of the kibbutz produce powerful cinematic texts in which they invest their own individual biographical experiences. At the same time, these personally anchored texts serve as a powerful revisionist critique of collective Israeli enterprises and priorities. In these films the traumas of unconventional communal practices such as collective sleeping in the "children's house" and the collective pressure on individuals (particularly nonconformist or "exceptional" ones) ensue from the private experience, which validates and authenticates the collective social memory. Dror Shaul's feature film *Sweet Mud* (*Adamah Mashuga'at*, 2006) and Ran Tal's documentary *Children of the Sun* (*Yaldei Hashemesh*, 2007) are award-winning examples of this trend.

The demand for authenticity of experience represented in recent Israeli films, and for a critique of Israeli history which is rooted in biographically invested fictional worlds, is one of the reasons for the unprecedented success of Israeli films both in Israel and in worldwide film festivals. It is my contention that one of the causes of the phenomenal popularity of *Turn Left at the End of the World* in Israel is its tapping into collective experiences and traumas shared by individuals from diverse ethnic heritages and different phases of Israeli history of "immigration booms." The personal and biographical coming-of-age story at the core of the film negotiates the experience of immigration in the collective Israeli memory. Furthermore, the cinematic rite of passage or initiation of the teenaged heroines in the film charges the fictional reality with universal dimensions of meaning that turn their personal traumas and experiences of immigration into objects of multicultural identifications, outside of Israel as well.

Although it refers to personal stories and biographies located in a seemingly specific time and place, *Turn Left at the End of the World* implies other stories, meanings, times, and places. The immigrants' story in the film resonates with the histories of others who came to Israel, Palestine, France, or America with a Russian/Polish/German/Iraqi/Moroccan Jewish or other name and changed it, reinventing themselves in the new country—the Promised Land. The film tells a personal and collective story of Mizrahi women, the communal story of the Mizrahi immigration to Israel, and the pains of its unique absorption and cultural integration. Yet it seems to be experienced as reconstructing a more generalized collective Israeli story of immigration and the traumas accompanying it. Kishon mediated his transit camp (Hebrew: *maʾabara*) traumatic immigration experience by using the Mizrahi male Sallah as his mask. In a similar way Avi Nesher, a male director of European heritage, uses the biography of Mizrahi females to mediate both his own personal negotiation of his immigrant parents' experience and the collective Israeli experience of immigration and its pains.

While *Turn Left at the End of the World* echoes a generalized story of immigration in the multicultural and postcolonial contemporary global context, the choice to tell this story from a feminine point of view is highly significant in the cultural Israeli context. The cinematic Israeli master narrative has constructed Israeli nationality and history in allegories of heroic males in crisis and in narratives of male protagonists' initiation. The grand narrative of nation building is told in Hebrew Israeli cinema from masculine points of view, in masculine stories and voices.[19] Nesher's choice to focalize his fictional account of the Israeli experience of immigration from a feminine point of view and base it on a narrative of women coming of age offers a counter-reading of the Israeli experience that goes in tandem with revisionist trends in Israeli cinema ever since the 1980s, and in particular regarding the masculine paradigm.[20]

Figure 24.1. The domestic feminine sphere: the Shusan family kitchen in *Turn Left at the End of the World* (Avi Nesher, 2004). Courtesy of Artomas Communications, Metro Communications, and United King Film.

Figure 24.2. The Israeli public collective sphere of folk dancing, victory, and re vival in *Turn Left at the End of the World* (Avi Nesher, 2004). Courtesy of Artomas Communications, Metro Communications, and United King Film.

Authenticity, Take Two: Nostalgia, Homecoming, and Israeli History

Shkhur's narrative goes back in time to 1972, not coincidentally the year when the Israeli Black Panthers movement changed Israeli consciousness regarding the oppression and frustration of Mizrahim. The film's narrative moves back and forth between two time zones: the present, in which the film heroine Khelli drives back south to her father's funeral, and the past that she painfully relives during that trip and in her childhood home—the realm of the demons, where her mother and her sister Pnina rule.

The film's narrative implies a nostalgic return to childhood, not in a trite nostalgic sense. "Nostalgia" is composed of two ancient Greek words that denote the pain (*algia*) of going back home (*nostos*). We tend to associate nostalgia with the yearning for a sweeter yesterday, a naïve and innocent one. Khelli's journey back home does not create the dialectics—typical of what sociologist Fred Davis characterizes as "primary nostalgia"—of a disillusioned present versus a past full of promise and potential. The alterations between past and present show the adult Khelli looking at herself as a child, on the screen, aware of the painful distance between the past, which is her origin in her flesh and blood family, and the present, which is what she has become. Khelli is doomed to reexperience the process of individuation as a painful separation, without being able to reunite with the plenitude of "origin," as Hall describes it, or meaning of her parents' world.[21]

The analogies between past and present in *Shkhur* create a pessimistic determinism that leaves Khelli aching for her mother's love as well as for her daughter's acknowledgment of her mothering and motherhood. At the end of the film Khelli's daughter, whose communicative skills are challenged, draws her mother's face for her. In her daughter's sketch Khelli is frozen, represented in the image of a child, forever preverbal, infantile: only in this manner is she able to become part of the "backward" world of her daughter, her mother, and her "retarded" sister Pnina. Hence Khelli is doomed to stay frozen in the liminal zone, between two impossible options. On the one hand: the cold, verbal, motherless world of television and "Westernized" Sabra-Israeli civilization. This is the visual, asensual, asexual silent world of progress and rationality, of the "Ashkenized" Israel and northern Tel Aviv, dominated by the symbolic law of the father, of language, of mediated media communication. On the other hand: the preverbal, pre-Oedipal southern, traditional world of her childhood—the sphere of the demons, of magic, and of the mother and father who keep their children away from progress (hence symbolically "retarded," blind, flawed, crippled). This world of the past is as inevitable and fatal as the closure of the narrative implies. Khelli's return home thus does confirm some kind of continuity, of a female dynasty, yet it is a paralyzing rather than a revitalizing, unifying experience of harmonic plenitude.

In opposition to *Shkhur*'s pessimistic and fatalistic meanings, constructed by the nostalgic movement between present and past, in *Turn Left at the End of the World* nostalgia can be theorized as producing a utopian and optimistic, albeit anachronistic, view of present and past. Slavoj Zizek describes nostalgia as the ultimately pure form of gaze-object relation.[22] The nostalgic view affords us the outlook of a naïve, hypothetical, mythic spectator who is still able to identify immediately with the universe of anachronistic genres. Israeli Bourekas films can be described as such an anachronistic genre. They have become the ultimate nostalgic object of Israeli spectators' gaze. These films afford Israelis the naïve outlook of 1960s–1970s audiences, still able to take seriously the genre's utopian vision, which integrates the diverse ethnic groups in the Israeli melting pot and settles social tensions and unjust power relations within formulaic closures of interethnic marriages and comic exchanges. It may very well be the case that the 450,000 Israeli viewers of the film *Turn Left at the End of the World* represent the fascinated nostalgic spectator that Zizek describes.

Applying Zizek's theorizing of the nostalgic gaze, I contend that Nesher's 2004 film affords Israelis a nostalgic gaze at their own spectatorship and allows them to "see themselves seeing" as they used to see in the 1960s and 1970s. Those "happy days" of integration and the openness of youth are reflected in those images of the 1968 southern small town in Israel. The retro images of late 1960s Israel in *Turn Left at the End of the World* reflect to viewers their own nostalgic gaze at the intercultural Israeli exchange in its utopian, popular Bourekas formulation and tradition. In addition, the film is focalized through the typically nostalgic point of view of youth, as Zizek conceptualizes it. It is filtered through the perspective of the young, naïve Sara, who admires her father, believes people are funny and fascinating, and thinks the story of these lost people who loved us needs to be told. The spectators are hence sutured into this retrospective nostalgic understanding of the time, of the film's fictional world and its protagonists, shared by the fictional female narrator in the fictional world (diegesis) and the (male) director on the extradiegetic, ideological level.

Fredric Jameson describes nostalgia as an apparatus for the recycling of retro images severed from their original historical context and operating connotations of "pastness" and pseudo-historical depth, in which the history of aesthetic styles displaces and replaces real history.[23] *Turn Left at the End of the World* manifests the retro aesthetics that Jameson theorizes as devoid of historicity in its visual quotations of earlier styles and images of the past, including movie posters, ice cream (Eskimo) logos, and fashion styles. Moreover, the film also creates a distinct retro aesthetics in its soundtrack based on 1960s hits, a retro aesthetics that characterized the George Lucas classic *American Graffiti* (1973) and its disciple, the 1978 cult Israeli film *Lemon Popsicle* (*Eskimo Limon*, Davidson, 1978).

As in the case of Nesher's Israeli classic *The Troupe* (*Halehaka*, 1978), however, the retro imagery and soundtrack are not "flat," empty simulacra pastiched randomly. Their selection and organization in the text are laden with historical and political meanings. Nesher chooses to locate *Turn Left* in the summer of 1968, one year after the 1967 Six Day War. Yoram Shayer (the film's art director) and Rona Doron (the costume designer) re-create a world that looks like 1968 in both Israeli and extra-Israeli (Western, European, American) contexts.[24] The 1968 look in the film is probably not how things looked for the real subjects who experienced 1968 in southern development towns or other Israeli locations of the time. Rather, the fictional world of 1968 is constructed around carefully designed spatial images of the past, with pseudo-historic connotations that have become mythologized. These images, self-consciously reconstructed through the mise-en-scène and musical score, re-create the 1968 Israel as inscribed in (official) Western collective memory. The sixties are remembered as a time of rebellion and the cutting edge of a new chapter in history: associated with the American pacifistic, revolutionary counterculture, the students' rebellion in Paris, and the sexual and feminist revolution. These subversive aspects of the 1960s are also reflected in Simone's and Nicole's proactive sexuality, in their insistence upon love as an ultimate value, and in the peace medallion that Sara wears, which Nicole mistakes for "an upside-down Y."

In collective Israeli memory this post-1967 era is specifically associated with the Six Day War and its glorious aftermath, a boom of national pride and international support, and a peak in Israeli militarism and nationalism. But Nesher chooses to ignore this national militarist and masculine zeitgeist (which he had criticized in his 1978 film *The Troupe*). Instead, he focuses on Euro-American pacifism; the counterculture; the sexual revolution; disco, rock, and ballroom dancing; and—last but not least—the family and the domestic sphere rather than the national-collective one. He chooses to tell the story of coming of age from a feminine perspective and focuses on the

Figure 24.3. Icons of the 1960s: an Eskimo in the desert in *Turn Left at the End of the World* (Avi Nesher, 2004). Courtesy of Artomas Communications, Metro Communications, and United King Film.

immigrant experience on the margins rather than on the masculine Sabra mainstream or the militarist nationalistic zeitgeist of the center. In a sense, Nesher displaces the immigrants' story from the traumatic post-1948 and early 1950s "correct" location in Israeli history and transplants it into the decade when the traumas of the war of attrition (Hebrew: *hatashah*) on the bank of the Suez Canal preoccupied Israelis and diverted the public agenda away from painful social injustices.

Subverting the militarist masculine-national time and official history, Nesher chooses to replace it with an alternative feminine time and history and focus upon the repressed aspects of collective and national history and the personal-domestic sphere. As Nicole's father comments about history within the film's fictional world, it may liberate but it might also imprison us. Nesher marginalizes the imprisoning aspects of history and brings its liberating potentials to the fore. Thus he constructs the sixties ethos of pacifism, civil rights movements, rebellion, and counterculture as articulated with the libidinal and sexual energies of Nicole and Simone, the unruly Mizrahi females. Nicole and Simone challenge the traditional conservative order and represent the revolutionary natural energies that their teacher Assaf quotes from Che Guevara.

The reference in Nesher's film to the Hollywood film *Wild in the Streets* (Barry Shear, 1968), which proposed to get rid of all parents and those older than thirty, articulates with the parents' insistence on their children's better future as worth their sacrifice and misery.[25] In this respect, the different interpretations in Hasfari's and Nesher's films of intergenerational relations as allegories for Israeli history and its teleology are telling. *Shkhur* creates a deterministic analogy between past and present, involving parents, daughters/sons, and granddaughter. Hence the traumas of the first generation inflict incompetence on the next generations and are in a determinist mode extended into the future—the trauma inescapable and the past paralyzing future integration.[26]

Turn Left at the End of the World, in contrast, proposes the optimistic (nostalgic, utopian) vision of the Bourekas while still acknowledging the trauma of displacement and marginalization. The next generation, the daughters, will realize the utopian vision of integration that their diasporic parents cannot live to accomplish; while the parents are doomed to the liminality of transition, the "exodus" of the desert generation, their daughters are able to choose their way into the new world of Hebrew Israeliness. Both Nicole and Sara speak (broken) Hebrew with each other, while their parents are unable to communicate outside of the family because of language constraints. Thus Nicole and Sara represent a possible vital, multicultural coexistence of different ethnicities, which characterized the Bourekas genre's utopian vision.[27] Moreover, the film's narrative prioritizes the personal, private, familial realm over the collective one. Although Sara experiences the painful loss of confidence in her father, who has been unfaithful to her mother and the family, both girls come to terms with their demanding mothers. Sara's future integration into Israeli society in the army is presented as an equally viable alternative to Nicole's assuming of her mother's roles and traditions, without blocking her possible future realization of the Tel Aviv/Israeli dream: to move from the margins to the center, to become famous, to become somebody, to become.

Conclusion: A Brave New World

Histories, as Stuart Hall has argued, have both material and symbolic effects. For those who were displaced, for those whose past was disrupted by history's traumas, the past is no longer a simple factual past. Our relation to it is like a child's relation to the mother, always already "after the break." The past, both personal and collective, is always constructed through memory, fantasy, narrative, and myth. The new (industrialized, globalized, postcolonial) world of displacement gives rise to an imaginary of plenitude that we constantly yearn for, re-creating an endless desire to return to "lost origins," to be one again with the mother, to go back to our roots.

Is it the mother as a metaphor for the suppressed ethnic and folkloric origins that we yearn for, through the medium of our films, escaping the haunting void of cut roots? Or is it the imaginary unity of the masculine national order that Israelis and possibly other cultures that negotiate this stable unity as well have lost, the cohesive egalitarian nation that substitutes for the lost ethnic history and origins? Both *Shkhur* and *Turn Left at the End of the World* represent feminine stories coming to terms with the mother and her tradition in the familial, domestic sphere. Yet both films either lament the loss of the father or ask for his forgiveness. Subliminally, the father still remains an object of nostalgic yearning, both for Hannah Azoulai-Hasfari and for Avi Nesher. But the stories that both films tell, the worlds they re-create, are about coming to terms with the mother, with the folkloric ethnic origins in the feminine kingdom of family and cooking and female solidarity and love, not war.

NOTES

1. Hall (2000: 705–706, 713–714).

2. Ibid., 714.

3. Talmon (1997, 2001).

4. Loshitzky (1996).

5. "Bourekas films" are a popular Israeli cinematic genre nicknamed after a Middle Eastern pastry, which dominated the Israeli cinema scene in the 1960s and 1970s. The films are characterized by comic exchanges, carnivalesque power reversals, and conflicts between ethnic stereotypes, Mizrahim and Ashkenazim. These films' plots resolve these interethnic exchanges in a utopian manner by integrating class and ethnic fissions, thus mediating the Israeli cinematic vision of the "melting pot," usually articulated through interethnic romance and marriage. The genre is also known for being very popular and loved by Israeli audiences while fiercely criticized by the film critics of the time.

6. An Israeli website titled "Couscous," devoted to the heritage and memories of the Moroccan Jewish community in Israel, defines the term *shkhur* as standing for mystics, dreams, and rituals.

7. Shohat (1989, 1990); Gertz (1993: 32–37).

8. See Shohat (1989: 138–139).

9. See Gertz (1993: 27–37).

10. *Shkhur* received the 1994 Israeli Film Academy awards for the following categories: best film, best director, best actress (Ronit Alkabetz), best supporting actor (Amos Lavy), best cinematography, and best art direction.

11. Sammy Smooha, *Ha'aretz* weekly supplement (February 1995): 60–62; Orly Levy in ibid., 68. The editor of the weekly supplement of the Israeli newspaper *Ha'aretz* at the time, Dov Alfon, whose parents immigrated to Israel from Tunisia, invited eight descendants of immigrants to Israel from the Middle East in the 1950s to comment on the film *Shkhur*. In February 1995 he published a series of articles concerning the film, representations of Mizrahim, and their shared collective biography. Orly Levy represents the attitude and discourse of the "second generation" to the traumatic immigration of Jews from North Africa to Israel in the 1950s, as Sammy Smooha wrote from a sociologist's point of view.

12. When *Turn Left at the End of the World* was released on DVD (in January 2005), 450,000 viewers had seen it in theaters. See Aviv Hofi, "The Cloud That Eclipses *Turn Left at the End of the World*," http://www.iwomen.co.il/item.asp?aid=88056, January 10, 2005. The film was notably a blockbuster in 2004, coming second in the Israeli box office ratings with its 450,000 viewers after *Shrek 2*, with 570,000 viewers in Israel, and bypassing *Lord of the Rings: Return of the King*.

13. Michal Ohaion, "Exposing the Wrongdoings" ("Khassifat Ha'avla"), *Ma'ariv*, September 8, 2004, 6; Dan Margalit, "Still Oblivious" ("Adayin Atumim"), *Ma'ariv*, September 7, 2004, 6; Naor Tzion, "They Remained in the Bubble" ("Hem Nish'aru Babu'ah"), *Ma'ariv*, September 6, 2004, 3; Meir Shitrit, "The Academy Has Missed the Point" ("Hahakhmatza Shel Ha'akademiah"), *Ma'ariv*, September 10, 2004, 8; Amnon Dankner and Avi Bettleheim, "A Cultural Scandal" ("Sha'aruria Tarbutit"), *Ma'ariv*, September 3, 2004.

14. Dankner and Bettleheim, "A Cultural Scandal" (my translation).

15. See, for example, Shohat (1991 translation by Anat Glickman: 138).

16. Although Shmuel Hasfari directed the film, equal authorial agency is assigned to Hannah Azoulai-Hasfari, who wrote the script. See, for example, Yaron Shemer's discussion in Chapter 10.

17. According to the Internet Movie Database the screenplay was written by Avi Nesher, Sara Eden, and Ruby Porat-Shoval. The latter two are women of Mizrahi heritage.

18. "Going to the Very End," interview with David Shalit, in *Globes*, June 24, 2004. Nesher claims in this interview that the film is very personal for him, even "private."

19. See Shohat (1990). See also Talmon (1997, 1999, 2001); and Gertz (2001).

20. As described in Talmon (1997, 1999, 2001); and Gertz (2001).

21. Davis (1979), which includes a discussion of the etymology of the term "nostalgia" and its theoretical social implications; Hall (2000: 714).

22. Zizek (2000: 527).

23. Jameson (1990).

24. Yoram Shayer and Rona Doron won the only two 2004 Israeli Film Academy Awards for this film, as recognition for their achievements in it.

25. Interestingly, in Israel the Hebrew title of the film was *Hano'ar Lashilton* (literally, "Power to the Youth").

26. Orly Lubin reads *Shkhur* as constituting an empowering, subversive dynasty of Mizrahi females, which marginalizes the Zionist-Ashkenazi nationalism and its hegemony. My own interpretation of the female-Mizrahi dynasty in *Shkhur* is different, yet I am indebted to her illuminating conceptualization of the feminine-domestic sphere as subverting the Zionist-national-masculine order. See Lubin (2001).

27. See Ben Shaul (1998 and 2005).

BIBLIOGRAPHY

Azoulai-Hasfari, Hanna. 2009. *Sh'chur (Shkhur: Hatasrit Vesheva Kriot Al Haseret)*. Tel Aviv: Yedi'ot Akharonot Vesifrei Khemed.

Ben Shaul, Nitzan. 1998. "The Implied Connection between the *Bourekas* Films and the [Israeli] Personal Cinema" ("Hakesher Hasamuy Bein Sirtei Habourekas Lasratim Ha'ishi'yim"). In Nurith Gertz, Orly Lubin, and Judd Ne'eman, eds., *Fictive Looks: On Israeli Cinema (Mabatim Fiktivi'im Al Kolno'a Yisra'eli)*, 128–134. Tel Aviv: Open University of Israel.

———. 2005. "The Euphoric Decade." *Journal of Modern Jewish Studies* 4, no. 2 (July): 233–243. London: Routledge/Taylor & Francis Group.

Davis, Fred. 1979. *Yearning for Yesterday: A Sociology of Nostalgia*. New York: Free Press.

Gertz, Nurith. 1993. *Motion Fiction: Israeli Fiction in Film (Sipur Mehasratim: Siporet Yisra'elit Ve'ibudeihah Lakolno'a)*. Tel Aviv: Open University of Israel.

———. 2001. "Gender and Nationality in the New Israeli Cinema." In *Assaph Kolnoa, Section D, No. 2*, 227–246. Ramat Aviv: Tel Aviv University, Faculty of Arts, Department of Film and Television.

Hall, Stuart. 2000. "Cultural Identity and Cinematic Representation." In Robert Stam and Toby Miller, eds., *Film and Theory: An Anthology*, 704–714. Malden, Mass: Blackwell Publishers, Inc.

Jameson, Fredric. 1990. *Postmodernism*. Durham: Duke University Press.

Loshitzky, Yosefa. 1996. "Authenticity in Crisis: *Shur* and New Israeli Forms of Ethnicity." *Media Culture & Society* 18: 87–103. London, Thousand Oaks, and New Delhi: Sage.

Lubin, Orly. 2001. "Distancing the Frame." In R. M. Friedman, Nurith Gertz, Orly Lubin, and Judd Neʾeman, eds., *Kolnoa-Assaph Section D, No. 2*, 213–225. Ramat Aviv: Tel Aviv University, Faculty of Arts, Department of Film and Television.

Niv, Kobi. 1999. "Shkhur." In *Five Screenplays: Studies in the Israeli Screenplay* (*Al Ma Haseret Haze*), 127–192. Tel Aviv: Dvir.

Shohat, Ella. 1989. *Israeli Cinema: East/West and the Politics of Representation*. Austin: University of Texas Press. Hebrew translation by Anat Glickman. Tel Aviv: Brerot Publishing, 1991.

———. 1990. "Master-Narrative/Counter Readings: The Politics of Israeli Cinema." In Robert Sklar and Charles Musser, eds., *Resisting Images: Essays on Cinema and History*, 251–278. Philadelphia: Temple University Press.

Talmon, Miri. 1997. "Nostalgia, Groups, and Collective Identity in Israeli Cinema" ("Khavurot Venostalgia Bakolnoʾa Hayisraʾeli"). PhD dissertation. Hebrew University of Jerusalem, Faculty of Social Sciences, Department of Communication and Journalism.

———. 1999. "Paradigms of Youth and Collective Identity in Israeli Popular Culture." In Sue Ralph et al., eds., *Youth and the Global Media*, 219–228. Luton, UK: Luton University Press.

———. 2001. *Israeli Graffiti: Nostalgia, Groups, and Collective Identity in Israeli Cinema* (*Bluz Latzabar Haʾavud: Khavurot Venostalgia Bakolnoʾa Hayisraʾeli*). Haifa: Haifa University Press and Tel Aviv: Open University Press.

Zizek, Slavoj. 2000. "Looking Awry." In Robert Stam and Toby Miller, eds., *Film and Theory: An Anthology*, 524–538. Malden, Mass.: Blackwell Publishers.

FILMOGRAPHY

Adamah Meshugaʾat (Sweet Mud). Dror Shaul, Israel, 2006.

American Graffiti. George Lucas, USA, 1973.

Eskimo Limon (Lemon Popsicle). Boaz Davidson, Israel, 1978.

Hakayitz Shel Aviya (The Summer of Aviya). Eli Cohen, Israel, 1988.

Halehaka (The Troupe). Avi Nesher, Israel, 1978.

Sallah Shabbati (Sallah). Ephraim Kishon, Israel, 1964.

Shkhur (aka *Sh'chur—Secrets and Magic*). Shmuel Hasfari, Israel, 1994.

Sof Haʾolam Smolah (Turn Left at the End of the World). Avi Nesher, Israel, 2004.

Velakakhta Lekha Isha (To Take a Wife). Ronit Elkabetz and Shlomi Elkabetz, Israel, 2004.

Wild in the Streets. Barry Shear, USA, 1968.

Yaldei Hashemesh (Children of the Sun). Ran Tal, Israel, 2007.

Contributors

ILAN AVISAR is an associate professor in the Film and Television Department at Tel Aviv University. He received his PhD degree from Indiana University and taught at several American universities as a visiting professor. His research focuses on the Holocaust, Israeli cinema, and Jewish films, exploring issues of historical representations, collective memory, trauma, national culture in a global context, and identity constructions. Avisar is the author of several books and numerous articles, including *Screening the Holocaust: Cinema's Images of the Unimaginable* (1988), *Visions of Israel: Israeli Filmmakers and Images of the Jewish State* (1997, 2002), *Film Art: The Techniques and Poetics of Cinematic Expression* (1995, in Hebrew), and *The Israeli Scene: Language, Cinema, Discourse* (2005, in Hebrew).

NITZAN BEN SHAUL is an associate professor in the Film and Television Department at Tel Aviv University. He received his PhD in the Cinema Studies Department at New York University. His publications include *Mythical Expressions of Siege in Israeli Films* (Edwin Mellen Press, 1997), *Introduction to Film Theories* (Dyonon, Tel Aviv University Press, 2000), *A Violent World: TV News Images of Middle Eastern Terror and War* (Rowman and Littlefield, 2006), *Film: The Key Concepts* (Berg, 2007), and *Hyper-narrative Interactive Cinema* (Rodopi, 2008). He is currently writing a study on optional thinking and narrative movies contracted by Berghahn Books.

YAEL BEN-ZVI-MORAD is a Kreitman Foundation Fellow at Ben-Gurion University of the Negev as a doctoral student in the Hebrew Literature Department. She has published articles on Israeli and Palestinian cinema. Her book *Patricide and Other Family Relationships in Contemporary Palestinian Cinema* is forthcoming from Resling. Ben-Zvi-Morad is also a writer and photographer, whose stories and photographs have appeared in various periodicals and exhibitions. Her short story collection *A Wedding in the Snow* was published in early 2008.

DAN CHYUTIN received his BFA in film production from Tel Aviv University's Film and Television Department and his MA in cinema studies from New York University before entering the PhD track in Film Studies at the University of Pittsburgh. He is currently working on his dissertation, which focuses on contemporary Israeli cinema's attitude toward Jewish religion and religious identity. In addition to his academic activities, he is also an accomplished filmmaker, whose short fiction and avant-garde films have been screened in various festivals worldwide.

URI S. COHEN wrote his PhD dissertation at the Hebrew University: *Survival: Senses of Death between the World Wars in Eretz Israel and in Italy* (published by Resling in 2007). He is currently assistant professor of Hebrew literature at Columbia University. He has published a novel, *Resting in Peace* (2003), and authored a documentary film, *Traces of Ida Fink* (2007), on the renowned author. Cohen is the author of scholarly publications on Hebrew literature and culture and has recently edited the Hebrew rendering of Giorgio Agamben (*Remnants of Auschwitz*) and Pier Paolo Pasolini. He is currently preparing a book on Israeli author Orly Castel Bloom and several articles on Israeli cinema and Uri Zohar.

NAVA DUSHI is an assistant professor of film studies at Lynn University, where she teaches film history, film theory, and international film. She earned her BFA in film and television from Tel Aviv University, where she is currently working on her PhD dissertation, entitled "Texts in Transition: Israeli Cinema in a Global Context," inspired by Kafka's idea of "minor literature" as interpreted by Gilles Deleuze and Félix Guattari.

ARIEL L. FELDESTEIN is the head of academic affairs at Sapir College in Israel. His field of expertise is Zionist ideology, the Zionist Movement, and relations between Israel and Diaspora Jewry. His recent publications include *Ben-Gurion, Zionism and American Jewry* (London, 2006) and *Pioneer, Toil, Camera: Cinema in Service of the Zionist Ideology, 1917–1939* (Tel Aviv, 2009, in Hebrew).

OLGA GERSHENSON is an associate professor of Judaic and Near Eastern studies at the University of Massachusetts in Amherst. She is the author of *Gesher: Russian Theatre in Israel* (Peter Lang, 2005) and co-editor of *Ladies and Gents* (Temple University Press, 2009). Her essays have appeared in the *Journal of Modern Jewish Studies, Multilingua, Western Journal of Communication, Journal of International Communication,* and other publications. She is now working on

a book about the Holocaust in Russian cinema. See her website: www.people
.umass.edu/olga.

NURITH GERTZ is professor emeritus of cinema and literature in the Department of Language, Literature, and Art at the Open University and head of the
Department of Culture—Creation and Production at Sapir College. Her books
include *Motion Fiction: Literature and Cinema* (Tel Aviv: Open University, 1993,
in Hebrew), *Not from Here* (Tel Aviv: Am Oved/Ofakim, 1997, in Hebrew), *Myths
in Israeli Culture* (London: Vallentine Mitchell, Parkes Center, University of
Southampton and Wiener Library, 2000), *Holocaust Survivors, Aliens, and Others
in Israeli Cinema and Literature* (Tel Aviv: Am Oved/Ofakim, Open University,
2004, in Hebrew), (with George Khleifi) *Landscape in Mist: Space and Memory in
Palestinian Cinema* (Tel Aviv: Am Oved and Open University, 2006, in Hebrew),
(with George Khleifi) *Palestinian Cinema* (Edinburgh University Press/Bloom-
ington: Indiana University Press, 2008), and *Unrepentant: Four Chapters in the
Life of Amos Kenan* (Tel Aviv: Am Oved, 2008, in Hebrew). Professor Gertz is a
recipient of the Brenner Prize for Literature for 2009.

GAL HERMONI teaches in the department of film and television at Tel Aviv University and Sapir Academic College. His interests are film theory, cultural and
critical studies, semiotics, and popular music. He is also a professional musician
who has released, produced, and played in several musical projects in the Israeli
alternative music scene.

JAN-CHRISTOPHER HORAK received his PhD in Communications from the
Westfalische Wilhlems-Universität in Munster, Germany. After being curator at
George Eastman House and director of the Munich Filmmuseum, he became
director of the UCLA Film & Television Archive. He has taught at the University
of Rochester, the Munich Film Academy, the University of Salzburg, and Wayne
State University's Program Abroad and is a professor at the University of California at Los Angeles. Horak's numerous books include *Making Images Move: Photographers and Avant-Garde Cinema* (1997), *Berge, Licht und Traum: Dr. Arnold
Fanck und der deutsche Bergfilm* (1997), *Lovers of Cinema: The First American Film
Avant-Garde, 1919–1945* (1995), *The Dream Merchants* (1989), *Anti-Nazi Filme
der deutschsprachigen Emigration von Hollywood* (1984), *Helmar Lerski—Lichtbildner: Fotographien und Filme, 1910–1947* (1982), and *Film und Foto der zwan-
ziger Jahre* (1979). He has published over 250 articles and reviews in English,
German, French, Italian, Japanese, Dutch, Hungarian, Spanish, Czech, Swedish,
and Hebrew publications. He is presently working on a book on designer and
filmmaker Saul Bass.

ERAN KAPLAN teaches history at Princeton University. His book *The Jewish Radical Right: Revisionist Zionism and Its Ideological Legacy* was published in 2003. He is the co-editor of *Zionism and the Yishuv: A Sourcebook* with Derek Penslar (University of Wisconsin Press, forthcoming). He has published several articles on Israeli history and culture in publications such as *Alpayim*, *Jewish Social Studies*, *Israel Studies*, and *Tikkun*.

ELDAD KEDEM was born and educated at Kibbutz Maagan, Jordan Valley. He earned his PhD at the Amsterdam School for Cultural Analysis, University of Amsterdam. He currently teaches cinema at the Open University of Israel. Kedem has published essays on Israeli cinema and on kibbutz films and edited a reader on the politics of Israeli cinema (in Hebrew).

SANDRA MEIRI is lecturer in the Department of Literature, Linguistics, and Art at the Open University of Israel. She has written on Israeli cinema in Hebrew and English. Her book *Any Sex You Can Do I Can Do Better: Trans-Gender in Cinema and Subjectivity* is forthcoming (in Hebrew).

YAEL MUNK is a lecturer in film and culture at the Open University, Israel. She has published articles in Hebrew, English, and French on issues in Israeli cinema. Her book *Exiled in Their Borders: Israeli Cinema between Two Intifadas* is forthcoming from the Open University Press (in Hebrew). Munk's research is concerned with colonialism criticism and postcolonial theory, the emergence of new and hybrid identities after the nation-state, postmodernism, women's documentary filmmaking, and gender studies in general.

DORIT NAAMAN is a film theorist and documentarist from Jerusalem, teaching at Queen's University, Canada. Her research focuses on Middle Eastern cinemas (primarily from postcolonialist and feminist perspectives). She is currently working on a book on the visual representation of Palestinian and Israeli women fighters. Her documentary work is about identity politics and politics of representation, and she has developed a format of short videos, DiaDocuMEntaRY. She has published in *Cinema Journal*, *Quarterly Review of Film and Video*, *Third Text*, *Signs*, *Hypatia*, and elsewhere.

JUDD NE'EMAN is emeritus professor at Tel Aviv University and has been a visiting professor at the New York University Tisch School of the Arts (2003–2005). He has an MD degree from the Hadassah School of Medicine at the Hebrew University in Jerusalem. He has served as combat surgeon in a paratroop reserve brigade and was decorated for bravery in combat in the 1967 Six Day War. Ne'eman is a laureate of the Israel Prize for cinema (2009), and his feature films and documentaries have been shown at festivals and on television. *The Dress* (1970), *Paratroopers* (1977), *Streets of Yesterday* (1989), *Nuzhat al-Fuad* (2007), and *Zitra* (2008) are some of the films he has directed and produced. He has published essays on Israeli cinema and on cinema and war.

GILAD PADVA is a scholar of film, television, sexuality, and queer theory who lectures at Tel Aviv University (Department of Film and Television) and Beit Berl College (Women and Gender Studies and the School of Education). His articles have been published in distinguished academic journals. He has also contributed to international encyclopedias and anthologies of cinema, art, sexualities, and masculinities.

YARON PELEG is an associate professor of Hebrew at George Washington University and the director of the George Washington Hebrew Program. His publications include *Derech Gever: Homoeroticism in Hebrew Literature, 1887–2000* (2003), *Orientalism and the Hebrew Imagination* (2005), and *Israeli Culture between the Two Intifadas: A Brief Romance* (2008). His articles on Israeli literature, cinema, and culture have appeared in *Prooftexts*, *Jewish Social Studies*, *Hebrew Studies*, and *Journal of Israel Studies*, among other publications.

YARON SHEMER is an assistant professor of Israel Cultural Studies at the University of North Carolina, Chapel Hill. He earned his PhD in Radio-Television-Film from the University of Texas at Austin in 2005. His published articles focus on contemporary Mizrahi films and on terrorism in Middle Eastern cinema. Shemer has produced and directed films in Israel, Poland, and the United States, including *Pilgrimage of Remembrance: The Jews of Poland* (1991) and *The Road to Peace: Israelis and Palestinians* (1995).

LIAT STEIR-LIVNY is a lecturer in the Department of Culture, Creation, and Production at Sapir College and a coordinator of Israeli Cinema and Culture courses in the Department of Literature, Language, and the Arts at the Open University of Israel. Her PhD, with distinction, was awarded for a dissertation entitled "A World of Difference: The Representation of the Holocaust, Holocaust Survivors, and Their Rehabilitation in the Films and Journalism of Zionist Organizations in Eretz Israel and the USA, 1945–1948" (Tel Aviv University, 2006). She is the author of *Two Faces in the Mirror: The Representation of Holocaust Survivors in Israeli Cinema* (Eshkolot-Magnes, 2009).

MIRI TALMON is a scholar of Israeli culture, cinema, and media who has taught at the Open University of Israel, at Tel Aviv University in the Film and Television Department, at the Hebrew University of Jerusalem and at Haifa University in the Department of Communication, at Wesleyan University (Connecticut), and as Schusterman Visiting professor for Israel Studies at the University of Wisconsin, Madison. Her PhD was awarded by the Hebrew University of Jerusalem, Department of Communication and Journalism. Talmon is the author of *Israeli*

Graffiti: Nostalgia, Groups, and Collective Identity in Israeli Cinema (Haifa University Press/Open University Press, 2001, in Hebrew) and has recently completed a new manuscript entitled "A State of Becoming: Transitions in Israeli Cinema and Culture." Her areas of specialization include Israeli cultural history, popular and folk Israeli culture, Israeli cinema and television, and representations of history and collective memory in Israeli culture.

RAZ YOSEF is an assistant professor and the chair of the cinema studies BA Program in the Department of Film and Television at Tel Aviv University, Israel. He is the author of *Beyond Flesh: Queer Masculinities and Nationalism in Israeli Cinema* (Rutgers University Press, 2004), *The Politics of Loss and Trauma in Contemporary Israeli Cinema* (Routledge, 2011), and numerous articles on issues of gender, sexuality, ethnicity, and nationalism in Israeli cinema. His work has appeared in *GLQ, Third Text, Framework, Shofar, Journal of Modern Jewish Studies, Camera Obscura,* and *Cinema Journal.*

ANAT ZANGER is an assistant professor in the Department of Film and Television and co-chair of the MA Program in Film and Television at Tel Aviv University. Her areas of expertise include Israeli cinema, mythology, collective memory, intertextuality, and space and landscape. Her articles have appeared in *Semiotics, Framework, Shofar, Journal of Modern Jewish Studies,* and *Feminist Media Studies,* among other publications. She is the author of *Film Remakes as Ritual and Disguises* (Amsterdam University Press, 2006) and is currently completing a book on landscape in Israeli cinema. This project is supported by the Israeli Science Foundation (ISF). In 2008–2009 Zanger was a visiting scholar at the Oxford Center for Hebrew and Jewish Studies.

YAEL ZERUBAVEL is a professor of Jewish studies and history at Rutgers and the founding director of the Allen and Joan Bildner Center for the Study of Jewish Life. She is the author of *Recovered Roots: Collective Memory and the Making of Israeli National Tradition* (University of Chicago Press, 1995), which won the 1996 Salo Baron Prize of the American Academy for Jewish Research, and numerous articles exploring the relations between history and memory, nationalism and collective identities, war and trauma, Israeli political culture, and the Jewish immigrant experience. She is currently completing a book entitled *Desert in the Promised Land: Nationalism, Politics, and Symbolic Landscapes* (University of Chicago Press, forthcoming).

Index